interpreting the postmodern

RESPONSES TO "RADICAL ORTHODOXY"

EDITED BY
Rosemary Radford Ruether and Marion Grau

t&t clark

NEW YORK • LONDON

Unless otherwise noted, all scriptural quotations in this book are from the New Revised Standard Version Bible. Copyright © 1989 by the Division of Christian Education of the National Council of the Churches of Christ in the United States of America. Used by permission. All rights reserved.

T & T Clark International, Madison Square Park, 15 East 26th Street, New York, NY 10010
T & T Clark International, The Tower Building, 11 York Road, London SE1 7NX
T & T Clark International is a Continuum imprint.

Cover design by Lee Singer

Library of Congress Cataloging-in-Publication Data

Interpreting the postmodern : responses to "radical orthodoxy" / edited by Rosemary Radford Ruether and Marion Grau.
    p. cm.
  Includes bibliographical references and index.
  ISBN 0-567-02880-1 (hardcover with jacket) — ISBN 0-567-02890-9 (pbk.)
  1. Philosophical theology. 2. Postmodern theology. I. Ruether, Rosemary Radford. II. Grau, Marion.
  BT40.I55 2006
  230'.046—dc22
                              2005016496

Printed in the United States of America

01 02 03 04 05 06 07 08 09 10   10 9 8 7 6 5 4 3 2 1

interpreting the
postmodern

Contents

Introduction

"Christianity" defined as "orthodoxy" rests uncomfortably on a history of inner conflict and persistent multiplicity. This intractable problem of diversity together with the ideological claim of unity only reinforces the cultural uniqueness or ideological paradox of Christian exclusivity in late antiquity.[1]

Historian Rebecca Lyman's words raise the question whether there has ever been such a thing as an orthodoxy, and, if so, whether it would have been a serious contender for theological hegemony without the support of the Roman Empire. Despite such imperial support, beginning with Constantine's promulgation of Nicene orthodoxy, a "persistent multiplicity" of doctrinal utterances, practices, and beliefs coexisted with assertions for orthodoxy throughout the centuries and millennia. The present time is no exception: Claims of orthodoxy continue to be enunciated in a space of multiple theological accounts. While some theologians have felt that the postmodern mood ended the reign of rationality and offers a *kairos* to reclaim traditional religious claims in a renewed and even stronger fashion, others continue to point out the attendant difficulties and trappings with such efforts. This volume intends to contribute to the discussions concerning the place and meaning of theological discourse in the contemporary setting.

Modernity and postmodernity are intensely contested interpretive spaces, as loaded with meaning as they remain notoriously resistant to neat definitions and generalizations. The terms "modern" and "postmodern" have become increasingly empty, except where they have been used by detractors and other "cultured despisers" of modernity's indeed rather fallible quests. In this context, which many in the industrialized world consider to be postmodern, how can we describe the space Christian and Jewish theologies occupy? What are its chances, its challenges, its hopes, and its limits?

A number of theological options have emerged since the middle of the twentieth century, or perhaps more accurately, the 1960s, many of which can be seen as formulating postmodern forms of theology. Political and liberation theologies, feminist and constructive theologies, and new currents in the study of the history of Christianity, in philosophy, and in Judaism have claimed a space departing in significant ways from modern theologies and have clamored into the spaces opened up by Enlightenment

---

1. Rebecca Lyman, "Hellenism and Heresy," *JECS* 11, no. 2 (2003): 211.

critiques of religion. These theologies, while being informed by the Enlightenment challenge to unquestioned authority, have also challenged many of the problematic phenomena of modernity.

In the early 1990s, a group of British Anglican writers emerged as another set of contenders to make postmodern theological meaning by proposing to reclaim the throne from which theology, formerly the "queen of sciences," had been toppled by claiming access to a "radical orthodoxy" built on a return to premodern sources. Designating a monolithically conceived modernity as a polluted space that must be overcome by a return to a premodern union of faith and reason, they set out to define the theological option of radical orthodoxy in stark contrast to other theological critiques of the Christian tradition, or of some of the problematic features of modern and liberal theologies. For this periodization, radical orthodox thinkers have partly relied on David Harvey and Fredric Jameson's work, which argues that postmodernism represents a manifestation of "late capitalism," is essentially descriptive and amoral, and hence in effect either aids and abets the structures of capitalism or offers no ethical stance from which to speak and act decisively.

If modernity equals the loss of a perceived premodern security and univocity, then postmodernity can be cast as either the complete degeneration of "truth" and "faith" or an opportunity for its resurgence. To generations of younger theologians that have absorbed deeply the questions of postmodernism but have felt that there is little ground to stand on from which to formulate self-confident constructive theologies, radical orthodox discourse may seem to offer a new self-confidence and place to stand. But does such a stance come at too high a price? Built upon such a unidimensional, if not modernist, conflation of modernity with nihilism and secularism, liberalism and even scientism, radical orthodoxy's reclamation of "creedal orthodoxy" occurs alongside wholesale dismissals of other theological options beyond modernity and the critical claims made by liberation theology, ecological theology, feminist theology, liberal theology, and even neo-orthodoxy. The movement's own modern contamination (to stay within its frame of interpretation) seems to be negligible and without consequence. But does not this crystalline periodization, this "either/or"[2] reading of theology and postmodernity, replicate and construct a straw image of modernity in discontinuity from the Middle Ages and contemporary times?[3] Is it possible that radical orthodoxy's discourse is at times caught in a very modernist discourse, despite the clear intent of moving beyond it?

Some would expect of a theology that claims to be postmodern an attempt to deconstruct and supplement the white-male logos of Western modern theological discourse. Unfortunately, radical orthodoxy offers no such iconoclasm but continues a very masculine, technocratic theology whose notion of contesting modernity hardly

---

2. John Milbank, "Knowledge: The Theological Critique of Philosophy in Hamann and Jacobi," in *Radical Orthodoxy: A New Theology*, eds. John Milbank, Catherine Pickstock, and Graham Ward (London: Routledge, 1999), 32.

3. For this argument, see also Gavin Hyman, *The Predicament of Postmodern Theology: Radical Orthodoxy or Nihilist Textualism?* (Louisville: Westminster John Knox Press, 2001), 67ff., esp. 70. Likewise, Hans-Georg Gadamer argued early that the German romantic recovery of pre-Enlightenment culture and literature was not only all too implicated in its rejection of the Enlightenment but also constructed a very particular vision of Enlightenment that was the mirror-image of romantic fears. See *Truth and Method*, etc. Cf. also Catherine Keller, *Apocalypse Now and Then: A Feminist Guide to the End of the World* (Boston: Beacon Press, 1997).

seems to consider that this means contesting notions of whose discourse gets to count as theology: women, African Americans, Latinos, peoples inhabiting the (former) colonies of the British Empire, to name a few. Hence, it might strike one as a rather limited project. What contemporary spiritual crises beyond the Euro-American body are missing from its discourse? Are radical orthodoxy's categories, themes and definitions only slightly shifted, while the language fails to reflect a change in epistemology that transcends some of the topics and problems of modernist discourse?

Proponents of radical orthodoxy take much of their ammunition from unidimensional misconstruals of liberation, justice, the gender of Christ, liberal theology, and poststructuralism. There are many who find things worth pondering in some of radical orthodoxy's critiques but who are disturbed by the superficial application of often flat and reductionist notions of what modernism or secularism is rather than a deep, sustained rethinking of what it might mean to move beyond modernism.

In the answers to the question raised above, the determining contexts are often already revealed. It is hardly ever remarked upon in discussions of postmodernity that its questions are often circumscribed in a European or, even more solidly, Euro-American conversation.[4] At the same time, around the edges of these "white mythologies," other centers of discourse are becoming enunciated.[5] The discursive context within which these questions are pondered is predominantly European and Euro-American, partly because that is the forum in which most of the discussions around radical orthodoxy occur. Thus, it is perhaps necessary that a group of writers mostly within the webs of current imperial centers engage these Anglo- and Anglo-American texts. But the impact of modernity, even more broadly disseminated through trade and colonialism than through literary, architectural, and postmodern art forms, reaches, for better and for worse, far beyond the European and Euro-American. At the same time, a solidly 'secularist' label attached to a problematic, uniform construct of modernism overlooks the ongoing eruption of "subjugated knowledge" both within a post-colonial context abroad and at home for nations that had either built their modern nation-states on the territories and/or the resources of their increasingly restless colonial spaces, without and within. As an expression of this eruption, a host of political and liberation theologies from Latin America, and created by feminist European and Euro-American women, African American men and women, indigenous peoples, sexual minorities, and an increasing number of ethnic minorities in the United States, have gained increased public visibility in Western media and academy. How do these theologies impact what is understood as modern and postmodern, and how do they relate to radical orthodoxy? Such questions have yet to be more fully explored.

Essays on the Possibility of Theology in Contemporary Space

Radical orthodoxy has provided many younger academic theologians with an exciting vision of sophisticated, complex, and intelligent theology, claiming its relevance in a

---

4. Compare the range of almost exclusively European and Euro-American contributions in Graham Ward, *The Postmodern God: A Theological Reader*, edited by Graham Ward (Oxford/Malden: Blackwell, 1997).

5. See, for example, the works of Derrida and Irigaray.

contemporary setting.[6] There are, however, other equally exciting ways of engaging the predicaments of our times. What are offered here are examples of constructive approaches to theology in postmodernity, approaches that are critical of the problems of modernity as well as mindful that we are also always building upon the gifts and poisons of enlightenment, reformation, and liberalism.

This volume represents a collection of approaches by a variety of authors whose work engages the present theological space, modern, postmodern, or otherwise, in ways that are in critical conversation with the claims of a radical orthodoxy but that claim alternative approaches. Many contributing authors share with John Milbank, Catherine Pickstock, Graham Ward, and others a critical and interrogatory approach to the heritage of modern epistemologies and theologies, but they are more careful in their conclusions about what responsible theologies, epistemologies, and actions might include. Hence, their constructive proposals will differ, sometimes subtly, sometimes significantly from those proposed by proponents of radical orthodoxy. The authors in this volume respond to radical orthodoxy's controversial claims about postmodern space in ways that aim to acknowledge the questions and critiques raised by Milbank, Pickstock, Ward, and others, but they propose different responses to issues crucial to contemporary theological discourse: the struggle against poverty and predatory capitalism; theologies of incarnation and of liberation; theological gender constructions; the radical nature of ethnic and cultural otherness; immanence and transcendence; feminist philosophy of religion; reconstructions of orthodox Judaism and Jewish women's concerns; theologies of gift, reciprocity, and economic exchange; and proposals for the recovery of a mystical activist ethics.

Questioning, as does Milbank, the "idea of an autonomous secular realm,"[7] alternative approaches to theology within postmodernity emerge as conversations between theology and discourses from other disciplines, such as literary and critical, social, and gender theories, yet in a vein that does not seek to rule over those discourses, as if that were a possibility, or even desirable. Many of the criticisms writers associated with radical orthodoxy have leveled at contemporary theologies have been directed toward selected texts and writers who are identified with liberation theology. In this volume, several writers contextualize liberation theology—then and now—differently and respond to the challenges voiced, widening North Atlantic views of liberation theology and making visible its contemporary contexts and complexity.

If this volume moves beyond orthodoxy, it attempts to do so in a spirit not of "denunciation" but of "enunciation," criticizing "without merely opposing."[8] This collection represents a collaboration between a Roman Catholic and an Episcopalian, and includes authors from Roman Catholic, Lutheran, Methodist, Anglican, orthodox Jewish feminist, and feminist philosophy contexts. Most of the contributors are European (British, German, and Scandinavian) and Euro-American women and men, others are Latin American. Some of the Europeans and Latin Americans theologize within North American seminaries and theological schools, others work in

---

6. For a critical and yet respectful reading of the contribution of radical orthodoxy, see also Clayton Crockett, ed., *Secular Theology: American Radical Theological Thought* (London: Routledge, 2001), 2–4.

7. John Milbank, *Theology and Social Theory: Beyond Secular Reason* (Oxford and Cambridge: Blackwell, 1990), 1.

8. See Keller, *Apocalypse Now and Then*, 19.

the contexts of British and Scandinavian universities. The majority of contributors are women. The prevalence of women may indicate (we have not taken polls or researched this in any depth) what might or might not be an interesting gender gap between those who are attracted by radical orthodoxy and those who share some of its critiques but who insist on the critical importance of insights from multiple centers of discourse, especially those that have become visible within the Western academy during modernity, the voices of colonized communities and women's voices.

What remains outside of this volume, for the most part, are the ongoing internal struggles in the Roman Catholic Church and the forces that appear to want to return to premodern terms and undo the coming to terms with modernity represented by the Second Vatican Council. The Vatican's effort to refute liberation theology by claiming it is a reduction to the political is echoed by many radical orthodoxy thinkers. More recently the Vatican has sought to refute Catholic feminist theologians by claiming that they lack a respect for the unique dignity and right ways of advancement of women. The writings of John Paul II on women are used to reaffirm traditionally essentialist dualisms of the masculine and the feminine, both to reject the possibility of women's ordination and also to privilege the pope's views as an expression of "true feminism." Many of these strategies of repristinated "orthodoxy" against liberation and feminist theologians parallel those of radical orthodoxy.

The authors of this book grapple in a variety of ways with the radical orthodoxy critique of liberation theologies and feminist theologies. They find much in common with its critique of modernity and capitalist consumerism but question its claims to have found the only true alternative by a return to the medieval church and its theology. Several authors question whether there is an unchanging "orthodoxy" to be ever redefined against "heresy."

Beyond Claims to Repristinate "Orthodoxy": Essays on Inhabiting Postmodernity

John Hoffmeyer's essay opens the collection with a plea to reconstruct an Augustinian *caritas* ethics that finds immediate application in a charitable reading of Milbank's love ethics. As characteristics of such a love hermeneutics Hoffmeyer names an open-ended, interrogatory character committed to ambiguity, a *theologia viatorum* that listens with gratitude to what is being offered. Such a dialectic, he submits, introduces respect for others as possible bearers of knowledge, thus inviting a practice of humble listening. Hoffmeyer's plea precedes the other essays in the hopes that this spirit may flow through the contributions in this volume.

Catherine Keller's essay pulls John Milbank into a contemplation of Jesus' encounter with the woman at the well, a "marvelous illustration of the asymmetrical reciprocity of the gift" he recommends in his writing. Keller argues that Milbank, while rightfully pointing out human participation in the work of forgiveness, does not sufficiently contemplate the depths of such a reciprocity, which includes a real mutuality and voluntary reception, despite the lack of symmetry and equality in the relations involved. At the well, Jesus asks the woman for a gift and thereby initiates an exchange that allows him to offer a gift in return, luring her thus to actively desire his gift in a positive feedback loop of mutuality. Thus, the asymmetrical gift does not generate dependence on an absolute unilateral power but stimulates an active mutuality.

Milbank's ultimately unilateralist notion of the Father who creates *ex nihilo* cannot, however, finally grasp such expressions of "ecstatic reciprocity."

Virginia Burrus's essay, "Radical Orthodoxy and the Heresiological Habit," examines two essays by the theologian Graham Ward in which he attacks feminist theologians on the issue of the masculinity of Christ and poststructuralist philosophers on the "sadomasochism" of the union of pleasure and pain in sacrificial spirituality. After examining the complexity of both of these themes in patristic thought, Burrus poses the question whether it is possible to theologize without the "heresiological habit"; that is, without caricaturing opponents one has labeled "heretics," while claiming a repristinated version of the same ideas that one claims to be *a priori* knowledge given by orthodoxy as an unchanging tradition.

Elina Vuola writes a trenchant critique of the superficial judgments among radical orthodox writers, such as Stephen Long and Daniel Bell, that Latin American liberation theology made grave intellectual errors from which it is now in crisis, if not dead, and that they have the recipes for a better liberation theology. Vuola demonstrates that such thinkers generally have little knowledge of the background from which liberation theology emerged in the late 1960s, nor of its dynamically continuing evolution into the twenty-first century, not only with new movements among feminists, blacks, indigenous peoples, and ecology, but also with new stages of criticism of global capitalism among thinkers such as Franz Hinkelammert. Most of all such North American radical orthodox thinkers ignore the reality of the roles of the church and of the United States government in world poverty and oppression.

Rosemary Radford Ruether, in her essay, "The Postmodern as Premodern," challenges the thought of the radical orthodox theologian Stephen Long, particularly his *The Goodness of God*. Ruether questions the simplistic dualisms on which Long's theology turns. On the one hand, everything from the late Middle Ages and particularly since Kant is seen as a decline and fall leading to irreparable nihilism. On the other hand, Thomistic theology and the Catholic Church of the thirteenth century are defended as virtually flawless and enjoying the divine gift of "indefectibility." The gains of modernity in areas such as human rights are not given adequate respect nor are the realities of the crimes of historical churches faced truthfully.

Joerg Rieger discusses various problems with the discourse of justice as employed by the American empire. He analyzes three notions of justice: as fairness, as order, and as preference. While preference may seem the least "fair" in terms of the U.S. discourse of fairness as justice, Rieger argues that this notion is the one most common in biblical texts and responds to inequality by focusing on its victims. This notion of justice as preference resists empire by giving an account of the injustices endured by people on the margins, producing an awareness of the power inequalities that prevent justice from being applied and a concern for broken relationships and their restoration.

Marcella Althaus-Reid's essay, "Sending Radical Orthodoxy to Ayacucho," echoes Elina Vuola's critique of its "radical Eurocentrism." More specifically, Althaus-Reid argues that radical orthodox thinkers have made a "class option" for those who benefit from the global system of wealth and power. She quotes liberation theologian Gustavo Gutiérrez that the most serious question one can ask is "how to speak of God in Ayacucho." This region of Peru where the population experienced horrendous violence stands as a test of the credibility of any theology today. Radical orthodoxy needs to measure itself by that standard.

Mayra Rivera's contribution offers a corrective to Milbank and Pickstock's neat and tidy delineation of transcendence as temporally and spatially discontinuous with the world. While they pit the transcendent against the void, marking a tight boundary that is bridged only in the crucial moment of eucharistic communion, Rivera delineates Ellacuría's notion of an immanent transcendent that relates to history, where God and humanity cooperate. Building on Ellacuría's designation of Jesus as a supreme form of transcendence in history, Rivera argues that developing liberative models of radical transcendence must include redefining our constructions of the divine and human as irreducibly transcendent—other—in diversity and complexity, as a community shot through with incarnate transcendence.

Marion Grau's essay argues that Milbank's critique of contemporary empires from a theological stance must go deeper than the indictment of an enlightenment ideology of the *homo sacer* as the imperialist subject of a secular, nihilist modernity. Rather, constructing an effective theological discourse pushing beyond empire requires that theologians engage the issue of theological complicity with imperial structures in premodern, modern, and postmodern times in depth. If the continued tragic entanglement of religion and empire would be rewritten, an exploration of the British civilizing mission must account for the complicity between capitalism and Christianity in missionary endeavors. As a case study, Grau offers a reading of Milbank's account of gift, giving, and reciprocity in the context of colonial encounters. Tracing a variety of ambivalent exchanges in Oceania, involving material, spiritual, erotic, and cultural "gifts," Grau suggests that reciprocal encounters beyond colonialist missionary dynamics must recognize that most colonized peoples were only badly described by terms such as "savage heathen" or "noble savage" and acknowledge them as agents in these colonial exchanges.

Lisa Isherwood weaves together a critique of Daniel Bell's attack on liberation theology with an outcry against the Bush administration's misuse of the September 11th terrorist attack to justify expanded U.S. economic and military imperialism. For Isherwood this U.S. misuse of September 11th reveals the dangerous position of humanity in the early twenty-first century of enslavement to a consumerist worldview that is at the same time impoverishing the majority of humans. Yet she sees Bell's solution to this situation by returning to twelfth-century theology and monasticism as compounding the problem, rather than offering a way out. Instead, she suggests a radically transformed Christology of the "flesh become word" that calls us to conversion to our neighbor as a real concern for one another's enfleshed realities.

The Catholic feminist theologian Mary Grey also grapples with radical orthodoxy's critique of liberation theology and by implication feminist liberation theology. She acknowledges that feminist theology and radical orthodoxy share many critiques of modernity but part company on solutions. Grey is also dismayed by the lack of deep anguish at the sufferings of the poor among radical orthodox thinkers, an anguish central to liberation theology. Gray sees the praxis of feminist liberation theologians, like that of liberation theologians, such as Gutiérrez and Ellacuría, as deeply rooted in a spirituality of compassion for and solidarity with sufferers. She explores the thought of Dorothy Day and Dorothee Soelle as examples of this deep union of mystical spirituality and action for justice.

Melissa Raphael's essay urges the expansion of a Jewish feminist theology whose reclamation of Judaism within modernity has been narrowed by the limited canon accessible to a post-*haskalah* Judaism preoccupied with the ethical justification of faith. Raphael observes that Judaism is largely non-creedal, is more concerned with orthopraxis than orthodoxy, and has different quarrels with modernity than has Christianity, since modernity both emancipated and destroyed European Jewry. Even so, she finds shared goals with radical orthodoxy in the need to reclaim the theological confidence to speak normatively and to refuse recognition to an autonomous secular sphere. Raphael differentiates Jewish approaches to theology, to feminist concerns, and to orthodoxy from those defined by the hegemonic Christian definitions and contexts. In doing so, she pushes the groundbreaking work of Judith Plaskow and others toward a Jewish women's theology that lies beyond an epistemology driven by the social needs of the community alone. In establishing its authority, Jewish feminist theology can then move toward a sense of the real presence of God as not only immanent to women's immediate experience but also as the transcendent *mysterium tremendum* under the dispensation of whose self-revelation all Jews, women and men, are assembled.

In her essay, Beverly Clack argues that the rejection of the Enlightenment, such as proposed by radical orthodox writers, is not the only way to articulate a religious perspective. Critiquing Graham Ward's application of Lacan to argue a subversive maleness of Christ that does not do much more epistemological work than undercut feminist criticisms, Clack grounds her feminist philosophy or religion on the use of Freud to rethink the nature of religious belief. Freud's more ambiguous account of religion and his intermediate position between modernity and postmodernity challenge the primacy of both reason and consciousness.

These approaches to theology and religion pursued in contemporary spaces and times, postmodern, postcolonial and other, mean to challenge and expand the task of interpreting the postmodern. They invite their readers to consider different answers to the challenges radical orthodoxy has leveled at theology and society. While many essays share certain critiques of modernity, empire, and capitalism with radical orthodoxy, they differ widely in their approaches to these issues, they employ approaches such as liberation theology, feminist theology, historical theology in conversation with contemporary theory, they expand themes differently, challenge the scope and contextualization of theologies in contemporary spaces and times.

Negotiating the hermeneutics of orthodoxy, some authors consider whether any successful imposition of a reigning orthodoxy must be propped up by the forces of empire, whether the heresiological habit of ferreting out and caricaturing one's opponents is a concomitant factor for theological dicourses of orthodoxy, or whether theological explorations should rather be guided by a hermeneutics of love, a practice of humble listening, open to consider also forms of orthodoxy within other religious contexts. Affirming the counter-imperial and counter-capitalist push of radical orthodoxy writers, authors ask which empires surround us at this time, what orthodoxies they espouse, and how theological discourse has been complicit with them in the modern colonial past and postmodern present. Expanding thus the quest for a challenge to empire some essays argue that truly radical theologies must also consider the impact of colonialism on the global scene and decolonize theology while contesting the vicissitudes of rampant capitalism and the marginalization of critical theological and ethical concerns in our societies. They aim to do so not in a spirit of dismissal of potential allies that erects false dichotomies and untenable periodizations but instead hope that these essays help readers to perceive multiple complex levels and locations of interaction between culture and theology, where theology, honoring its religious socialist connections forms alliances across schools of thought in order to formulate critically relevant and ethically pertinent responses to the crises of our places and times, beyond the narrowly defined confines of European and Euro-American modernity. If colonialism and civilizing missions are also products of modernity, then postmodern theology must resist attempts to reinstate the rule of a theological Britannia over the waves of culture and society, but rather account for its imperial past and enter into subversive coalitions that challenge the rule of contemporary empires. To this effect, theologians must consider the effects of colonialism, theological and social, and must do so by fully appreciating the range of experiences in different locations and contexts, hearing many voices to make up a fuller picture of the increasingly mutually effected global locations we inhabit. Furthermore, it must abandon the notion that simply because contemporary Europe seems secularized, there is not a great resurgence of Christianity in the landscapes and contexts of former colonial territories. Appreciating the vitality and many shadedness of liberation theologies in Latin America as well as in the North, can help continue to forge alliances for contesting problematic dynamics in society and theology, without radical orthodoxy's seeming option for those who benefit from global capitalism over those who are impoverished by it, and hence honor further the radical demands of otherness on theological discourse. The challenge of otherness is heightened by the voices of women who find radical orthodoxy's approach to gender and embodiment little more than a simple undercutting of feminist theological critiques, claiming a subversive maleness of Christ, a transcorporeality that once and for all does away with the challenges to masculine and heterosexist theology.

This work, we hope, will be further facilitated by essays that offer discussions of gift and reciprocity critiquing the lack of symmetry and equality in radical orthodox texts, aiming to deepen the consideration of varieties of mutual exchange between human and divine agents, to acknowledge colonized peoples as agents in colonial exchanges, and outline a theology of reciprocal giving that does not generate dependency on a unilateral power. Other doctrinal interventions include a challenge to too tidy delineations between transcendent and immanent, the narrow point of encounter between them as located by radical orthodox writers in the eucharistic communion, pushing towards an understanding of community shot through with incarnate transcendence.

These considerations are supplemented by a discussion of the difference between justice and fairness, a mystical spirituality of action for justice, a feminist Jewish approach to radical orthodoxy's challenge to modernity that pushes the boundaries of what is considered orthodox and of Jewish feminism, a theological response to September 11 in the light of liberation theology and radical orthodoxy, and a forceful argument that a rejection of enlightenment is not the only way to articulate a contemporary religious perspective. Thus we hope that this volume will stimulate further discussions of issues of theology and orthodoxy, radical and other, in postmodernity, post-coloniality and beyond.

PART I

interpreting bodies

1. Charitable Interpretation

—John F. Hoffmeyer

Radical orthodoxy has produced profound and innovative readings of Augustine. Augustine is so important for John Milbank, the preeminent figure in the radical orthodoxy movement, that a few years ago he accepted the phrase "postmodern critical Augustinianism" as a fitting description of his theological endeavor.[1] One of the Augustinian themes most dear to radical orthodoxy is *caritas*. Milbank in particular has appropriated Augustinian "charity" to articulate an ontology of nonviolence rooted in Christian narrative. In our age of "wars and rumors of wars" (Mark 13:7), any attempt to cultivate nonviolence is an occasion for gratitude. Milbank's work is far more than a commendable attempt in a laudable direction. It is a brilliant and creative project whose virtues are too numerous to delineate here.

This essay does not seek to explicate the main lines of Milbank's work. Still less does it seek to mount a critical attack upon fault lines, real or imagined, in his theoretical edifice. Instead my goal is to build upon the foundation that Milbank has laid, extending his proposal for a "charitable" ontology in what I hope will be a constructive direction. Specifically, I will commend the practice of charitable interpretation. This commendation will have three primary elements. First I will discuss the nature and some identifying characteristics of charitable interpretation. In the light of these identifying characteristics I will then consider some of Milbank's positions, with some reference to those of other radical orthodox thinkers. I will be looking both for resources for charitable interpretation in the work of Milbank and other radical orthodox theologians and for ways in which more charitable interpretation could strengthen that work. Finally, I hope that my own interpretive practice in this essay is more charitable than not.

Charitable Interpretation and Its Marks

Although Martin Luther is neither a prominent nor a particularly positive figure in Milbank's version of Western intellectual and theological history, I am a Lutheran theologian, so let me begin with Luther's *Small Catechism*. Discussing the eighth

---

1. John Milbank, "Postmodern Critical Augustinianism: A Short 'Summa' in Forty-Two Responses to Unasked Questions," in *The Postmodern God: A Theological Reader* (ed. Graham Ward; Oxford: Blackwell, 1997), 265.

commandment "not to bear false witness against your neighbor," Luther says that this means that "We are to fear and love God, so that we do not tell lies about our neighbors, betray or slander them, or destroy their reputations. Instead we are to come to their defense, speak well of them, and interpret everything they do in the best possible light."[2]

In Luther's view, telling the truth requires a choice among interpretive possibilities. These possibilities are not confined to the extremes of two diametrically opposed alternatives: either true or false. In the metaphor employed by the English translator, Timothy Wengert, different interpretive possibilities involve different shadings. One can interpret the neighbor's deeds in different "lights." Telling the truth—not bearing false witness—requires interpreting the neighbor's deeds in "the best possible light."

The English wording "interpret everything they do in the best possible light" reflects the German *alles zum Besten kehren*.[3] A literal translation would be "turn everything to the best." This wording suggests the English idiom "making the best" of something, but that idiom carries the negative overtone of "making the best of a bad situation." The saying "making the best of a bad situation" sharply divides the subject who will "make the best" from the negatively evaluated object, the "bad situation." Luther's point is that we are to "turn everything to the best" in the very evaluation of our neighbor's words and deeds. One might say that telling the truth involves turning the neighbor's words and deeds so that they are seen in the best possible light.

One might also say that telling the truth requires giving a charitable interpretation to our neighbor's words and deeds. Such an interpretation is charitable in the sense that it is an expression of charity, not in the thinned-out contemporary sense of that word as giving leftovers to persons in economic need, but in the sense of Augustine's *caritas*. A charitable interpretation is one that instantiates charity in the sense that the King James translation of the Bible uses in rendering 1 Cor 13 a hymn to charity. According to Paul in that famous chapter, charity or love "rejoices in the truth" (v. 6). This rejoicing demonstrates that charity is power for observing the eighth commandment not to bear false witness. Charity rejoices in the truth not by celebrating that it has the winning argument or the superior position, not by "insist[ing] on its own way," but by being "patient" and "kind," rather than "boastful or arrogant or rude" (vv. 4–5).

It hardly requires a leap to move from this Pauline notion of rejoicing with patience and kindness in the truth to Luther's vision of turning our neighbors' words and deeds so that they are seen in the best possible light. What Paul adds to Luther's approach is a specific word for naming the power at work in such "rejoicing in the truth," in "not bearing false witness" in the interpretation of the neighbor's words and deeds. That power is charity, or as contemporary usage would say, love. Love is the principle of charitable interpretation.

Advocating charitable interpretation and invoking love as its principle can open the door to suspicions that niceness is trumping rigor, that warm fuzziness is supplanting critical edge. Can charitable interpretation be rigorous? If so, what are the marks

---

2. Robert Kolb and Timothy J. Wengert, eds., *The Book of Concord: The Confessions of the Evangelical Lutheran Church* (Minneapolis: Fortress Press, 2000), 353.

3. *Die Bekenntnisschriften der evangelisch-lutherischen Kirche* (Göttingen: Vandenhoeck & Ruprecht, 1982), 509.

of that rigor? In what follows I propose not an exhaustive list of such marks, but a reflection upon four important ones.

The first such mark is the interrogatory character of charitable interpretation. The interpreter asks questions, sometimes hard questions, of that which is being interpreted. An insightful question opens up a perspective that might otherwise have remained hidden. Insightful questions make possible revealing answers. Asking good interpretive questions is a skill. Like all skills, honing it requires disciplined work. This may be part of what John Milbank has in mind when he says somewhere that exegesis is relatively easy, while interpretation is difficult.

Perhaps the most difficult interrogatory element in the work of interpretation is that a good interpreter is alive to her own questionability. Theories of interpretation in the past century have devoted much attention to hermeneutical circles. One of the most important hermeneutical circles is the questioning of the questioner. In the act of interpretation, the interpreter can find her own perspective called into question. Almost two centuries ago, G. W. F. Hegel's *Phenomenology of Spirit* provided one long demonstration that a subject can not seek the truth of its object without its own truth coming into question. In the late 1960s and early 1970s the famous debate concerning the "hermeneutical" approach of Hans-Georg Gadamer and the "critical theory" approach of Jürgen Habermas presumed that good interpretation requires that the interpreter be open to coming into question. The debate revolved around how such coming into question might happen.[4]

To many critics and proponents alike, Christian theology has not seemed to cultivate the interpreter's sense of his own questionability. Christian dogmatics has seemed, well, "dogmatic." (It is worth remembering that the pejorative sense of "dogmatic" in contemporary English is not true of the word and its parallels in all times and places. Friedrich Schleiermacher preferred the term "dogmatics" to "systematic theology" because he felt that the former called attention to the fact that the beliefs or "dogma" of a Christian community were tied to a specific historical situation, while the term "systematic theology" suggested an inflexible, ahistorical edifice. In other words, "dogmatics" better preserved a sense of its own questionability.) The Christian bumper sticker "God said it; I believe it; that settles it" does not encourage Christians to be open to the questioning of their theological formulations.

In his essay "The Finality of Christ," Rowan Williams writes that the church's "institutional life is committed to the preservation, by word and sacrament, of its own questionability, and the ambiguity of all systematized schemes of religious meaning, all attempts at finished religious ontologies. And because of this, it is not free to claim finality for itself; there are things it does not say, meaning it does not carry."[5] Theology is never final. It is *theologia viatorum*, theology in process, theology always open to being questioned. For Christian theology the finality of Christ precludes the finality of any ideas about Christ or formulations of Christ's being or significance.

For Williams there is a further christological reason for theology's questionability, its inherent ability to be questioned. One could think that Christ embodies and

---

4. See the exchange between Gadamer and Habermas, as well as contributions from other authors, in Karl-Otto Apel et al., *Hermeneutik und Ideologiekritik* (Frankfurt am Main: Suhrkamp Verlag, 1980).

5. Rowan Williams, "The Finality of Christ," in *On Christian Theology* (Challenges in Contemporary Theology; Oxford: Blackwell, 2000), 100.

symbolizes all that essentially needs embodiment and symbolization, so that theology is always questionable because it can never adequately express this fullness of Christ. Williams argues for a different view of Christ. He says that "the meaning of Jesus is not the container of all other meanings but their test, judgement and catalyst. . . . His 'universal significance' is a universally crucial question rather than a comprehensive ontological scheme."[6]

To the extent that this is true, theology has the task of posing that "universally crucial question." Since Christ is a universal question,[7] theology itself not only is called to pose that question in different specific circumstances, but is itself questioned by that question. Theology cannot be the master of the question that it poses. Its posing of the question of Christ is just as much a "letting be" of that question, a speaking that is just as much and in fact first and foremost a listening.

Listening is so important that it deserves separate treatment as a second mark of charitable interpretation. In one sense, the claim that listening is a mark of charitable interpretation is so obvious as to be trivial. The interpreter tries to hear what the author or speaker is saying—rather than, for example, simply projecting the interpreter's ideas onto the author or speaker. Beyond that it is important to distinguish between two poles on the spectrum of listening. One pole is listening to discern the fault lines in what is being interpreted, to analyze its structure so that one can use it for one's own purposes, to discern its possible weak points so that one can attack it, to highlight its possible dangers so that one can sound the alarm against them. The other pole is listening with gratitude for this opportunity to learn from the other, with openness to what the other might give. This type of listening seeks to discern possible strengths so that it can benefit from them, possible beauties so that it can celebrate them.

This is an interactive rather than an exclusive polarity. To listen with gratitude and openness by no means precludes critical judgments and rejections of positions under interpretation. But an approach marked by gratitude and openness does preclude coming to the interpretive task armed for battle, primarily seeking ways to shoot down the other's arguments.

One could use the language of conversion to frame the difference between polemical listening and open, grateful listening. In its Latin etymology, "conversion" is a "turning." The former approach to listening seeks to convert the other to one's own point of view by showing the inferiority of the other's point of view. The latter approach to listening recognizes that any and all parties may need conversion. This approach also rejects the idea that any one point of view, any one "scheme of meaning" as Rowan Williams would say, is the goal toward which all are to turn in conversion.

The positive expression of this rejection is humility, the third mark of charitable interpretation. Christian theological tradition has some strong "humility checks" to guard against any particular theology claiming that it adequately articulates the goal of conversion. Karl Barth insisted that Jesus Christ, not any Christian claim about or understanding of Christ, was "the one Word of God." He argued that the Christian

---

6. Ibid., 94.
7. For an important meditation on the relation of an interrogatory mode of theology to Jesus' own predilection for asking questions, see Ched Myers, "'I Will Ask You a Question': Interrogatory Theology," in *Theology Without Foundations: Religious Practice and the Future of Theological Truth* (ed. Stanley Hauerwas, Nancey Murphy, and Mark Nation; Nashville: Abingdon Press, 1994), 91–116.

"statement of Jesus Christ as the one Word of God in reality has nothing to do with . . . a self-glorification of Christians in comparison with other human beings, or of the church in comparison with other institutions and arrangements, or of Christianity in comparison with other conceptions of the world. . . . Since Jesus Christ is the content of this statement, those who confess it do not in any way separate themselves from those who do not confess it."[8] One of the central points of Christian eschatology is that "now we see in a mirror, dimly, but then we will see face to face" (1 Cor 13:12). When Christians are tempted to be too definitive in our theological claims, we need to remember that we do not even know the truth of our own lives. As Paul wrote to the Colossians: "Your life is hidden with Christ in God. When Christ who is your life is revealed, then you also will be revealed with him in glory" (Col 3:3–4).

Of course Christian faith also claims that in knowing Christ we know the truth of our lives. Christian theology would betray its calling if it degenerated into a caricature of negative theology that simply threw up its hands and said, "We have no claims to make and no insights to share, since our lives are hidden with Christ in God." But eschatological reserve enjoins upon Christian theology the humble recognition that our claims about God's truth are by no means identical with that truth. The best of Christian theology has always honored the humble dialectic of knowing and unknowing.

The dialectic of knowing and unknowing introduces a fourth mark of charitable interpretation: respect.[9] If one is aware of the limited and questionable nature of one's own knowledge, one respects others as quite possibly bearers of knowledge and insight that oneself does not have. Listening, already discussed as a mark of charitable interpretation, is one of the most powerful enactments of respect. The person who listens to others says in effect: "I want to hear from you. I think what you have to say is important. It is important not simply as raw material to be processed, improved, and corrected by fitting it into my point of view. It is important in its own right within the context from which it emanates, the context of your life and person. I think that you as a speaker are important."

Charitable Interpretation, Milbank, and Radical Orthodoxy

The current essay responds to radical orthodoxy by taking the latter's emphasis upon charity as a spur to develop a theory of charitable interpretation. My primary focus is not any claims or interpretations advanced by Milbank or other theologians identifying with the radical orthodoxy movement. I do, however, want to bring some of my proposals into conversation with moves that Milbank and some other radical orthodox

---

8. Translation mine. "Mit einem Selbstruhm der Christen anderen Menschen, oder der Kirche anderen Anstalten und Einrichtungen, oder des Christentums anderen Weltkonzeptionen gegenüber, hat der Satz von Jesus Christus als dem einen Wort Gottes in Wirklichkeit nichts zu tun. . . . Indem Jesus Christus sein Inhalt ist, trennt sich also der, der ihn bekennt, in keiner Weise von denen, die ihn nicht bekennen" (Karl Barth, *Die Lehre von der Versöhnung: Jesus Christus, der wahrhaftige Zeuge* [vol. IV/3/1 of *Kirchliche Dogmatik*; Zollikon-Zurich: Evangelischer Verlag, 1959], 100-101).

9. As I was writing this article, I was happy to find that my emphasis on charitable interpretation bears important similarities to positions advanced by the admirable pragmatist thinker Jeffrey Stout in his recent book *Democracy and Tradition* (Princeton, N.J.: Princeton University Press, New Forum Books, 2004). My listing of "respect" as a distinct mark of charitable interpretation is dependent upon Stout's appeal to respect in that work.

theologians make in their work. This has two purposes. One is to elucidate my proposals by moving from generalities to specifics. The other is to engage Milbank's own practice of interpretation, and to a lesser extent that of other radical orthodox writers, in a constructively critical way.

Earlier I introduced a polarity between two approaches to interpretive listening. One pole was bent on converting others by showing the inferiority of positions other than one's own. The opposite pole gave major attention to the real possibility of one's own need for conversion. Of course these two poles are not the only options. They mark out a spectrum that includes various shadings of the two poles. One of my uncertainties in reading Milbank concerns his position on the spectrum. Critical readings of Milbank often locate him in the direction of the prior pole, short on humble listening and long on the polemical attempt to demonstrate the inferiority of other positions.

In his contribution to the volume *Christian Uniqueness Reconsidered: The Myth of a Pluralistic Theology of Religions*, Milbank proposes that Christians replace interreligious "dialogue" with both "mutual suspicion" and "conversation."[10] On the surface, the proposal to replace dialogue with mutual suspicion sounds repugnant. But to use that initial reaction as the jumping-off point for a critique of Milbank would be unfair. Milbank's proposal depends upon a particular understanding of the concept of dialogue, which he develops in the course of his essay. He takes dialogue to be a discursive exchange that assumes that what the dialogue is about is an idea or value fundamentally shared by the participants in the dialogue. Since he holds that such fundamental commonality is absent in interreligious discursive exchange, he thinks that the name "dialogue" is inappropriate.

Even if one grants both Milbank's notion of dialogue and his understanding of interreligious discursive exchange, replacing "dialogue" with "mutual suspicion" holds little promise for charitable interpretation between religions. If questioning (including one's own questionability), listening, and humility are marks of charitable interpretation, a fundamental posture of mutual suspicion is a mark of uncharitable interpretation. How can one listen with the openness to learn from the other, to let the other call one's own position into question, if one's basic attitude toward the other is suspicion?

Fortunately Milbank uses a second term for what he thinks should replace interreligious dialogue: "conversation." Unlike "mutual suspicion," the general sense of the term "conversation" is not incompatible with charitable interpretation. For my reading, Milbank's reference to conversation stands as a corrective to his appeal to mutual suspicion. Just how to interpret this corrective is unclear, though, since he lets these two formulations stand in juxtaposition, without commenting on their relation. My guess is that "conversation" better expresses Milbank's intention, since he privileges that term over "mutual suspicion" for the remainder of the essay.

Fleshing out his understanding of interreligious conversation, Milbank observes: "In the course of such a conversation, we should indeed expect to constantly receive Christ again, from the unique spiritual responses of other cultures."[11] This is a lovely

---

10. John Milbank, "The End of Dialogue," in *Christian Uniqueness Reconsidered: The Myth of a Pluralistic Theology of Religions* (ed. Gavin D'Costa, Faith Meets Faith; Maryknoll, N.Y.: Orbis Books, 1990), 189–90.

11. Ibid., 190.

statement of charitable interpretation as humble listening. In interreligious conversation, Christians can expect themselves to be converted anew, to "receive Christ again." This is not just a possible occasional benefit, under the best possible circumstances. Milbank says that Christians engaged in interreligious conversation should "expect to *constantly* receive Christ again."

Milbank immediately proceeds: "But I do not pretend that this proposal means anything other than continuing the work of conversion."[12] Here questions rush in. When Milbank speaks of conversion, is he referring to the conversion of both (or all) participants in the conversation, or does he mean more narrowly the Christian work to convert others? If Milbank means the former, which would continue the line of interpretation I began in the preceding paragraph, why does he begin the sentence with "But"? If expecting "to constantly receive Christ again" and "continuing the work of conversion" stand in an adversative relation, they must be talking about different things.

Above I supposed an identity between the two. I supposed that receiving Christ again was ongoing conversion. In doing so I am following Martin Luther's understanding of Christian life as daily baptism: "Thus a Christian life is nothing else than a daily baptism, begun once and continuing ever after." The daily renewal of Christian life is a daily turning, a daily conversion, from the "old Adam" to Christ.[13]

Treating the continually renewed reception of Christ by Christians as a form of the ongoing labor of conversion need not assume that it is the only form of such labor. Persons of other faiths engaging in interreligious conversations with Christians can also undergo conversion. In the history of Christian interaction with persons of other faiths, Christians have primarily thought of such conversion as the move from other religions to Christianity. However, might not persons of other faiths experience a conversion analogous to the renewal Christians experience by "receiving Christ again"? Analogously to the renewed Christian turning from "the old Adam" to Christ, might not a Muslim experience conversion as a renewed submission to the sovereign will of God? Could not interreligious conversation lead both parties to a deepening and renewal of their own religious lives that does not involve a switch from identification with one religious tradition to identification with the other?

Further pursuit of this question is beyond the scope of the current essay. One of the points to be explored would be the realization that the very practice of interreligious conversation makes it inaccurate to speak of the religious traditions involved as wholly separate and distinct. The Christian who "receives Christ again" in conversation with a Hindu experiences conversion to a deeper Christian faith that is no longer wholly explicable without reference to Hinduism.

My purpose here, though, is simply to point to some of the directions in which one might go in thinking about conversion in interreligious conversation. Milbank recognizes in a profound way that interreligious conversation is not a one-way street when he speaks of expecting "to constantly receive Christ again, from the unique spiritual responses of other cultures." However, when he immediately goes on to say, "But I do not pretend that this proposal means anything other than continuing the work of conversion," it is hard to see how conversion here might function other than as a one-way

12. Ibid.
13. Kolb and Wengert, *Book of Concord*, 465.

street. More narrowly, Milbank might be reserving "conversion" to refer to the move from another religious faith to Christianity. In that case, Milbank would also be affirming that other faiths have "unique spiritual responses" to contribute and that these responses can deepen and renew Christian faith, but he would reserve "conversion" for the narrow sense just specified. More broadly, Milbank might be including that deepening and renewal of Christians' faith as part of the "work of conversion," along with the movement of persons from other faiths to Christianity. The conversion street would still be ultimately one way, since its goal would be the cultivation of Christian faith.

If charitable interpretation is to govern interreligious conversation, then it is essential that Christians be ready to respect the "unique spiritual responses" of persons of other faiths. Milbank models charitable interpretation still further by claiming that Christians should enter interreligious conversation expecting to be renewed in their Christian faith precisely through the gift of the unique spiritual responses of persons of other faiths. The humility and respect characteristic of charitable interpretation urge a further step. The unique resources of other faiths are not only gifts with the power to renew Christian faith. Respect requires that the Christian interpreter honor the possibility that the resources of another religious faith put its practitioners in a position to be open to the "unique spiritual responses" of Christians and to be renewed and deepened in their faith by those Christian gifts, without themselves having to "convert" to Christianity.

I claimed early in this essay that the charitable interpreter is essentially open to the questionability of her own views. This openness to the questionability of one's own views is not obvious in Milbank's claim that, from his Christian perspective, interreligious conversation is about "continuing the work of conversion," coupled with his apparent assumption of what I have called the "one-way" directionality of that conversion. Perhaps I am misreading Milbank here, since elsewhere, when giving a programmatic summary of his approach, he says, "Christianity should not draw boundaries, and the Church is that paradox: a nomad city."[14] Then my question is this: In interreligious conversation, what does the church's nomadic wandering look like? Does Milbank's nomadism do the work that I am trying to accomplish by insisting on the interpreter's openness to the questionability of her own views? Does nomadic Christian participation in interreligious conversation include the possibility that all participants might be converted to something that would be new to all of them, since it would respond to questions that only take shape in the course of the conversation?

Graham Ward, along with Milbank one of the editors of the volume *Radical Orthodoxy*, takes this approach. In the epilogue to his *Cities of God*, Ward argues that "the real questions about the relation of different faith communities and traditions only emerge as we learn to live together without fear. We cannot presuppose the outcome. . . . We cannot solve the complexity of the relation before the real questions have emerged. And the real questions only emerge in the practices of our everyday living alongside each other."[15]

---

14. Milbank, "Postmodern Critical Augustinianism," 269.
15. Graham Ward, *Cities of God* (Radical Orthodoxy; London: Routledge, 2000), 258.

To my knowledge Milbank has only written one essay on interreligious conversation. A vastly more extensive resource for exploring his approach to interpretive listening lies in his discussions of authors, movements, and epochs across the centuries of Western intellectual history. Milbank can be a valuable teacher for those who would learn the ways of charitable interpretation. One of his finest interpretive accomplishments is his reading of Hegel. This is not to say that I always agree with his reading of Hegel, because I do not. Yet Milbank's reading of Hegel is exemplary because here Milbank combines nuanced appreciation of the perceived strengths of the material he is interpreting with incisive criticism of its perceived weaknesses. This is true in the chapter that Milbank devotes to Hegel in *Theology and Social Theory*, appropriately entitled "For and Against Hegel,"[16] as well as in his essay "The Second Difference."[17]

At the same time, critics have charged Milbank with succumbing both to dualism and to sweeping generalization, neither of which is conducive to charitable interpretation. Before examining this criticism more closely, it might be worth acknowledging that Milbank is by no means the only radical orthodox writer to be charged with dualistic or overgeneralizing interpretation. Most likely some examples of such criticism will appear in other contributions to the volume in which this essay appears. To cite one of the most strongly worded examples already in print, Ellen Armour has the following to say about Catherine Pickstock, whose *After Writing: On the Liturgical Consummation of Philosophy* was the first book other than Milbank's to arise out of the radical orthodoxy movement: "Continental philosophers serve only as straw enemies for her. Pickstock's readings of Derrida and Levinas, in particular, are in my view unconscionable and irresponsible."[18] Even Gerard Loughlin, himself a contributor to the volume *Radical Orthodoxy*, has contrasted "what often seems her [i.e., Pickstock's] relentless hostility to Derrida" with Graham Ward's "generous and appreciative reading of fashionable theorists—above all, of Derrida."[19]

Naturally the mere existence of a critique does not confirm that it is well grounded. Although to some ears the label "radical orthodoxy" may suggest a rigid dualism, a division of the house into the "orthodox" and the "heterodox," Ward distances himself from such an understanding when he writes: "Because of the nature of analogical world-views, there can be no tight and policed boundaries around any of them."[20] Milbank himself declares that "Christianity should not draw boundaries."[21] The sound advice against the drawing of dualistic boundaries is unfortunately difficult to follow consistently in practice. One ironic contemporary example is the tendency for some "anti-dualistic" thinkers to divide the field between those who operate with "binaries" and those who supposedly eschew them.

16. John Milbank, *Theology and Social Theory: Beyond Secular Reason* (Oxford: Blackwell, 1998), 147–76.

17. John Milbank, *The Word Made Strange: Theology, Language, Culture* (Oxford: Blackwell, 1999), 171–93.

18. Ellen T. Armour, "Beyond Belief?: Sexual Difference and Religion after Ontotheology," in *The Religious* (ed. John D. Caputo; Blackwell Readings in Continental Thought; Oxford: Blackwell, 2002), 224.

19. Gerard Loughlin, "Rains for a Famished Land: Catherine Pickstock's Alternative to the 'Polity of Death,'" *Times Literary Supplement*, April 10, 1998, 13.

20. Ward, *Cities of God*, 257.

21. Milbank, "Postmodern Critical Augustinianism," 269.

Radical orthodox thinkers—some more than others—have their own difficulties in staying away from dualistic boundaries. Take for example one of the basic elements of radical orthodoxy: its critique of secular modernity. To a large extent the expression "secular modernity" seems to be redundant to radical orthodox authors. The dominance of the secular defines modernity. In his recent book *Democracy and Tradition*, Jeffrey Stout argues that radical orthodoxy fails to distinguish between modern, secular, democratic societies and a particular philosophical understanding of those societies: namely, a "liberal secularist" understanding. Liberal secularism, whatever that exactly is, is only one element of modern, secular, democratic societies. By conflating the two, radical orthodoxy treats modern, secular, democratic societies as much less heterogeneous than they actually are.[22] This oversimplification makes it too tempting for Milbank and at least some of the other radical orthodox writers to state the relation of their own project to secular modernity in a way that sounds like an "us-them," "good-bad" dualism. As Stout puts it, "radical orthodoxy's critique of the secular tends, under current circumstances, to reinforce the sort of boundary-drawing it officially opposes. . . . From within radical orthodoxy's refuge of aggressive like-mindedness, prophetic denunciation of the secular 'other' and the unmasking of liberal theological error ritually reinforce the enclave boundary, rather than healing the world."[23]

One can rightly object to the reference to "aggressive like-mindedness" as unfairly overstated. The difference indicated above between Graham Ward and John Milbank with regard to Christianity's relation to other religions is but one example of differences among radical orthodox thinkers. The basic concern about a dualistic and over-generalizing relation to secular modernity is well founded, though. As Stout argues, when Milbank finds thinkers who lived chronologically within the modern period but who sound more "radical orthodox" than "secular modern," he does not take them as reason to construct a more heterogeneous view of modernity.[24] Instead he assigns them to a "counter-modernity" that "continues to shadow actual, secular modernity."[25] Why not speak instead of minority traditions within modernity? Why decide that one bundle of modern traditions is more "actually" modern than another?

In his essay "The Programme of Radical Orthodoxy," Milbank states his relation to modernity in a somewhat different way: "Radical Orthodoxy, although it opposes the modern, also seeks to save it. It espouses, not the premodern, but an alternative version of modernity."[26] Is this alternative version of modernity Milbank's wish for how modernity might have developed and his proposal for how we might still develop it? Or is it an actually existing but underappreciated strand of modernity? If the latter, then Stout's challenge is an apt one: Why not give modernity credit for enabling this "alternative" development as well? The project of "saving" modernity by espousing this "alternative version" would then not present itself as a project simply external to modernity. It would be in an important sense a modern project, openly using resources of modernity even in criticizing major elements of modernity.

---

22. Stout, *Democracy and Tradition*, 100–107.

23. Ibid., 115.

24. Ibid., 106.

25. Milbank, *Theology and Social Theory*, 4.

26. John Milbank, "The Programme of Radical Orthodoxy," in *Radical Orthodoxy?—A Catholic Enquiry* (ed. Laurence Paul Hemming; Aldershot: Ashgate, 2000), 45.

In critical debates concerning radical orthodoxy in general and Milbank in particular, no one side holds a monopoly on overgeneralizing dualism. Some critics have responded to Milbank's polemical stance toward secular modernity with a false dualism of their own, in which they accuse radical orthodoxy of seeking a return to medieval Christianity. Milbank makes clear from the beginning of *Theology and Social Theory* that "the book offers no proposed restoration of a premodern Christian position."[27] On a closely related note, some critics have lamented Milbank's supposedly broadside attacks upon the European Enlightenment. Yet when Milbank attempts a programmatic summary of his theology, he can state clearly that "any claim of outright Christian opposition to enlightenment is bound to be an oversimplification."[28] Critics who are quick to accuse Milbank of "Enlightenment bashing" need to take notice of Milbank's clarification on this point. At the same time, Milbank needs to ask himself why thoughtful readers can suspect him of "outright Christian opposition to enlightenment." In the heat of trying, as he would say, to "out-narrate" Enlightenment narratives, does Milbank tend toward the oversimplification against which he elsewhere warns?

Beyond any particular material position, some critics have objected to Milbank's style. Gavin Hyman, by no means a polemical opponent of radical orthodoxy, has commented that "John Milbank in particular is notorious for his penchant for hyperbole, his tendency to make the sweeping statement and the gigantic claim."[29] Laurence Paul Hemming, editor of the fine collection *Radical Orthodoxy?—A Catholic Inquiry* and himself a contributor to the volume *Radical Orthodoxy*, says that radical orthodoxy in general invites "respectful rudeness" by "its refusal to be apologetic . . . its pugnacity, and its seemingly unshakeable convictions of inerrancy." Hemming argues that these features of radical orthodoxy "all function as stimuli to debate, if correctly understood." He links them to the tutorial tradition at Cambridge (among other British universities and colleges), where radical orthodoxy had its birth. Acknowledging that these stylistic features have their roughness, he defends them as "generosity in disguise." They push the interpreter/respondent to think, and they can lead to a serious debate about issues in which both parties grow.[30]

Hemming's comments provide helpful instruction in charitable interpretation. One can read Hemming as honoring the concern of those for whom the self-assured polemics of Milbank and some other radical orthodox authors come across as arrogance and a lack of sympathetic openness to other views. At the same time, Hemming looks for a more charitable reading of Milbank and other radical orthodox theologians stylistically akin to him in this regard, a reading that will make it less easy to close one's mind to their arguments.

Still, if "pugnacity" and "seemingly unshakeable convictions of inerrancy" are "generosity in disguise," the burden ought not fall disproportionately upon the interpreter to divine that the disguise is just a disguise. A polemical writer needs to provide clues that will invite the reader to discern the generosity behind the disguise. For example, the

---

27. Milbank, *Theology and Social Theory*, 2.

28. Milbank, "Postmodern Critical Augustinianism," 268.

29. Gavin Hyman, Review of John Milbank, Catherine Pickstock, and Graham Ward, eds., *Radical Orthodoxy: A New Theology*, *New Blackfriars* 80 (1999): 426.

30. Laurence Paul Hemming, "Introduction: Radical Orthodoxy's Appeal to Catholic Scholarship," in *Radical Orthodoxy?—A Catholic Enquiry* (ed. Laurence Paul Hemming; Aldershot: Ashgate, 2000), 4.

polemical essayist Wendell Berry includes these words in the preface to his collection *Sex, Economy, Freedom, and Community*: "An essayist not only has no right to expect complete agreement but has a certain responsibility to ward it off. If you tell me, dear reader, that you agree with me completely, then I must suspect one or both of us of dishonesty. I must reserve the right, after all, to disagree with myself."[31] Berry begins one of the book's essays, originally given as a lecture at a theological seminary, with the words: "An essayist is, literally, a writer who attempts to tell the truth. Preachers must resign themselves to being either right or wrong; an essayist, when proved wrong, may claim to have been 'just practicing.'"[32]

Berry explicitly acknowledges that his conclusions are fallible enough that he may have to disagree with them himself. He admits that he may be proven wrong. He employs humor, generously at his own expense as well as at the expense of the preachers in his audience, to keep his polemics from becoming too "warlike." In Hemming's language, Berry provides reminders that, if his polemical style sometimes evinces "seemingly unshakeable convictions of inerrancy," the seeming is not the reality. If Hemming is right about Milbank's "generosity in disguise," then Milbank's interpreters need not take umbrage at his "pugnacity" and "seemingly unshakeable convictions of inerrancy." But Milbank needs to provide his readers sufficient reminders that the "seeming" is only seeming, and that the disguise is only a disguise.

Two Proposals

As stated earlier, my governing purpose in this essay is not to judge the validity of criticisms made against Milbank in particular or radical orthodoxy in general but to commend the practice of charitable interpretation. In this concluding section I offer two proposals for charitable interpretation in the ongoing development and critique of Milbank's work in particular and of radical orthodoxy in general. The first proposal I will discuss at length; the second will be more succinct.

First Proposal

Critiques of radical orthodoxy should eschew broadside attacks, even when the rhetoric of radical orthodox writers invites such attacks, if a careful reading of radical orthodox texts shows that such attacks are unwarranted. For example, there may be problems with the way in which Milbank appeals to premodern Christianity in his attack upon secular modernity, but that does not justify the simplistic claim that he advocates a return to premodern Christianity. Paul Lakeland takes a more helpful approach when he says that much of his unease with Milbank's vision "derives from the shaky marriage between the premodern and postmodern."[33] Lakeland sympathetically observes that Milbank, far from evincing a simple nostalgia for the premodern, seeks "to overcome the speculative and deductive theologies of premodernity and modernity."[34] Yet some readers might not get this far in Lakeland's discussion, or might

---

31. Wendell Berry, *Sex, Economy, Freedom, and Community* (New York: Pantheon, 1993), xix.

32. Ibid., 93.

33. Paul Lakeland, *Postmodernity: Christian Identity in a Fragmented Age* (Guides to Theological Inquiry; Minneapolis: Fortress Press, 1997), 71.

34. Ibid., 73.

not get there with an open mind, because he does not resist the temptation to introduce his discussion of Milbank's project with a broadside remark characterizing it as "a shameless reassertion of the premodern superiority of Christendom."[35]

Like Lakeland when guided by his better lights, Grace Jantzen expresses discomfort with Milbank's relation to premodern Christianity but without simplistically identifying Milbank's vision with a return to the premodern: "There can be no going back to a medieval or premodern religion of certainties and securities (if there ever was such a thing); nor indeed should its substitute in 'radical orthodoxy' be desired where doctrines or revelations are given or premised without equally radical engagement with the ways in which such orthodoxy has been death-dealing."[36] Rather than making the sweeping charge that radical orthodoxy is a return to premodern Christianity, Jantzen describes radical orthodoxy as a substitute for premodern Christianity. That description in itself is certainly debatable, but Jantzen quickly turns the debate in a constructive direction when she specifies what she means. Her objection is to the fact that radical orthodoxy has not yet produced "equally radical engagement with the ways in which such orthodoxy has been death-dealing." Had she claimed that radical orthodoxy simply ignores the death-dealing ways of past orthodoxies, her critique would have lacked bite, since Milbank and others have said very critical words about the church's failure to live in accordance with "the Christian narrative" of peace.[37] Instead Jantzen issues in effect a challenge: If you are going to talk "radical orthodoxy," be as profound in your critique of the ills that have gone under the name of Christian orthodoxy as you are of secularist departures from Christian orthodoxy.

It is of course equally important for radical orthodox writers to resist the temptation of engaging in broadside attacks that distort complex relations into simple dualisms and that block constructive collaboration by creating unnecessarily stark oppositions. Radical orthodoxy, as is often the case for movements that foreground their attachment to orthodoxy, has shown a penchant for dualisms. An extreme example is Milbank's judgment upon Latin American liberation theologians: "In making the merely algebraic equation, liberation = salvation, they still celebrate a hidden working of divine design through purely immanent processes. What they really say is what they claim not to say: namely that Christians should say their prayers, be decent citizens, and otherwise just accept society as it is."[38] As Nicholas Lash eloquently comments, "Mindful of so many deaths, of such bereavement and imprisonment, and of so much patient suffering generously sustained in peaceful struggle by people some of whom I am privileged to count as friends, [this passage] strikes me as not only false but tasteless."[39]

As the debates about radical orthodoxy proceed, I hope that proponents as well as critics of radical orthodoxy will forego broadside attacks and simplistic dichotomies. One encouragement in this direction is Catherine Pickstock's invitation "not to regard Radical Orthodoxy as a discrete edifice which purports to be a stronghold. For it is by

---

35. Ibid., 68.
36. Grace M. Jantzen, "'Barely by a Breath . . .': Irigaray on Rethinking Religion," in *The Religious* (ed. John D. Caputo; Blackwell Readings in Continental Thought; Oxford: Blackwell, 2002), 228.
37. See, e.g., Milbank, *Theology and Social Theory*, 432–33.
38. Milbank, *Theology and Social Theory*, 245.
39. Nicholas Lash, "Not Exactly Politics or Power?" *Modern Theology* 8, no. 4 (October 1992): 357.

no means this. Radical Orthodoxy is a hermeneutic disposition and a style of meta-physical vision; and it is not so much a 'thing' or 'place' as a 'task.'"[40] Part of the work of heeding this invitation will be for radical orthodox writers to demonstrate more awareness of how their appeals to "the Christian narrative" can create the appearance of precisely a discrete edifice. It is important for radical orthodox appeals to "the Christian narrative" to bear in mind two cautions.

First, there are many Christian narratives. Although I do not think the plurality of Christian narratives makes it necessary to give up reference to "the" Christian narra-tive, that plurality does make it necessary to be aware of the limitations and pitfalls of the singularizing reference. Otherwise the impression can arise that diversity of Christian narratives can be unproblematically reduced to one, or that theologians can extract the best Christian narrative from the diversity. In either case the result is a false "discreteness" that ignores the messy complexity of diverse Christian narratives, each with its strengths and weaknesses. The existence of this messy complexity is also a rea-son to be circumspect about the use of the very term "Christian orthodoxy"—not to forego altogether, but to be circumspect.

Second, in the contemporary Western context in and for which radical orthodox theologians write, Christian narratives never exist in discrete isolation from other nar-ratives. Stories engage other stories, are influenced by them, appropriate elements from them, make accommodations to them even in the apparent act of subsuming them or rejecting them, and so forth. In this sense, no narrative tradition keeps itself "pure." Encounter with other narratives "contaminates" it. The very idea of the preservation of a discrete, unsullied narrative tradition in the face of other narratives is a misunder-standing of the nature of stories. Stories are temporal processes. Preservation of a nar-rative tradition is not preservation of a static deposit. It is continuity in temporal flow. Thus Catherine Pickstock can write: "Those who offer a criticism of Radical Orthodoxy on the grounds of its alleged nostalgia are misunderstanding our inten-tions altogether; we are seeking to mediate between finitude and transcendence by way of time."[41] Graham Ward, the theologian who most clearly and consistently avoids giv-ing the impression that radical orthodoxy is a "discrete edifice," articulates the point that I am trying to make here when he refers to "a movement beyond the narrative which binds Christian practice and formation through a deepening sense of the rich interpretative openness of that narrative. The Christian community always waits to receive its understanding, waits to discern its form."[42]

Second Proposal

Provocative words and grand rhetorical gestures are not always inappropriate, but they have a quite limited usefulness for constructive debate. I have discussed above the impression that Milbank sometimes creates of advocating a wholesale rejection of modernity. I have tried to show that, in Milbank's better moments, he makes explicit a more nuanced attitude toward modernity. He can even say that "modernity has often extended the drive toward liberty, equality, fraternity, individual expressiveness,

---

40. Catherine Pickstock, "Radical Orthodoxy and the Mediations of Time," in *Radical Orthodoxy?—A Catholic Enquiry* (ed. Laurence Paul Hemming; Aldershot: Ashgate, 2000), 63.

41. Ibid., 64.

42. Ward, *Cities of God*, 258.

romantic love, historicity, and the celebration of the spatially- and temporally-bound ordinary and local, all of which were indeed already manifest in the early to high Middle Ages, and yet not explicitly released."[43] Unfortunately I had to read many hundreds of pages by Milbank, wondering all the while whether he really was blind to these advances of modernity, before I came across this passage. Milbank could help his readers by placing qualifying statements of this type more frequently and more prominently in his work. Doing so would sacrifice some of the thrill of rhetorical provocation, but it would advance constructive debate.

Augustine's heading for the first chapter of the fifth book of his treatise "On the Trinity" admonishes him and his readers to be sober in reflecting on the mystery of the triune God: "How modestly and soberly ought human beings, to whom the nature of their own mind is inexplicable, think about the substance of God."[44] Such sobriety is a form of the humility that I have proposed as one of the marks of charitable interpretation. Augustine's admonition to sobriety can remind radical orthodox theologians and their critics not to get carried away by sweeping claims and polemical rhetoric. Charitable interpretation operates on the assumption that truth is never so neatly apportioned and packaged. This does not mean that charitable interpretation is governed by a spirit of timidity about debate and truth seeking. It does mean that the path to deeper interpretive insight is marked by questioning, listening, respect, and humility. Such a path can be slow and even messy. But as the great religious thinker Vincent Harding says: "I am so happy for a messy God. . . . those messy Gods seem to have love oozing out all over."[45]

---

43. Milbank, "Programme," 44–45.

44. "Quam modeste ac sobrie debeat homo cui etiam suae mentis natura inexplicabilis est de dei substantia cogitare" (Aurelius Augustinus, *De trinitate* [Corpus Christianorum: Series Latina 50; Turnhout, Belgium: Brepols, 1968], 9).

45. Remark made by Vincent Harding at a session in his honor at the annual meeting of the American Academy of Religion and the Society of Biblical Literature, Atlanta, Ga., November 2003.

2. Is That All?

Gift and Reciprocity in Milbank's Being Reconciled

—*Catherine Keller*

For there to be a gift, there must be no reciprocity, return, exchange, countergift, or debt.

—Jacques Derrida[1]

If there is a gift that can truly be, then this must be the event of reciprocal but
asymmetrical and non-identically repeated exchange.

—John Milbank[2]

If you knew the gift of God, and who it is that is saying to you, "Give me a
drink," you would have asked him, and he would have given you living water.

—John 4:10[3]

Our primal memories of hope, love, and festivity come wrapped in associations with
gifts. Of course, accompanying those memories come the holiday-coded family tensions. I remember my ten-year-old heart sinking when my little siblings, having torn
through a great mound of Christmas packages, some painstakingly selected and
wrapped by me, looked up and asked, "Is that all?" The little ingrates: yet clearly I
expected something in return, if only gratitude. That sense of spoiled glut may represent the peculiar economic socialization of U.S. culture—where we annually perform
the greatest incarnation of consumption and debt in human history. But the interplay
of childlike delight and childish greed, of love and expectation, of excess and obligation, infuses the notion of gift with conflictual feelings discernible in any human context. I suspect that this childish ambivalence is not extrinsic to the theoretical paradox
of "gift" itself: "If the other gives me back or owes me," there will not have been a gift
as such.[4] As Jacques Derrida radicalizes this now famous aporia: even if the recipient
recognizes the gift as a gift, "if the present is present to him as present, this simple

---

1. Jacques Derrida, *Given Time: I. Counterfeit Money* (trans. Peggy Kamuf; Chicago: University of
Chicago Press, 1992), 12.
2. John Milbank, *Being Reconciled: Ontology and Pardon* (New York: Routledge, 2003), 157.
3. This and future citations taken fron the *New Revised Standard Version.*
4. Milbank, *Being Reconciled*, 12.

recognition suffices to annul the gift."[5] Why? For if there is any expectation of return, even of gratitude—then the gift is annulled.

The aporia of the gift, theistically amplified in Jean Luc Marion and theologically disputed in John Milbank, would be this: that a gift must remain independent of its reception in order to be a gift at all. A true gift does not come with strings attached. No expectation of thanks, indeed no catering to expectation, and thus no ritual or gesture of exchange would fail to taint the gift. If a gift is given with the expectation of a gift in return, then it is no gift at all but an economic transaction. Embarrassment at empty-handed reception betrays the impurity of our notion of gift. For instance when I first visited South Korea and was ashamed not to have known to bring gifts to exchange, as everyone I visited had a gift for me. In fact culturally there is an expectation of a reciprocal gesture. So it is not inappropriate that I in my crude North American ignorance of a custom was ashamed. These were traditional marks of social reciprocity—productive, as the anthropologist Marcel Mauss argued in the work that stimulated the philosophical conversation, of sociality itself. No doubt my gender further exposed me to this sense of shame, as women (whose labor is itself traditionally freely given) do not coincidentally bear disproportionate responsibility for rituals of gift exchange.[6] Later reading of the gift discourse might retroactively redeem me: these weren't really gifts at all! These were strings of obligation, tying up the gift in a transitional circle of exchange. For Derrida this sociality of reciprocation compromises the gift and its radical promise, its unpredictable difference—it marks the gift as "the impossible."[7] But if I join in a deconstruction of such gestures—gestures I experienced as modest, disarming events within a connective tissue of hospitality—am I not extending my ethnocentric vulgarity? Am I disrespecting others of my gender?

These questions may only show that I do not "get" the gift.[8] This much, however, I do take in: the gift given with expectation of reciprocation is precisely an *expectation*—to whom much is given, much will be expected (Luke 12:48). Such an expectation is close, very close, to a demand—quite the opposite of a gift. In this I concur with Derrida. The coloring of gift by expectation—that of the giver, or that of the recipient—indeed contaminates the purity of the gift. But as I hope to demonstrate, this impurity is not extrinsic but rather constitutive of gift giving—at least from a certain New Testament perspective. This would not surprise Derrida, for whom Christian promises of reward in heaven already compromise the purity of even the most self-sacrificial gift. Indeed I would argue that the *purity* of the gift may be beside the point. Its radical gratuity may precisely hinge not upon a unilateral purity but upon a reciprocity, a relationality, that by its very nature already contaminates the pure, the simple, the absolute. Indeed the very style of the present argument, with its homiletical appeal to examples, its biblical hermeneutic, means to disturb the transcendental purity by which the gift-discourse is currently sustained.

---

5. Derrida, *Given Time*, 13.

6. This paper omits explicit feminist engagement of the discourse of the gift. For a delightful queering of early Christian and contemporary theo-economics, cf. Marion Grau's "trickster hermeneutics" in *Of Divine Economy: Refinancing Redemption* which influences every level of the present reading.

7. Derrida, *Given Time*, 10.

8. To whatever extent I do get it, I am indebted to present and former students working on the philosophical and theological problematic of the gift: Taekyun Ahn, Mario Costa, and again, Marion Grau.

In this essay I want to suggest that the particular biblical text that may be read as the *locus classicus* of "the gift of God" folds a certain set of impurities into a pneumatological event: the gift-event is spirit-event. Its impurities stem from a mix of asymmetrical differences of culture, gender, and tradition. The *spirit* in which a gift is offered (to a woman in particular) effects an indelible theological event. I would like to suggest that in its *ur*-context this gift—"the gift of God"—is offered neither in unilateral purity nor in manipulative egotism but in a spirit of radical reciprocity. And this asymmetrical reciprocity is colored, indeed charged, by expectancy. *Expectancy*, however, should not be identified with *demand*, as for repayment or countergift, in kind or at least in gratitude. Much may be expected that can precisely *not* be demanded. Expectancy may comprise *hope* rather than debt. Of course hope itself can be tainted by demand, want, manipulation: "hope not, for hope would be hope for the wrong thing."[9] The lack of a certain expectancy—that the gift will be received, realized, enjoyed—would indeed comprise a lack of reciprocity. But wouldn't it also signify a chilling lack of care that the other take pleasure in the gift? Gratitude is the expression of joy in receptivity. Of course I have some expectant desire that the recipient of a gift will feel grateful, will have that pleasure: if I did not, would my disinterest in the character of the reception signal not so much generosity as indifference? I may or may not thereby desire gratitude as a return, a repayment, a recognition. But to emulate the absolute anonymity of giving—anonymity even to oneself, as giver—would according to Derrida characterize a pure gift, and indeed characterize it as the impossible. And such purity absolves the giver therefore from relationship itself; it emulates the absolute self-presence of an Unmoved Mover, of one not subject to reciprocity, to influence, to interdependence.

This is an argument I am not hoping to win against Derrida, even with the help I hope to garner from Milbank, for it will only confirm the impurity of "the gift, if there is one." But I want to put out there, as an offering—attaching to it the strings of further and future theological exchange, beyond what this essay can deliver—that neither gratitude nor hope of gratitude annuls the gift. An implicit *demand* for gratitude does. Of course we cannot tell the difference. What remains undecidable in human exchange throws itself on grace in theology. Indeed the margin of mystery surrounding the motives of the human other suggests precisely the "inter-human transcendence"[10] that can only be absolved or purified of relationship by an imaginary of unilateral fiat. An absence of reciprocity defines the form of subjective independence corollary with power, and particularly with the *unilateral power* that only gives, influences, or donates—but that does not or cannot receive. Finally a relational theology resists both the deconstructive unilateralism of the transcendental gift and the supernatural transcendence of Milbank's proposed alternative. Yet not without gratitude for the gifts each contribute to the debate.

---

9. T. S. Eliot, "East Coker," in *Four Quartets* (New York: Harvest, 1943, 1971), 28.

10. I thank Mayra Rivera for this phrase, as well as the idea of a "relational transcendence," which she has articulated in conversation with Levinas, Latin American liberation thought, and Luce Irigaray. Cf. *The Touch of Transcendence*. Unpublished Dissertation, Drew 2005.

Giving Gifts, Taking Poison

Strangely enough, perhaps aporetically, such a theology of the gift, with its evident kinship to process, feminist, and/or ecological theologies of radical relationality, comes close to a certain argument of John Milbank. I find myself in agreement with him when he avers that "there can only be more than egotism, there can only be love, if there is ecstatic reciprocity and interplay of characters. . . ."[11] Indeed it is precisely in his critique of the poststructuralist gift discourse of Derrida and J. L. Marion, as he begins to formulate his own theological alternative, that I find an opening for a wider conversation on and within radical reciprocity. Milbank may be right when he finds both Derrida and Marion "trapped within Cartesian myths of prior subjectivity after all."[12] For he recognizes as they do not, but as Mauss, whom they are revising, *did*, that "gift-giving is a mode (the mode in fact) of social being." This recognition of a root sociality of interdependence is a step in the direction of recognizing the constitutive—ontological?—reciprocity of all subjects, as it is manifest and performed in the exchange of gifts. Whether Milbank himself breaks out of the trap of the substantial subject remains to be seen. He intends to rescue a certain festive fullness of human experience, beyond the ethics of self-sacrifice, by his christological appeal to the ultimate reciprocity of love. That ultimacy takes on a character of eschatological expectancy that charges the present with the hope of resurrection.

Yet in the sentence cited above, Milbank goes on to specify the reciprocating "characters" as those "who naturally 'belong together.'" What would such a "natural belonging" consist of? Surely it wouldn't happen to display such "natural" marks of belonging as shared ethnicity and culture? Surely an elite of Christian intellectuals, belonging together by virtue of a certain orthodoxy, is not actually envisioned? Yet he argues that "In this way, the chain of affinity, beyond nature, discovers a higher nature (the supernatural, the gift of grace)." Why, having just announced such a promising turn to reciprocity, does it behoove him to insert without argument a dualism alien not only to postmodern but to biblical sensibility?[13] Does the supernaturalization of this grace function to set apart the "natural" affinity-group, serving as a hedge against the indiscriminate excess to which grace is prone? I will argue that it is the incapacity of his doctrine of God to accommodate a robust reciprocity—of both the radical gratuity of grace and the sensitivity of God to its reception—that cramps his christological gesture.

Milbank's gift to theology is from the start difficult to receive. Its orthodoxy, like all orthodoxies, threatens to renege on its own gift unless it is received as exclusive truth: the one Truth of the nature of things, supernaturally donated to the privileged affinity group. Indeed hermeneutically speaking one is hard pressed to accept a gift that is delivered in effect as a *threat*: "any 'contemporary garb' for Christian truth is of course the most puerile form of betrayal."[14] Such a claim is confusing, coming from

---

11. Milbank, *Being Reconciled*, 203.
12. Ibid., 156.
13. Ibid., 203.
14. John Milbank, *The Word Made Strange: Theology, Language, Culture* (Oxford: Blackwell, 1997), 1.

an altogether contemporary theology, indeed one at pains to remain *au courant* (however grumpily) with French philosophy. Does it mean to perform the *naked* truth? Or to insist on consuming it *l'ancien*? But isn't such costuming itself altogether "contemporary" in fabrication? So is the point really to rule out of bounds the feminist and 'other' heterodoxies that don't play by the rules of a classical confessional language game? Who with our barbarisms have disrupted the brotherhood of affinity, contaminated the harmony of theological symposia? Perhaps I am (predictably) too suspicious. Let me resist the temptation of returning ressentiment in kind: how quickly exchange turns toxic. The gift, famously, "can also be bad, poisonous (*Gift, gift*)."[15]

I am still hoping, if not for natural belonging, for support in strengthening the avowal of reciprocity as proper to the gift. Milbank's version of Christian truth poses a *hermeneutical* problem: It refuses to be *received* interpretively, in the terms of the recipient—*ipso facto* in terms that are strange, other and always only now emerging: that is, "contemporary." A gift that thus dictates the terms of its reception would certainly not survive the Derridean deconstruction. But I am more interested in whether Milbank's own avowal of *reciprocity* can survive such a controlling grace. How can there be reciprocity—if reciprocation happens only in freedom—in the face of a gift that cannot be received in the terms of the living, contemporary, recipient? A truth that presumably can only circulate within the pre-established network of a single, past and supernatural language? Perhaps it will be most helpful to retain focus on the more recent *Being Reconciled*, which actually, in the spirit of its title, seems relatively free of the accusatory assertions of orthodoxy characterizing Milbank's prior opus.

In noting the tension in his move toward a radical divine/human reciprocity, my primary interest is however neither to receive nor to reject Milbank's still developing discourse of the gift. In this he already provides a needed supplement to the deconstructive unilateralism of the gift. Yet these two strands of postmodern gift rhetoric together conspire to send me back to the source of the metaphor. I turn then to a biblical hermeneutic that will indeed wear its contemporary clothing (if always already a bit out of fashion, eclectic, with hand-me-downs of deconstruction and threads of various orthodoxies): no pretense here to the naked truths of either biblicism or orthodoxy. Rather I am wondering how—in a robust spirit of reciprocity and in relation to the current debate—to receive the gospel itself, to receive in particular its originary narrative of "the gift." Perhaps the indirection of a biblical theopoetics will at the same time permit a reception of that tendency in Milbank's thinking which avows, wonderfully: "Before a gift can be given, it must have already started to be received."[16]

A Hot Exchange

If John Milbank's meditation on the gift takes place in a Shakespearean mid-winter, let us journey temporarily to a hot desert midday of John's Gospel. For this drama, Jesus is sitting alone by Jacob's well, "tired out by his journey," thirsty and without access to the water. When a Samaritan woman shows up his thirst takes priority over social taboos. "Give me a drink." It is not the woman's soul but her bucket that interests him.

---

15. Derrida, *Given Time*, 12.
16. Milbank, *Being Reconciled*, 156.

Instead of simply and silently obeying his request, she talks back: "How is it that you, a Jew, ask a drink of me, a woman of Samaria?" (4:6–9). The grammar of a question resists his flat imperative. Now suddenly she has his attention. Her *hutzpah* in challenging both the taboos he embodies and the taboos he breaks, teasingly and succinctly posing her question, shows a lively subjectivity. By surfacing their strangeness one to another, their relation of alien/nation across gender and ethnicity, she has made possible a sudden intimacy. As is Jesus' wont, he springs into the present. He wants to expose himself to this mouthy woman (not by shedding his contemporary garments, surely); but not too directly, not in the immediacy of a full presence. Not as a unilateral revelation. He wants her to ask. He desires her desire.

In the complex grammar of his desire is articulated the key locution of any Christian theology of the gift: "If you knew the gift of God, and who it is that is saying to you, 'Give me a drink,' you would have asked him . . ." (4:10). One must estrange the text from its traditional drone, where Jesus sounds smug, superior, vaguely chiding her for having failed already to "know the gift," pointing her toward higher things, beyond mere H_2O: ". . . and he would have given you living water" (4:10). But I hear nothing condescending in this response. Revise the tone. *He* is the one who wanted plain water. He has been drawn into some highly charged repartee by her bold, perhaps flirtatious, challenge. And he characteristically ups the ante, charmingly, disarming her "you a Jew" with "if you knew who I am." He is a mystery man, provocative in return, making riddles out of the dust. The rhetorical conditional "if you knew . . . then you would have . . ." shifts his speech from the blunt need of his opening imperative into a grammar of invitation—from "give me" to "he would have given you": meaning "I still might, if you ask; but this gift you must first desire; it will be nothing at all if you do not feel first the thirst for it." In the steep asymmetry in which the literal water turns to metaphor of salvation, the reciprocity *holds*.

There unfolds an elaborate dialogue, its fluid metonymy welling up from the gift given by Jacob, the ancestor shared by these peoples who, as the text reminds us, "do not share things in common" (4:9). Encoding the water of life as a bottomless source, an eternal flow, the "if" itself is the hook on the bucket of eternal life, the lure to a possibility that is infinitely preceded and utterly unprecedented. (I mean "lure" almost in the technical sense of a Whiteheadian divine Eros, the "initial aim from God.") This "gift of God" is the very water of life, and for those who accept this gift, who drink of this water, it "will become in them a spring of water gushing up to eternal life" (4:14). It is an extraordinary metaphor: the sip that becomes a spring; a source that comes from beyond them and yet opens "in them" an endless flux of life. It "gushes up": no buckets are required for this excessive flow from below!

Caught in the spirit of what may surely be described as "ecstatic reciprocity and interplay of characters," Jesus and the Samaritan woman press each other further. She then chooses to expose her own devastatingly vulnerable life to him. Or had he been testing her with "call your husband" (4:16)? I don't read him as a cat to her mouse; no, he may just have wanted to have a larger audience if he were going to preach anyway. Besides, he could see his disciples walking toward them, just moments away, seeing already ("astonished," says John) this incorrect intensity with a woman. No doubt neither he nor they relished spats about his scandalous spontaneities. I had best mention that I wasn't there (and neither was John, and I don't know if Jesus was either), but I hear it this way: the Johannine Jesus then read her honest "I have no husband" (4:17) with his exceptional extrasensory perception—no totalizing omniscience, please, but a brilliant, somewhat invasive, sensitivity, a *gift*, not a given. He names the conjugal series that would have been impossibly painful for her to share with a stranger. And still there rises from the text not the least tone of judgment, nor—more to the point—of any *forgiveness*—which would itself presuppose judgment. For, as Milbank suggests, forgiveness may be nothing but a transcendent fiat offering exoneration whether or not it was sought. His resistance to such a model of power is welcome: he means to deconstruct the persistence of a model of "oriental despotism, protracted to infinity in the late mediaeval reconception of God as a reserve of absolute, infinite untrammeled power and will."[17]

Yet how obsessively the tradition has cast her as sinful, assuming in amazing ignorance of context that somehow she had chosen a series of divorces and then free cohabitation with a man.[18] This is precisely what biblical scholars show happened in the more infamous but tellingly parallel case of Mary Magdalene. For John, Mary is the first witness of the resurrection. For the classical tradition she could only be read—with literally no textual evidence—as the holy harlot, the great sinner.[19] The subtle eros of these disclosive exchanges has been twisted by the tradition into shaming confrontations between a sinfully oversexed but salvageable woman and the judging/forgiving, anerotically divine Man.

It is the Samaritan's engaging honesty, not her sexual morality, that interests Jesus: "What you have said is true!" (4:18). As he has read her more correctly than she could have imagined, she reads him—*reciprocally*—with her own uncanny (and like him delicately ironic) accuracy: "Sir, I see you are a prophet" (4:19). In other words she responds with no defensiveness at all, since no judgment was implied.[20] She returns to him such forceful insight into *his* gift, or talent, that there unfolds in this pericope the first serious theological conversation of the Gospel, reciprocal at every stage—capped off by his first and only self-disclosure as "the messiah." But this "I am he" statement (4:26) becomes grimly grandiose when lifted out of this conversational context. It has been useful, like the rest of this Gospel of signs, for the dysrelational closure of meaning. It only *opens* its meaning within the intersignifying force field of *dis/closive* reciprocity—indeed of something very like Milbank's ecstatic reciprocity. But of course the power of this text still to refresh its reader lies in its openness to being read differently, to being itself refreshed. The reader is then returning something to the text,

---

17. Ibid., 48. Glad as I am for an intra-orthodox critique of a certain doctrine of omnipotence, I am of course not underwriting this discourse of the "oriental."

18. "Perhaps the woman, like Tamar in Genesis 38, is trapped in the custom of levirate marriage and the last male in the family has refused to marry her. Significantly, the reasons for the woman's marital history intrigue commentators but do not seem to concern Jesus." Gail R. O'Day, "John," in *The Women's Bible Commentary* (ed. Carol A. Newsom and Sharon H. Ringe; Louisville: Westminster/John Knox, 1992), 296.

19. Cf. my forthcoming "She Talks Too Much: Magdalene Meditations," *Toward a Theology of Eros: Transfiguring Passion of the Limits of Discipline* (ed. Virginia Burrus and Catherine Keller; New York: Fordham University Press, 2006). Cf. also Jane Schaberg, *The Resurrection of Mary Magdalene: Legends, Apocryphy, and the Christian Testament* (New York: Continuum, 2002).

20. "Significantly, the reasons for the woman's marital history intrigue commentators but do not seem to concern Jesus. Nor does Jesus pass moral judgment on the woman because of her marital history and status. . . . When interpreters speak of the woman as a 'five-time loser' or a 'tramp' (as has been the case in recent scholarship), they are reflecting their own prejudices against women, not the views of the text." (O'Day, "John," 296.)

as indeed the Samaritan is returning something to the thirsty Jew: "The fuller, more abundant life is a return of life always afresh, always differently."[21]

Preferring John

Milbank has an insight into the Johannine Jesus specifically relevant to the present reading. He contrasts John's Gospel to that of Luke, with its test imperatives of nonreturnable love—invite only those to the banquet who are too poor to return the invitation; and love the enemy, who by definition will not return the sentiment. While not rejecting the synoptic perspective, Milbank prefers John's Gospel, "where there is no mention of loving enemies, where love seems to ceaselessly circulate amongst friends—I in you, and you in me, where there are erotic gestures (between Jesus and Mary of Bethany) and where the disciples are described as the Father's 'gift' to the Son, just as the Son is his gift to the disciples."[22] There is indeed refreshment in this line of thinking. For those stretched into networks of relationships edged with impossible demands, haunted by a globalizing ethic of multiple others mutely demanding some *other* other's sacrifice—friendship sounds like a restorative model. Yet the gift of (super)natural affinities among a like-minded spiritual elite—definitively male, yet not misogynist, complemented by an occasional exceptional woman—comes with a price.

Milbank privileges this version of the Platonic eros *over* the sort of outreach to the stranger emphasized by the discourse of difference. Or dramatized at the well. Indeed Milbank's Johannine preference is posed not only against Luke but also against Derrida, temporarily conflated with Luke. The Lukan unilateralism of love is designated as "Derrida's favoured focus for the Christian essence."[23] He thus situates the heart of his argument against the poststructuralist gift within a scriptural difference. He does not dismiss Derrida, Levinas, and Marion as in any sense "unbiblical." Milbank suggests historically that the "one-way operation proceeding downwards from the King towards those in need—'the widows and orphans'"—represents a Near Eastern idea that Derrida and Levinas (all too Jewishly?) share. It is this idea that Milbank finds "qualified in the inter-testamental period by the influence of Greek notions that good can be done by anyone—even a slave—and is more reciprocal or exchangist in character."[24] I would have thought that the tradition of covenant, indeed the blessings purveyed even by unfortunates like Hagar and Ishmael, would suggest a thoroughly Hebrew reciprocalism—no less hierarchical, to be sure, than the Greek. Moreover, Milbank's reading of Hellenism as purveying (via John) a Socratic ideal of "dying for friends rather than the city"[25] may fly in the face of other readings of Hellenism, in which the friendship idea is precisely urban and not imperial,[26] as well as of the New Testament, with its urban intertestamental apocalypse of the (New) Jerusalem.

---

21. Milbank, *Being Reconciled*, 156.
22. Ibid., 160.
23. Ibid.
24. Ibid.
25. Ibid.
26. Cf. Gilles Deleuze and Felix Guattari on "geophilosophy" and the deterritorializing function of the Greek City *vis à vis* philosophical friendship. (*What is Philosophy?* [trans. H. Tomlinson and G. Burchell; New York: Columbia University Press, 1994], 85ff.)

Nonetheless Milbank rightly points out that the unilateralism of divine power, mirroring an Eastern imperial model of the God-King, infected the biblical imagination more than it did Athenian theology. Easy as it is to decry the hellenizing "ontotheology," indeed to piggyback on older Protestant and Troeltschian projects of de-hellenization, one should be aware that the construct of divine omnipotence cannot be derived from Greek theology. This is not Milbank's point, but one that intersects with it meaningfully: that doctrine of omnipotence is at least as responsible for the unilateralism of divine love in classical theology as are the more specifically Hellenistic elements such as *apatheia* and impassibility. It is the concern of a theopoetic relationalisn—*ipso facto* heterodox, even in its appeal to Scripture as *other* than orthodoxy—to deconstruct the doctrine of omnipotence. But Milbank's tracing of ancient and postmodern streaks of unilateralism is nonetheless helpful. If Milbank resists Derrida's idealization of the pure gift as instantiated in the Lukan love of the enemy, it is because it idealizes a self-sacrificial giving that by definition cannot be returned.

Milbank at any rate does line up Patocka, Levinas, Derrida, and Marion as representing a view that "now enjoys a wide consensus,"[27] that is a view that believes it escapes "the sacrificial economy of *do ut des*,"[28] of giving up the lesser for the greater. But Milbank argues that it in fact performs the self-sacrificial view at its logical extreme, as sacrificing the self for the other, the absolute other, with no hope of any "return" for the self.[29] If even gratitude immediately nullifies the gift as such, turning it into an exchange tainted by interest, where the gift can have no return if it is to count as gift, of course for Derrida this means no true gift is possible. Yet the gift in its impossibility, its purity, remains nonetheless the ideal or standard for all gift giving. Milbank finds, I think insightfully, in Derrida and Marion (and so irrespective of the question of theism) a reduction of "exchange" to "contract" and thus an inability to think of ethics in terms of reciprocity.[30] The gift remains the ethical gesture par excellence, construed precisely as one-way donation. It is thus the impossible, difference itself, that is for Derrida infinitely, for Marion eschatologically, postponed. Marion especially seems to fall prey to Milbank's critique. Milbank, who cites parsimoniously, must have had such a passage as the following in mind: "Only the enemy makes the gift possible; he makes the gift evident by denying it reciprocity—in contrast to the friend, who involuntarily lowers the gift to the level of a loan with interest. The enemy thus becomes the ally of the gift, and the friend its adversary."[31]

Milbank structures his own position as a third way beyond the deadlock between an Aristotelian ethical eudaemonism and a Kantian "other-regarding" morality. The first attempts to secure happiness, although it cannot finally protect against the vagaries of fortune without enclosing itself in a Stoic tranquility, lacking therefore, precisely, in joy. The second, in its attempt to place the other before the self, erects a construct of pure duty, disregarding happiness, which can only implode—for the

---

27. Milbank, *Being Reconciled*, 139.
28. Ibid.
29. Ibid.
30. Ibid., 156.
31. Jean Luc Marion, *Being Given: Toward a Phenomenology of Givenness* (trans. Jefrey L. Kosky; Berkeley: Stanford University Press, 2002), 89.

happiness of the other cannot be ignored. Milbank would locate Levinas and, more cautiously, the poststructuralists, in the tradition of an other-regarding moralism that bows to its abstract "other," who must at once be a subject but cannot be. Feminist critics of Levinas concur here, that the pure subservience to an absolute other is not only akin to a familiar feminine self-abnegation, but that it cannot acknowledge the subjectivity of the other without then in turn acknowledging the rights of the ethical subject as well.[32]

Milbank tries to capture all of his continental "others" in this aporia: "Modern ethics, just because it enthrones altruism, is pathological in its degree of obliteration of the possibility of consummation or of the beginning of beatitude in a time to be enjoyed, and a conviviality to be celebrated by the living self."[33] In other words, he seems to offer a certain Christian eudaemonism that would not secure happiness as the attribute of a self-possessed self, but that would "participate" in happiness through the gift that is experienced as luck but which is "secretly" grace.[34] But his grace is—rather winningly—predicated on a simple refusal of "all Protestant accounts of grace as mere imputation" along with an espousal of a strong doctrine of sanctification.[35] This may be his Anglo-Catholicism speaking; on this point it corresponds rather well to my Methodism. Wesley was among those Protestants who just as firmly repudiated the notion of grace as mere unilateral and so juridical imputation. For him there was a constant "return" to God inspired, indeed made possible, by grace but not *caused* by it. Our free response to divine initiating grace is the *sine qua non* of the sanctifying grace; "God does not continue to act upon the soul unless the soul reacts upon God."[36] The doctrine of sanctification traditionally safeguards human spontaneity, ethical responsibility, and the possibility of growth in well-being—during our lifetimes. Derrida's series of transcendental impossibles—democracy to come, messianicity, the secret, the gift—arguably exhibits the sharp binary structure not just of the Kantian ethical transcendental but also of the Protestant grace that precedes it.[37] For the imputational grace is perceived as not only unconditional but also unilateral in its purity. The purity of the gift is maintained at the price of the recipient's abjection, as purely undeserving. Thus the reformation dualism of unmerited supernatural grace versus sinful human "nature" haunts the binary formed by the impossibility of the gift and the endless deferral of its return.

Milbank argues convincingly that to reduce *exchange* to *contract or to debt* is to reinscribe the dualism between unilateral gift and abject recipient. And perhaps more fundamentally, it reinforces a quasi-Cartesian separation of subject (giving or receiving) and other (receiving or giving). Does any life-giving reciprocity under conditions remain impossible? For even the reciprocity involved in the apprehension of another's

---

32. Claire Elise Katz, *Levinas, Judaism, and the Feminine: the Silent Footsteps of Rebecca* (Bloomington & Indianapolis: Indiana University Press, 2003).

33. Milbank, *Being Reconciled*, 144.

34. Ibid., 161.

35. Ibid., 138.

36. John Wesley, "The Great Privilege of those that are Born of God," Vol. III.3–4, *Works* (Nashville: Abingdon Press, 1984) 1:442. Discussed in C. Keller, "Salvation Flows: Eschatology for a Feminist Wesleyanism," *Quarterly Review* (Winter 2003).

37. Cf. Catherine Keller and Stephen D. Moore, "Derridapocalypse," in *Derrida and Religion: Other Testaments* (ed. Yvonne Sherwood and Kevin Hart; London and New York: Routledge, 2005).

prospective reception of my gift breaks the purity of giving and attaches strings—at least as measured by the purity of a merely one-way grace-event. It may indeed be the case, as Derrida demonstrates, that the mere awareness of giving "sends itself back the gratifying image of goodness or generosity, of the giving-being who, knowing itself to be such, recognized itself in a circular, specular fashion, in a sort of auto-recognition, self-approval, and narcissistic gratitude."[38] Indeed one could spot such specular auto-recognition in the "I am he" of John's Jesus; and the woman no doubt exhibits narcissistic gratitude. But from what ideal of selfless purity would such judgment proceed?

Does this implied stance of the "pure giver" (impossible of course, yet transcendentally imagined) not only remove the self-approval to a higher level—that of the *author's* specular gaze? A circle of its own, suspiciously reminiscent of the circularity of the eternally self-contemplating God of ontotheology? Is there any way out of this circle? Avoiding the illusion of presence, is every present tense of the gift—the *present* after all—denied? With Kierkegaard, Derrida claims that "in any case, the 'present' (*présent*) of the gift is no longer thinkable as a now, that is, as a present bound up in the temporal synthesis."[39] This is not only a deconstruction of a substantialist self-presence but of any now-moment as the gift-present. So we are perhaps indeed left with a timeless deferral, circular rather than eschatological, purified indeed even of the gift-time of "eternal life," and thus as Milbank would have it, an ultimately empty "perpetual postponement"?[40] Is the alternative then to "aim for reciprocity, for community, and not for a barren and sterile self-sacrifice (which . . . is the alternative of both nihilists and Levinasian moralizers who take capitalist exchange to be the definitive form of exchange"?[41] Or is this way out—requiring a tired identification of deconstruction as nihilism—itself a misleading shortcut?

Not surprisingly deconstruction factors in its own risk. It is onto the danger of its own endless and therefore circular deferral.[42] John Caputo slides in here to ask about this deconstructive distance between "the present" and "the gift": "Does that mean, when one desires the gift, that one is grasping at a specter or a ghost? Does one succumb to a 'transcendental illusion' in which a concept (which determines something *present*) loses its empirical traction and is allowed to spin freely on its own in the empty air of ideality. . . ? Would not everything in deconstruction then go up in smoke or turn to ash? The secret, the gift, justice, the democracy to come, *avenir*—would they not all become a transcendental illusion?"[43] Derrida answers this dilemma with what Caputo calls a "double risk." According to Derrida "it is a matter—desire beyond desire—of responding faithfully but also as rigorously as possible both to the injunction or the order of the gift . . . as well as to the injunction or the order of meaning . . . know what you intend to give, know how the gift annuls itself, commit yourself [*engage-toi*] even if commitment is the destruction of the gift by the gift, give economy

---

38. Derrida, *Given Time*, 23.

39. Ibid., 9.

40. Milbank, *Being Reconciled*, 156.

41. Ibid., 169.

42. And indeed precisely as a post-Kantian dilemma for its own "hyper-ethics." Jacques Derrida, *The Gift of Death* (trans. David Wills; Chicago: University of Chicago Press, 1995), 71.

43. John Caputo, *The Prayers and Tears of Jacques Derrida: Religion without Religion* (Bloomington & Indianapolis: Indiana University Press, 1997), 170.

its chance."[44] To "give economy its chance" is as I read it to distinguish, or to begin to distinguish, *exchange* from *contract, debt* or *demand.*

At this point Derrida also distinguishes his moves significantly from the "Levinasian moralizers," whose logic of exterior transcendence does undercut reciprocity (as Milbank suggests): "for finally, the overrunning of the circle by the gift, if there is any, does not lead to a simple exteriority that would be transcendent and without relation. It is this exteriority that sets the circle going, it is this exteriority that puts the economy in motion."[45] Milbank's charge that Derrida ontologizes the sinful condition of economic circularity[46] may be right but somewhat beside the point, which is after all not that of a paralyzing and moralizing impossibility but of a faithful engagement, beyond certainty.

Certainly Derrida does not offer theologically satisfactory signs of reciprocity, relationality, or community, let alone participation in the divine. I agree with Milbank that the problem of the astringent unilateralism of his gift-ideal remains, and with it the absence of a festive sociality. And there may remain the trace of a Cartesian subjectivity, a self-possession that can become open to the other through a self-sacrifice, or sacrifice of the concept of the subject and thus of the possibility of its reconstruction. But in Derrida there is also always the trace of the other in the subject, the beginning at least of a radically relational alternative. Moreover, by distinguishing the gift from a grace that descends from a dysrelational and external transcendence (divine or merely ideal), Derrida opens a space of irreducible responsibility. This responsibility is for him not reducible to ethics. The charge of empty nihilism seems to miss the Kierkegaardian intensity of this double risk—unless "nihilism" is itself a circular notion, a catch-all for whatever stands outside of the boundaries of a confessional orthodoxy, as the other definitive of an orthodox same.

Orthodox Nihilism

Milbank's critique of deconstruction comes perhaps too soon. For he has from the start read deconstruction as a nihilism. I am not concerned to defend deconstruction as such—it has formidable strategies of escape. The theological tendency to reduce difference (however spelled) to the nihil is worrisome on *theological* grounds. Theology, in its needed resistance to various modernist voids of meaning, may itself have recourse to a *theistic* form of nihilism. I do not simply mean the nihilism that certain theisms need in order to establish their own orthodoxy, but a nihilism infecting their most positive confessions: "We give up everything, but not for the terrestrial city, and not even primarily for others: here we give up everything 'absurdly' to God in order to confess our inherent nothingness and to receive life in the only possible genuine mode of life, as created anew."[47] Our "inherent nothingness" is a discourse that entered orthodoxy early, as in Athanasius's argument for *creatio ex nihilo*. And in this hyperbolic form it does not so much radicalize as compromise the creation-affirmative faith of Genesis. For by denying all *intrinsic* worth to the creature—in a fashion that would be

---

44. Derrida, *Given Time*, 30.
45. Ibid.
46. Milbank, *Being Reconciled*, 153.
47. Milbank, *Being Reconciled*, 161.

intensified by the Augustinian and then Reformation dualism—it undermines the goodness of the creature. It lacks the capacity to differentiate tenderly between creaturely conditions, indeed to discern amidst our utter interdependencies and impure reciprocities our potentiality for renewal, for new creation. If that potentiality can only be actualized in grace—that grace need no longer be conceived as merely extrinsic to a sinful, sealed off, and proto-Cartesian, nature. For as Milbank also avows, that nature itself always already participates in the infinite.

Milbank wants to find a Christian eudaemonism in the eucharistic anticipation of "the eschatological banquet and the cosmic nuptial." Yet then again he wants to affirm the "beginning of beatitude in a time simply to be enjoyed, and a conviviality to be celebrated by the living self."[48] This is possible through eschatological anticipation. And in this I concur: the expectancy that charges all gift exchange may be impure, but the exchange it enacts is irreducible to symmetrical contracts or self-sacrificial hopes. The present of all expectancy is tinged by a hope that ultimately encompasses the entire creation—a hope for a *convivencia* of all creatures in a future in which I too will somehow, as some-body, participate. Milbank ups the ante: "to be ethical therefore is to believe in the Resurrection, and somehow to participate in it."[49] Yet if this were a prescription *for Christians* it might leave open enough hermeneutical space for that faith to take place as an offering of love rather than threat. But not untypically he follows it by the menacing pronouncement: "and outside this belief and participation there is, quite simply, no ethical whatsoever." Thus, "quite simply," the gift turns to poison, grace to shibboleth: the power discourse of the world's majority religion reasserts itself.

Indeed it is only in the "resurrection of the dead" that inter-human reciprocities can actually partake of the gift-event. Due to our sinful incapacity, expressive of nothingness of the present/presence, Milbank espouses a deferral if anything more total than Derrida's—except of course after death. It is only eschatologically that the dead one "appears in the space of living exchange as surprising gift, beyond our life now in time which is always the mere pursuit of security."[50] Because Milbank uses Hermione of *A Winter's Tale* as his figure of resurrection, the prefiguration and liturgical foretaste seem to endow the present with a greater richness than do his "Levinassian moralizers." Yet rather than redistributing the resurrection *within* time, as Shakespeare does, the drama becomes a literary allegory of a literal, doctrinally correct *eschaton*.[51] The theoretical magic is Milbank's: the gift of life set against our craving for security offers the ultimate security of an afterlife. Rather than letting the resurrection serve as a lure to the "eternal life" *welling up within this* life, Milbank performs the standard eschatological postponement. Yet he takes away with the right hand the gift the other has given.

To the contrary: "our life now in time" is indeed never the *mere* pursuit of security, however much we do as societies and individuals try to make it so. The pursuit of security is sinful not as such but as the appropriation of all the creaturely goods—of love, of hospitality, of health, of abundance, of mutual protection, that it manipulates and deforms. Indeed in our craving to secure the present, and our compensatory adventures into destruction, we may choke the very spirit of life. But the temporality of life

---

48. Ibid., 144.
49. Ibid., 148.
50. Ibid., 151.
51. Ibid.

will not have been the cause of our sin, nor escape from it the answer. Life in time pulses with the fragile and fierce tempo of the creation. Within the creation, the extent and boundaries of which lie beyond the most advanced calculation, flow bottomless streams of renewal, offered to us ever again—not from outside the creation but from outside our entrapped, self-possessive subjectivities. They flow into a new inside, dis/closed from below, from whence the spirit *gushes.* The point is not to deny the surge of those waters beyond the boundaries of individual lives or indeed beyond the bounds of the four known dimensions. At this point, "supernature versus nature" is a crude organizing principle for the complexity of the spatiotemporal continuum, indicative of boredom with the earth more than interest in its transfiguration.

My specific contention with Milbank may boil down to this: the reciprocity he seeks to reinstate as the basis of an alternative theology of the gift needs a deeper, and so more radical, theological ground than either poststructuralist groundlessness *or* an orthodox foundationalism can provide. How does the ontology of participation stretch all the way into the constitutive reciprocities of "life now in time," except as a supernatural donation, from the transcendent outside, beyond, after all? While he seeks to unhinge the imaginary of the unilateral gift from its secular moorings, he refurbishes its premodern superstructure. He offers his anti-modernism with an in-your-face final flourish: thus "super-hierarchical transcendence offers us its gift."[52] Even in the end one senses a poisonous atmosphere of threat and demand surrounding this "gift." But of course—and this would be Derrida's and Marion's point—the notion of reciprocity can function perfectly well along a vertical axis. Indeed exchange characterizes the patronage system of hierarchy.

If Milbank's movement toward an inter-human conviviality, an affinity of loving interplay, seems to invite, indeed, require a more radical mutualism, he does not offer an ontology, phenomenology, or even thick description, of interrelatedness sufficient to the task. Some serious account of the dynamics of reciprocity would be needed to construct the alternative subjectivity he rather fitfully seeks. He is too impatient with "immanence" to trace and test the dusty, on the ground interchanges where a gift of truth, a flow of spirit, indeed a "relational transcendence," might take place. Of course such impatience with most everything within the cosmos characterizes any *aggressively* orthodox Western Christianity. It routinizes its fancy that theological vision can escape its creaturely condition. So it need not attend seriously to the emergencies of city or earth—except as parables of "I told you so." And therefore it will reduce the earthling moments of ecstatic reciprocity to dust and nothingness. As though it has opened up all these material and social realities, only to ask: "is that all?"

The reciprocity reads as radical because it is constitutive of both the giver and the receiver: they do not exist as self-sufficient substances prior to and independent of the gift-event. It acquiesces in neither a Cartesian substantialism nor a Platonic essentialism. Theology was ousiologically framed from the start, and so the deconstruction will be a long and delicate operation, precisely in its radicality. To appreciate that participation is not just in ideas but also in each other and therefore also in God. The point is not to purge theology of metaphysics or indeed of Platonism but rather to liberate it from the classical binarism. This sense of participation draws on alternative Platonic

---

52. Ibid., 211.

traditions, such as that of Nicholas of Cusa, whose articulation the principle for radical relationalism in theology cannot be surpassed: "therefore to say that 'each thing is in each thing' is not other than to say that 'through all things God is in all things' and that 'through all things all are in God.'"[53] It is only through this transcosmic panentheism that the reciprocities of all creatures, in their exchange of the breath of life and all its gifts, finds its proper theological context.

Bottomless Reciprocity

Inasmuch as postmodern ideas of "the gift" do privilege a transcendental unilateralism, a one-way flow that trumps rather than fosters mutuality, Milbank's insistence on a transfiguring reciprocity contributes new life and nuance to the discussion. Indeed it may stimulate a robust concept of love, enhancing not only our interpersonal affinities but also funding the struggle for planetary justice and sustainability. Everything depends for Christian theology upon a claim that Milbank has carefully situated in the tension between the Lukan/poststructuralist unilateralism and the Johannine reciprocalism: "Now it may very well be argued that Christianity has combined both perspectives on giving, but if it has done so it is surely more fundamentally under the aegis of reciprocity, even though the eschatological character of this goal requires 'an absolutely unilateral' moment for the gift in our fallen present time."[54]

I want to agree. Grace is a meaningless notion apart from its unconditional gesture. But I fear that "the absolutely unilateral moment"—the moment of "super-hierarchical transcendence"—again jeopardizes reciprocity itself. The whole argument of *Being Reconciled* depends upon the "fundamental" claim of reciprocity. This entails, surely, a *theological* reciprocity. But then is he prepared to think seriously about the reciprocity between God and the world? What he offers at this juncture is "the incarnation of the Logos, as the return of humanity to the Father." This conflation of incarnation with ascension could perhaps symbolize and empower a fundamental reciprocity. But it seems instead to settle for a Trinitarian sleight of hand. The Logos serves here as a mere Athanasian stand-in for humanity, rather than as a christological mediation of real human interrelatedness with said "Father." Relationality is thereby reduced or absorbed into the circularity by which the incarnation of the second Person eternally returns to the first Person of God. This wintry abstraction seems rather far removed from the hot midday interchange at the well, in its—admittedly Johannine—interhuman thirsts and satisfactions. Milbank takes a further step: "Likewise, God ceases to be a gesture of lonely superabundant giving, but instead his gift which is the Holy Spirit only results from, and is the manifestation of, the perfect mutuality of Father and Son."[55] The perfect mutuality of the "divine economy" seems then to fall prey to the Derridean warning about the economic circularity: the relationality of God is reduced to a mere immanent trinitarianism, the original trope of economic circulation.

How does such reciprocity within the deity improve upon a unilateral overflow, which might in its excess at least touch the creation directly? Indeed this triangle is nailed shut by this uncritical re-assertion of the *filioque*, the very clause that drove the

---

53. *Nicholas of Cusa: Selected Spiritual Writings* (trans. H. Lawrence Bond; Mahwah, N.J.: Paulist Press, 1997), 140.

54. Milbank, *Being Reconciled*, 160.

55. Ibid.

final wedge between eastern and western orthodoxy.[56] "And finally, the Son offers himself *not at all* for the earthly city, and not at all as the giving up of something for the sake of an even greater something else, not even himself for the sake of the cosmos or the other."[57]

Not at all? Where do these hyperboles take us? Certainly away from the anti-imperial struggles that Milbank himself advances with one hand. On that score, he may be right when he argues that "local resistances to globalization" will only be "finally effective and liturgical if they blend, universally, to encompass the globe as a sacred locality."[58] But the other hand taketh away: the solidarity must be defined and supervised by a triumphant Christianity, indeed a Christianity of his liturgical preference; and so, not surprisingly, redemption escapes beyond the very cosmos. The gift is given *not at all* for a renewed city, for a new Jerusalem of this earth, for this earth transfigured. What for, then? "The manner in which 'he dies for his friends' is indeed not that they should live their self-possessed lives while he has lost his—as if he had saved them from drowning or defended them in war."[59] True, John's Jesus is not exchanging his life for theirs, whatever retrieval we want to make of exchange, "but rather in defense of the truth he has secretly proclaimed to them ... the truth of which is the absolute creative power of the Father, a truth only maintained and indeed fully taught in Christ's resurrected return."[60]

Perhaps for some there is living water in this revelation. I am left thirstier than before, indeed parched and perplexed. For how can we read the "absolute creative power of the Father" as anything but the ultimate closure of reciprocity? Absolute creative power, as pure activity, pure act, brooks no space in the divine in which we—*we*, not just our humanness platonically "assumed" by the logos—might be received. There is here no receptivity in God, no moment of divine reception *of us*, in which God too might—if we use personal images at all, rather than a consistent apophasis—be imaged feeling our feelings, desiring our desire, thirsting in our thirsts, embracing our finitudes. Then of course the moment of absolute divine unilateralism is eternal: there is no rhythm by which God and world, creator and creature, come into "affinity." Yet in the last chapter he argues quite pleasingly for that *oikeosis* (becoming at home with) via Gregory of Nyssa and the *imago Dei*.

He declares that "affinity is the *mysterium*," the "absolutely non-theorizable," "almost ineffable." Mystery may of course be the traditional cover for theological oxymoron. But if affinity and a fundamental mutualism remain incoherent in the face of this Father-God of absolute creative power, mystery works differently for a theology of *radical reciprocity*. It melts off the tones of certainty, while heightening the articulability of our complex cosmic networks of relation. To speak of God at all, beyond sheer negation, is to decouple divine creativity from absolute power and thus to begin to think reciprocity with theological consistency. The "ecstatic reciprocity" needs by his own account a divine home—an *oikeosis* of a two-way love. Without some version of what Whitehead called "the consequent nature of God," some way of thematizing the

---

56. Even such a confessionally orthodox theologian as Jürgen Moltmann has been at pains to undo the western bias of the filioque clause. Cf. *The Spirit of Life: A Universal Affirmation* (Minneapolis: Fortress, 2001).

57. Milbank, *Being Reconciled*, 160, emphasis mine.

58. Ibid., 186.

59. Ibid., 160.

60. Ibid.

temporal, receptive, passionate life of God, I fear that this entire argument on behalf of reciprocity is undermined precisely where it matters most: in its doctrine of God. God remains impassive, apathetic, and absolutely active—that is, more Aristotelian than biblical. But for a supremely exceptional incarnation, rather than an incarnation that opens all flesh to its logos, reciprocity obtains within the Godhead, and within the world, but not between them.

Such a supremely self-centered divine immutability, wearing a paternal face, will only generate sons in His image, "prior subjects" every one. An alternative subjectivity, in which subjects arise moment to moment as events of inter-becoming, constituted for good or ill in our interrelations, calls for a theology of radical reciprocity. To put it conversely, only a God imagined as enjoying infinite reciprocity with the universe will lure from us an ethic adequate to our own gruesomely vulnerable, festively gifted interdependence one with another. That enjoyment is marked as "ah, good!" in the first chapter of Genesis, as Elohim lures forth a great complex, richly delegated process of co-creativity.

The problem lies in part in the nonbiblical machinery of the *creatio ex nihilo*. It seems to trap theology in a theological dualism that does not so much (as its modern defenders insist) protect newness, creativity, and difference so much as it reduces difference to the separation of Creator and creation. The "gift of God" is indeed, as Milbank avows, always already being received. But might this "always already"—unlike that of Milbank or Derrida—signify that creation is itself absolute gift?[61] The cosmos as explosive, radiant, endlessly generous, unfolds within its intergeneses infinite reciprocities. It thereby offers infinite opportunities for the gift of the spirit to come, to come differently, asymmetrically, anew. Creation is the genesis-field, in which the gift opens our perception to—what? Something *outside* of it? Surely that imaginary of a transcendence outside the world would be our self-delusion, the dulling delusion of those who think they can imagine what lies beyond imagining, while failing to open their eyes to what lies before them: "now I see with my eyes," confesses Job. The transcending of any particular immanence does not draw us outside of the open-ended spatio-temporality of the creation but into its deep inside. There, what precedes and exceeds the creature transfigures the creaturely *present*.

To reopen spiritual perception within the closures of a dulling, violating empire of sameness, a sameness not of creation but of sin, requires art, drama—and even theology. Indeed it requires the gift with which to receive the gift.

> Thou that hast giv'n so much to me,
> Give one thing more, a grateful heart.
> See how thy beggar works on thee
> By art.[62]

The ultimate gift—the one worth teasing, wheedling, begging, and flirting for, in the lyrical reciprocalism of art itself—is the gratitude with which to perceive the gifts

---

61. Anne Primavesi, *Sacred Gaia: Holistic Theology and Earth System Science* (London and New York: Routledge, 2000), and its development in *Gaia's Gift: Earth, Ourselves, and God after Copernicus* (London and New York: Routledge, 2003), for the emergence of an ecofeminist theological discourse of "life as gift event."

62. George Herbert, "Gratefulness," *The Complete English Works* (New York: Knopf, 1995), 88.

already given. If creation is the gift of gifts, it is a creation whose warp is life and woof is death. So we have been given the sign of the death of death, the future-present of a remembered resurrection, to re-enliven life, not to take it beyond life in time but precisely to reawaken the time of our lives: "such a feast, as mends in length."[63] This gift *takes time; indeed it takes*: the actualizing of all of our gifts, the resurrection of each of us in the surging life of the Body, reciprocally realizing our many odd and asymmetrical gifts. It takes the continuing commitment to that actualization, that activity, in the face of the repeated dulling and disappointing of hopes. The gift *takes*. The reciprocity is costly and celebratory.

I would offer in place of the *creatio ex profundis* an iconic concept I have developed at length elsewhere.[64] It may prove truer to Milbank's insight into the primacy of reciprocity over unilateralism than is his own resort to the absolute creativity of supernatural transcendence. Though creation from the deep, the chaos, is in fact more biblical, I am not proposing a biblicist return to Genesis. Yet if theological ex-nihilism is predicated upon a nihilistic reading of creaturely life as nothingness, it misses the rhythmic interplay of genesis and kenosis, becoming and perishing, that would open up a more biblical version of Platonism. That would be nothing new: creation from the *khora*, the Timaean chaos, translated into the sheer flux of the biblical *tehom* would follow a path not taken, a possibility signaled by Christian Platonists such as Justin and Hermogenes. The "truth of the absolute creative power of the Father" is the truth of the path taken, the wide path of Christendom. The absolute is precisely that which is absolved from relations, from reciprocity. Its supernaturalism arises as a perennial defense, a dam, of "Truth" against a great pluralist flood, threatening under imperial circumstances to wash out depth and difference. But then this paternal power of the absolute, all the more imperious, proceeds, as dams usually do, to clog the subtler subterranean streams, even to channel and block the living waters.

The truth of living waters, however, suggests another, subtler flow, the way neither of a timeless truth nor of a truthless time: a way of *timely* truth. Beyond the mirrorplay of ex-nihilism and nihlism exists a "worship in spirit and in truth." This spirit deterritorializes every city, every site, movement, church, or dogma that would confine truth within a boundary—or a bucket. Milbank may be right, that "the only way . . . to escape restricting terrain is to refuse even the opposition of territory and escape."[65] But recourse to "supernatural transcendence" against "pure flux" only reterritorializes spirit, trumping its reciprocity. Theology could instead remember the path of the *bottomless spring*: infinite flux within creaturely limits. The radical reciprocity of Spirit generates its new subjects precisely at the interfluency of those limits. The truth of this Spirit and the gift of this life, far from offering escape from the creation, *immanates* from its bottomless flux. It flows unconditionally into the conditions of intracosmic interchange. But the agapic generosity of the unconditional does not— no more than the rain and the sun that stream upon all—imply an unmoved Giver. If the encounter in Samaria offers the gift with a grammar and a grace that, remaining asymmetrical, never appears as unilateral, then indeed "we would have to name it universal gift."[66]

---

63. Herbert, "The Call," *The Complete English Works*, 153.
64. Catherine Keller, *Face of the Deep: A Theology of Becoming* (London & New York: Routledge, 2003).
65. Milbank, *Being Reconciled*, 210.
66. Ibid., 169.

3. Radical Orthodoxy and the Heresiological Habit

Engaging Graham Ward's Christology

—*Virginia Burrus*

Orthodoxy enters the stage of history hand in hand with heresiology. From the perspective of the early apologists and their Nicene and post-Nicene successors, the truth of Christian doctrine becomes articulable only when provoked by heresy's stubborn refusal of that same truth. The delineation of falsehood in its manifold guises—the work of heresiology—is, then, also the delineation of the one true faith. In his groundbreaking study of the birth of "the notion of heresy" in the second century, Alain Le Boulluec has suggested that the discursive relation of orthodoxy to heresy that emerges in the works of ancient theologians such as Justin and Irenaeus is at once oppositional and mimetic, like the relation of a photographic image to its "negative."[1] More recently, Rebecca Lyman has introduced a slightly different metaphor, via an invocation of Homi Bhabha's postcolonial theory of mimicry: the ancient discourse of orthodoxy, she suggests, represents heresy less as the oppositional negation of orthodoxy than as its flawed or perverted imitation; heresy is, then, "not quite" orthodoxy, as menacing in its resemblance as in its dissimilarity.[2]

Whether we read the representation of heresy as negation or (as I would prefer) as mimicry, it must be admitted that orthodox discourse thereby addresses a number of real problems. Among these is the problem presented by the practice of theology itself. It is, after all, difficult to justify ongoing theological production where doctrine—represented as divinely granted revelation transmitted via apostolic succession—is presumed to be both fully accessible and utterly unchanging. The need to refute heresy supplies such justification, allowing doctrine to break out of its self-consigned stasis by providing the church fathers both pretext and cover for their own immensely innovative theologizing. Yet the temporality of orthodoxy must bend and split in order both to accommodate and to repress the historicity, and thus the inventiveness, of theology. Christian truth is by definition prior, in the terms of the orthodox script: it always already *is*. It is, however, also necessary (by the terms of that same script) that the

---

1. Alain Le Boulluec, *La notion d'hérésie dans la littérature grecque IIe–IIIe siècles* (Paris: Études augustiniennes, 1985).

2. See Rebecca Lyman, "Hellenism and Heresy," *Journal of Early Christian Studies* 11, no. 2 (2003): 209–22, and "The Politics of Passing: Justin Martyr's Conversion as a Problem of 'Hellenization,'" in *Conversion in Late Antiquity and the Early Middle Ages: Seeing and Believing* (ed. Kenneth Mills and Anthony Grafton; Rochester, N.Y.: University of Rochester Press, 2003), 36–60.

heretics see it first, albeit through distorting lenses: the negation or perversion of orthodox truth by heretics is understood to *precede* its doctrinal articulation by the orthodox fathers. Yet in practice orthodoxy and heresy must always be spoken in the same breath, *at the same time*: paradoxically, there is no orthodoxy without heresy, no confession without negation, no original without mimicry. (This "paradox," of course, begins to undo the claims of orthodoxy, even as it also sustains them by supplying endless grist for the heresiological mill.)

Here I want to explore the shifting temporality of doctrine that arises at the historical roots of Christian orthodoxy by considering two essays by Graham Ward, one of the founding fathers of the recent—indeed self-consciously "postmodern"—theological movement dubbed "radical orthodoxy." The question that motivates me is this: Why does Ward's "radically orthodox" Christology—consisting in nuanced reflections on the topics of gendered embodiment and erotic suffering—apparently need to represent itself as both preceding and superseding the assertions of identified "heretics," whether wrong-headed "feminists" or pathological "sado-masochists"? (Why must his orthodoxy and his heresiology be uttered in the same breath?) Put otherwise: How stubborn is theology's heresiological habit? These issues press me with particular urgency because I both admire much about Ward's constructive project and at the same time align myself with the agenda of advocates of both the radical feminism and the radical sexual politics so stridently opposed by Ward. Ward seems to fear, as the ancient fathers also feared, that without the threat of heresy theologians have nothing to say. Can this be true?

Engaging Ward's two essays sequentially in the two parts of my own essay, I will also be reengaging the teachings of the fathers regarding the gender of Christ and the erotics of suffering.

The Heresy of Feminism and the Doctrine of the Multi-gendered Body of Christ

In "The Displaced Body of Jesus Christ," Ward proposes that classical Christology "displaces" the body of "Jesus the gendered Jew" in such a way that it becomes "multi-gendered." Beginning by delicately distancing himself from Karl Barth's resurrection-centered theological position—which, he assures his readers, he would also not wish "to contradict"—he moves swiftly to focus on other theologians whose mistaken opinions, it would seem, *require* contradiction. He charges that "questions such as 'Can a male Saviour save women?' and modern investigations into the sexuality of Jesus, which simply continue the nineteenth-century rational search for the historical Jesus, fail to discern the nature of corporeality in Christ."[3] For Ward, the incarnation must be interpreted from the perspective not only of the resurrection—in which is revealed the body's "inability fully to be present, to be an object to be grasped, catalogued, atomized, comprehended"—but also of the ascension of Christ, which supplements the resurrection, accomplishing the "final displacement of the body of the gendered Jew."[4] From this Gospel-based vantage point, specifically masculinized representations of the

---

3. Graham Ward, "The Displaced Body of Jesus Christ," in *Radical Orthodoxy* (ed. John Milbank, Catherine Pickstock, and Graham Ward; London and New York: Routledge, 1999), 163.

4. Ward, "Displaced Body," 175.

divinity of Christ—for example, the privileged trinitarian trope of Sonship—appear expendable (even self-deconstructing) within the traditional framework of doctrine.[5] In contrast, feminist theologians such as Rosemary Radford Ruether—whom Ward intends to supersede by invoking a prior truth—have claimed that the human maleness and the divine masculinity of Christ have been tightly and even causally linked in the history of theology. (Furthermore, if the masculinity of Christ's divinity is either expendable or self-deconstructing, why does almost no one seem to have noticed?) Ward reads the tradition differently: The "relation of [the multi-gendered body of Christ] to the body of the gendered Jew does not have the logic of cause and effect. . . . One abides in and through the other. The body of the gendered Jew expands to embrace the whole of creation."[6]

Ward's critique—and his optimism—notwithstanding, I do not think that Ruether's question, "Can a male Saviour save women?" (for the question is in fact hers), simply overlooks the implications of Christ's posited transcendence by perpetuating a reductively historicized and humanistic (thus ineluctably modernist) representation of Christ. I wonder if Ward actually believes that it does—and thus I also wonder why he needs to attack Ruether so directly.[7] If anything, Ruether's analysis is in danger of taking Chalcedon for granted: for her, the two-natured Christology established as orthodoxy in the fifth century retrospectively clarifies the ambiguous forces at work in the previous centuries, whereby the long-standing feminine figure of Wisdom was suppressed in favor of the Word or Son. When two natures are made one person, the human maleness of Jesus is all too easily translated into a divinized masculinity, she suggests. "The unwarranted idea develops that there is a necessary ontological connection between the maleness of Jesus' historical person and the maleness of *Logos* as the male offspring and disclosure of a male God."[8] Ward, agreeing that such an idea is "unwarranted," is nonetheless more interested in criticizing the feminists for their supposedly low Christologies than the fathers for their highly patriarchal theologies: as long as theologians take the ascendancy of the divinity of Christ seriously enough, he seems to believe, the salvation coded as "multi-gendered" will become available to all humankind.

Despite Ward's insistence on a rhetoric of contradiction, both he and Ruether agree, I think, that the human maleness of Jesus does not in itself pose an insurmountable problem for feminist theology. I myself would go further and add that Jesus'

---

5. This is my inference. Ward, it should be mentioned, does not directly address the masculinizing language of Nicene-Chalcedonian orthodoxy—in part because he is attempting to reframe Christology in less "patristic" terms. He states explicitly that his study begins "not with those concepts philosophically and theologically honed by the ante- and post-Nicene Fathers but with the gendered body as scripture presents it to us and as the Church has reflected upon it" ("Displaced Body," 163). Clearly, however, his intent is not to subvert either the authority of tradition—represented in the figure of the church as body of Christ—or the particular validity of two-natured Christology, which is (it seems to me) not only assumed but defended.

6. Ward, "Displaced Body," 177.

7. In fairness, I must record Ward's own comment: "I do not intend this essay to be an attack on Ruether herself" (Ward, "Displaced Body," 177, n.1). It remains the case that he positions his essay initially as a refutation of a position demarcated by a well-known citation from Ruether's work in a rhetorical context that, it seems to me, subtly misrepresents her argument.

8. Rosemary Radford Ruether, *Sexism and Godtalk: Toward a Feminist Theology* (Boston: Beacon Press, 1983), 117.

human maleness has its theoretical advantages, from a feminist perspective, insofar as it disrupts the gendered terms of cosmological dualisms that masculinize transcendence and feminize particularity and thereby restores to masculine gender its rightful "particularity."[9] The divine masculinity of the Son *is*, however, a major stumbling block. Here I resist Ward's postfeminist stance, while sharing his commitment to a philosophically nuanced rereading of traditional Christology that attempts "to show how a masculinist symbolics can be refigured in a way which opens salvation through Christ to both (if indeed there are only two, which I doubt) sexes."[10]

In order to take the full measure of the Son's manhood, "he" must be distinguished from the comparatively undersexed pre-Nicene Word. No doubt the tendency to privilege Logos at the expense of Sophia in the earlier period reflects the politics of patriarchy, among other factors, for example, the exegetical;[11] nonetheless, the subtle attraction of the grammatical gender of the Word to the embodied maleness of Jesus remains merely implicit. In contrast, the exclusive masculinism of trinitarian Son Christology is not only explicit but also inherent to the articulation of the Nicene position. It is by erasing sexual difference from the Trinity that the fourth-century fathers affirm the essential difference of a sublimely masculine God from an ambivalent creation not "begotten" by God but "made" out of nothing: it is by eliminating the distinction between mother and child that they assert the sameness of father and son, by abjecting a feminized materiality that they push the spirit to new heights. If this is the logic of paradox, it is also the logic of "belief," which is founded upon the exchange of bodily presence for absence and absence for real presence, indeed upon the atoning principle of substitution itself. In the play of such enacted "displacements," manhood becomes the measure of a humanity that aspires to transcend its own nature, to be what it is not; corporeality itself is refashioned as a diaphanous veil, both hiding and revealing what lies beyond, above, or within.[12] Elsewhere I have attempted not only to expose Nicene doctrine to feminist critique but also to explore the subversive possibilities contained within a radically transcendentalized theology that is, paradoxically, framed in "essentially" gendered, sexualized, and indeed pluralized terms.[13] What is perhaps still needed, however, is a nuanced analysis of the gendered structure of the

---

9. This becomes evident when one contrasts the insidious *ease* with which a two-natured Christology subjects Jesus' Jewishness to the terms of Christian supersessionism, under the sign of a "multi-ethnic" Christ who is frequently silently reinstated as "white"—the colorless non-ethnicity of Euro-America. From this perspective, Jesus "the gendered Jew" strikes me as a slippery designation. Why not Jesus "the male Jew"? What is here elided, and to what end?

10. Ward, "Displaced Body," 177, n.1.

11. Regarding the exegetical matrix of Logos-Sophia theology, see the important argument of Daniel Boyarin, "The Gospel of the Memra: Jewish Binitarianism and the Prologue to John," *Harvard Theological Review* 94, no. 3 (2001): 243–84.

12. In an essay entitled "Belief Itself," Luce Irigaray rereads Jacques Derrida's rereading of Freud's famous discussion of "the *fort-da* of little Ernst": "The most important *fort-da*—as you know, even, or especially when you refuse to believe it—refers, past the mother's presence, in the mother, beyond-veil, to the presence of God, beyond the sky, beyond the visual horizon. . . . It moves . . . away from the mother's presence, then, toward that of god beyond and in heaven. All the threads and all the sons come and go between these two places of the invisible. . . . And what is being sent of hers . . . is not some phallus she guards jealously—even if this is a condition he depends on—but rather the mystery of a first crypt" (Luce Irigaray, *Sexes and Genealogies* [trans. Gillian C. Gill; New York: Columbia University Press, 1993], 32).

13. Virginia Burrus, *"Begotten, Not Made": Conceiving Manhood in Late Antiquity* (Figurae: Reading Medieval Culture; Stanford, Calif.: Stanford University Press, 2000).

relation of the fully divine Nicene Son to the human man Jesus in subsequent incarnational Christology, the terms of which were hotly debated among fourth- and fifth-century theologians. The two-natured Christ affirmed at Chalcedon—who is also "one person"—is not, after all, simply the sum of his manly and more-than-manly parts. The foregrounding of the incarnation within post-Nicene Christology results in a profound reconceptualizing of the subjectivity of Christ at a level of complexity that is not easily theorized. Chalcedon, it seems, demands a new math, a calculus that exceeds the logic of addition and subtraction, of fractions and wholes. Have we found it yet?

I would suggest that we require not only a new theory of subjectivity but also an accommodation of the analysis of gender to a more complex understanding of power and positionality. For this purpose, it may be worth recalling the political circumstance in which two-natured Christology was first articulated. The historian Peter Brown comments on the widening chasm that separated an increasingly autocratic—and also Christian—emperor from even the most privileged of his subjects by the early fifth century, a development that is likely to have had the strongest impact on elite men, who now found themselves "*mere men.*" Under the conditions of autocratic rule, it was no longer effective to appeal to the emperor for justice on the basis of the cultural values transmitted by a shared *paideia*; one could only hope that he would exercise mercy. "The emperor was to show *synkatabasis*, condescension, to his subjects, as the rich stooped to hear the cry of the poor and as God himself had once stooped to join himself, through his Incarnation, to the impoverished flesh of the human race." Brown continues by underlining the relevance of the experience of autocratic power for the controversies that produced the doctrine of the two-natured Christ. "It is, perhaps, no coincidence that the first generations in which the inhabitants of the imperial capital had to face the permanent and overwhelming presence among them of a godlike autocrat were marked, in Constantinople and elsewhere, by vehement christological debates (associated with the councils of Ephesus and Chalcedon, in 431 and 451) on the precise manner in which and, above all, on the precise extent to which God had condescended to join himself to human being in the person of Christ."[14] (Consider, for example, the following articulation of Chalcedonian doctrine: "That self-emptying of his . . . was a drawing near in mercy not a failure in power" [*Tome of Leo* 3].) Can Brown's insightful suggestion that fifth-century Christology is, in part, a cultural effect of empire be pressed further? What might this tell us about Christ's "mere" and "more than" manhood?

It is at this point that a specifically *postcolonial* concept of hybridity may helpfully supplement the postclassical doctrine of the doubled—or "two-natured"—subject. For theorist Homi Bhabha, hybridity emerges in the "interstitial passage between fixed identifications"[15] and is closely related to what he calls "mimicry," that inevitably imperfect or incomplete imitation by which the colonized subject *almost* reproduces the colonizer's discourse, in an act of aping that carries the ambivalence of both envy and mockery, assimilation and subversion, resemblance and menace. The colonial subject as Bhabha describes him is marked by a subtle lack, "almost but not quite" a single, whole essence; less than one, "he" is also more than one—and yet this hybridity is

---

14. Peter Brown, *Power and Persuasion in Late Antiquity: Towards a Christian Empire* (Madison: University of Wisconsin Press, 1992), 155.

15. Homi K. Bhabha, *The Location of Culture* (London: Routledge, 1994), 4.

by no means the result of combining discrete cultural essences. Rather, it is the effect of the disruption of the colonial itself through the doubling, and doubling back, of a productively flawed mimesis that introduces difference to trouble the rule of the one and the same. The authority of colonial discourse is challenged in the "process by which the look of surveillance returns as the disciplining gaze of the disciplined, where the observer becomes the observed and 'partial' representation rearticulates the whole notion of *identity* and alienates it from essence."[16]

Not wanting to make a mockery of either theory or theology (the latter always already "a hybridized form"),[17] I will nonetheless risk a deliberate act of discursive mimicry. Does not the indwelling God—the fully divine Son—enact his transcendence in part by pitching his tent in a "nativity" ("born in the last days from the Virgin Mary," "Jesus the gendered Jew"), a localized particularity that He can be represented (to His own advantage) as otherwise lacking? Is not the native ("colonized") humanity—"mere manhood"—itself always produced as such from the perspective of transcendence, produced as a necessarily inexact imitation of the creator, a divinized nature that is "not quite" God but nonetheless made "in the image"? (Adapting Bhabha's language: "To be divinized is *emphatically* not to be divine.")[18] In the christologically refracted dualistic cosmology of Chalcedon, if humanity is "not quite" divine, God—who condescends to be born, crucified, and buried—in turn is "not quite" human (though the relation is anything but symmetrical): both "natures," in asserting their "completeness" in Christ, are also forced to acknowledge lack to the extent that they understand themselves as (less than) "one." Viewed against the backdrop of Bhabhan postcolonial theory—which in turn highlights the backdrop of the late antique politics of empire—the two-natured Christ is the very figure of the borderland, the site of ongoing specula(riza)tion, in the ambivalent play of dominance and subordination wherein the integrity of the subject is ever again dying and rising. Not simply a *tertium quid*—the "third *thing*" that horrified the orthodox fathers—the hybrid Christ may yet be a "Third *Space*," a "split-space of enunciation."[19]

Working, provisionally, within this postcolonial concept of hybridity—with its attention to imbalances of power as well as to the interdependence of subjectivities not so much reproduced ("begotten") in mimesis as produced ("created") in mimicry[20]—it may be possible to achieve a somewhat more precise description of where and how masculinity is generated within the two-natured Christ, a drama enacted, as we have seen, on the stage of empire. The "source" or "cause" of Jesus' sex, I would suggest, is nowhere and everywhere, dispersed in the interstitial passage between "natures," an eroticized effect of the heightened play of sameness and difference produced in the forced and forceful exchange of images—the mis-speculations of "identity"—across the chasm separating divine omnipotence from the abject weakness of a creation

---

16. Ibid., 89.

17. Ibid., 226.

18. Cf. Ibid., 87: "To be Anglicized is *emphatically* not to be English." Gnosticism takes this notion of creation-as-imitation over the edge into outright parody, as the misbegotten Demiurge and his unhappy cosmos are mockingly represented as poor mimics of the perfect Monad and its divine Fullness. Orthodox understandings of creation and fall likewise, I am suggesting, retain the hint of a proleptically postcolonial doctrine of human subjectivity as divine mimicry.

19. Ibid., 38.

20. Cf. the distinction between representation and repetition (mimesis and mimicry) in ibid., 88.

materialized *ex nihilo*. Does it "start" with the flesh, with "Jesus the gendered Jew," with Jesus the colonized *man*? On the one hand, yes, for only the mortal body can bear the cutting mark of gendered particularity, according to the dictates of ancient cosmology. On the other hand, no, for that mark—the subjugating, even feminizing mark of circumcision?—first becomes visible, theologically, when viewed from the God's-eye perspective of Christ's full divinity—or rather, when viewed with the double vision of a fully two-natured Christology. It is when placed on the "split screen,"[21] juxtaposed with the majesty of his divinity, that the finitude of Jesus' sexed (and therein also ethnicized) body becomes painfully evident and evident precisely as a *mimicry of masculinity*: there, our eyes are guided less to the acts of his life than to the irreducible fact of his material subjection to birth and death, as he is caught up in the throes of the maternal body, pierced by the nails of imperial domination. But it is also through the opposite movement, through speculative "displacement" onto his divinity, that Jesus' masculinity can finally achieve its swelling destiny in patristic thought: "The expansive bloom of the flower is not the effect of the bud, but its fulfillment," to borrow Ward's poetic phrasing.[22] (If this does not seem to be a very manly metaphor, it is nonetheless traditional. The fathers too spoke of the Son as a flower: for example, Origen, *Commentary on the Song of Songs* 3.4.) Mimicking what is thereby constructed as "human nature," the resurrection gets the divinely sexed body of Jesus "up" and the ascension finalizes the act of "fulfillment"—arguably distinctly *phallic* displacements (not least in the extent to which they reflect an envious appropriation of the ambiguously feminized body and a greedy colonization—spatialization?—of *place*). The forcefully transcendentalized body of Christ is not, then, *merely* the effect of Jesus' maleness, but it *is* unthinkable without it, and it is also, I suspect, unthinkable outside the intensely dualistic and hierarchical ontology conveyed by Chalcedonian Christology. Multifaceted and unstable, even vulnerable, in its complex and interstitial masculinity, Christ's body may *approximate* the "multi-gendered." It does so *not*, however, by a doctrinal sleight of hand ("the Church is now the body of Christ")[23] that recovers the singularity of a sex that "can only play its role as veiled"[24] but rather in a performative unmasking of the man's hybridity, the aim of which is "not to deny or disavow masculinity, but to disturb its manifest destiny—to draw attention to it as a prosthetic reality—a 'prefixing' of the rules of gender and sexuality; an appendix or addition, that willy-nilly, supplements and suspends a 'lack-in-being.'"[25]

The Heresy of Sadomasochism and the Doctrine of the Suffering *Jouissance* of Christ

A second essay by Ward, entitled "Suffering and Incarnation," displays its polemical edge even more nakedly. "The concern of this essay lies with a comparison and, ultimately, a confrontation between two cultures: the secular and the Christian with

---

21. Ibid., 114.
22. Ward, "Displaced Body," 177.
23. Ward, "Displaced Body," 177.
24. Jacques Lacan, "The Meaning of the Phallus," in *Feminine Sexuality: Jacques Lacan and the École Freudienne* (ed. Juliet Mitchell and Jacqueline Rose; New York and London: W. W. Norton, 1982), 74–85.
25. Homi K. Bhabha, "Are You a Man or a Mouse?" in *Constructing Masculinity* (ed. Maurice Berger, Brian Wallis, and Simon Watson; New York and London: Routledge, 1995), 57.

respect to the character and economies of pain and pleasure, suffering, sacrifice, and ultimate satisfaction."[26] Here the split and doubled temporality of orthodoxy is forcefully inscribed onto the very structure of the essay, as Ward begins with an account of "contemporary pain and pleasure," followed by an exposition of "Christian pain and pleasure." (What, I wonder, is the implied temporality of the "Christian," if not both prior and superseding, and thus also "the same," that is, contemporaneous?) Ward concludes with the staging of "the confrontation." There is, of course, no suspense regarding who will emerge the winner in this near-classic performance of the aggression of apologetic theology. Confrontation itself is, moreover, crucial. At the conclusion of the essay, Ward reminds his readers: "The method of my argument is confrontational, not simply analytical. And the Christian theological nature of that confrontation is important, for . . . Christianity has a 'subversive core,' a radicality inseparable from its orthodoxy."[27] Orthodoxy, in other words, *requires* a confrontation with heresy.

The "heretics" summoned by this essay are not other theologians but rather a broad spectrum of poststructuralist philosophers. As was the case with his reading of Ruether, here too Ward seems to have to work hard—even at points deliberately to misread the philosophers—in order to set himself off from the opposition (or, more precisely, in order to construct an "opposition"). He observes that "intellectual debates concerned with the economies of desire . . . have been oriented around the notion of *jouissance*." Fair enough. He continues with his description, homing in on the "problem": for the philosophers, "suffering constitutes itself as the lack or absence of *jouissance*"—a lack that may, however, be construed as pleasurable. By the end of the same paragraph he has distilled his complaint regarding the particular "sacrificial logic" of the philosophers' conceptions of desire into the following concise accusation: "It has the structure of sado-masochism."[28] It has the structure then, of a sacrifice, of a pleasure (a "joying"?) complicit with suffering, complicit (*perhaps*) even with the suffering of lack—but certainly not simply with "the lack or absence of *jouissance*"— unless one wants to define *jouissance* differently, as I think perhaps Ward does. But the success of his argument is difficult to judge, given both his conflation of quite diverse philosophers (some of whom, Deleuze for example, explicitly reject the concept of desire as "lack") and his flatly reductive reading of all of them—both being traditional heresiological tactics, particularly well exemplified by Irenaeus, who likewise aligns heresy with philosophy. (Discernment is further hindered by the way that Ward's own theological position so often seems to mimic that of the philosophers, as we shall see.) According to Ward, poststructuralist philosophy's "economy of sacrifice" (based on deferral and the fantasy of limitless productivity) is complicit with capitalism: "Sacrifice as enjoying one's own suffering, in this immanent economy of desire, sustains current developments in globalism."[29] Elsewhere, he makes his charge still more baldly: "The sado-masochistic economies of desire, profoundly at work in contemporary culture, are pathological."[30] These are scarcely insignificant, unprecedented, or even altogether unfounded claims.

---

26. Graham Ward, "Suffering and Incarnation," in *The Blackwell Companion to Postmodern Theology* (ed. Graham Ward; Oxford: Blackwell, 2001), 193.
27. Ibid., 205.
28. Ibid., 194–95.
29. Ibid., 197.
30. Ibid., 205.

They are, however, framed in such a way as to elide the fact that many, if not most, of the philosophical economies of sacrifice that Ward invokes are themselves explicitly offered as critical subversions of the capitalist economy and the politics of globalism that are complicit therewith. Consider, for example, the contemporary philosopher Karmen MacKendrick's (broadly poststructuralist) critique of an implicitly capitalist economy of desire: "In the everyday (nonecstatic) economy of investment, expenditure is loss (and desire is lack, founded upon the need to fill what is empty, replace what is lost). This is precisely the economy of productivity, the teleological economy found in the security of the center." MacKendrick contrasts the "transgressive economy of excess" reflected in both Christian asceticism and current theories and practices of sadomasochistic eroticism: "Within the economy of joy, power seeks expenditure; materially, as force, the body expends itself. But in expenditure is its increase; the more it expends itself (its energy, its vitality, its strength) the more powerful it becomes."[31]

Ward goes on to articulate his own distinctly Christian, indeed "radically orthodox," understanding of a divine suffering and sacrifice that begins in creation (itself issuing "from a certain kenotic giving, a logic of sacrifice") and culminates in the passion of Christ, in which the emptying of kenosis is matched by "a filling and a fulfilling, not only of Christ but of each believer with respect to Christ." Lack, Ward points out, "is now being satisfied."[32] The deferral inscribed by Christian eschatology should not, in other words, be confused with the deferral inscribed by the sadomasochistic economy of sacrifice, which promises no satisfaction. Yet Ward acknowledges the ongoing power of erotic suffering affirmed by the Christian ascetic tradition (astutely citing Gregory of Nyssa in particular) and wonders aloud how it differs from sadomasochism "since the internalization of a pleasurable pain is common to both." Indeed. He artfully defers answering his own question: "For a moment let us allow that question to hang and draw. . . ."[33] (An exquisitely "sado-masochistic" suggestion!) And here, reading both with Ward and against his denunciation of the philosophers of "sado-masochistic" desire ("allowing the question to hang and draw"), I return again to the Christology articulated by the Christian fathers of late antiquity, with particular attention to the convergence of gender and eroticism in the suffering body of Christ.

Christ, as we have already seen, gets more "sexy gender-y" as his two natures get more pronounced; his ontological hybridity constitutes a kind of threshold or portal through which his sex becomes more visible.[34] And yet, in itself, Chalcedonian

---

31. Karmen MacKendrick, *Counterpleasures* (SUNY Series in Postmodern Culture; Binghamton: State University of New York Press, 1999), 126. Admittedly, MacKendrick may be a bit too "contemporary," as Ward unfortunately does not cite or seem to know her work. He is, however, clearly familiar with the work of some of the philosophers on whom MacKendrick draws most heavily.

32. Ward, "Suffering and Incarnation," 197–99.

33. Ibid., 202.

34. This "technical" term is borrowed from Eve Kosofsky Sedgwick, "'Gosh, Boy George, You Must Be Awfully Secure in Your Masculinity!'" in *Constructing Masculinity* (ed. Maurice Berger, Brian Wallis, and Simon Watson; New York and London: Routledge, 1995), 16, 18. Sedgwick suggests that "not only are some people more masculine or more feminine than others, but some people are just plain more gender-y than others—whether the gender they manifest be masculine, feminine, both, or 'and then some.'" She goes on to speculate that becoming visible as a sexed subject, entering "onto a map of sexy gender-y-ness," does not involve incremental increases along a dimension of "masculinity," for example, but rather requires "crossing over a threshhold" or passing through a "portal" of what may seem to belong in a different dimension entirely. "Sexy gender-y-ness" is thus likely to be an impure or complex product, becoming

Christology is, perhaps, a relatively modest portal. The real *coming out* of the sexed Jesus is through the gateway labeled "asceticism" and decorated with biblical erotica clipped from the Song of Songs. What he is wearing as he emerges is none other than his resurrected body. (The fathers do, after all, tend to linger there, rather than following Ward to the final "displacement" of Jesus' body in the ascension.) This resurrected body is the body that everyone desires. It is the body to suffer and die for. It is the body with something for everyone (hybrid—and then some?). It is the body of the bridegroom.

Of course, the portal only exists for those with eyes to see—which is to say, with the eyes of a bride. Origen was one of the first Christians to enter the sacred bridal chamber, through the portal of his *Commentary on the Song of Songs*. There the bridegroom "revealed His breasts" to the bride (1.2), who was overwhelmed by his extraordinary beauty (3.2), drawn into his "clefts" (3.15). Origen's bridegroom is not "*all* man," as Stephen Moore observes: "And not only because he is also God, but because he is also a woman." Referring to the Eusebian report of Origen's self-castration, Moore quips, "Clearly, Origen's own gender indeterminacy has communicated itself, somehow, to the Bridegroom."[35]

If Origen opened the (flood)gates of fantasy, Gregory of Nyssa's *Homilies on the Song of Songs* spread them still wider to accommodate the ever queerer sex and more radically unorthodox sexuality of the Savior. For Gregory, the shocking violence of the second watchmen's scene (Song 5:7) becomes an interpretive key to the Song of Songs' larger meaning, unlocking the infinite mysteries of divine eros. Like the smitten woman (or so he imagines), Gregory knows that pain and ecstasy coincide in desire and that the only true goal for a lover is found in love's unending detours and deferrals; thus the most violent frustration of desire—the stripping, beating, and wounding of the searching "bride"—is reconceived by him as the source of the soul's deepest pleasure. Gregory not only rejoices in the agony of his own unfulfilled desire, he actively wills that the pain be intensified. "Perhaps these may seem to some to be the words of one who grieves rather than of one who rejoices—'they beat' and 'they wounded' and 'they took away my veil'; but if you consider the meaning of the words carefully, you will see that these are utterances of one who glories greatly in the most beautiful things" (*Homilies on the Song of Songs* 12.1359). With her veil removed, the soul can at last see clearly, and the beating, in the course of which she is stripped of her obscuring veil, is thus "a good thing," he assures us (going on to compile an impressive list of biblical beatings) (*Hom.* 12.1361–62). "The soul that looks up towards God and conceives that good desire for his eternal beauty constantly experiences an ever new yearning for that which lies ahead, and her desire is never given its full satisfaction" (*Hom.* 12.1366), he declares serenely, thereby leaving the yearning woman to wander the dark streets and alleyways ad infinitum, confident that the watchmen, like stern guardian angels, will find her and whip her, again and again—and this too is "a good thing." "In this way she is, in a certain sense, wounded and beaten because of the frustration of what she desires." But "the veil of her grief is removed when she learns

---

visible in the borderlands or at the points of intersection of disparate registers of gender; such registers might include much of what is not typically thought of as "gender"—ethnicity, for example ("Jesus the gendered Jew"), or even corporeality itself.

35. Stephen D. Moore, "The Song of Songs in the History of Sexuality," *Church History* 69, no. 2 (2000): 335–36.

that the true satisfaction of her desire consists in constantly going on with her quest and never ceasing in her ascent, seeing that every fulfillment of her desire continually generates another desire for the transcendent" (*Hom.* 12.1369–70). Here clearly the binary of "satisfaction" and "lack" reinscribed by Ward is decisively deconstructed—as it arguably also is in at least some contemporary "sado-masochistic" philosophies of eros.

The erotics of deferral are not confined to the second watchmen's scene in Gregory's reading of the Song. They feature still more intensely in Song 2, as he interprets it (*Hom.* 4). "Stay me with sweet oils, fill me with apples: for I am wounded by love. His left hand is under my head, and his right hand embraces me," chants the woman (Song 2:5–6, LXX). Gregory takes this to mean that the bride has been wounded by the divine groom's dart of desire. "O beautiful wound and sweet beating!" she exclaims. Pricked by the potent arrow and infected with insatiable desire, she herself *becomes* an arrow: the divine archer's right hand draws her near to him, while his left hand directs her head toward the heavenly target (*Hom.* 4.127–29). Making his way to the end of Song 2, Gregory points out that the bride seeks a place of repose "in the cleft of the rock" (*Hom.* 6.178; cf. Song 2:14). This image merges with an earlier one in the same chapter, in which the bridegroom is imagined as an apple tree into whose shade the bride has entered (v. 3), evoking for Gregory Moses' theophanic climax in "the cleft of the rock" (Exod 33:22; cf. Exod 20:21), which in turn facilitates his rescripting of the apple-tree scene as wedding-night lovemaking, replayed and thereby prolonged (on his reading) by the first watchmen's scene of Song 3:1–4: "thinking to achieve that more perfect participation in her union with the divine Spouse," she finds herself, "just as Moses" did, enveloped in the secret inner space of a sacred darkness (*Hom.* 6.181).[36] Subtle gender ambiguities and reversals (the bride as arrow resting in the bridegroom's cleft) are thus overlain by a queer image of Moses penetrating God's cleft, which then renders the original exchange (between bride and bridegroom) queerer still, as Gregory interprets the bride's experience "in the cleft" as a surprise honeymoon encounter with an unexpectedly feminine lover who teasingly leaves her ravenous for yet more heavenly delights. "Far from attaining perfection, she has not even begun to approach it," Gregory asserts (*Hom.* 6.181), in seeming admiration at the divine top's consummate skills. Immortality, for Gregory, is undying desire; and so the desire that suffuses the Song, on his reading of it, can only be the kind that does not admit of satiation; yet that refusal of satiation is its own kind of ever-unfurling "satisfaction."[37]

---

36. This is not the only time that Gregory supplements his reading of Moses' entry into the "darkness" of God in Exod 20:21 with an invocation of the "cleft of the rock" of Exod 33:22, in which God is depicted as announcing to Moses, in response to Moses' request to see him face to face, "I will put you in the cleft of the rock . . . and you shall see my back; but my face shall not be seen"; cf. his *Life of Moses* 2.230, discussed in my *"Begotten, Not Made,"* 127–28, 130.

37. See Virginia Burrus and Stephen Moore, "Unsafe Sex: Feminism, Pornography, and the Song of Songs," *Biblical Interpretations* 11 (2003): 24–52, for a discussion of Gregory's homilies in the context of contemporary feminist interpretations of the eroticism (and troubling sadomasochism) of the Song of Songs. Concerning "transgendering" in Gregory's homilies, see also Michael Nausner, "Toward Community Beyond Gender Binaries: Gregory of Nyssa's Transgendering as Part of His Transformative Eschatology," *Theology and Sexuality* 16 (2002): 55–65.

Perhaps all of this seems excessive—multigendered, oversexed, sadomasochistic, and then some. To be sure, other Christians of late antiquity (less "Greek" in orientation)[38] found such queerly unstable Christs a bit *lacking*—they expected more substance from the resurrection body than could be borne by such allegorical flights of fancy. Indeed, for a "not quite" millennialist like Augustine[39] Christ's heavenly manhood could *almost* be "grasped, catalogued, atomized, comprehended."[40] Were such relatively literal-minded anti-Origenists getting straighter (and more "vanilla") sex from the bridegroom? Well, let's take a closer look.

It is Jerome who tweaks aside the loincloth of the resurrected Lord, informing his readers authoritatively that Jesus "must have also had the whole body formed of [all the members], and that not a woman's but a man's; that is to say, He rose again in the sex in which He died." Jerome makes this assertion in the process of refuting an unnamed Origenist "heretic" who argues that the resurrected body will be spiritual, transcending (transgressing?) physical marks of distinction—including the "distinction of sexes." By introducing the case of Jesus, Jerome intends to buttress his argument that the Pauline doctrine of the resurrection of humanity necessarily implies the continuity of identity through the preservation of physical difference. He represents himself as successfully bullying his opponent: "Do you believe, said I, that there will be a resurrection of the dead or do you disbelieve? He replied, I believe. I went on: Will the bodies that rise again be the same or different? He said, The same." (Evidently Jerome cannot imagine that anyone would want to deny the possibility of a continuous and unified "self.") Now he moves in for the rhetorical kill: "Then I asked: What of their sex? Will that remain unaltered or will it be changed? At this question he became silent and swayed his head this way and that as a serpent does to avoid being struck." The sexed body is thus located at the center of the debate about "identity," as Jerome scripts it; avoiding the cutting blow of the distinction of sexes, his opponent wavers, serpent-like, as if performing the very indeterminacy of gender that his position on the resurrection implies. With manly vigor, Jerome finishes him off: "As you have nothing to say I will answer for you and will draw the conclusion from your premises. If the woman shall not rise again as a woman nor the man as a man, there will be no resurrection of

38. See Elizabeth A. Clark, "The Uses of the Song of Songs: Origen and the Later Latin Fathers," in *Ascetic Piety and Women's Faith: Essays on Late Ancient Christianity* (Studies in Women and Religion; Lewiston, N.Y.: Edwin Mellen Press, 1986), 386–427, on the influence of Origen and subsequent developments in Songs exegesis among Latin writers (Aponius, Gregory of Elvira, Jerome, Ambrose, and Augustine). Although Jerome and Rufinus both translated Origen's works, none of these Latin authors actually produced extended commentaries of their own; their interpretations emerge largely in the contexts of their ascetic writings. Augustine notably had little interest in the book, apart from using it to develop an anti-Donatist ecclesiology. David G. Hunter, "The Virgin, the Bride, and the Church: Reading Psalm 45 in Ambrose, Jerome, and Augustine," *Church History* 69, no. 2 (2000): 281–303, offers a complementary analysis of Latin exegesis of another biblical passage with strong bridal imagery.

39. On Augustine's near-millennialism and its implications for gender, see my "An Immoderate Feast: Augustine Reads John's Apocalypse," *Augustinian Studies* 30, no. 2 (1999): 183–94. Elizabeth A. Clark, *The Origenist Controversy: The Cultural Construction of an Early Christian Debate* (Princeton, N.J.: Princeton University Press, 1992), provides a lucid and illumining account of the Origenist controversy as a debate about difference, highlighting the significance of Jerome as a link between the Origenist controversy in the East and the Pelagian controversy in the West, in which Augustine came to figure so prominently.

40. Cf. Ward, "Displaced Body," 175.

the dead. For the body is made up of sex and members." He continues his wondrously circular argument: "But if there shall be no sex and no members what will become of the resurrection of the body, which cannot exist without sex and members? And if there shall be no resurrection of the body, there shall be no resurrection of the dead." Anyone who doubts the resurrection of the sexed body is like Thomas, Jerome further insists. And yet—oddly—it is not Jesus' male member but the gash in his side to which our eyes and hands are drawn, with Thomas's, in this exploration of the Lord's sexed carnality. "How do you explain the fact that Thomas felt the hands of the risen Lord and beheld His side pierced by the spear?" demands Jerome. "I wonder that you can display such effrontery when the Lord Himself said, 'reach hither thy finger, and behold my hands; and reach hither thy hand and thrust it into my side . . . ,' 'handle me and see . . .'" (*Epist.* 108.24). Our Lord's sex is here rendered queerly penetrable.

This passage occurs in Jerome's "Life of Paula," composed as a letter of consolation to Paula's daughter Eustochium on the occasion of her mother's death. At first glance the polemical exchange appears out of place—an annoying intrusion even. At second glance, however, one realizes that the sex of Jesus' resurrected body is *always* on view in the ancient "Lives" of female saints. In marked contrast to male hagiographies, in which Jesus scarcely figures at all, female hagiographies inevitably cast the Savior in a leading role as heavenly bridegroom. In other words, we are, in the "Lives" of women, once again witnessing a staging of the Song of Songs, but this time not all of the actors are male and the interpretation of the script—including its element of erotic violence—is a bit more literal. This accounts in part for the shyness of the bridal gaze: we do not actually see much of the groom's private parts, though we are assured that he is appropriately endowed. "Since therefore it is admitted that He had all the members which go to make up the body, He must have had the whole body formed of them, and that not a woman's but a man's. . . ."

Thus modestly shrouded in the indirection of anatomical abstraction, the body of the bridegroom is further veiled through a series of horizontal displacements. Here displacement itself is a rather literal affair: Jesus' body is mapped not onto an idealized landscape (as in Gregory's allegorical eroticizing of the Song of Songs) but rather onto a particular *place*—the land of his birth and death, a land once colonized by Rome and subsequently recolonized as "holy" by Christians.[41] But it is the Roman-Christian *woman* who is in perpetual motion *between places*. As she sets sail from Italy on the winds of desire, Paula's mobility becomes an icon of her insatiable love for the body of her Lord. She is ever rushing on to yet another site: "In visiting the holy places so great was the passion and the enthusiasm she exhibited for each, that she could never have torn herself away from one had she not been eager to visit the rest." The place of Christ's passion arouses her own: "before the Cross she threw herself down in adoration as though she beheld the Lord hanging upon it"; "she kissed the stone which the angel had rolled away from the door of the sepulchre"; "ardent" and "athirst," "she even licked with her mouth the very spot on which the Lord's body had lain." "What tears she shed there, what groans she uttered, and what grief she poured forth, all

---

41. Andrew Jacobs, *Remains of the Jews: The Holy Land and Christian Empire in Late Antiquity* (Divinations: Rereading Late Antique Religion; Stanford, Calif.: Stanford University Press, 2003), offers a nuanced—and explicitly postcolonial—analysis of "the ways in which Christian empire could be built on the remains of the Jew," discussing the role of literal and literary relics in the imaginary recolonization of Jewish Palestine as the Christian Holy Land.

Jerusalem knows," summarizes Jerome (*Epist.* 108.9). At Bethlehem, Paula's propensity for biblically inspired (and strikingly empathetic) visions, anticipated at Golgotha, comes to the fore. "She protested in my hearing," reports Jerome, "that she could behold with the eyes of faith the infant Lord wrapped in swaddling clothes and crying in the manger. . . . She declared that she could see the slaughtered innocents, the raging Herod, Joseph and Mary fleeing into Egypt" and she cried out "with a mixture of tears and joy" (*Epist.* 108.10). A tireless pilgrim, Paula traverses the Holy Land "and then some," finally reaching the ascetic settlements at Nitria in Egypt. "Was there any cell that she did not enter?" Jerome queries rhetorically. "Or any man at whose feet she did not throw herself?" Seeing the ascetics, "she believed that she saw Christ Himself." "Forgetful of her sex," as Jerome puts it (meaning perhaps the opposite), she even entertains thoughts of living more permanently among these colonies of male hermits, who so closely resemble Jesus. Feeling drawn by a "still greater passion for the holy places" of Jesus' homeland, she returns, however, to Palestine. Soon thereafter, Jerome reports with surprising brevity, she decides to dwell permanently in Bethlehem, establishing monastic communities at the site of Christ's nativity. Here Jerome concludes the "narrative" portion of his account of Paula—a "narrative of the journeys" (*Epist.* 108.14). Propelled by a love even greater than her already excessive love for her children, Paula is set in motion, released from her ancestral Rome; and in a sense she *remains* in motion, not because her love is too slight to bind her in place (on the contrary) but because still greater loves intervene. The point is not just that her path from Rome to Bethlehem does not run straight but that her searching for the incarnate Lord knows no end.

Having thus narrated less in order to bring Paula to her goal than to set her loose on the power of her passion, Jerome pauses to describe the virtues of this lover. Introducing a portion of his account that thematizes Paula's excessiveness ("her self-restraint was so great as to be almost immoderate" [*Epist.* 108.17]), he insists "I am no flatterer; I add nothing; I exaggerate nothing; on the contrary I tone down much . . ." (*Epist.* 108.15). Paula's regime of self-improvement is quickly sketched: she dressed like a servant, never ate with a man, rarely bathed, and slept on the ground—to the extent that she slept at all. She prayed constantly, and prayer for her was lamentation: "Her tears welled forth as it were from fountains, and she lamented her slightest faults as if they were sins of the deepest dye." If there is a surprising hint of irony in Jerome's mountains-out-of-molehills depiction of Paula's tearful self-flagellations, he nonetheless represents himself (without detectable irony) as solicitous of her health: "Constantly did I warn her to spare her eyes and to keep them for the reading of the gospel." Sparing herself, however, is hardly what Paula has in mind, and Jerome comes off looking a bit foolish (or is it level-headed?). Her response: "I must disfigure that face which contrary to God's commandment I have painted with rouge, white lead, and antimony. I must mortify that body which has been given up to many pleasures. I must make up for my long laughter by constant weeping. I must exchange my soft linen and costly silks for rough goat's hair. I who have pleased my husband and the world in the past, desire now to please Christ" (*Epist.* 108.15). It becomes clear that what Lynda Coon has dubbed "the patristic theology of the cosmetic"[42] is more than a

---

42. Lynda L. Coon, *Sacred Fictions: Holy Women and Hagiography in Late Antiquity* (Middle Ages Series; Philadelphia: University of Pennsylvania Press, 1997), 108.

matter of simple inversion. Seeming to swap beauty for ugliness and pleasure for pain, Paula is making herself over as the bride of Christ. Her fasts are heroic (*Epist.* 108.17), her illnesses frequent (*Epist.* 108.19). Face furrowed by grief, body practically a corpse, her mortal flesh betrays an immense desire; good looks disordered, her power to please is out of this world. If the Lord is sexed and sexy, so too, we realize, is Paula. Already in the process of acquiring her own resurrection body, Paula is almost too hot an item for her hagiographer to handle.

So long postponed (not least by his intruded debate with the heretic), Jerome's grief finally overwhelms him. "What ails thee, my soul? Why dost thou shudder to approach her death? I have made my letter longer than it should be already, dreading to come to the end and vainly supposing that by saying nothing of it and by occupying myself with her praises I could postpone the evil day." If praise is possible only while grief is deferred, the deferral of grief makes the letter long, longer than it should be. And yet grief cannot be postponed indefinitely: the praise of a woman must claim its price. "For who could tell the tale of Paula's dying with dry eyes?" Now it is Jerome who weeps. Yet, although he has stolen Paula's tears, Jerome remains an outsider in relation to his own grief: Mother and daughter are enfolded in a single embrace by Paula's impending death, and Jerome—now writing to the daughter—is an awkward intruder on this stage of female intimacy (*Epist.* 108.28). "Why do I still linger and prolong my suffering by postponing it?" he asks again, as if unable to release Paula's already cooling body, caught up within his narrative performance of re-membering. It is Paula who helps him over the edge, as he tells it, by opening the door onto the Song of Songs. "As soon as Paula heard the bridegroom saying: 'Rise up my love my fair one, my dove, and come away: for, lo, the winter is past, the rain is over and gone,' she answered joyfully 'the flowers appear on the earth; the time to cut them has come' and 'I believe that I shall see the good things of the Lord in the land of the living'" (*Epist.* 108.29). Finally, the veil will be removed (!).

The glamorous Paula's funeral drew throngs of bishops, the entire urban population of Palestine, and every single monk and virgin, lasting for days, as Jerome tells it. As her body lay on a bier in the center of the Bethlehem church, "the paleness of death had not altered her expression; only a certain solemnity and seriousness had overspread her features." Jerome adds (gazing with the eyes of a bridegroom?), "You would have thought her not dead but asleep." Jerome insists that "no weeping or lamentation followed her death" but only the chanting of psalms. Vying with this touted decorum, however, he reports also that "the destitute cried aloud that they had lost in her a mother and a nurse" (*Epist.* 108.29) and—naming his addressee, Eustochium, in the third person—that "Paula's daughter . . . , 'as a child that is weaned of his mother,' could not be torn away from her parent." Elaborating the scene, he adds, "She kissed her eyes, pressed her lips upon her brow, embraced her frame, and wished for nothing better than to be buried with her" (*Epist.* 108.30).

Jerome finally acknowledges quite explicitly that he has borrowed Eustochium's sorrow in order to sing Paula's praises, writing of her death as a "martyr" in order to articulate the passion that could scarcely be contained by a "Life" (*Epist.* 108.32). "I have spent the labour of two nights in dictating for you this treatise; and in doing so I have felt a grief as deep as your own," he addresses the daughter who desired only to be buried with her mother. Jerome laments with the woman, like a woman, here at the end. Through Eustochium's mediation, he makes Paula's remarkable grief his own. "I say in 'dictating,'" he continues, "for I have not been able to write it myself. As often as I have taken up my pen and have tried to fulfil my promise; my fingers have stiffened, my hand has fallen, and my power over it has vanished." Grieving Paula, Jerome is unmanned. But grief also gives rise to a new "Life," and *a newly sexed life*, for both woman and author. "In this letter, 'I have built' to your memory 'a monument more lasting than bronze,'" Jerome quotes triumphantly, "which no lapse of time will be able to destroy." The metaphor is almost literalized, in the last, hardening lines of appended text: "I have cut an inscription on your tomb, which I here subjoin."

The holy woman thus becomes publicly representable, but only in the moment of her dying, the moment when she meets her bridegroom—who thereby also becomes representable as sexed. Subject of lament, her "romance"[43] is narrated from death's vantage point, her "Life" is memorialized in the rituals of mourning. Correspondingly, a woman's "Life" can only be written by one who can be seen to grieve. The authors of early female "Lives" are inevitably men, and, more than that, they are men who represent themselves as standing in privileged relationships with their subjects. The same is not typically the case for the writers of male saints' "Lives."[44] The disclosure of the woman's story is a delicately public performance of an ostentatiously private grief. In this it is quite distinct from the public delivery of a funeral oration, that tearless celebration of the quintessentially masculine dead. The hagiographer himself seems to play the role of ersatz bridegroom in relation to the holy woman, and he does so with the awareness of his transgression, equally awed by her power and by his own violence. Intruding under the cover of his grief into a private and distinctly feminine world, in which the primary bonds are between women, most typically between mothers and daughters, he opens space for a hetero-eroticism of an uncommon order.[45]

---

43. Elizabeth Clark critically interrogates the influence of the romance on female hagiography in the face of the overwhelming maleness of the biographical genre: "Although the *Vitae* of early Christian women stress their overcoming of femaleness and subsequent incorporation into a world of 'maleness,' it is still dubious whether the classical *bioi* furnished any fitting models for these *Lives*. And if they did not, did any other form of ancient literature, more focused on women, suggest itself as a more suitable model? Might not the Hellenistic romance, with its concentration on lively heroines, provide a better paradigm for a Vita like Melania's?" (*The Life of Melania the Younger: Introduction, Translation, and Commentary* [Studies in Women and Religion; Lewiston, N.Y.: Edwin Mellen Press, 1984], 155). Returning to the question more recently, Clark reaffirms that "the Vitae of early Christian women saints share many features with the relatively new genre of novels or romances popular in this period rather than with classical biography that focused on the public activity of statesmen and generals: women did not operate in a public, political sphere." She also points out, however, the influence of the philosophical biography, as measured by the fact that all ancient female hagiographical subjects are represented as teachers and purveyors of wisdom (Elizabeth A. Clark, "The Lady Vanishes: Dilemmas of a Feminist Historian After 'the Linguistic Turn,'" *Church History* 67, no. 1 [1998]: 16, 22).

44. See Elena Giannarelli, "La biografia femminile: Temi e problemi," in *La donna nel pensiero cristiano antico* (ed. Umberto Mattioli; Genoa: Marietti, 1992), 231–35, and "Women and Miracles in Christian Biography (IVth–Vth Centuries)," *Studia Patristica* 25 (1993): 377. As Arnaldo Momigliano points out, Gregory of Nyssa, even when composing a funeral oration on his brother Basil, elides rather than emphasizes his close relationship to his male subject: "While Macrina is brought near by a biography, Basil is made distant by a panegyric" ("The Life of St. Macrina by Gregory of Nyssa," in *On Pagans, Jews, and Christians* [Middletown, Conn.: Wesleyan University Press, 1987], 339).

45. See my *The Sex Lives of Saints: An Erotics of Ancient Hagiography* (Divinations: Rereading Late Antique Religion; Philadelphia: University of Pennsylvania Press, 2004), 53–90, for a fuller treatment of the erotics of female hagiography.

Making a woman the subject of a "Life," the hagiographer thus makes a man of himself—but what kind of sex is this? (This is the urgent question that drives Jerome to lift Jesus' loincloth in such a seemingly inappropriate place.) It is *Jesus' sex*, the sex and the members, the sex and the holes, the piercings, the holy caves explored by a woman in the land that is also Jesus' body. It is *Jesus' sex*, resurrected sex, sex after death, sex as death, death as sex, eros as joyous suffering, suffering as *jouissance*. (For the female "Life" presupposes and supplements the deaths of virgin martyrs, those exuberantly masochistic viragos who give witness to their own sharp desire to encounter their bridegroom in the thrust of an executioner's sword.)[46] *Jesus gets sexed* in the bridal chamber, threshold of thresholds, where his human-divine, dead-alive body encounters difference in the body of a desiring woman at the moment of her own violent passage from life to death—the moment of her own resurrection. *Jesus gets sexed* with Paula in much the same queer way that he gets sexed with Origen and Gregory, after all. Paula, in turn, gets sexed in much the same queer way that Origen and Gregory get sexed. In the bridal chamber (that "split-space of enunciation"), *all* subjects are transformed in and by the suffering of a divine desire that keeps on coming. There suffering is indistinguishable from joying, *jouissance* incompatible with a satisfaction—for who could get enough? If this is, in Ward's terms, "pathological," it is a pathology with a distinctly Christian lineage. It is also a pathology that is curiously difficult to differentiate from Ward's own positive articulation of a sacrificial self-emptying that is at once "a filling and a fulfilling, not only of Christ but of each believer with respect to Christ."

Between Sex, Beyond Orthodoxy

Homi Bhabha calls for the conceptualization of "an *inter*national culture, based not on the exoticism of multiculturalism or the *diversity* of cultures, but on the inscription and articulation of culture's *hybridity*." He adds: "To that end we should remember that it is the 'inter'—the cutting edge of translation and negotiation, the *inbetween* space— that carries the burden of the meaning of culture."[47] Similarly, I have desired to uncover in the "Third Space" of Jesus' gendered and eroticized body—of Christ's *hybridity*—a theological basis for reconceptualizing "sex" that would provide an edgier (and more sharply feminist) alternative to the liberal embrace of the exoticism of "multigenderism" or the *diversity* of "sexualities" that abide in "the church." At the same time, Bhabha's "Third Space" may be an apt metaphor for the space of theology itself, a terrain constituted by the endless acts of translation and negotiation between discourses and disciplines that mark theology's inherent hybridity—and thus potentially mark it as something other than an "orthodoxy."

Historically, Jesus has not been represented as simply "(multi)gendered" but rather as complexly masculine. To ignore the sexism inhering in the formative texts and formidable doctrines of Christianity and to imagine that it can be eliminated seem equally flawed responses. Avoiding those dangers, it may become possible to turn the power and complexity of the masculinized Christ to our advantage, feeling for the

---

46. See my "Reading Agnes: The Rhetoric of Gender in Ambrose and Prudentius," *Journal of Early Christian Studies* 3, no. 1 (1995): 25–46.

47. Bhabha, *Location of Culture*, 38.

fracture lines, the sites of reversal, the effects of ambivalence that expose the partiality of the God-Man (and thus also of both Manhood and Godhead) and uncover not only the perverse desire for violence that sustains essential difference as difference-in-power but also the violence of divine desire that may productively pervert such ontologized hierarchies—via the practices of "sadomasochistic" eroticism performed in the literature of Christian asceticism, for example. There is no *safe* sex with Jesus but there may be some good sex in the split-space of transcendent flesh, the passage between (gendered) natures, the suffering of sacred eros.

I finally believe—or rather, I confess that I want very much to believe—that it is possible to theologize without resort to the heresiological habit, via creative and creatively ambivalent reappropriations of a complex and diverse tradition, in dialogue (in acts of translation and negotiation) with whatever other voices may seem most helpful and relevant in a given moment. (This I have tried, however sketchily and imperfectly, to model in my own "historical theological" interpretations of the patristic tradition, though I am not a theologian but a historian by training and profession.) I think Ward could do so if he chose: but then the theology would not be "orthodox," much less "radically orthodox." It would not need to justify its own claims by proclaiming (by seeming to "expose") the falsehoods of others—feminists, humanists, "secular" philosophers, sadomasochists, and so on. (It would "analyze" without staging a "confrontation.") It would open itself more fully both to others and to the otherness of the future, as well as the past. It would suffer its own radical, sometimes even violent, opening, boldly affirming that (to borrow Ward's words) "only God can discern and distinguish what is true suffering"[48]—what, in other words (words close to Ward's own), is a suffering that is not only a lack but also a filling, even a joyous overflowing, *beyond* mere "satisfaction," an extension or transcendence in and of theology itself.

---

48. Ward, "Suffering and Incarnation," 202.

PART II

considering
liberation
theologies

4. Radical Eurocentrism

The Crisis and Death of Latin American Liberation Theology and Recipes for Its Improvement

—*Elina Vuola*

Most readers of this book have probably heard several times that Latin American liberation theology[1] is either in crisis or dead.[2] The death announcements often go hand in hand with declarations of other tragic deaths, such as those of history, God, the subject. However, very seldom do we see such obituaries combine the sense of respect for the deceased and that of loss and grief. Hardly ever do we see results of autopsy, done by professionals able to detect the causes of death, which makes one suspect that either there is no corpse at all or if there is, the circumstances of death are covered up or ignored. This brings us to the logical questions: Why does this situation exist? Who are those interested in these death announcements, even when they might be premature? Even if the corpse is found and liberation theology is identified as dead, what did it die of? Was it a suicide, natural causes, or a murder? Was euthanasia involved? It is clear even by a very superficial glance that those most interested in declaring liberation theology dead are those who either never saw it alive or those who ardently wished for its death from the beginning.

There are also those who say liberation theology did not die but is fatally ill, in crisis, that it is weak, impotent, unable to rise from its sickbed to its previous glory, condemned—implying that it will die, sooner or later.[3] Again, I am interested in asking

---

1. In this essay, I concentrate on Latin American liberation theology, despite the fact that liberation theology today is best understood as a global phenomenon with so many different forms that it would be best to speak of it in the plural. Claims about the present status of "liberation theology" would look very different if analyzed in the global context and would in fact make Latin American liberation theology look somewhat different, too. It also would become more complicated to speak of the "crisis of liberation theology" in the simplistic ways in which it is often done. More emphasis would be placed on the method, the historical commonalities (as well as differences) of colonialism, and the role of the Christian church and theology in defining good parts of humanity as inferior than to easy "ideological" or "intellectual" explanations of the relationship between Marxism and liberation theology, between European thinkers and liberation theologians, and so forth.

2. I wish to thank Dr. Teivo Teivainen, director of the Program of Democracy and Global Transformation at the University of San Marcos, Lima, Peru, and Dr. Franz Hinkelammert, researcher at the Departamento Ecuménico de Investigaciones in San José, Costa Rica, for their comments on this essay.

3. According to Stephen Long, "We have not yet witnessed the demolition of liberation theology, but it is inevitable" (Long, *Divine Economy: Theology and the Market* [London and New York: Routledge, 2000], 115. His argument for this is that "one of [liberation theology's] pillars, a socio-scientific analysis of poverty grounded in dependency theory, has been knocked down." This calls for a more thorough

the logical questions: What does this fatal illness consist of? How did liberation theology become infected by it? Is the diagnosis done by adequate tools and professional skills? What sort of medicine would liberation theology need? Do we want its recovery at all?

A Better Liberation Theology from the North

The questions above bring me to the most relevant issue in the context of the radical orthodoxy movement's assessment of Latin American liberation theology: even if liberation theology is not outright declared dead or in serious crisis, there are those who in one way or the other are offering recipes for an improved, better version of liberation theology. That in itself can be part of honest and open intellectual dialogue in any field, aimed at a common and true understanding of the phenomenon in question. I might very well count myself among those who simultaneously take liberation theology seriously but who are also critical of some of its aspects. Nevertheless, especially for someone not originally from Latin America, who does not share the immediate context of liberation theology—in the 1970s or today—to make his or her critique legitimate and credible, there are two serious prerequisites or conditions. First, a more epistemological condition: to be fully aware of the history, the intellectual and political context, and the contemporary developments of liberation theology. Second, and this condition is also of an ethical character: to test one's theories and analyses with those one names "liberation theologians," meaning also that one gives credit to those one is "consuming." This, again, is part and parcel of traditional academic practices, but for reasons as trivial as lack of language skills or geographical distance, the practice is not often applied to Latin American liberation theologians. In other words, they are treated as if dead, unable to be asked, checked, challenged, communicated with, listened to, and known, including why they think as they do. To be able to do that, one might have to exchange Latin or German for Spanish or Portuguese or learn (well) another foreign language in the first place.

Fewer and fewer writings by liberation theologists—or other intellectual discourses in Latin America—in Spanish and Portuguese seem to be translated into English. Even though translations by companies such as Orbis Books, which earlier did an important job of making Latin American liberation theologians known in the United States and elsewhere, were not always without problems, the current translation situation simply ignores a vast intellectual production. It becomes more serious if new generations of scholars conclude from the lack of translations that "if it does not exist in English, it does not exist," and base their analysis on the meager and limited amount of translations.[4] Further, by reading only the early classics of Latin American

---

analysis than what can be done in this essay, especially for at least three reasons. First, there are many who would ask for further qualifications about the claim that dependency theory has been "knocked down." Second, there are many who would question Long's claim about dependency theory as being one of liberation theology's "pillars." It was important, but so were many other theories. Third, the causal explanation between the fate of an economic theory and a phenomenon as multifaceted as liberation theology needs similarly detailed arguments for its support as in the case of the relationship between the collapse of socialism and the presumed crisis in liberation theology.

4. The availability of English translations of scholarship written in Spanish and Portuguese also serves South-South dialogue by making Latin American intellectual production more easily known in Asia and Africa.

liberation theology, be they in English, Spanish, or Portuguese, one does not get an adequate understanding of the development and current situation of liberation theology. All of this leaves one wondering if part of the proclaimed crisis and stagnation of liberation theology is in fact based on a lack of access to sources, especially in the United States. This lack of access is related to a widespread acceptance that one does not have to read intellectuals from other cultures in the original language.

What this means is that liberation theologians are not considered serious partners of dialogue, but rather objects of first world monologues. Only this latter, unfortunately very common among first world academic theologians, do I call Eurocentrism. In this essay, I will mainly pay attention to one book, that of Daniel M. Bell Jr., whose *Liberation Theology after the End of History: The Refusal to Cease Suffering* (2001) is not only published in Routledge's Radical Orthodoxy series (which is why I take it as a representative of that movement) but is also acclaimed by the publisher as "the most thorough account to date of the rise, failure, and future prospects of Latin American liberation theology." I could not disagree more strongly with this statement, even if it is meant only to sell the book.

Of course, I am not saying that liberation theology could or should not be critiqued, but I argue that there are more serious and fruitful ways to do that than by the type of critique represented by Bell's book. Nor am I pretending to offer a detailed theological critique of his book or any other radical orthodoxy text on liberation theology, as necessary as that would be. Rather, I am interested in looking at some of the premises and presuppositions of those texts, including their sometimes striking gaps and errors. By presenting Latin American liberation theology through a very selective amount and use of texts, omitting the most recent developments, the radical orthodoxy interpreters of liberation theology have risked misunderstanding the scope and importance of liberation theology altogether.

I have critiqued liberation theology myself for its understanding of praxis and its lack of substantial dialogue with some new social movements and theories, especially feminist concerns of the intersection of poverty and (poor) women's lack of reproductive choices, and the sometimes uncritical attitude liberation theologians have toward the political and social role of the Catholic Church in Latin America in issues of sexual and reproductive ethics.[5] I claim that there are ways of engaging liberation theology critically while also respecting it for what it is. I am a living example of the fact that all of this can also be done by someone who is not a Latin American, and in fact, I question the essentialist sort of positioning of oneself in locked contexts. To be aware of the possibilities and limitations of an "outsider" position is however of utmost epistemological importance. For example, my sensitivity to the importance of language

---

5. Elina Vuola, "El derecho a la vida y el sujeto femenino," *Pasos* 88 (2000): 1–12; *Limits of Liberation: Feminist Theology and the Ethics of Poverty and Reproduction* (Sheffield: Sheffield Academic Press; New York: Continuum, 2002); this title also published in Spanish as *La ética sexual y los límites de la praxis: Conversaciones críticas entre la teología feminista y la teología de la liberación* (Quito: Abya-Yala, 2001); "Remaking Universals? Transnational Feminism(s) Challenging Fundamentalist Ecumenism," *Theory, Culture, and Society* 19, no. 1–2 (2002): 175–95; "Option for the Poor and the Exclusion of Women: The Challenges of Postmodernism and Feminism to Liberation Theology," in *Opting for the Margins: Postmodernity and Liberation in Christian Theology* (ed. J. Rieger; Oxford and New York: Oxford University Press, 2003), 105–26; "Seriously Harmful for Your Health? Religion, Feminism, and Sexuality in Latin America," in *Liberation Theology and Sexuality: New Radicalism from Latin America* (ed. M. Althaus-Reid; London: Ashgate, 2005).

stems from the fact that my mother tongue, Finnish, is spoken by five million people. I never assumed I could have an intelligible dialogue with people from other cultures and countries without knowing the language in which they think and write. This holds true for me also in English, the language of the radical orthodoxy movement.

The Church and Liberation Theology

There are some themes in Bell's book that seem to be central in most radical orthodoxy writings, especially that of ecclesiology. It is about what the church should look like, what its role should be in the contemporary, often secularized world, and who has the power to decide. In many radical orthodoxy writings, there seems to be an odd mixture of overestimating the force and depth of secularization—in need of a new orthodox response from Christian theologians—and underestimating or avoiding the new and growing public role of religion, in Christian as well as in non-Christian cultures.[6] This new public role is often about a new type of fundamentalist interpretation of the tradition in question, easily used to fuel a presumed "clash of civilizations." Liberation theology, with all its shortcomings and flaws, has been one form of thinking about the public (and even political) role of religion without this fundamentalist bend.[7]

In the case of Latin America, the most important historical contexts for liberation theology, the repressive military dictatorships of the 1960s and 1970s, on the one hand, and the five hundred years of colonization (including the role of the Catholic Church in both the conquest itself and the following centuries of colonialism), on the other hand, disappear in an analysis that refuses to take seriously the amount of violence inherent *in* the Christian churches and their dominant theologies throughout the centuries. The link between the Christian church in its real historical, social, and political context of power—even today—and its deeply woven ties to capitalism, Eurocentrism, racism, and sexism is missed in an attempt to "save" the church(es) from the "secular" world. To acknowledge and critically analyze that link has been the insistence of liberation and feminist theologies since their beginning. Latin America with its more than five hundred years of "evangelization" is a perfect example of a colonial(ist), imperial(ist) interpretation of Christianity, in which it is practically impossible to separate the

---

6. See, for example, José Casanova, *Public Religions in the Modern World* (Chicago and London: University of Chicago Press, 1994). Regarding the ways in which this new "social fundamentalism" is intimately tied to issues of women's rights, sexuality, and the family, see my "Remaking Universals?", in which I call it fundamentalist ecumenism, visible in the actual leadership of the Catholic Church, in some Muslim interpretations of their tradition, as well as in fundamentalist Protestant groups (mainly) in the United States.

7. The feminist philosopher of religion Grace Jantzen points out how most Anglo-American philosophers of religion center their approach on the creedal statements of western Christianity, making their understanding of "religion" much narrower than that of most feminist scholars interested in religion. She refers to Julia Kristeva's understanding of western Christianity as maintaining itself by insisting on the centrality of *belief* (production of doxy) (Grace M. Jantzen, *Becoming Divine: Towards a Feminist Philosophy of Religion* [Manchester: Manchester University Press, 1998], 24, 197). I would add that what she says about Anglo-American philosophy of religion very much holds true for the radical orthodoxy movement as well. The difference in liberation and feminist theorizations of religion lies primarily in how religion is not interpreted only through its formal institutions, creeds, and dogmas. Also, holding different religious institutions accountable for their social and political roles in different times and in different societies is central in different liberation theologies.

interests of the church and the state. This makes the radical orthodoxy type of restoration of a "pure" Christianity combined with its critique of liberation theology especially problematic. Any contemporary theology, especially those that would restore a more prominent role for Christianity, should start with a critical reflection of the ways Christianity, Christian theology, and Christian churches, based on their positions of authority, have been key players in opposing civil and human rights, especially those of women and non-European peoples by defining them as inferior, and of the still prevalent sexism, anti-sexuality, and hierarchical structures in the very organization of the churches.[8]

In the radical orthodoxy writings in general and in their assessments of Latin American liberation theology in particular, practically no attention is given to the wide array of Christian churches and theologies. One is left wondering if "the church" and "Christian theology" mean primarily the Catholic Church or also (but how exactly?) the different Protestant and Orthodox churches. In Latin America, in spite of the predominant role of Catholicism, liberation theology has always been and is ecumenical, some of its major proponents being Protestants (such as José Míguez Bonino, Rubem Alves, Elsa Tamez, and Luis Rivera-Pagán). Further, the rapid growth especially of Pentecostalism in the subcontinent in the last decades is a challenge for both classical and *iglesia popular* types of Catholicism.

I am not going to give a review of Bell's book; rather, I will look at some of the more general presuppositions that are characteristic of his work on Latin American liberation theology, even if they are by no means exceptional but rather the rule among the radical orthodoxy movement. This centering on issues regarding liberation theology's death and crisis seems to be the dominant discourse, even if sometimes in an implicit form.

The Declared Crisis of Liberation Theology

It is clear that Latin American liberation theology is not the same as it was decades ago. It would be more than odd if it would be, taken the enormous political and ecclesial changes in the continent and in the world. Liberation theologians are the first to admit this.[9] It would be absurd to see changes as signs of decadence, weakness, and loss of relevance and meaningfulness, be these intellectual or sociopolitical changes. Why name these necessary changes a "crisis"?

One very common line of reasoning in the case of Latin American liberation theology—even in those basically sympathetic to it—is that the crisis and disappearance

---

8. According to Steven Shakespeare, radical orthodoxy has "an absurdly inflated ecclesiology which refuses to receive truth from others," implying "an aggressive refusal of all that is not-Church." Most importantly for the sort of liberation and feminist theological critique that my essay wishes to represent, this "idealization of the Church . . . takes no account of the sometimes violent history of the Church" (Steven Shakespeare, "The New Romantics: A Critique of Radical Orthodoxy," *Theology* 103, no. 813 (2000): 167, 171.

9. See, for example, Franz Hinkelammert's short description of the evolution of liberation theology from the 1960s to today, in which both continuity and ruptures can be discerned. Interview with Germán Gutiérrez in José Duque and Germán Gutiérrez, eds., *Itinerarios de la razón crítica: Homenaje a Franz Hinkelammert en sus 70 años* (San José: Editorial DEI, 2001), 33–34. See also Pablo Richard, "La iglesia y la teología de la liberación en América Latina y el Caribe: 1962–2002," *Pasos* 103 (2002): 29–39."

of "historical socialism" and the Soviet Union is the main reason for the weakening and crisis of liberation theology. The proponents of this thesis see a strong causal connection between liberation theology in Latin America and historical socialism in Eastern and Central Europe; further, they see that link primarily in ideological or theoretical terms ("Marxism is dead, so liberation theology is dead or in crisis"). These two premises can be held simultaneously by their proponents, but often the latter is the one that is stronger. There is no space to analyze this in detail here, nor is it my main interest. I rather want to point out some problems in the reasoning.

What exactly is the relationship between the collapse of socialism in European countries and the contemporary forms of Latin American liberation theology? If there is a causal relationship, one would presume it could be shown, but I have not yet seen a study that has done so. Most liberation theologians have had a reserved or negative relationship to existing socialism, probably with the exception of their "own" Cuba. This does not exclude the fact that many—but not all—liberation theologians and intellectuals close to them have had a serious dialogue with Marx as a philosopher and, in some cases, an affinity to leftist parties and groups in different countries. This is true for many intellectuals in western European countries as well, but that does not yet reveal any easy causal relationship between one's intellectual exercise, one's concrete political commitments, and one's relationship to historical socialism. Nor has it meant the delegitimization of major European thinkers and their work—as it of course shouldn't.[10] So, why is this delegitimization so easily done in the case of liberation theologians? I assume that it is a result of the sort of Eurocentrism in which only thinkers from the North are taken really seriously (even when criticized), on the one hand, and a lack of knowledge of political processes both in Latin America and the former socialist countries, especially those of central Europe, on the other hand. There are links between what happened in the two regions, but I propose they are not those usually mentioned. Let me explain.

First, if one sees what happened in those regions from the perspective of democratization—which happened to some extent at the same time in these two regions—the link between socialism, theology, and the churches can be highlighted, although in a very different way than what is usually done. There are similarities between the regions in the process of radicalization of the civil society from the 1990s onward. Ordinary people rose to resist authoritarian regimes and their human rights violations. Second, the role of the churches—Catholic, Protestant, and Orthodox, especially the first two—with all their differences had the common element of offering a space, often limited, for this resistance and reorganizing of the civil society. The role of the church changed from that of a power holder to a representative of the civil society, with the concomitant role of defending people's rights against authoritarian regimes. In both socialist (anti-capitalist) Europe and right-wing (anti-communist) Latin America, this role of the church was a contested one, mostly marginal, and by no means did it indicate a total conversion of the church from its previous role, but the similarities are there nevertheless. Of course, there are also vast differences between the roles of the churches—such as that of the Catholic Church in socialist Poland, the Evangelical Church in the former GDR and Estonia, and the Russian Orthodox Church in the former Soviet

---

10. The situation in western Europe is different from that of the United States, where the relationship of intellectuals and activists to the Marxist legacy and the very word "leftist" have very different connotations from those in Europe.

Union. Here, I merely highlight some of the similarities in order to make the point that a claim of causality between the fall of socialism in Europe and phenomena such as liberation theology in Latin America should not be made too easily. To make this link between what happened in the socialist countries and Latin American liberation theology, one needs to take seriously the schism and conflict inside the churches vis-à-vis repressive societies (South Africa under apartheid could be yet another example) and the changing role of the institutional churches in them.

The now deceased pope John Paul II misunderstood liberation theology. His Polish background made him see communism in places where there was none, but curiously also close his eyes from the similarities between what happened in Eastern Europe and Latin America. The Polish priest, Father Jerzy Popieluzko, was murdered by the then military junta of General Jaruzelski in Poland in 1984 for causes well-known by Latin American radical priests: for being a dangerous anti-state fanatic. His state was the atheist and communist bureaucracy machinery of Poland. In Latin America, the state was the "Christian" right-wing national security state. Both were run by military forces that saw the primary enemy in their own people. The Solidarnosc movement of Poland was a labor union, in which the harbor workers of Gdansk organized themselves illegally, an activity close to John Paul II's heart. However, he could not understand similar activities in Latin America, in which workers' rights and organizing were opposed with a different ideology. The Vatican interpreted people's quest for freedom, democracy and basic rights, even the churches' opposition to horrendous human rights violations, as "communism," because the formal state apparatus was Christian and Western and anti-communist, even if illegitimate and undemocratic. This ideological Cold War setting was the framework in which the U.S. government, the Vatican, and the Latin American national security states all operated, together with the repressive governments of Eastern Europe. In that setting, liberation theology is clearly on the other side. Together with others, liberation theologians took the side of those representing the fragile and threatened civil society.

Third, another important link, directly related to the most important claims made by liberation theology ever, is that between worsening economic conditions in Latin America and the collapse of the Soviet Union. This link is explicitly made by several economists and liberation theologians but is hardly ever quoted in studies that only see the "ideological" link as if that would be obvious and (more) direct. These very concrete effects include the withdrawal of Soviet financial support and investments from third-world countries,[11] starting already during the perestroika period (in Latin America, fatal for Cuba), and later, the lessening of Western investments in the South because of the new markets in former socialist countries and the channeling of parts of Western development aid to Eastern Europe instead of the poor countries of the South. The so-called second world disappeared, and "for the first time, the Third World is totally alone."[12]

Fourth, it is important to take into account the changes in U.S. foreign policy toward Latin America after the late 1980s. The United States financed and supported right-wing military coups and regimes, as well as counterinsurgent groups such as the *contras* in Central America, but it also had the unilateral power to cease those conflicts

---

11. It is practically impossible to get trustworthy statistics from the Soviet era.

12. Hinkelammert in an interview with Benjamín Forcano and Manuel García Guerra in Duque and Gutiérrez, *Itinerarios de la razón crítica*, 97.

by withdrawing its military and financial support. Thus, there is again a link and causality between what happened with historical socialism in Europe and what happened in Latin America, but this link existed most importantly in the thoughts of U.S. foreign policy leaders. Central American peace processes and democratic changes elsewhere in Latin America were possible only after an ideological change *in the United States*. When the communist threat and the Cold War setting disappeared, the United States could allow limited democratization processes in its presumed backyard.

Fifth, the importance of different social movements in Latin America cannot be downplayed. Human rights movements, labor unions, land reform movements, women's movements, the popular church, and in many cases also armed insurgent groups all had an important role in the democratization process, again similarly to at least some former socialist countries. Both external and internal reasons for the democratization of Latin American countries are thus true and should not too easily be separated. To ignore the relevance of these changes to the way in which liberation theology has changed and to how those changes should be evaluated is another example of the "ideological" type of explanation in which an abstraction of "Marxism" is given more weight than local political and social changes, including interpretations of Marxism that cannot easily be lumped together with the communist regimes of the Soviet Union and Eastern Europe.

It is sometimes said that after the disappearance of historical socialism liberation theology has not created sociopolitical theories and practices that would be able to offer a credible alternative to today's global capitalism. First, even when true, it is not true only for Latin American liberation theologians but for intellectuals anywhere, not least for us in Western Europe or North America. Second, in the specific case of Latin American liberation theology, what it became and what it did not become is also reflective of the expectations that were put on it in the 1970s. Here, it is especially important for academic theologians from the North to be self-critical. All the (romanticized) hopes for a revolutionary Christianity were placed in a group of theologians who worked in extremely difficult situations of forced exile, political repression, and lack of support from church leadership. Third, the huge global problems that we all share in one way or the other—global inequality, poverty, racism, militarization, sexism, ecological destruction—are challenges for all of us, intellectuals or not. The results of these problems are most serious and immediate in the South, thus making classical liberation theological claims more relevant than ever. Fourth, liberation theologians and intellectuals close to it have at least taken on themselves the responsibility to think seriously about and from this global situation, something that cannot be said of many first world theologians. Liberation theologians intend to rethink the present situation, and these intents bring liberation theologians close to the worldwide movement of globalization critics and proponents of alternative forms of globalization (*otro mundo es posible*, according to the World Social Forum movement). The works of Latin American intellectuals such as Franz Hinkelammert are serious intents to rethink critically the current crisis, even when they do not pretend to be total solutions to it, and to reduce Hinkelammert's massive production (as Bell does) to a few separate texts simply misses the point—about theology and the church, about economy, about the state, about capitalism vis-à-vis socialism, about liberation theology.[13] And fifth, that

---

13. Bell's (mis)use of Hinkelammert is an example of my more general critique of how liberation theology is depicted among the radically orthodox. Hinkelammert is a major theorist for the contemporary

works such as Hinkelammert's (and many others') are not known and adequately assessed in the United States or western Europe, tells more about us in the North than about any "current crisis" in Latin American liberation theology.

It is important to notice that there are internal problems and inadequacies in liberation theology (like in any human enterprise). According to my judgment, some of the most challenging ones have by and large been acknowledged by liberation theologians themselves, such as avoiding issues of sexism, sexuality, and sexual ethics; concentrating on issues of power only on the macro level of society; lack of dialogue and interaction with new social movements such as the ecological movement, the feminist movement, indigenous and black movements, as well as gay and lesbian movements— all important and flourishing in the contemporary array of social movements in Latin America. The wave of conservatism in the Catholic Church globally has also hit liberation theologians hard. Not only have they been censored and silenced, but there is nowadays practically no institutional support in the church for them, a situation different from that of the 1970s and the 1980s. Of course one could say that liberation theologians themselves should have made their differences with the leadership of the church clearer and kept more distance from it, but at the same time we have to remember the individual costs of that kind of a move. Today, all these issues are discussed among liberation theologians, even when it is also true that part of the loss of influence of liberation theology is certainly related to the issues mentioned above. Most importantly, there is a rather general agreement among liberation theologians that whatever we call liberation theology, it is not the same today as the one thirty or twenty years ago. Any critical dialogue with "liberation theology" has to make clear if it is discussing works written decades ago, if it is engaging contemporary intellectuals, or if it is doing both. The lack of this clarification is a major problem in many scholarly works on liberation theology, including the books of Daniel Bell and D. Stephen Long.[14]

Bell quotes some liberation theologians to support his claim that they themselves perceive and recognize the crisis "of their vision,"[15] not taking into account that the people he is quoting are not talking about the same thing. Even less so, they would never agree with Bell's analysis of the causes and solutions to the crisis. If one reads widely and attentively enough what liberation theologians in fact say about the "crisis," the result is very different from what Bell says. Liberation theologians talk of a crisis of the entire globe, of all its people, most acutely of those in the impoverished South, a

rethinking of liberation theology in the larger sociopolitical, economic, and philosophical context of Latin America. This is why I give a lot of space to his thoughts in this essay, even if he is not strictly speaking a (liberation) theologian at all. In spite of his importance in Latin America, very little of his work has been translated into English.

14. Long, *Divine Economy*, is marketed in its first page as "the first book to directly address the need for an active dialogue between theology and economics" without the necessary addition "in English" (even in English, this is not true). More importantly, however, it should be mentioned that books discussing liberation theology and economics simply ignore the most important liberation theological writings on the subject, such as those of Franz Hinkelammert, Hugo Assmann, Jung Mo Sung, and others. This is another example of truly radical Euro/Anglocentrism, which should not be accepted as good scholarship. Again, based on the same Eurocentrism, it seems that this is accepted in Northern universities only in the case of first world evaluations of third world intellectuals. In Long, *Divine Economy*, and John Milbank, *Theology and Social Theory: Beyond Secular Reason* (Oxford: Blackwell, 1994), there is not one liberation theological book quoted or referred to in Spanish and Portuguese in comparison to Milbank's use of several sources in German and French.

15. Daniel Bell Jr., *Liberation Theology after the End of History: The Refusal to Cease Suffering* (London and New York: Routledge, 2001), 42–43.

crisis produced by several factors, not least by the sort of neoliberal global capitalism that destroys both humans and their environment. Bell reads what liberation theologians have said about Latin American (or other) intellectuals "being in crisis" as a diagnosis of a specifically liberation theological crisis, when in fact what they try to do is to analyze a larger cultural, religious, economic, and political crisis. In other words, liberation theologians acknowledge that something is fatally wrong with our situation as human beings. It is simply wrong to interpret this acknowledgement as "liberationists' own recognition that their vision is in crisis."[16]

In short, my responses to the question of the crisis of Latin American liberation theology are the following. First, if there is a crisis, we all share it with liberation theologians. Second, liberation theology is not the same today as it was thirty years ago—and should or could not be, given the vast changes in Latin America. Third, the most important current forms of liberation theology are not (well) known outside Latin America, for which I already have given several reasons. It is a serious scholarly mistake to assume that liberation theology does not exist or that it is in crisis if its contemporary proponents have not been as widely translated into English as its classics from the 1960s and 1970s. Fourth, anybody who declares liberation theology to be in crisis or dead should be able to give detailed and well-founded arguments for his or her claim. By and large, this does not happen.

Too Radical or Too Conservative for Radical Orthodoxy?

Against this background, I will take up some issues that Daniel Bell discusses in his book. It aims at an improved version of liberation theology that would be sufficiently radical (now it is "insufficiently radical"[17]) and become a "therapy of forgiveness as a form of resistance to capitalism."[18] In addition to the already mentioned reasons for the supposed crisis of liberation theology (all of which Bell does not necessarily agree with), he has theses of his own for liberation theology's crisis. According to him, liberation theology is in crisis because its hope is misplaced (in the state),[19] because liberation theologians "have succumbed to the capitalist order" by embracing the modern vision of "politics as statecraft."[20] Liberation theologians have been advocating an apolitical church and hitching the revolution to the state, all this reflecting "a failure to perceive the true nature of both the struggle and the resources God may have."[21] Bell locates both the cause and the potential solution to the crisis in "in liberationists' understanding of the Church,"[22] a point that indicates why he probably feels affinity

---

16. Ibid., 42.
17. Ibid., 3, 42.
18. Similarly, Stephen Long, referring to John Milbank, criticizes liberation theology for the "inability to *properly* theorize ecclesiology," i.e., "*failing* to develop the social ecclesiologically" (Long, *Divine Economy*, 130; my emphasis). This sort of language seems to imply that the radical orthodoxy response, whatever it is, is the properly theorized successful truth. Especially in this context, it is worth remembering that the theology they are dismissing for failure is the one that more than any other theology in our time has radically re-elaborated both ecclesiology and the role between the church and society.
19. Bell, *Liberation Theology*, 43.
20. Ibid., 44.
21. Ibid.
22. Ibid., 42.

with the radical orthodoxy movement and its wishes to restore the church to the center of contemporary societies. Differently from the critique that blames liberation theology for politicizing the church (I assume he speaks of the Catholic Church in the Latin American context), Bell's critique is the exact opposite: liberation theologians' false vision of politics and the church has led them to depriving the church of a forthright political presence.[23]

I already commented briefly on the problems with the radical orthodoxy vision of the church. Again, I think what makes any liberation theology (including feminist and black theologies) epistemologically so at odds with that vision is that the very birth and raison d'être of different liberation theologies lie in the realization of how the church and dominant theology have been constructed to support and legitimize sexism, racism, capitalism, and colonialism. We cannot put away the centuries of outright oppression and the "forthright political presence" of the church. Instead, especially in societies such as those of Latin America, what is acutely needed is in fact the deprivation of the (Catholic) church of its political presence.

In the sort of critique of liberation theology that I have been carrying on myself, together with many others,[24] the historical context of Christianity in Latin America is taken seriously, not in order to introduce a new status of authority to the (Catholic) church in the society but quite to the contrary: to question that role both in the past and in the present. Critical theology can help to construct a discursive space that questions the de facto political role of the Catholic Church in today's Latin America. Liberation theology has done this to a great extent, while at the same time omitting some areas of conflict, most importantly the direct political, moral, and financial influence of the Catholic Church on governments and international organizations (including the United Nations) regarding issues of sexuality and reproduction. The role of women and their rights is especially crucial, since not only are they the poorest among the poor but also because so many of the different "truth restoration" and "back to the (authentic) roots" projects in different religions have the control of women's bodies, minds, and reproductive capabilities as their primary focus. Bell totally ignores the very active, often aggressive, intervention of the Catholic Church in present day politics, of which we have examples from almost all Latin American countries.

Bell traces the evolution of liberation theologians' view on the apolitical church, according to him problematic, back to the social teaching of the Catholic Church and the related lay movement Catholic Action, both of which were influential in Latin America in the first part of the twentieth century. The most significant influence, according to Bell, on the development of the New Christendom model (commitment to an apolitical church and politics as statecraft) is found in the work of the French

---

23. Ibid., 44.
24. Of the feminist critique of liberation theology, see, for example, María Pilar Aquino, *Nuestro clamor por la vida: Teología latinoamericana desde la perspectiva de la mujer* (San José: Editorial DEI, 1992); Marcella Althaus-Reid, *Indecent Theology: Theological Perversions in Sex, Gender, and Politics* (London and New York: Routledge, 2001); Ivone Gebara, *Teología a ritmo de mujer* (Madrid: San Pablo, 1994); and Elsa Tamez et al., *El rostro femenino de la teología* (San José: Editorial DEI, 1986). On issues of whiteness and syncretism in liberation theology, see, for example, Josué A. Sathler and Amós Nascimento, "Black Masks on White Faces: Liberation Theology and the Quest for Syncretism in the Brazilian Context," in *Liberation Theology, Postmodernity, and the Americas* (ed. D. Batstone, E. Mendieta, L. A. Lorentzen, and D. N. Hopkins; London and New York: Routledge, 1997).

Catholic lay philosopher Jacques Maritain.[25] However, Bell does not give any detailed arguments for how Maritain's visions and thoughts were taken up by liberation theologians. Obviously, Maritain was important to a pre-liberation theology generation, especially in Chile, Argentina, and Brazil. Nevertheless, to trace the intellectual legacy of liberation theologians' view of the church and politics back to (only, mainly) him is problematic. Maritain was influential in the formation of Catholic intellectuals and politicians elsewhere, too—including the United States, leaving one wondering if the relationship between Maritain and U.S. liberation theologians holds true in that country as well. Why would it be so (only) in Latin America? Every book on the history of the church and theology in Latin America mentions Maritain but mostly together with several other influential thinkers and with two important qualifications: first, that Maritain was important really in the three countries mentioned above; and second, that there were serious discussions about the validity of his thoughts for the Latin American reality.[26]

Most importantly, Bell ignores the fact that some of the most influential liberation theologians—such as Gustavo Gutiérrez, Leonardo Boff, Juan Luis Segundo, José Comblin, Pablo Richard, and Jon Sobrino—either do not mention Maritain in their works at all or mention him only incidentally.[27] In his *Teología de la liberación*, Gutiérrez in fact distances himself from Maritain and his view of the church by saying that (in Maritain) "a view of the Church as a power in front of the world is strongly nuanced. But it continues to be, in a certain way, at the center of the work of salvation. A certain ecclesiastical narcissism remains."[28] Gutiérrez, too, pays attention to the limited and controversial reception of Maritain among Latin American Catholic intellectuals.[29] Most liberation theologians thus seem either to pay no attention to Maritain at all or to see him in the proper historical context: he was one important philosopher, who saw the role of the (Catholic) church in society in new terms, but, decades later, liberation theologians do not see themselves as embracing his view of the church, to a large extent irrelevant for the post-1960s Latin America.

According to Bell, "liberationist thought is in crisis because it does not grasp that capitalism . . . is not simply an economic system."[30] Since liberation theologians do not grasp this, they "endorse politics as statecraft,"[31] failing to see that "the conflict between capitalism and Christianity is nothing less than a clash of opposing technologies of

---

25. Bell, *Liberation Theology*, 45–46.

26. See, for example, Josep-Ignasi Saranyana, dir., *El siglo de las teologías latinoamericanistas* (1899–2001) (vol. 3 of *Teología en América Latina*; Madrid: Iberoamericana; Frankfurt am Main: Vervuert, 2002), 26, 205, 227; Enrique Dussel, ed., *The Church in Latin America: 1492–1992* (Maryknoll, N.Y.: Orbis Books, 1992), 13, 140. In his other book on Latin American church history, Dussel only shortly mentions Maritain. See his *Historia de la iglesia en América Latina* (Bogotá: Universidad Santo Tomás, 1984).

27. In the most important works of Sobrino, Comblin, Richard, Boff, and Segundo, Maritain is not mentioned at all.

28. Gustavo Gutiérrez, *Teología de la liberación: Perspectivas* (14th ed.; Salamanca: Ediciones Sígueme, 1990), 106.

29. Ibid., 105 n. 8, 107. Gutiérrez mentions Maritain in the context of the birth of Social Christian parties, which only had importance in some countries (Gustavo Gutiérrez, *La fuerza histórica de los pobres* [Salamanca: Ediciones Sígueme, 1982], 240–41. Liberation theologians distanced themselves from the Catholic parties all over the continent.

30. Bell, *Liberation Theology*, 44.

31. Ibid.

desire."[32] Now, without going into detail about what he means by concepts such as (technology of) desire and statecraft—not made very easy to grasp in the book—what is surprising in Bell's assertion is that in spite of having read intellectuals such as Hinkelammert, he seems to ignore the fact that a major (if not the most important) combining thread in Hinkelammert's thinking is exactly the intent to see capitalism (and, in fact, socialism as well) as something beyond a "mere" economic system. For him, socialism and capitalism are two sides of Western modernity, "the society without alternatives," which presents itself in utopian terms. For Hinkelammert, both capitalism and (Soviet) socialism are deeply modern and western, and both have a theological-religious metastructure, which he has set himself to analyze critically. It is not only about economics, it is about the future of humanity in relation to the future of Western society (*sociedad occidental*). It is impossible to understand Hinkelammert's thoughts if one omits his basic thesis on the profound similarity between capitalism and socialism as expressions of Western, Christian modernity. In front of the present crisis, which is not simply that of liberation theology or any other theory, "we do not have recipes, and that is our most profound problem."[33] Universal anti-humanism, together with its universal anti-utopianism, is the dominant ideology today, and they should be of primary concern for theologians. Critical theology from the third world, not just from Latin America and not just Christian, rethinks that universal anti-humanism and anti-utopianism of the present dominant system. Their global importance lies in the fact that the future of humanity is determined in the third world.[34]

Similarly, all discussions on the role of the state, and the differences between different intellectuals close to liberation theology on that role, are simply omitted by Bell by letting us know that (all) liberation theologians have a vision of "politics as statecraft." This statement is even more problematic when one takes into account under what kinds of terrorist states the sort of politics that liberation theologians ever endorsed was created, what the role of the Catholic Church was during the military dictatorships, and what impact the process of democratization has had.[35]

---

32. Ibid., 2.

33. Hinkelammert in an interview with Germán Gutiérrez in Duque and Gutiérrez, *Itinerarios de la razón crítica*, 38. In this context, he in fact makes a direct (amused) reference to the presumed death of liberation theology: "Once they invited me to Cologne to a meeting called "Is liberation theology dead?" The conference hall was full, they had to open the adjacent, much bigger, hall for us to discuss if liberation theology was dead. And it was not a meeting of theologians" (39).

34. Hinkelammert in an interview with Raúl Fornet-Betancourt in ibid., 59.

35. There are several works that do not treat state formation and the specific history of Latin America separately, for example, works of Anibal Quijano. For his part, Guillermo Nugent speaks of a "tutelary system" (*orden tutelar*) as a way of understanding the conflict between issues of sexuality and public policy in Latin America, based on a belief in the necessity of representation: groups seen as unable to represent themselves need the tutelage of others. In Latin America, the most influential institutions in supposedly representing the interests of large social groups have been the army and the Catholic Church (Guillermo Nugent, "El orden tutelar: Para entender el conflicto entre sexualidad y políticas públicas en América Latina" [unpublished ms, 2002]; and "De la sociedad doméstica a la sociedad civil: Una narración de la situación de los derechos sexuales y reproductivos en el Perú," in *Diálogos sur-sur sobre religión, derechos, y salud sexual y reproductiva: Los casos de Argentina, Colombia, Chile, y Perú* [comp. C. Dides; Santiago: Universidad Academia de Humanismo Cristiano, Programa de Estudios de Género y Sociedad, 2004)]. His research makes more understandable the curious situation of the Latin American Catholic Church, which, with its inner division in the 1960s and 1970s, simultaneously does and does not represent civil society. Liberation theology played an important role in naming and analyzing this contradiction.

There is no space here to do the sort of critical and close reading of Bell's book that it definitely calls for. One general reason for several mistakes and misunderstandings in his book seems to stem from the fact that his reading of liberation theologians is so selective and narrow—even though he at least seems to read texts published in Spanish, unlike many others. But there is an entire new form and way of doing liberation theology that he seems not to be aware of. And it is exactly these newer discourses that are most relevant for issues Bell is interested in, such as capitalism, the state, the pretended autonomy of economic theory.[36]

Liberation Theology Today, Alive

Of the discussions that are characteristic of contemporary liberation theology's assessment of economy, politics, the role of the church, capitalism, and the poor, I merely refer to the writings of Franz Hinkelammert and, more broadly, that of the Equipo de Investigadores del DEI (Departamento Ecuménico de Investigaciones) in San José, Costa Rica, wherein Hinkelammert works, but which also has had regularly organized continent-wide multidisciplinary meetings of theologians, philosophers, economists, and social scientists during the last twenty-five years.[37] I will give a very short overview of these new discourses and contrast them with Bell's assessment of liberation theology. I will consciously omit such new forms of liberation theology as feminist liberation theology, black liberation theology, ecological liberation theology, and indigenous liberation theologies, which Bell does not mention at all, in spite of the fact that their critiques of the first generation of liberation theologians have been catalysts to later developments. I concentrate here on those issues in liberation theology that radical orthodoxy critics have considered of importance.

The thought about the primacy of the poor has long roots in Christian, especially Catholic, theology. In Latin American liberation theology, the rebirth of this thought has always been ecumenical, both in theory and practice. Even when the option for the poor became standard church teaching in the Catholic Church, the critical analysis of the reasons for poverty and the commitment to its eradication in society, together with other social and political actors, are held in common by Protestant and Catholic liberation theologians. Liberation theological understanding of "the poor" has over the years become more varied, more detailed, less bound to mere economic and class-related explanations. Material poverty hits indigenous and black people harder, likewise women and children.

One major specification in this direction has been the discussion on the (repressed, oppressed) subject or agent (*sujeto*) in relation to the sacrificial elements in both our

---

36. See, for example, Hinkelammert's comment in an interview with Germán Gutiérrez in Duque and Gutiérrez, *Itinerarios de la razón crítica*, 197–200, on the state, which is impossible to interpret as some sort of "politics as statecraft," which Bell claims to be a central problem in liberation theology. According to Hinkelammert, the contemporary form of globalization needs repressive and submissive states combined with an anti-state ideological discourse. "Stalinism was anti-state, fascism was anti-state, globalization is anti-state. And they create the most ferocious states, the most absolute states. The anti-state ideology is a myth which serves to promote blind, inoperative states, operative only for those who need the state for their strategies of power.... The anti-state ideology is an ideology of absolute states" (ibid., 198).

37. Overviews and compilations of papers presented at these workshops can be found in various issues of the journal *Pasos*.

religious and economic traditions. The poor are, on the one hand, victims of a system that excludes masses of people, entire populations, as unnecessary for the efficiency and rationality of the system (*exclusión*). On the other hand, the system is sacrificial, because so many human beings and their cultures are seen as necessary human sacrifices (*sacrificios humanos*) for the functionality of the system, which sees itself in utopian terms. This utopian element is something that both capitalism and socialism have in common, according to Hinkelammert. Both of them, as well as Christianity, are profoundly modern and western.[38] Theologically speaking, the sacrificiality is about idolatry: money has taken the place of god. The god of the poor, the god of life (*el dios de la vida*), thus becomes a necessary reference point for liberation theologians in their defense of the life of the poor against the sacrificial system. In this thinking, capitalism is by no means seen only as an economic system—it is a symbolic discourse, it is a philosophy, it is a theology, it is a utopia, it is an ideology.

The reconstruction of the human being as a subject, a concrete, bodily, historical subject of necessities, has become the starting point in this new configuration of liberation theology (since the 1980s) as a radical critique of the sacrificial and totalitarian system that crushes human life.[39] There is a marked difference to an earlier understanding of the term *sujeto* as the social subject, as a class or as a social movement.[40] The human being as subject affirms her or his life as a radical alternative to both economic and religious fundamentalism.[41] The task of any critical thinking from the South, including liberation theology, is to base its discourse on the corporality and dignity of this (negated) subject.[42] The option for the survival of humanity is on the continuum with the option for the poor of earlier liberation theology, but it is also more encompassing.[43]

The demands for bringing politics (back) to the economic sphere and for the democratization of economic decision making, including the rethinking of the role of the nation-state in different contexts and alternative forms of globalization, are not inventions of liberation theology. The religious-theological analysis, however, brings an important and critical element to those demands, which is why I tend to comprehend contemporary liberation theology most naturally as part of the global movement against neoliberal capitalist globalization. The so-called globalization critics come

---

38. See, for example, Germán Gutiérrez's interview with Hinkelammert in Duque and Gutiérrez, *Itinerarios de la razón crítica*, 38. Also in another interview by Norbert Arntz in the same book, Hinkelammert states how the utopian structure and space is what liberal and socialist thinking have in common, including the refusal in both to recognize themselves as profoundly utopian. This is why Hinkelammert speaks of anti-utopian utopianism.

39. See Richard, "La iglesia y la teología," 103, 37; and the following titles by Franz Hinkelammert: *Cultura de la esperanza y sociedad sin exclusión* (San José: Editorial DEI, 1995); "La teología de la liberación en el contexto económico y social de América Latina: Economía y teología o la irracionalidad de lo racionalizado," in *Por una sociedad donde quepan todos* (ed. J. Duque; San José: Editorial DEI, 1996), 53–85; *El grito del sujeto: Del teatro-mundo del evangelio de Juan al perro-mundo de la globalización* (San José: Editorial DEI, 1998); "El sujeto negado y su retorno," *Pasos* 104 (2002): 1–12; and *El retorno del sujeto reprimido* (Bogotá: Universidad Nacional de Colombia, 2002).

40. Hinkelammert, "El sujeto negado," 1–2.

41. Ibid., 9–10.

42. Hinkelammert in an interview with Raúl Fornet-Betancourt in Duque and Gutiérrez, *Itinerarios de la razón crítica*, 59–60.

43. Hinkelammert in an interview with Germán Gutiérrez in Duque and Gutiérrez, *Itinerarios de la razón crítica*, 34.

from all regions of the world, but because of the unique place of Latin America in the world-system, it has produced theories such as dependency theory (according to Hinkelammert, in need of rethinking and revitalization[44]) and liberation theology. The latter has never been only about theology. It has always aimed theological critique as phenomena considered a-theological (such as economic theory) but without the radical orthodoxy kind of view of theology as the queen of sciences and as a Eurocentric, exclusively Christian form of truth. Liberation theology has always been transdisciplinary in the best sense of the word—today it can be and is a partner in discussions on a variety of subjects: modernity from a Latin American perspective (for example, the works of Enrique Dussel[45]); the (ir)relevance of postcolonialism in the Latin American context; and post-occidentalism (a term originally from Roberto Fernández Retamar) and not postmodernity or postcolonialism as having more explanatory power in the case of contemporary Latin America (for example, the works Walter Mignolo). What all these thinkers share with each other is an understanding of how the colonial experience has been constitutive of modernity not only in the Americas but also in Europe,[46] the Americas thus representing "the extreme West" (Occidentalism).[47] According to Edgardo Lander, "perspectives that go beyond Eurocentric interpretations of the crisis of modernity, such as subaltern studies and postcolonial theories, create possibilities for new intellectual strategies to address the challenges posed by the crisis of modernity for Latin American critical theory."[48] (I would count liberation theology, broadly speaking, as part of such an intent.)

In this sense, the presumed crisis in and of liberation theology can thus, more critically and more constructively, be assessed in the context of a larger intellectual and political crisis, not only in Latin America but globally. There are no easy solutions in sight. However, Latin American intellectuals such as the ones mentioned above, together with liberation theologians and intellectuals close to them (such as Hinkelammert), are offering interesting answers to questions that we are all facing. Are those declaring these intents to be dead in fact speaking of themselves and their own academic settings or are they just blind to the existence of alternative forms of thought? Is the necessity to negate alternatives an expression of the last breaths of

44. For example, in an interview with Henry Mora in Duque and Gutiérrez, *Itinerarios de la razón crítica*, 177–78.

45. According to him, "If one understands Europe's modernity—a long process of five centuries—as the unfolding of new possibilities derived from its centrality in world history and the corollary constitution of all other cultures as its periphery, it becomes clear that, even though all cultures are ethnocentric, modern European ethnocentrism is the only one that might pretend to claim universality for itself. Modernity's Eurocentrism lies in the confusion between abstract universality and the concrete world hegemony derived from Europe's position as center" (Enrique Dussel, "Europe, Modernity, and Eurocentrism," *Nepantla: Views from South* 1, no. 3 (2000): 471.

46. See, for example, Walter D. Mignolo, *Local Histories/Global Designs: Coloniality, Subaltern Knowledges, and Border Thinking* (Princeton, N.J.: Princeton University Press, 2000), 50.

47. Ibid., 58. On recent transdisciplinary forms of trying to theorize Latin America in the context of globalization, including the role of Christianity, see, for example, various essays in Santiago Castro-Gómez and Eduardo Mendieta, coord., *Teorías sin disciplina: Latinoamericanismo, poscolonialidad, y globalización en debate* (México D.F.: Miguel Angel Porrúa; San Francisco: University of San Francisco,1998).

48. Edgardo Lander, "Eurocentrism and Colonialism in Latin American Social Thought," *Nepantla: Views from* South 1, no. 3 (2000): 525. See also Anibal Quijano's works, especially his theorizations on coloniality (*colonialidad*). In English, for example, Anibal Quijano, "Coloniality of Power, Eurocentrism, and Latin America, *Nepantla: Views from South* 1, no. 3 (2000): 533–80.

Eurocentric hegemonic reason (often Christian and masculine) on its deathbed? The Western culture as we have made it is the one in obvious crisis. We might face unseen large-scale destruction before it gives up. This is what Hinkelammert calls "the culture of hopelessness" (*la cultura de la desesperanza*), which is "the crisis that we are living."[49] Politics, especially economic policies, have become mere applications of techniques, ripping politics of its autonomy.[50] It is important to notice, however, how Hinkelammert thinks not only in these terms but also in those of "resurrection of hope," and here he explicitly mentions the World Social Forum and the "movement for the recuperation of the globality of humanity and the earth," wrongly called an *anti-globalization* movement.[51] "The total market" of globalization needs a total(itarian) political system to create hopelessness and to block resistance. This system he locates primarily in the present global anti-terrorist war, which has become some kind of global security dictatorship.[52] To think of an alternative is to think how to subvert the legitimacy of such a system, not an easy job for opposition movements, but necessary.[53]

Justice and Forgiveness: Learning from the Victims

It is clear to anybody knowing contemporary Latin America that post-dictatorship democracies have failed to pursue justice for the crimes committed under dictatorships. Truth commissions in Guatemala, Chile, and Peru have made serious attempts at a truthful assessment of the past, but in most countries special amnesty laws have been introduced to protect those responsible for human rights violations during the military regimes. In Chile, the process of prosecution of ex-dictator Augusto Pinochet has lasted years and no trial has been held yet. Human rights organizations remind the new democracies of how fragile their base will be if the past is simply "forgotten." In relationship to Bell's theses on liberation theology, one wonders how any discourse on justice and forgiveness in Latin America can (again) simply ignore these very recent times and events. Even if one would agree with his theory about the need to change demands for justice to the gift of forgiveness (presented by Bell as opposing polarities), one is left wondering what exactly that would mean in the case of most Latin American societies. Is "the refusal to cease suffering" Bell's answer for victims of torture, forced disappearances and exiles, genocides of entire indigenous villages, and other atrocities of full-scale repression? He does not pay any attention to how Latin American societies (and churches) have tried to come to grips with their horrendous past, and how in that process they might have given some new understanding to concepts such as (social) sin, forgiveness, suffering, and reconciliation. Liberation and feminist theologies have for years produced writings on how to rethink justice and sin in relationship to such faceless systems as racism, sexism, poverty, and capitalism. What we read in Bell's book is that no such attempt is (good) enough: "Their [the liberationists'] justice was unable to break the cycle of violence that torments humanity. Specifically, it was incapable of

---

49. Franz Hinkelammert, *El asalto al poder mundial y la violencia sagrada del imperio* (San José: Editorial DEI, 2003), 27.
50. Ibid., 25.
51. Ibid., 28–29.
52. Ibid., 30. This language of "assault on the world" is profoundly religious, according to Hinkelammert (ibid., 37).
53. Ibid., 31.

eliminating the conflict that arises from the inevitable clash of rights and it legitimated violence in the name of justice."[54] Did he expect the liberation theologians to be able to do that? Why (only, primarily) them?

As I said earlier in this essay, even the most modest forms of democratization in Latin America were possible only after changes in U.S. foreign policy. This does not mean downplaying the role of Latin American resistance, of guerrilla and social movements. It is true that "liberation theologians' justice" was not able to break the cycle of violence, but that is simply because they have had no such power in their hands. That power lies closer to Bell's home than theirs. For many, at least in Latin America, Bell's thoughts would sound blatantly like the "blame the victim" mentality, which is reflective of how intellectuals in the United States very seldom are able to bring critical distance to the fact that some of the worst atrocities in contemporary Latin America were funded and planned by their government. The amount of violence is not understandable for us who did not experience it, and especially for anybody who does not bother to step down from a "forgiveness-as-God's-gift-for-those-who-stop-demanding-impossibilities" throne. People who have lived under terrorist states should be seen as the masters of forgiveness from whom we others might have something to learn in our theorizations about justice and forgiveness. What is even more complicated is how exactly should poor people "forgive capitalism," women "sexism," nonwhites "racism" and slavery, and so forth? Historically seen, the Christian church and its dominant theology have been some of the legitimizers and defenders of all those systems.

Thus, we read toward the end of Bell's book that forgiveness is not even meant to happen, because "the truth of the therapy of forgiveness as a form of resistance to capitalism, to echo Foucault, is in the future. It is in a future where the tears are wiped away, where those who are hungry now are filled. . . . This is to say, the truthfulness of forgiveness as the Christian form of resistance to capitalism is contingent upon the consummation of redemption, when suffering will indeed cease."[55] Here, he makes no reference to liberation theologians' extensive work on the kingdom of God, its relationship to utopia and to contemporary society, or to the relationship between liberation and salvation.

Conclusion: State(s) of Fear

As someone with long-term experience of both the ex-socialist countries, the United States, and various parts of Latin America (especially of Central America), from the early 1980s onward, I will conclude my essay by reflecting on some odd similarities between states as different as the Central American right-wing military states of the 1980s (Guatemala, El Salvador, Honduras), the communist one-party surveillance states (Soviet Union, former GDR), and today's anti-terrorist Patriot Act state of the United States, and how they appear to a foreign visitor with a Finnish passport. In spite of differences in the ideology and proposed aims (anti-revolution and anti-communism, anti-capitalism, anti-terrorism) of these regimes, there are striking similarities between them. In all three regions—and nowhere else—have I been so thoroughly suspected, inspected, and documented when entering a country. Only in

---

54. Bell, *Liberation Theology*, 149.
55. Ibid., 194.

today's United States am I also forced to be photographed and fingerprinted. By saying this in the context of a critical evaluation of some radical orthodoxy viewpoints on Latin American liberation theology, I want to point out that in any (theological, ethical) analysis of globalization, liberation theology, religion and politics, and economics, a critical evaluation of the contemporary hegemonic role of the United States should not be left aside. It would be especially crucial for U.S. intellectuals—theologians and others—to assume that task. In the process, they might learn something from their colleagues in other regions, especially Latin America, the promised land of U.S. military interventions for decades. The same questions that scholars such as Bell direct at liberation theologians could as well be directed at theologians working in the United States, a country that combines a weak state (in public services) with a super strong state (surveillance, militarism, unilateralism) and which offers an openly public political role for (certain kinds of) religious doctrines.

Only blindness to the destructive sides of our liberal democracies, our "Western" versions of Christianity, and our Eurocentrism can lead intellectuals to claim a new "radically orthodox" status to (some forms of) Christianity and Christian theology and declare other intents to take Christianity seriously in today's world as insufficient or dead.

5. The Postmodern as Premodern
The Theology of D. Stephen Long
—Rosemary Radford Ruether

D. Stephen Long is an American systematic theologian who adopted in the 1990s the framework of radical orthodoxy for his theological perspective, having been influenced particularly by the thought of John Milbank.[1] He is the author of two major books written from a radical orthodoxy perspective, *Divine Economy* and *The Goodness of God*.[2] In *Divine Economy*, Long discusses three contemporary traditions about the relationship of theology and the economy. He calls these the dominant tradition, the emergent tradition, and the residual tradition. The dominant tradition seeks to reconcile theology and the neoliberal market economy, exemplified by thinkers such as Michael Novak, Max Stackhouse, and Philip Wogaman. The emergent tradition consists of liberation theologies. Here he discusses Gustavo Gutiérrez, Jon Sobrino, James Cone, and me. The residual tradition encompasses Catholic social teachings, exemplified in the social encyclicals of Leo XIII and in the writings of the Jesuit Bernard Dempsey and the German Catholic Hans Urs von Balthasar.[3]

Long is scathingly critical of the dominant tradition of neoliberal economics, which he sees as having sold out any authentic understanding of virtue rooted in divine goodness for a notion of freedom of choice that caters to the market economy. He is more favorable to liberation theologies, but ultimately he sees them as having capitulated to a modern idea of freedom. He favors the Catholic tradition of the social teaching of the church that retains the subordination of the market to divine goodness revealed in Jesus Christ present through the church, although he finds that Catholicism too allows a space for a natural theology disconnected from revelation, something which he disapproves.[4] His key theme is the priority of the church over the market as the source of truth and relation to God, which must order other human institutions.

---

1. Long is currently professor of systematic theology at the Garrett-Evangelical Theological Seminary in Evanston, Illinois, a Methodist institution. Long did his master of divinity and doctoral work at Duke University under the tutelage of Stanley Hauerwas. Long is the author of the article on radical orthodoxy that appeared in the *Cambridge Companion to Postmodern Theology* (ed. Kevin J. Vanhoozer; Cambridge: Cambridge University Press, 2003), 129–44.

2. Long, *Divine Economy: Theology and the Market* (London and New York: Routledge, 2000); *The Goodness of God: Theology, Church, and Social Order* (Grand Rapids, Mich.: Brazos Press, 2001). See Long's website under www.Garrett.edu for his major bibliography.

3. Long, *Divine Economy*, 177–260.

4. Ibid., 182–83.

In the first part of his book *The Goodness of God*, Long develops his theological critique of modernity's basic flaw, the subordination of theology to ethics. Under the part title of "Beyond Evil and (Toward an Enchanted) Good" he discusses his basic understanding of ethics as participating in the goodness of God. He then embarks on his central critique of Immanuel Kant's "ethical revolution against religion," wherein he defines Kant's philosophy as the epitome of the basic flaw of modernity that splits the noumenal and the phenomenal and subordinates knowledge of God to ethics or practical reason. He then delineates his understanding of how Christian thought needs to move "beyond evil through the beauty of holiness" to a recovery of "true God and true humanity." Here he contests the modern view of humanity, which he sees as leading to nihilism. Under the part title of "Christian Ethics as Repentance" he defines a restored doctrine and practice of penance as the way back to the reestablishment of right relation between ethics and God and the church.

In the second half of the book on "the church and other social formations" he outlines his ecclesiology, defining the church as the institution that should order all other institutions. He then discusses how the church should order these other institutions: the *oikos* or family and household, the *agora* or market, and the *polis* or state. These chapters allow him to critique strongly what he sees as the great sources of the evils of modern society: capitalism, the free market, and warfare. He also engages in analysis and denunciation of what he sees as two major expressions of evil in modern society, the acceptance of homosexuality and abortion.[5]

Long builds particularly on his interpretation of the Thomistic theological understanding of the relation of humanity and the creation to God as one of *analogia entis* or analogy of being. God is supreme goodness in whom alone essence and existence coincide. We humans participate in goodness by participating in God. This is made available to us solely through Jesus Christ, who incarnates and makes concrete the goodness of God prolonged through the sacraments of the church, baptism and the Eucharist. Here the body of Christ is continually made present for us.[6]

Long views Thomistic thought as the definitive theology that most fully expresses the truth of the relationship between the human desire for the good and the goodness of God made available through the incarnation of Christ present in the sacraments of the church. Everything about the theology of Thomas Aquinas is defended as giving us the correct view of creation's relation to God. He rejects what he sees as later Thomisms that allow a space for natural theology apart from supernatural revelation and redemption as misunderstanding Thomas. For Long almost all theology from the fourteenth-century nominalism of Duns Scotus to today is seen as a decline and fall from this perfect moment in Thomas Aquinas, although he is mostly positive about Karl Barth, with the reservation that Barth failed to realize that he actually agreed (should have agreed) with Thomas Aquinas.[7]

According to Long, the decline and fall of theology is due to the desire for autonomous reason, individualism, the quest for freedom and the desire to claim the good as one's own possession rather than as a gift from God. Long claims that the Reformation had some good initial insights, but these were vitiated because they led to

---

5. Ibid., 204–12, 218–22.
6. This theme is found throughout Long, *The Goodness of God*. See, for example, 133–35.
7. Ibid., 44–46.

autonomous reason and individualism.[8] Luther rightly critiqued the corruption of the late medieval Catholic Church that sought to turn the priority of the church over state into a power relation in which the church ruled like a state. But Luther took this critique in the wrong direction as a subordination of the church to the state.[9] But the prime culprit responsible for the corruption of Western thought is Imanuel Kant.

Kant's thought, by splitting the noumenal from the phenomenal, led to a social constructionist view of knowledge. On the one hand, he posited the knowledge of God and eternal life for the sake of a morality, denying the possibility of any sensual experience of God's presence. On the other hand, Kant saw the universal church as simply a forerunner to be superceded by the universal state that alone can bring perpetual peace. For Long, Kant's views are the source of the false and idolatrous concept of the universal state and the universal market that marginalizes the only universal institution, the church, and leads to all forms of modern violence and tyranny.[10]

For Long all forms of liberalism (never clearly defined) and modernity are quests for an autonomous reason and individual freedom without roots in truth and goodness, which are found only in God through the Jesus Christ present in the sacraments. Thus they all finally lead to nihilism. Nietzsche is the logical culmination of the liberal quest, although liberals are too fuzzy-minded to realize it. When God is dead, there is no good and evil, but only the will to power.[11] Postmodernism deconstructs the liberal claims to universal human rights and freedoms by privileging difference, but this is only a cover-up for the sameness of the market. This masking of the sameness of the market as respect for difference is exemplified in the food court of the shopping mall where one can choose from different kinds of "ethnic foods" homogenized and subjugated to the same logic of market consumerism.[12]

Radical orthodoxy makes use of the postmodern deconstruction of Enlightenment universalism and liberalism, but this is a temporary alliance that must lead back to the only thought system that rightly subordinates ethics to faith. This is Catholic orthodoxy rooted in revelation and best expressed in the theology of Thomas Aquinas. Thus radical theology understands itself as a recovery of a theology normative for all times, not as a "modern theology" that overcomes the past.[13]

Long's critique of modernity, especially liberalism subordinated to the logic of the market and to use values, has considerable merit. Contemporary critics of neoliberal market economics could find some helpful insights in his unmasking of the failure of the global market to deliver justice and the "good life." But Long's criticism is too simplistically biased against all modern movements of thought and social practice. Long's method of thought exaggerates Western history of thought into a dualism of normative truth, goodness, and beauty (Aquinas and an idealized church located in a utopian moment of undetermined historicity) on the one hand, and fallacious modernity that justifies an alienated self that leads to nihilism on the other.

---

8. Ibid., 142–48.

9. Ibid., 478–79; see also his critique of Luther's view of penance, 143.

10. Long's critique of Kant is found particularly in his second chapter of the *Goodness of God*, 53–104, but it occurs throughout this book, as well as in *Divine Economy*. See indices of both books.

11. For Long's use of Nietzsche as the culmination of modernity, see *Goodness of God*, 124–26, 284–85 and *passim*.

12. Ibid., 250, 251–52; see also 258–59 on his condemnation of the neoliberal view of the market.

13. See Long's article on radical orthodoxy in the *Cambridge Companion to Postmodern Theology*, 126–27.

This dualism of good Christian Catholicity and bad modernity is accomplished by a tendentious and selective mode of analysis of both pre- and post-fourteenth-century Western thought. Negative elements, such as oppressive authoritarianism, are largely removed or underplayed in any history he sees as normative; that is, the Bible, the church fathers, and Thomas Aquinas, as well as the actual practices of the patristic and medieval church. Long concentrates his praise largely on Western Catholicism, especially Augustine and Aquinas, ignoring almost entirely Eastern Christianity, as well as other Western patristic and early medieval writers.

At the same time, Long mostly eliminates positive elements from all the movements that he sees as modern and leading to nihilism. This includes most of Protestantism from the Reformation on, especially liberal Protestantism, including Niebuhr and Tillich, and all secular liberalism. The modern is by definition destructive and leads to nihilism because it believes in progress in ideas that can create improved social practice. The idea of progress for Long is an absurdity based on the belief that truth can be improved through time by new scientific discoveries and criticism of past injustices. For orthodox Christians, the good as the basis of truth has been fully revealed in Jesus Christ and expressed definitively by Thomas Aquinas. He speaks of Aquinas as "offer[ing] an alternative path out of the dead end in which we find ourselves at the end of modernity. . . . Aquinas' quest for the good took place alongside a quest for truth and beauty which understood them all as related to each other and secure in God. . . ."[14]

All change from this standard is decline. Theology should only again and again recover this definitive truth, not seek to improve it. Long does not explain how this recovery of Aquinas and the practice of the medieval church can meet modern concerns for human rights of women, racial minorities, and religions other than Christianity. How does a thought system that believed in women's natural inferiority and lack of a complete humanity allow for women's civil rights in society, much less for their ordination in the church? Long ignores all the accomplishments of liberalism and modernity in the areas of universal human rights. Indeed he vilifies the very idea of any "rights" possessed by humans as part of their "human nature" as a false effort to claim an autonomous self that possesses goodness apart from God manifest in Christ (and the sacraments).

This elimination or underplaying of any problematic elements in high medieval thought and practice leads Long to some extraordinary defenses of medieval papal autocracy. Since the church is superior to the state and should "order" the state, Pope Gregory VII only spoke the truth when he declared in his *Dictatus Papae* in 1075 that the Roman Church is founded by God alone, that the Roman pontiff alone is rightly to be called universal, that he alone may use the imperial insignia, that he is the only one whose feet are to be kissed by all princes, that his name alone is to be recited in churches, that his title is unique in the world, and that he alone may depose emperors.[15]

These claims by the pope are essentially true for Long because the church is the sole font of relation to God, is alone in contact with God and hence with what is truly good, and so should order all other human institutions: the state, the family, and market. The

---

14. Long, *The Goodness of God*, 20.
15. Ibid., 256. Long draws on Brian Tierney, *The Crisis of Church and State: 1050–1300* (Englewood Cliffs, N.J.: Prentice-Hall, 1964), 49–50, for this excerpt of the *Dictatus Papae.*

pope did, Long admits, make a slight mistake in expressing this preeminence of the church over the state and right to order the state as a coercive power relationship. The church orders all other institutions, not by appropriating political or other kinds of coercive power but by nonviolent "witnessing" to the state, the family, and the market and by providing the sacraments through which right relation to God and participation in God's goodness are mediated.[16]

Indeed the proper role of Protestantism is simply to protest against the Catholic Church's appropriation of coercive power "like a state." Once the Catholic Church finally gets this key Protestant message, and reforms itself to remove all vestiges of coercive power, Long seems to think that Protestants should rejoin the Catholic Church and submit to the papacy since the papacy alone has successfully expressed the universality of the church. Thus he says, "Only one such universal form has had an effective presence in the modern world: that embodied in the papacy. All other conciliar efforts to produce such a universal form have failed. Is it time (for Protestants) to abandon them and recognize that the church cannot be catholic without the papacy?"[17]

How the church can succeed in witnessing to, teaching, much less "ordering" the state and other social institutions without any power is unclear in Long's thought. Surely any public power by which the church can shape other social institutions, such as control of education, public media of communication, or economic power through control of property and investments, are forms of power to influence others, even if they are not seen as "violent" or "coercive" power.

Long also defends the truth of the idea of the "indefectibility" (inability to depart irreparably from God) of the church. He understands this as God's promise that God has founded the Church of Jesus Christ and will ever be with it, and the "gates of hell will never prevail against it." Such a notion of the church's indefectibility does not necessarily mean that the church cannot err in its public teachings on faith or morals or fall into serious sin as an institution. It could be understood simply as a faith that God will be with us no matter what our sin or error.

Long suggests that the papal doctrine of infallibility as defined by the 1870 declaration, while not quite the right way to say it, is rightly rooted in this basic faith in the church's indefectibility. Thus he states,

> First, indefectibility is not mere Constantinianism, but arises from the biblical witness itself. It is part of the promise which Jesus gave to Peter that the power of hell would not prevail against the church (Matt. 16:18). The church can claim *indefectibility* because it is not merely a human social process but has present within it the power of the Holy Spirit to prevent it from falling into complete and inescapable error. The particular form given that indefectibility by Pius IX in the doctrine of infallibility may be objectionable, but even that dogma does not prevent the church from admitting wrong. . . .[18]

Protestantism, in contrast, can't seem to get anything right. Long is very hostile to Paul Tillich's idea of the Protestant principle, seeing it as leading to endless criticism

---

16. See Long, *The Goodness of God*, 264.
17. Ibid., 277.
18. Ibid., 93; see also his remarks on the infallibility of the church in *Divine Economy*, 255, 257.

and revision of ideas, without a clear ability to affirm truth. Yet Tillich proposed the need for a dialectical relationship between the Protestant principle and Catholic substance.[19] Long does not mention Tillich's affirmation of Catholic substance (the sacramental presence of God in the church), but he attacks the idea of a Protestant principle that must ever dissent from any absolutizing of the relative. For Long the Protestant principle denies that God is fully present in church through the church's sacraments. He believes that Christians can only restate this truth, not endlessly dissent from it and try to restate it better.[20]

This apologia for Catholic tradition means that Long brushes away the problematic aspects of much of traditional thought and church practice. Its patriarchalism and misogyny are underplayed. They are ignored entirely when speaking of Thomas Aquinas, who taught that women were "misbegotten men" and that this lack of full humanity precluded their being ordained or exercising public leadership of any kind.[21] Although Long himself is enough of a "modern" to reject misogyny, if not patriarchy, as well as other problems, such as classical Christian anti-Semitism, he apparently thinks that these "defects" can be put aside without mentioning them as a significant challenge to the tradition's indefectibility.

Long's apologetic for the classical Western tradition of theology contains many questionable interpretations. For example, in speaking about Augustine's view of marriage he glosses over Augustine's view that celibacy is superior to marriage and his defense of the goodness of marriage only as second best. He defends Augustine's view that concupiscence is the root of sexual sin by interpreting concupiscence as "lust" in the sense of a dominating and instrumentalizing use of women.[22] But Long fails to recognize that the problem with Augustine's description of concupiscence lies in the fact that he collapses "lust" into any sexual pleasure, thus making concupiscence qua sexual pleasure something that arises only in the fall, becoming the means through which original sin is transmitted through sexual acts, even in faithful and fruitful marriage.[23]

This Augustinian conflation of sexual pleasure with sin makes all sexual intercourse, even in marriage, sinful, although venially so (forgiven) if it is done only for procreation or to keep from illicit sexual acts outside marriage (fidelity).[24] But any sexual act, even in marriage, undertaken only for pleasure, while impeding procreation, is wholly sinful and equivalent to fornication. This Augustinian view of sexual pleasure is the basis of the rejection of birth control in Catholic ethics. Long himself is hostile to birth control and apparently thinks that couples should not seek to limit births. He interprets birth control as a Malthusian desire to limit the numbers of the poor.[25]

---

19. For Paul Tillich's understanding of the Protestant principle, see particularly his *The Protestant Era* (Chicago: University of Chicago Press, 1957), xi–xxix.

20. Long, *The Goodness of God*, 211 and 283.

21. See Thomas Aquinas, *Summa Theologica* 1.92.1 ad. 1; also 1.99.2 ad. 2. For a comprehensive view of Aquinas's view of women, see Kari Borreson, *Subordination and Equivalence: The Nature and Role of Women in Augustine and Thomas Aquinas* (Washington, D.C.: University Press of America, 1981).

22. Long, *The Goodness of God*, 127–29 and 195.

23. See especially Augustine, "On Marriage and Concupiscence," in *Anti-Pelagian Works: Select Library of the Nicene and Post-Nicene Fathers* (2nd series, vol. 5; New York: Charles Scribner's Sons, 1902), 258–308.

24. See Augustine, "On the Good of Marriage," in *Fathers of the Church*, 27:9–53, and "On Marriage and Concupiscence."

25. See Long, *The Goodness of God*, 118, 222, 315–16 n. 32; also *Divine Economy*, 151.

That poor women and men themselves (as well as middle-class couples) might want to limit births both for women's health and to care adequately for their children is not discussed. That there might be a legitimate need today for population control, with a rapidly expanding population of the human species relative to finite resources on the planet, is for him incompatible with divine abundance and goodness. We will return to this theme when we discuss his particular rage against abortion.

Long's apologia for classical Catholic thought is matched by his erasure of any positive virtues from modern liberal thought. For Long, all liberal traditions are unequivocally rooted in a quest for personal freedom without a basis in truth or goodness derived from God, thus leading to rationalistic utilitarianism and finally to nihilism, violence, and death. He roundly condemns neo-Protestantism (liberal Protestantism) as utilitarian and finally nihilistic. He sees Niebuhr's view that we have only a partial grasp of truth and that finite things cannot contain the infinite as a rejection of the incarnation of God in Jesus Christ prolonged in the sacraments,[26] while he views Tillich's Protestant principle as pure liberal nihilism.

Orthodox Christians should reject liberal tolerance and epistemological "humility" in order to assert and claim the fullness of truth, which they know in Jesus Christ. In one article Long even speaks of humility as a "violent vice," an expression of an inability of liberal Christians to affirm the truth that they know in Christ boldly and decisively.[27] No human sphere, family, market, or state can be autonomous or a place of human rights possessed as intrinsic to human "nature." Only through Christ present in the sacraments do we have contact with and participate in our true potential for goodness. This is why the church alone has contact with God and can and should "order" all other human spheres.

Long's polemic against "natural theology" or "creation theology," as well as his dismissal of any notion of "progress" that assumes new or improved ideas and practices, implies a collapse of the creational and eschatological poles of classical Christian theology into the single moment of the historical incarnation of God in Jesus Christ, which is then prolonged "indefectibly" in the church's sacraments through ongoing history to the end of time. This relation to God given in Jesus' incarnation cannot be improved upon nor is it available from any other source, such as reason, human experience apart from the church's sacraments, or from other religious traditions. By concentrating relation to God solely on Jesus Christ and his presence in the sacraments, Long's theological perspective limits both the creational pole in which God as Logos is present throughout creation and in every quest for truth and also the redemptive pole in which the redeemed future is expressed in the millennial hope and eschatology.

On the creational side of Christology, Long fails to reckon with the classical patristic theologies of the Logos that affirmed that the Logos of God incarnate in Jesus is the same Logos through which the world was created. Humans and indeed all creation participate in the goodness and being of God through their creation. Church fathers spoke of this presence of God through the creating Logos as present even in the birds and the fish, not just in humans. They confidently drew on the truths of Greek philosophy and Hebrew Scripture, even though both preceded the incarnation in Jesus, based

---

26. Long's critique of Reinhold Niebuhr is found in *The Goodness of God*, 66, 92–93, and *passim*.

27. Ibid., 282–93; Long, "Humility as a Violent Vice," *Studies in Christian Ethics* 12, no. 2 (fall 1999): 31–47.

on their belief that all truth is rooted in God in whose being we participate through the creational Logos. Greek philosophers and Hebrew prophets and sages were in touch with the Logos of God even before Christ appeared.[28]

Long himself draws heavily on Greek philosophy, both the works of Plato and Aristotle. He constantly speaks of the divinity present in Christ as revealing God as goodness, truth, and beauty, a classic Greek philosophic phrase. How did Plato and Aristotle know about a divine being that discloses truth, goodness, and beauty without Christ and the sacraments? The Christian church took over both Hebrew religion and Greek philosophical traditions and constructed a synthesis of the two, a synthesis Long continues. But by collapsing all access to God to the one historical incarnation of Christ prolonged in the sacraments, he rejects any space for a "natural" or "creation" theology that expresses this continuing relation to God through creation that is not mediated historically through Christ. Classical and modern Catholic theologies, in contrast, allow such a distinction and thus make a space for true knowledge of God and virtuous living mediated through creation, even to those who do not know Christ. Long, does not discuss indigenous or contextual theologies outside of the Greco-European tradition.

Long's rejection of any natural theology and hence any idea of goodness or truth possessed by humans apart from Christ present in the church's sacraments seems to be hung up on a semantic problem in classical Catholic theology itself. Although this theology recognized relation to God throughout creation apart from Christ, it defined this distinction in terms of faith and reason, the particular and the universal, revelation and nature. Modern Western liberal theology and philosophy have drawn on this same duality, but favoring reason over faith, the universal over the particular, the natural over the revealed. Long rejects this distinction and hence the basis of modern natural theologies by insisting that all relation to God is contextual, experienced in particular historical situations.

But while insisting on the particular and the historical as the context for any encounter with truth, he reduces historical particularity to one event, the incarnation in Jesus continuing to be made present in the church's sacraments. But clearly Plato's and Aristotle's insights were no less expressions of historical cultures and contexts. Each religion has its particular historical development, often privileging particular moments of experience, such as the Buddha's enlightenment and Muhammad's reception of the revelatory word of God manifest in the Qur'an, as the place and time of transcendent disclosure. In reality we construct what is called "universals" through interaction with many historical particularities, not by having one exclusive particularity incarnate in Christ over against generic, timeless, "universal truths" present through "reason" and "human nature."

Today those engaged in dialogues between world religions are rejecting this classical Christian dualism between faith and reason, particularity and universality, revelation and nature, recognizing that all insights are particular historical constructions. We construct "larger" commonalties only through dialogue and tentative synthesis between several particularities. True universality, in the sense of truths that transcend any particular context or unite all contexts, is impossible, just as it is impossible to

---

28. See especially D. S. Wallace-Hadrill, *The Greek Patristic View of Nature* (New York: Barnes & Noble, 1968).

speak all languages and unite the insights of all cultures. But we may come to a working "global ethic," as is the case with the Parliament of the World's Religions,[29] by synthesizing the insights common to many religious traditions. Catholic Christianity did that two millennia ago by synthesizing two particular worlds of thought, Hebrew and Greek.

On the future dimension of Christology, much of modern thought, liberal and liberationist, has been rooted in forms of Christian messianism that see God continuing to come to us from the future, not simply completed in the past. Christ has a future dimension culminating in the reign of God, as well as disclosing the Logos of God through which the world was created, present throughout creation and in every person and culture. Although this Logos of God finds its normative expression in the incarnation in Christ for classic Christian theology, Christian theological reflection from its beginnings in the New Testament did not think that the reign of God had come fully through Christ's incarnation. The crucifixion demonstrated that the powers of evil still reign. Christ's resurrection in one sense triumphs over this reign of evil that killed Christ but in a way that looks forward to a future completion. This future completion can be seen as both the return of Christ in clouds of glory definitively ending the reign of evil and also an ongoing process (progress) within history by which we grow into better lives that more fully realize God's redeeming and transforming presence in creation.

Modern liberal and liberation movements, including theological expressions of these movements, such as the American Social Gospel and Latin American liberation theology, focus on a future reign of God. Indeed all modern ideas of progress draw more or less consciously on this future messianic dimension of Christian hope. They recognize that evil and ignorance have not been overcome and indeed often appear to have been particularly entrenched in the historic church. They see new insights from science and social criticism of injustices as disclosing new dimensions of truth that may bring in a better society, ultimately that reign of God where every tear is wiped away and every form of ignorance overcome. Every claim of progress and hope for the possible superiority of the "new" draws, even in the most debased form, as new and better cars and computers, but also in highly exalted and visionary forms, as a new world of justice and peace, on this inexhaustible font of future hope unleashed by Christianity itself, as well as by its parent faith, Judaism.[30]

Although Long recognizes that the church and its practices have hardly demonstrated a reality by which every tear has been wiped away, and indeed have become major sources of continuing and new oppressions, he seems to think that the incomplete side of human redemption in Christ does not require any new insights but only a process of repentance that continually restores what is already fully present in the one historical incarnation of Jesus maintained through the sacraments. But this flattens the volatility of the messianic dimension of Christian faith and positions his response to

---

29. The Global Ethic was developed by the Parliament of the World's Religions at its 1993 meeting in Chicago and edited by the Catholic theologian Hans Küng. For a copy of the ethic with Küng's remarks, see http//astro.temple.edu.~dialogue/Center/kung/htm.

30. For the relationship between secular Western future hope and biblical messianism, see Rosemary R. Ruether, *The Radical Kingdom: The Western Experience of Messianic Hope* (New York: Harper & Row, 1970).

all modern hopes for a better future solely as denunciations of apostasy from his peculiarly truncated notion of orthodoxy.

Long thinks that the church as the one universal institution has the presence of God through the sacraments by which it can commune with the fullness of divine truth and goodness. It should claim this truth unapologetically and without humility. But he does not think that the church should order other people and institutions coercively. All coercion and violence have been overcome by the cross, and Christians should never exercise coercion in testifying to the truth that they alone have. Christians should claim the truth as witness, not coercion. But this assumes that Christians constitute a single community where there is a clear consensus of what is truth, something that does not exist and has never existed. From the earliest Christian communities there were a diversity of interpretations of the meaning of the faith. He decries "liberal" Christians who create a neutral space where different views can be tolerated and suggests that they are actually intolerant since they implicitly exclude Christians like himself who commit the one intolerable sin for the tolerant, namely intolerance. This idea is elaborated in his attack on liberals in the United Methodist Church who argue for the support of gay marriage and ordination.[31]

Long's ecclesiology is a peculiar synthesis of Anabaptist and Catholic, a combination that is not inappropriate for Methodism with its synthesis of Anglican and Moravian traditions. It is Catholic in its view of the church as universal body of Christ through which God is securely present in the sacraments. It is Anabaptist in its desire for a pacifist, gathered, and disciplined community that witnesses to the world but without incorporating itself within the world and taking on the means of coercion "like a state." But Long puts the two together in a way that most United Methodists would find hard to understand, especially his stress on the indefectibility of the church and his view of the objective workings of the sacraments. Thus he speaks of the church accomplishing the Eucharist as a "divine-human exchange" that "alone is sufficient to order our lives through God's goodness."[32]

Long's understanding of the church does not seem to leave any space for ways of communing with God outside Christianity, although he does not discuss relations with non-Christian faiths. At a time when the world's religions are not just situated in other regions of the world far away from the daily life of Christians but are part of one's neighborhood, this makes Long's church something of a fortress over against most other humans, non-Christian believers as well as the secular world. He verbally claims Judaism to be the roots of Christianity, even speaking of Christianity as a "sect" of Judaism.[33] But it is not clear how Jews would in fact be able to relate to Christianity as anything other than an apostate sect, as indeed is the traditional orthodox Jewish view of Christianity.[34] A Christian church that sees faith in Jesus Christ and communion in the sacraments as the one aperture through which God is present leaves Judaism as a superceded forerunner that should some day convert to Christ.

---

31. On the covert intolerance of liberals, see Long's "Ecclesial Disobedience or Ecclesial Subordination to Liberal Institutions," in *Staying the Course: Supporting the Church's Position on Homosexuality* (ed. Maxie D. Dunnam and H. Newton Malony; Nashville: Abingdon Press, 2003), 41–55.

32. Long, *The Goodness of God*, 236, 239.

33. Ibid., 218.

34. See R. J. Zwi Werblowsky, "Christianity," in *Encyclopaedia Judaica* (Jerusalem: Macmillan, 1972), 5: 506–15.

Long's politics bring together moral claims that presently are polarized between conservatives and radicals. As a pacifist who rejects voting in a corrupt state,[35] as one who critiques the market and the capitalist system as destructive of true human community, he would seem to fall on the "left" of the political spectrum, while his repudiations of abortion and rejection of homosexual unions fall on the "right." In the United Methodist context Long has aligned himself with Good News evangelical United Methodists who have rejected "holy unions" and decried "reconciling" congregations that welcome gays and lesbians as members.

Long has expended considerable energy in attacking the theological and biblical arguments of other United Methodists, such as the Scripture scholar Victor Furnish, who have defended homosexual unions.[36] He has supported a group of twenty-eight conservative United Methodist clergy and laity in calling for the progressive "reconciling" bishop C. Joseph Sprague of the Northern Illinois Conference of the United Methodist Church (now retired) either to renounce publicly his contrary teachings or resign and surrender his ordination credentials.[37] He also joined with conservative United Methodists, such as Maxie Dunnam of Asbury Seminary and H. Newton Malony of Fuller Seminary, in a volume entitled *Staying the Course: Supporting the Church's Position on Homosexuality* (2003).[38] In a section of his book *The Goodness of God*, he critiques Furnish and other writers of the volume *The Loyal Opposition: Struggling with the Church on Homosexuality* (2000).[39]

Long is particularly annoyed at Furnish's view that new scientific information and new understandings of human relations might relativize biblical teachings on topics such as homosexuality. For Furnish these teachings were set within a patriarchal framework that is now obsolete. Also the ancients had no understanding of sexual orientation as a part of one's nature that disposes some to heterosexual relations and others to homosexual relations. Long is irate at the idea that any new information might supercede biblical teachings, which are timeless and unchangeable. To think we might know better than biblical revelation on any topic is the essence of a modern arrogance that trusts autonomous reason rather than God. He dismisses the idea of sexual orientation as a part of one's created nature, and hence as divinely given, as a spurious "natural theology."

---

35. Stephen Long's rejection of voting was made known to me by personal communication while he and I were professors at Garrett-Evangelical Theological Seminary, 2000–2002.

36. For Long's attack on Victor Furnish and the "Loyal Opposition" to the Methodist teachings on homosexuality, see *The Goodness of God*, 205–11.

37. See Leon Howell, *United Methodism at Risk: A Wake-Up Call* (Kingston, N.Y.: Information Project for United Methodists, 2003), 115. For Bishop C. Josephs Sprague's defense of the theological and biblical basis of his views, see his *Affirmations of a Dissenter* (Nashville: Abingdon, 2002). Long wrote several statements attacking Bishop Sprague. See his "Open Letter to Bishop Sprague," http://www.orthovox.org/orthovox/slongbish.htm; also his statement, "Here I Stand: Risking Methodism Means Gaining a Common Life," www.reporterinteractive.org/news/071603/hs071603. Long's involvement in Northern Illinois Methodist politics against Bishop Sprague is evident in the June 20, 2003, news article in *The Illinois Leader*, "Methodist Teaching and the Northern Illinois Methodist Conference at Odds," www.illinoisleader.com/news/newsview.asp?c-6500.

38. See note 24, above.

39. Victor Furnish's article, "The 'Loyal Opposition' and Scripture," was published in *The Loyal Opposition: Struggling with the Church on Homosexuality* (ed. Tex Sample and Amy E. Delong; Nashville: Abingdon, 2000), 33–42.

Yet Long reverts to his own natural theology when he insists that humans are created male and female, and that this means they are intended by their biological natures to relate only heterosexually.[40] One might question this assumption by citing the scientific evidence that humans are not as securely created either male or female as he assumes. The fetus is initially female and testosterone shapes roughly half of them to become male in the process of gestation.[41] This sometimes is incomplete and at least one in two thousand are born with ambiguous genitalia. Doctors in the United States generally assign such infants to be females, surgically removing the penis, while doctors in India assign such infants to be males, on the grounds that it is harder to be a female than a male, since the first responsibility of females is to bear children. Many such infants grow up to be uncomfortable with their assigned gender. At some point in their development some individuals decide they have been assigned the wrong gender and opt to identify with the other gender, some seeking surgical change and others simply living socially as the other gender. Today some doctors argue against such surgery, and in favor of allowing the individuals to grow up and decide on their own gender.[42] Thus gender difference is more complicated that Long assumes.

Long might argue that such "scientific" evidence should not top God's clear decree that we are "created male and female." But this Genesis declaration is coupled with the divine command that they should procreate, "be fruitful and multiply and fill the earth and subdue it" (Gen 1:28). Long has no difficulty in accepting the patristic argument that this command has been superceded in Christ. Augustine and other church fathers argued that polygamy and the command that all procreate was given only to the pre-Christian era in order to produce the abundant families of Israel from which Christ was born. Now that this has been done, it is no longer necessary for all to procreate and indeed it is better to be celibate in order to anticipate heaven, "where there will be no more marrying and giving in marriage."[43]

Long affirms this argument claiming that the family itself is reshaped by the Christian church to allow different options: celibacy, singleness, and the adoption of non-kin into new family configurations.[44] If the church may reshape the "natural" in these cases, why is it so difficult to imagine that perhaps some new thing is also appearing with "holy unions" between people of the same gender? If the criteria of Christian marriage is not procreation, but faithfulness and love for one another and service to others, then gay Christians (and non-Christians) are today giving abundant witness to both their capacity for and their commitment to such holiness and service.

One of the striking aspects of the recent permission of legal marriage for people of the same gender in the city of San Francisco and then in Massachusetts has been the testimony of long-standing fidelity of many decades from those who took advantage

---

40. See Long, *The Goodness of God*, 204, 216.

41. See Mary Jane Sherfey, "Embryology and the Nature of Bisexuality," in *The Nature and Evolution of Female Sexuality* (New York: Random House, 1972), 30–53.

42. See Claudia Kolker, "The Cutting Edge: Why Some Doctors Are Moving Away from Performing Surgery on Babies with Indeterminate Gender," posted June 8, 2004: http://slate.msn.com/id/2102006.

43. See Long, *The Goodness of God*, 191, 194.

44. Long approves the idea that the church reshapes marriage: see *The Goodness of God*, 189, 204, 232; also his article "The Language of Death: Theology and Economics in Conflict," in *Growing Old in Christ* (ed. Stanley Hauerwas, Carole Bailey Stoneking, Keith G. Meador, and David Coutier; Grand Rapids, Mich.: William B. Eerdmans, 2003), 146–50.

of the offer of legal marriage.[45] What has convinced many Christians who today have come to support holy unions is less the arguments about the naturalness of different "sexual orientations" than the testimony of the faithful and loving quality of life of those one knows in such relationships. Long himself says that "the church should at least argue that a faithful gay couple is preferable to the indiscriminate and promiscuous consumer sexuality that pervades both hetero- and homosexuality at present."[46]

Long's rejection of abortion seems more irate and uncompromising than his views on homosexuality. He speaks of abortion as the "sacrament" of the capitalist free market's global power and as the epitome of the "commodification of human flesh."[47] He uses a "seamless garment" argument that the cross and resurrection of Jesus Christ forbids Christians any recourse to violence, and this means an absolute prohibition of abortion. Drawing on the writing of Catherine MacKinnon, he argues that abortion makes women vulnerable to male sexual aggression, since they cannot argue that they must reject sex in order not to become pregnant.[48] Abortion is at hand to remedy undesired pregnancies. One wonders why such arguments have never restrained male sexual aggression when abortion was not available? Also he argues that abortion and birth control are promoted by the free market to limit the number of workers.[49] Those who want to regulate the work force promote abortion. Again one wonders why such free market promoters as the current Bush administration are against it?

Rather than blaming women as "callous creatures who desire sexual pleasure without child raising" (Long's phrase caricaturing pro-life views) in the manner of social conservatives, Long prefers to see pregnant women who seek abortion as victims who need to be helped by caring Christians who would surround them and help them raise their children.[50] While such help from caring Christians for women with more children than they can care for is certainly to be desired, it is hard to see this as an argument for forcing women to have children they do not choose or want to have. Long's argument against abortion is complicated by his hostility to birth control. It should be obvious that if birth control is not available and encouraged, this increases the likelihood of unchosen pregnancies and hence the recourse to abortion.[51]

Long's vehemence against abortion is not correlated with real and effective policies to reduce the use of it, given the problem of an unchosen pregnancy in circumstances where a pregnant woman lacks the material and psychological resources to raise the child. Feminists committed to legal and safe abortion do not argue that abortion is in

---

45. The first couple to be married when marriage was made legal in San Francisco in 2004 was the lesbian activists Phyllis Lyon, seventy-nine, and Del Martin, eighty-three, who had been a couple for fifty-one years. See http://www.cnn.com/2004/LAW/02/12/gay.marriage.california.ap/.

46. Long, *The Goodness of God*, 218.

47. Ibid., 218.

48. Ibid., 221–22, citing Catherine A. MacKinnon, *Feminism Unmodified: Discourses on Law and Life* (Cambridge, Mass.: Harvard University Press, 1953), 99.

49. Long, *The Goodness of God*, 221–22, also 315–16 n. 32.

50. Ibid., 223.

51. There is ample evidence that when birth control is discouraged the rate of abortion increases. See Sushella Singh and Gilda Sedgh, "The Relationship of Abortion to Trends in Contraception and Fertility in Brazil, Colombia, and Mexico," *International Family Planning Perspectives* 23, no. 1 (March 1997): 4–14. Also see http://www.plannedparenthood.org/global/Education/viewer/asp?1D=54.

itself a "good thing."[52] No one claims that abortion is in itself a "wonderful experience that every woman should have" to fulfill her life. Rather it is a painful and sad remedy for what are seen as worse options, bearing children one did not choose to have in bad circumstances. Thus real reduction of recourse to abortion calls for reduction of those circumstances that create the need for it; namely, unchosen pregnancies. This means both developing cultures that curb male sexual demands on women when women do not desire them and also effective means and use of birth control, together with legal and safe abortion. These solutions Long rejects, thus promoting the very effects that he opposes.

Other elements of Long's social ethics would seem to put him in the company of the left. As a pacifist he signed a statement of one hundred Christian ethicists opposing the American invasion of Iraq.[53] As critics of capitalism, the opponents of the global neoliberal economy, such as the NGOs that gather at the World Social Forum and economists such as David Korten, who looks for a post-corporate economy,[54] might find this aspect of Long's thought congenial. But his need to apologize for the correctness of the biblical witness complicates his anti-war witness.

When speaking of the violence and war that are endemic in Hebrew Scripture, Long claims that the advocacy of the killing of all the residents of conquered cities found in Lev 27:29 and Josh 6:17 should not be condemned as "ethnic cleansing."[55] In the case of the ancient Hebrews he claims that such killings were carried out under pious obedience to God, understanding the dead as sacrificial offerings to God. Long seems oblivious to the way in which these biblical precedents have been used by both Christians and Jews to justify ethnic cleansing today.[56] Such an apology for ancient biblical violence is startling in the mouth of an avowed pacifist. In a time when much of the violence of the world is promoted by religious claims, can we imagine that religious motivations alleviate the horror of such violence? Does the fact that the Al Qaeda terrorists who piloted the planes into the World Trade Center, the Pentagon, and the ground of Pennsylvania saw themselves as carrying out a pious duty to God justify their destructive acts? One wonders if Long would have written such an apology for biblical ethnic killing if he had been writing after September 11th, although surely it should have been evident before that time that religious motivations generally worsen violence, rather than lessening its virulence. This recognition of the worsening effect of religious motivations for violence was the basis of the decision of the recent Parliament of the World's Religions (held in Barcelona, Spain, July 6–13, 2004) to

---

52. I first heard this clarification from Maureen Fiedler of the Quixote Center (personal communication, ca. 1992). See also the article by Ann Pat Ware, SL, "What Pro-Choice Means," in *Courage: Newsletter of the Loretto Women's Network* (July 2004): 1.

53. See the list of names of those who signed this statement in the *Sojourners* website: www.sojo.net/index.cfm/action=action.ethicists_statement.

54. On the current critique of the corporate globalization by the World Social Forum and by the economist David Korten, see Rosemary Radford Ruether, *Integrating Ecofeminism, Globalization, and World Religions* (Lanham, Md.: Rowman & Littlefield, 2004).

55. Long, *The Goodness of God*, 271.

56. See the book by Michael Prior, *The Bible and Colonialism: A Moral Critique* (Sheffield: Sheffield Academic Press, 1997) and "Ethnic Cleansing and the Bible: A Moral Critique," *Holy Land Studies: A Multi-Disciplinary Journal* (2002): 1:37–59.

make "overcoming religiously motivated violence" one of the key themes for dialogue between world religions.[57]

Long's theology is, to say the least, provocative. His critique of modernity follows a long tradition of critical thinkers who see in the modern world a falling away from the virtues of an earlier world of faith and community. But his dogmatic claims for biblical authority and a repristinated Catholic orthodoxy found in its fullest expression in Thomas Aquinas often entail a strained and questionable apologia. His church politics dispose him toward alliances with right-wing Catholics and evangelicals, such as the Pro Ecclesia group,[58] and also with Good News Methodists who may share his hostility to abortion and homosexuality but hardly the totality of his theological perspective.

Although many aspects of his thought have merit, Stephen Long's style of communication, both written and oral, is often confrontational and contemptuous of those with whom he differs. To be persuasive, one must cultivate an attractive mode of discourse that draws out the best of what those with other truth claims are saying and shows how it agrees with your own views, while gently pointing out the aspects of the others' thought that lead in negative directions. But Long's style of argumentation is the opposite of such attractive persuasiveness. By assuming an adversarial stance toward those with whom he differs, giving a polemically one-sided account of their views, he antagonizes and polarizes, rather than seeking common ground. In church bodies increasingly rent into hostile camps, this is a disturbing pattern that bodes ill for the future of Christianity.

---

57. See the website of the Parliament of the World's Religions, www.CPWR.org.

58. Long, "Fetishizing Feuerbach's God: Contextual Theology as the End of Modernity," *Pro Ecclesia* (fall 2003). Pro Ecclesia was founded by the conservative Lutheran theologian Carl E. Braaten and describes itself as a group that nurtures Catholic and evangelical theology that is "obedient to Holy Scripture and committed to the dogmatic, liturgical and institutional continuity of the church" and that "challenges the churches to claim their identity as members of the One, Holy, Catholic and Apostolic Church." See www.e-ccet.org.

6. "That's Not Fair"

Upside-Down Justice in the Midst of Empire

—Joerg Rieger

Few terms have had a more mixed history of reception than the notion of justice. Our own times demonstrate the confusion. While the notion of justice is called into question by various postmodern sensitivities, the call for justice has been revived as the rallying cry for both empires and liberation movements. In the midst of all this, the metamorphoses of the U.S. empire under President George W. Bush have led to connections with popular understandings of justice that have been all but overlooked by everybody else.

At a time when the postmodernists have rightly called our attention to the problems of universal norms and values of justice—with some radical orthodox voices chiming in on the problems of "liberal rights language"—and the liberation movements have rightly focused on the blatant injustices that rob millions of livelihood and lives, something else has fermented in popular U.S. discourse. Not worried about universal norms and values, liberal human rights, or blatant injustice, popular U.S. discourses on justice promote notions of "fairness" that seem to work without metaphysical safety nets, are completely oblivious to differentials of power, and promote justice through flat tax and death penalty. Belief in the myth of individualism is another major component of these popular discourses.

In what follows I will develop more constructive notions of justice that might aid in the resistance to empire, keeping in mind the contemporary critiques of the concept and not losing sight of the predominant notions of justice in empire. Alternative notions of justice emerge, I will argue, in a reversal where we look at things from the other/Other side.[1] Theological discourse is of particular importance here not because theology would be once again ready to be crowned the "queen" of the academy but because the main discourses about justice are all theological in their own ways, even though often only between the lines. Justice as proposed by the U.S. empire, for instance, cannot be understood as a purely "secular" discourse. Images of God are frequently invoked by its supporters, and the formal concept of justice as "fairness" is guaranteed by particular images of God that overrule alternative Christian concepts to such a degree that not the slightest doubt remains that *God* wants us to go to war or

---

1. For the connections between other people and the divine Other—and an argument that without respect for others there might be no respect for God as Other and vice versa—see my book *God and the Excluded: Visions and Blindspots in Contemporary Theology* (Minneapolis: Fortress Press, 2001).

that *God* wants us to apply the death penalty (keep in mind that chaplains are present in both cases to the bitter end).

Justice as Fairness and the U.S. Empire

The notion of justice that has come to dominate the commonsense logic of the U.S. empire might be summed up as "fairness." At first sight, this type of fairness appears to be a completely formal principle that states that everybody should be treated exactly alike, both positively and negatively. The same rules should apply to everybody in the same way, everybody should be measured with the same yardstick without consideration of differences, and any action should receive its response in kind. According to this idea of fairness, things like affirmative action and progressive taxation seem utterly unfair because they take into consideration certain differences and do not treat everybody the same. At the same time, flat tax and death penalty seem utterly fair; a flat tax would treat everybody the same by requiring billionaire and pauper to pay the same percentage of tax, and the death penalty is seen as responding in kind to those who kill other human beings. Thus, the Bush tax cuts for the wealthy are not only not a problem but appear as a step in the right direction.

In this perspective, the wars against Afghanistan and Iraq (and any other war) can also be considered fair if they are seen as war against terrorists—we simply kill the people who are out to kill us. All the current talk about the "liberation of Iraq" is not much more than frill, the kind of stories that we tell because we believe others want to hear them. No fairness-minded American would accept the need to spend funds on the liberation of anyone, as demonstrated not long ago in the resistance to U.S. military actions in Bosnia and the Sudan under the Clinton administration; a similar spirit is at work even in the welfare debates at home. In fact, the Bush government had planned to name the war against Afghanistan "Operation Infinite Justice" and only refrained from doing so "amid fears that the Muslim world, already leery of U.S. intentions, would object on the basis of Koranic teachings that only God can provide infinite justice."[2] The new name was, not surprisingly, "Operation Enduring Freedom," precisely the sort of frill that covers up the underlying vision of infinite justice that is backed up by the infinite—Godself.

While "freedom" is now on everybody's mind—to the point that obituaries for U.S. soldiers killed in Iraq claim that they died fighting for our freedom (from the slavery to which Saddam Hussein committed us?)—the deeper reason for the war is "Infinite Justice." The Iraq war is not about the ownership of oil (the Iraqi oil resources continue to be owned by Iraq and not by the United States) but about some sort of justice. The war against terrorism justified (literally: "made just") the venture in Iraq. Justice in terms of the Iraqi oil means that leaving these oil resources in the hands of a regime that follows its own rules rather than our rules of fairness would perpetuate an unjust situation. This same notion of justice can be found when people in the U.S. Southwest are concerned that if water rights belong to Native Americans who do not follow our rules of fairness, immediate catastrophe will ensue. Only if water and oil are in the

---

2. Reuters news report, "U.S.'s 'Iron Hammer' Code Name 1st Used by Nazis," November 18, 2003, via http://www.commondreams.org/headlines03/1118-12.htm.

hands of systems that guarantee "fairness," that is, a "free market" system without visible restraint, can we rest assured that justice will prevail. In the Southwest, the tendency is therefore to transfer water rights to investment companies that operate on the basis of the "fairness" of the market; and in Iraq, a U.S.-type democracy that likewise promotes the "fairness" of the market and happens to be pro the United States accomplishes the same thing.

These popular notions of fairness provide a strong basis for the justice of the U.S. empire. In this context of empire, the fact that justice is qualified as "infinite" is significant. "Infinite" could simply mean that there is no justice that can trump or transcend the justice of the empire. This is certainly assumed, and there is now not even a question of possible variations in the notion of justice; there is now no recognition that different concepts of the term justice exist. But there is another aspect to which the qualifier "infinite" seems to point: to the self-confidence of Bush's America that we are the nation chosen by God and that our justice is ultimately God's own justice. The basic message is that this is the way the world works, that our fairness is backed up by what Paul Tillich would have called "ultimate reality." No doubt, the Rumsfelds, Wolfowitzes, and Cheneys that prop up the Bush government not only see themselves, but are widely seen, as what might be called "ultimate realists"; at the same time they are also seen as people who operate on the basis of faith, confident that "ultimate reality" is on their side.

Our children demonstrate to us how deeply this understanding of justice is entrenched in our lives. Many of them, too, act as if fairness were the ultimate measuring stick for the world—another indication that we are dealing here with what has become a seemingly "natural" and "ultimate" understanding of justice. What is often overlooked, however, is that while children might apply the notion of fairness to their immediate peers and are quick to utter the complaint "that's not fair," they would have no trouble understanding why a race between a three-year-old and a nine-year-old might not be "fair," or that a high school student would be at a different stage of development than a kindergartner and for this reason cannot be measured by the same standards.

Obviously, an understanding of justice as fairness is not harmless. Neither is such an understanding a purely formal criterion. Equating justice with fairness requires a substantial set of propositions, most importantly the assumption of a level playing field. If all start on the same level, fairness might indeed be just. If there were no power differentials, fairness might also be just. If human beings were completely unbiased and neutral, fairness might be just. If everybody looked and acted exactly the same, fairness might be just, and the list goes on. One of the most important presuppositions for defining justice as fairness is an individualistic outlook. Fairness is, thus, a situation where individuals can do as they please and where they reap the fruits of their efforts without limitations being imposed on them. What is overlooked, however, is that this individualism is mostly a myth of the powerful—it is the story that the powerful tell about their success. By presenting themselves as self-made persons, the powerful can perpetuate the myth of their own personal powers and virtues; in addition, by refusing to acknowledge their dependency on others, they do not have to share their power or wealth.[3]

---

3. One of the few exceptions are those children-turned-stars whose parents reap the financial benefits of their careers, precisely because they cannot present themselves as "self-made" individuals.

A final comment: Unless we acknowledge this struggle for justice as fairness as genuine, we cannot do much to overcome it. The majority of people really believe in justice as fairness, without too many second thoughts about the matter. Likewise, economic theory depends largely on this notion as well by assuming that those who are successful have earned their success and that even the huge gaps in compensation in the contemporary economic situation are somehow "fair."[4]

Justice as Order: Reordering the Empire

The justice of the U.S. empire is clearly insufficient. The equal treatment of unequals may well be the greatest injustice of all,[5] particularly if there is a severe power differential and a playing field that is not level. The popular sentiment against affirmative action as expressed in California and other places, for instance, does not lead to greater justice for all. It mostly leads to a cover-up of inequalities in opportunity (harking back to the American dream that "anybody can make it") and thus to an advantage for those who have greater opportunity, the benefit of better connections, and a more sheltered environment that gives them some advantages on the playing field. Those who started life with significant advantages are often the ones who are most adamant about the fact that anybody can make it. One of the most telling recent examples is billionaire Donald Trump's television show *The Apprentice* where Trump picks whom he sees as the most capable person, that is, the person who is most like him, to get a chance to become even more like him. What is covered up is that Trump, modeling the self-made person for those aspiring to be like him, started his own career, it is said, with a substantial investment put down by his father.[6]

In this context, Aristotle's classical definition of justice as *suum cuique*—to each his or her own, or to each what is due—might lead us a step beyond the empire's simplistic and clearly faulty ideas of justice and fairness. This is also the notion taken up by some theologians whose work has appeared in the Radical Orthodoxy Series, particularly Stephen Long and Daniel Bell, both in their own ways inspired by their teacher Stanley Hauerwas and his widely popularized claims that justice is a "bad idea."[7] Both Long and Bell argue that Aristotle's notion of justice, when taken up by

---

4. The economist Friedrich von Hayek's understanding of justice as fairness can be seen in his critique of the notion of "social justice." Justice means "the fair and impartial application of legal, moral and perhaps customary rules. But precede it with the word 'social' and everything changes. Social justice may require redistributing property and treating people unequally. In this way the word 'social' empties the nouns it is applied to of their meaning" (Friedrich A. von Hayek, *The Fatal Conceit: The Errors of Socialism* [ed. W. W. Bartley III; Chicago: University of Chicago Press, 1988], 116–17).

5. Aristotle addressed the problem in his own way: "It is when equals have or are assigned unequal shares, or people who are not equal, equal shares, that quarrels and complaints break out" (Aristotle, *Nicomachean Ethics* 5:III [trans. J. A. K. Thomson; New York: Penguin Books, 1955], 178).

6. Richard Conniff reports how Trump makes fun of people who inherited money, although his own father's estate was worth more than $150 million (*The Natural History of the Rich: A Field Guide* [New York: W. W. Norton, 2002], 266).

7. See Stanley Hauerwas, *After Christendom: How the Church Is to Behave If Freedom, Justice, and a Christian Nation Are Bad Ideas* (Nashville: Abingdon Press, 1991). The projects of both Bell and Long are easier to understand on the grounds of Hauerwas's claims, even though these claims are rarely quoted in their work. Consider the following statement by Hauerwas, which can be seen as the nucleus of Bell's work on Latin American liberation theology: "The salvation promised in the good news is not a life free from suffering, free from servitude, but rather a life that freely suffers, that freely serves, because such suffering and service is the hallmark of the Kingdom established by Jesus" (53). All three, Hauerwas, Bell, and Long,

medieval theology, incorporates the notion of justice into Christian visions of the common good and of charity—understood as the love of God.[8] While they do not develop the notion of justice in resistance to the empire's own ideas of the common good and charity ("compassionate conservatism" comes to mind) but in resistance to modernity and some forms of "secular" liberal capitalism (there is little recognition that we might be up against another sort of theology[9]), their notion of justice does provide a certain challenge to the status quo.

Bell offers the more sustained argument, starting with the Cistercians whose monastic order is seen as exemplary for devising a "divine pedagogy whereby desire underwent not annihilation but rehabilitation"[10] through the love of God. While he is not arguing for a direct return to the monastic orders, he is concerned about "the lack of persons who are willing to place themselves in the types of relations with others and with God that characterized Cistercian life."[11] It seems that by sheer power of will people might overcome the problems of modernity and return to happier circumstances.[12] Bell recognizes, with Alasdair MacIntyre, that justice defined as giving "to each what is due" is pluriform, since "what is due" depends on different factors and social systems.[13] Thomas Aquinas's definition of justice as giving "to each one his right" draws on the classic model but, as Bell points out in a footnote, transforms it into a position that is not based on merit (for Aristotle merit relates to virtue) but on God's "unmerited grace."[14] Justice in this sense is "a matter of righteousness, of conformity with the common good." Aquinas's vision of justice was, in the words of Bell, "most clearly displayed in medieval monastic communities . . . insofar as they were ordered toward nurturing a shared love or solidarity in the common good." The problem with modernity (and modern Thomism) is, therefore, its move away from ordered communities to "justice as a fundamentally distributive force that secures rights in societies distinguished by the absence of anything but the thinnest of conceptions of the common good." The "rich medieval vision of the common good as shared love, embracing material, social, and spiritual goods," Bell concludes, has been reduced "to the temporal good of the state."[15]

---

draw heavily on Alasdair MacIntyre, *Whose Justice? Which Rationality?* (Notre Dame, Ind.: University of Notre Dame Press, 1988).

8. See, for instance, D. Stephen Long, "Charity and Justice: Christian Economy and the Just Ordering of the Commandments," *Communio* 25 (spring 1998): 14–28. This essay is the same as Long, *Divine Economy: Theology and the Market* (Radical Orthodoxy Series; London: Routledge, 2000), 233–40. See also ibid., 228–29.

9. For an argument that late capitalism promotes its own kind of theology see Joerg Rieger, "Gott und die globale Marktwirtschaft," in *Oikos Europa zwischen Oikonomia und Oikumene: Globale Marktwirtschaft, EU-Erweiterung und christliche Verantwortung* (ed. Dietmar W. Winkler and Wilfried Nausner; Innsbruck and Vienna: Tyrolia Verlag, 2004), 73–85.

10. Daniel M. Bell Jr., *Liberation Theology after the End of History: The Refusal to Cease Suffering* (Radical Orthodoxy Series; London: Routledge, 2001), 92.

11. Ibid., 97.

12. Here is a curious blind spot in Bell's relentless struggle against modernity and liberal capitalism, since his own proposal depends on people having the autonomy and willpower to place themselves in different relationships.

13. Bell, *Liberation Theology*, 101. He gives some credit for this insight also to Latin American liberation theology.

14. Ibid., 102, 135 n. 76.

15. Ibid., 103–4. According to Bell, this is the problem not only of modern Catholic social teaching of the nineteenth and early twentieth centuries but also of Latin American liberation theology, which he sees as basically copying and only slightly modifying these approaches.

These references to the Middle Ages might be seen as an antidote to the U.S. empire's emphasis of individualism. Referring to a common good goes against the individualistic tendencies of modernity. Nevertheless, and here we run into the first problem, this reminder about the common good takes individualism at face value and fails to address the fact that it is never more than a myth, that even in a postmodern economy where fragmentation and diversity rule there are deep connections and relationships on which the system is built. Furthermore, this position creates some problems that tend to go unrecognized by those theologians who work mainly within the realm of ideas. The "rich medieval vision of the common good" implies a divine order of the universe that is certainly beautiful and unified, as Bell points out, but also strictly hierarchical. Order is the key to justice in this model. The embeddedness of justice in an all-encompassing order presupposes a stratified society in which everything has its preordained place. Aristotle's *suum cuique*, as picked up by Thomas Aquinas, assumes such a well-structured order. The ancient Greek idea of the tripartite society (naturalized by Plato in analogy to the metals of gold, silver, and iron or brass), according to which God made some rulers, some auxiliaries, and some peasants, artisans, and laborers, is reflected in this notion of justice. Justice is realized when each person does "one job, the job he was most naturally suited for." Otto Gerhard Oexle has aptly summed up this position as "harmony through inequality."[16]

A story from the life of Hildegard of Bingen illustrates what is at stake in medieval notions of order, the common good, and justice. In the middle of the twelfth century, Hildegard was challenged about the socially exclusive nature of her convent, which did not admit people who were not nobility or had no wealth. Another nun, Tenxwind of Andernach, argued that Christ had chosen his apostles from fishermen, the lowly, and the poor. With reference to Paul's first letter to the Corinthians, Tenxwind argues that God has chosen only few of noble birth; rather, God has chosen mainly those who are low and despised in this world (1 Cor 1:26ff.). In her reply, Hildegard maintains that it is God's will that the lower estates should not rise above the higher one; that the order of creation was stratified, as shown by the animal kingdom, and that failure to respect this order resulted in Adam's original sin against God, and that chaos will ensue if this order is broken. Nevertheless, Hildegard does not doubt that "God loves all" in their different states. Although directly challenged by Tenxwind to do so, Hildegard is not able to provide biblical images for her position; she refers to virtue instead, and the highest virtue is to submit to God's hierarchical order.[17]

While medieval theology might well have a substantive notion of the common good, one wonders whether it is very helpful in the empire in which we live. In a later

---

16. Otto Gerhard Oexle, "Perceiving Social Reality in the Early and High Middle Ages," in *Ordering Medieval Society: Perspectives on Intellectual and Practical Modes of Shaping Social Relations* (ed. Bernhard Jussen; trans. Pamela Selwyn; Philadelphia: University of Pennsylvania Press, 2001), 98–99. See Plato, *The Republic* III, 414c. Already Augustine can be found in this tradition, when he points out that order—on which justice rests—is "the disposition of equal and unequal things in such a way as to give to each its proper place" (Augustine, *The City of God against the Pagans* XIX:13; ed. and trans. R. W. Dyson; [Cambridge: Cambridge University Press, 1998], 938).

17. Alfred Haverkamp, "Tenxwind von Andernach und Hildegard von Bingen," in *Institutionen, Kultur und Gesellschaft im Mittelalter* (ed. Lutz Fenske, Werner Rösener, and Thomas Zotz; Sigmaringen: Jan Thorbecke Verlag, 1984), 520, 533, 536. Hildegard adds that since God is powerful, God cannot possibly have rejected people who are powerful.

essay, Bell moves on to Anselm, who unites charity and justice in Christ's "sacrifice" in order to "deliver us to the City of God,"[18] which once again emphasizes the medieval sense of order. "Christ's sacrifice," Bell argues, creates a situation in which "the divine plenitude spills over with the result that sacrifice becomes gain (Luke 9:24) and we can give ourselves as a gift of love to our neighbors."[19] Apart from the fact that Anselm does not talk about Christ's "sacrifice" but about Christ's death in the broader framework of the restoration of God's honor (satisfaction and sacrifice are two different matters), Bell's claim that Anselm's model provides an alternative to capitalism may be correct insofar as Anselm's model promotes a feudalist order rather than a capitalist one. The superiority of Anselm's model might even be supported by the fact that Anselm was opposed to the Crusades; this insight would save Bell some of the troubles he has with Bernard of Clairvaux.[20] Yet Anselm was opposed to the Crusades not because he rejected violence (he would even lead the king's soldiers into battle on other occasions) but because Christianity did not really need the Crusades. The medieval Christian feudal social order, in Anselm's day another rising empire, was secure in its superiority. In his book *Cur Deus Homo* Anselm celebrates the restoration of God's order of creation in Christ and uses it to push further against the wall the "infidels" of his day, both Jews and Muslims.[21]

The radical orthodox commitment to justice in terms of divine order and the common good is, thus, at least a mixed blessing since the traditional views of order and their elitist presuppositions cannot easily be eclipsed.[22] On the positive side, taking seriously the question of order might be helpful if it pushes us to take a closer look at how order and the common good shape up in the U.S. empire. Looking at the case of Donald Trump in terms of order would at least point us to the underlying order of things, such as the substantial class differential, and thus expose the illusion that simply "anybody can make it." In struggles concerning affirmative action, an awareness of the order of things would help clarify the different levels of the playing field, and opponents would have to be clearer and more up front about the fact that they do not appreciate the leveling of playing fields. These kinds of order and the related common goods are far from being naively materialistic or "economic" (as Bell seems to assume, which is probably why he does not take this order seriously); various spiritualities, values, and ways of life (*habitus*) are at stake here too. If order and common good were thus recognized, individualism could potentially be exposed as the myth that it is.

---

18. Daniel M. Bell Jr., "Sacrifice and Suffering: Beyond Justice, Human Rights, and Capitalism," *Modern Theology* 18, no. 3 (July 2002): 344.

19. Ibid., 347.

20. Bell takes on Bernard's support of the Crusades, insinuating that he should not have taken up the "sword of justice" but embraced suffering (*Liberation Theology*, 134 n. 50 and 150). But this seems to be a minor flaw, apart from some political mischief, in a Christian hero who was otherwise on the right track (see 88–96).

21. See Anselm of Canterbury, *Why God Became Man*, in *Anselm of Canterbury: The Major Works* (ed. Brian Davies and G. R. Evans; Oxford: Oxford University Press, 1999), 265, 355.

22. Christian theologians cannot escape the problem as easily as MacIntyre in regard to Aristotle, who simply claims that Aristotle's preference for a virtue-based aristocracy is "independent of any thesis about what kinds of persons are or are not capable of excellence" (*Whose Justice?*, 104–5). The particular forms of justice, order, and virtue promoted by medieval theology cannot be separated from their theological proposals, as demonstrated for instance by Anselm's presuppositions about God's honor in *Cur Deus Homo*.

One way to rewrite medieval notions of order and the common good—which unlike contemporary empire have at least the advantage that they are more open and honest about God as being at the very top of the hierarchical chain of being—would be to reject the hierarchy in favor of equality. Equality is in vogue, and there appears to be a widespread sentiment these days that the Trinity is a model for equal rather than hierarchical relations.[23] Bell, too, ultimately seems to have a different order in mind when he talks about "giving ourselves as a gift of love to our neighbors." Yet the problem is that at present quite a few of our neighbors would feel much happier if U.S. Christians and other pious elites stopped seeing themselves as a "gift to the world," no matter how benign and loving. The problem is that the deeper distortions of empire are not dealt with here, and thus empire might find ways of sneaking in through the back door. The churches' mission trips are the best example of how well-meaning efforts at giving ourselves to others as gift can easily become the first messengers of empire.[24] Here, theology needs to dig deeper and, in a self-critical mode, reflect on how the power structures of empire can make use of even the most well-meaning efforts of the church, including its visions of order and of equality in the Trinity.

Nevertheless, emphasizing equality rather than hierarchy, the *suum cuique* might be another preliminary step in the resistance against empire, if it is reinterpreted as "to each according to his or her needs" rather than as "to each according to his or her merits." This interpretation would be a significant improvement over the empire's notion of fairness. Perhaps this is what Bell means in his own reversal of the *suum cuique*, when he says that God's redemption is "an act of injustice" because it does not proceed according to right and merit but according to grace.[25] Justice with a focus on people in need has the potential to challenge the empire's notion that there is a level playing field and that "anybody can make it." This model of justice would, furthermore, match some of the postmodern concerns about diversity. Justice, understood as "to each according to his or her needs," is able to respect diversity and to uphold it as a positive value.

Justice understood as "to each according to his or her needs" might, furthermore, be seen as restorative justice, a term that became fashionable in the aftermath of South African apartheid and that is gaining prominence in the United States. In a situation of empire, restorative justice takes the edge off some pressures and promotes forms of healing and restitution that include both victims and offenders.[26] Those most in need

---

23. See for instance the work of Catherine Mowry LaCugna. Long, "Charity and Justice," seems to assume that this equality can already be found in medieval theology (16) and proposes that there is equality "in the communion practiced at the Eucharist" which is "subject only to the condition of one's baptism and willingness to repent and seek reconciliation" (19). The requirement of baptism for communion is odd for a Methodist theologian.

24. For a more extended argument see Joerg Rieger, "Theology and Mission in a Postcolonial World," in *Mission Studies: Journal of the International Associaton for Mission Studies*, 21:2 (2004): 201–227.

25. Bell, *Liberation Theology*, 131.

26. According to the Prison Fellowship International Centre for Justice and Reconciliation, restorative justice is a systematic response to wrongdoing that emphasizes healing the wounds of victims, offenders, and communities caused or revealed by criminal behavior. See www.restorativejustice.org. For the South African perspective see John W. de Gruchy, *Reconciliation: Restoring Justice* (Minneapolis: Fortress Press, 2002), 204, which describes restorative justice as "renewing God's covenant and therefore the establishing of just power relations without which reconciliation remains elusive." De Gruchy thus proposes a more holistic understanding; yet the difficulty in the actual South African processes includes the fact that reconciliation between "victims and perpetrators" was ultimately interpreted as little more than forgiveness (Audrey R. Chapman and Bernard Spong, eds., *Religion and Reconciliation in South Africa: Voices of Religious Leaders* [Philadelphia: Templeton Foundation Press, 2003], 12).

receive special attention; they are the focus of love and grace, as expressed in Jesus' parables of the Lost Sheep, the Lost Coin, and the Prodigal Son (all in Luke 15). Justice as "to each according to his or her needs" can also be found as informing various welfare strategies and social programs. The problem, however, is that this justice often stays within the system and supports that which is recognized as order and the common good. Those with the greatest needs receive special attention in order to recuperate and to be restored to a better place within the system. The system as such is not necessarily questioned—there is no reflection on what is defined as crime, for instance, and no sustained reflection on the causes of inequality in references to restorative justice in the United States. Affirmative action, likewise, can be seen in this light as geared to integrate those into the system who might not make it otherwise. Resistance is not an option.

In this sense, even justice as "to each according to his or her needs" remains a top-down approach, not unlike justice as "to each according to his or her merits." There is an idealism here that claims faithfulness to certain issues but fails to raise questions about the system as such, just like medieval theology was unable to raise questions about its own hierarchical system; based on this system, Anselm's Christology could pose as rational and offer reasonable proof even to those who were truly other, Jews and Muslims. If order as such is not questioned, however, the flow of power is not questioned either. While justice as order in the sense of "to each according to his or her needs" can mitigate the excesses of those in power to a certain degree and promote more equal relations, it cannot reverse the flow of power. In this model, not even God can go against the system; God cannot associate with the powerless in order to challenge the powerful. When individualism is mentioned here, it is granted the status of reality and thus things usually end in moral appeals to be less individualistic, to accept some notion of the common good and order, and to look out for others.

The U.S. empire is not fundamentally challenged here. If justice is defined as divine ordering—whether in terms of social or ecclesial hierarchies or in terms of a society of equals (even if only among the baptized) where all are responsible for their neighbors—we must not forget that the empire also claims divine order. While some modernists and Enlightenment thinkers may have indeed rebelled against ideas of divine order, a position that has left strong residues in European politics and culture, this does not seem to be the problem of the U.S. empire in the past and it certainly is not now.[27] It is not inconceivable that the empire can appropriate various notions of justice as order by compartmentalizing them in different departments, such as faith-based welfare programs (need based), economics (merit based), and education (value based). Of course, while empire emphasizes justice as "fairness," justice as *suum cuique* is not at all out of place in a capitalist framework either. In John Rawls's definition of justice, "social and economic inequalities . . . are just only if they result in compensating benefits for everyone, and in particular for the least advantaged members of society."[28] That's what capitalism wants us to believe—that some economic inequalities are good for the system because "a rising tide lifts all boats" and wealth tends to "trickle down."

27. It should not be overlooked that Enlightenment resistance to the divine, which is much more common in Europe, assumes its own access to some sort of "ultimate reality"; nevertheless, here is a definite difference between the contexts of the United States and of Europe, which should make us wonder how readily the principles of radical orthodoxy can be imported/exported into different contexts.

28. John Rawls, *A Theory of Justice* (Cambridge, Mass.: Harvard University Press, Belknap Press, 1971), 14–15. This is Rawls's second principle; the first is equality.

Justice as Preference: The Empire Upside-Down

At first sight, to define justice as preference implies a stark contradiction in terms. Justice as preference is the model farthest removed from the commonsense logic of the U.S. empire and thus seems the least fair. I will argue, however, that this notion of justice, understood as "being in solidarity with those who experience injustice," and as "taking the sides of those who have been marginalized and excluded from relationship," is required to produce true opposition to the injustices of the status quo. This notion of justice is more radical than mere rejections of the status quo's notions of justice as fairness because it leads to unexpected reversals, implying not only attention to needs but closer attention to those pressured by injustice, and reminds us of alternative sorts of agency and energy that are often overlooked. This perspective introduces a moment that is self-critical in the truest sense of the word, since it critiques the self formed by the U.S. empire by revealing its hidden relation to the other/neighbor—not simply some neighbor in need of gifts but that neighbor on whose back the self (even the Christian self) has built its identity through a process of repression.[29] In other words, the relationship to the other is not first of all a moral imperative (like "care for your neighbor," or "create a loving relationship") but a reality that is always there even though it is more and more covered up.

Furthermore, justice as preference is the notion of justice that is most common in biblical texts of both the Old Testament and the New Testament. In many biblical texts, justice refers not to the empire's notion of fairness, nor primarily to a predetermined order, but to the covenant, that is, to a relationship between God and humanity that is dynamic and responsive. This relationship is expressed in terms of God's faithfulness, which implies God's special concern for those pushed to the margins of the covenant and excluded by some who are under the mistaken impression that they are closer to God.[30] Justice has to do, therefore, with a particular concern for the restoration of relationship with those who are being pushed to the margins of the covenant, such as the proverbial widows, orphans, and strangers of the Old Testament, and the fishermen, prostitutes, and tax collectors of the New Testament. In this context, restoration of relationship with the marginalized is not simply a social issue—the quality of our relationship to God is inextricably connected to this matter as well. Distortions in our relations to others get reproduced in distortions in our relations to God, and vice versa. Justice as preference for those who experience injustice and who are excluded from the covenant by those who feel closer to God (whether owing to their success, their power, or their religious privilege) provides resistance to the empire in the following ways.

First, such upside-down justice is linked to a detailed account of the kinds of pressures that people on the margins have to endure in their lives.[31] Here a sharper

---

29. This notion of repression is developed in my *Remember the Poor: The Challenge to Theology in the Twenty-First Century* (Harrisburg, Pa.: Trinity Press International, 1998), chapter 3.

30. Most interpreters are now agreed on the centrality of the covenant and of relationship in the understanding of the biblical notions of justice. See, e.g., Christopher D. Marshall, *Beyond Retribution: A New Testament Vision for Justice, Crime, and Punishment* (Grand Rapids, Mich.: William B. Eerdmans, 2001); and Walter Kerber, Claus Westermann, and Bernhard Spörlein, "Gerechtigkeit," in *Christlicher Glaube in moderner Gesellschaft* 17 (Freiburg: Herder, 1981).

31. Karen Lebacqz proposes to begin with injustice not because it "offers better 'theoretical insights' but because it is the only honest place to begin, given the realities of our world" (*Justice in an Unjust World: Foundations for a Christian Approach to Justice* [Minneapolis: Augsburg Publishing House, 1987], 11).

understanding of the dangers and injustices of the empire emerges since people on the margins experience them in their own bodies, and thus much more directly than anyone else. Viewed from the perspectives of those pushed to the margins, there can be no illusion of equality or a level playing field and a structural understanding of injustice emerges. From this perspective, there cannot be a grand theory based solely in the world of ideas. This attention to the pressures that people have to endure requires a very close look at the claims of individual achievement in empire. Individualism is questioned at the most fundamental level here: Does it really exist or is it the myth of the powerful? Is the wealth of corporate America built single-handedly by a few prominent CEOs, as their compensation seems to indicate, or is it rather tied to the labor of billions around the globe who labor under constantly worsening conditions? From the perspective of workers, for instance, pressed to sell their labor for less and less money, the individualism displayed by the top-level CEOs is easily exposed as fraud. From this perspective, relationship is not first of all a moral demand but a suffocating reality because of a severe asymmetry of power that pervades corporate America. The challenge for the system is, thus, not to become "less individualistic" but to become aware of the relationships already in place, to put an end to the cover-up, and to form less asymmetric relationships. This insight has important implications for our relationship to God as well; as those in power misrecognize their relationship to other people, they are also prone to misrecognize their relationship to God. Neither a well-meaning communitarian approach nor the insistence on equal rights makes much of a difference here—in fact both communitarianism and equal rights might be harmful since both discourses often cover up differences in power.[32] This implies a very different awareness of empire and the urgency of the situation; the problem of "modernity," as identified by radical orthodoxy, is much deeper and much more severe.[33]

Second, upside-down justice that is aware of power transcends distribution and takes into account productivity. Injustice is tied not just to distribution as such but to the dramatic differences in the valuation of productivity. The productivity of a CEO, for instance, is valued much higher than the productivity of a worker. According to recent statistics, the average CEO earns 531 times more than the average worker.[34] Upside-down justice provides an adjustment of the value attached to various forms of productivity. Such justice has nothing to do with the giving of alms, neither is it primarily concerned about social programs or even advocacy for the marginalized. Justice in touch with the lives of the marginalized leads to a new awareness and valuation of the productivity of the margins—and thus it might lead also to a new awareness of God's own mysterious productivity in places where we least expect it, even on a cross. Once the empire's myth of individualism gives way to an awareness of actual relationships, the true productivity of the marginalized can be seen. This productivity bears a certain family resemblance to the kind of energy that is set free at the personal level

---

32. "Between equal rights, force decides" (Karl Marx, quoted in David Harvey, *Justice, Nature, and the Geography of Difference* [Oxford: Blackwell, 1996], 399).

33. Bell misunderstands Gutiérrez's call for liberation from the "oppression being carried on in the name of 'modern liberties and democracy,'" thinking that this has to do with a gap between what modernity proclaims and what it accomplishes (*Liberation Theology*, 113). Yet Gutiérrez seems very clear: there is something inherently wrong with modern liberties that result only in "new and more refined forms of exploitation of the very poorest" (ibid.).

34. Editorial, *Dallas Morning News*, September 5, 2001; the numbers are up, from 419:1 in 1999 and 70:1 in the late 1980s.

once persons connect with their repressions. Below the surface, at the level of what has been repressed, lie tremendous energies that push toward transformation and justice, not primarily in its punitive or redistributive forms but as creating a space for alternative productivity. It should go without saying that these energies must not be romanticized or idealized.[35] Here we have arrived at the level of desire, since our desires are ultimately formed in moments of repression, as Freud pointed out; any hope for transforming desire needs to take into account our repressions.[36] Elsa Tamez reinterprets Paul's doctrine of justification by faith in a parallel way, as focusing on productivity: "Insofar as it is by faith and not by law that one is justified, the excluded person becomes aware of being a historical subject and not an object."[37] Put slightly differently, God's own productivity is what shapes human productivity, and this gives a whole new dimension to the doctrine of justification.

Such productivity, set free by upside-down justice, is one of the things that radical orthodoxy is unable to deal with. Bell, for instance, acknowledges the "option for the poor" of Latin American liberation theology, but this mainly amounts to a moral imperative.[38] Justice, however, that recognizes and values the productivity "from below" is not a moral imperative; such justice pushes beyond justice as distribution and beyond justice as order: justice that recognizes a different sort of productivity does not depend on activation by well-meaning proponents, is often surprising, and cannot easily be controlled.[39] Unlike justice conceived as order, justice that celebrates a different productivity is not predetermined but based on relationships with the margins. As distorted relationships are restored and new forms of productivity take hold, God's reign of justice gains hold, overcoming the injustices of empire.

Third, justice as preference, taking the sides of those marginalized and excluded, is concerned about broken relationships. Its main concern is not distribution but the restoration of relationships, which include both victim and offender. The initial step in the context of broken relationships is a search for solidarity. Solidarity in the midst of the current situation is highly complex owing to various types of pressure and differences along the lines of gender, race, age, and sexual orientation. In the midst of a globalizing economy, however, the point of connection and solidarity might be seen in the reality of economic pressures endured across the board. Economic pressures broadly

---

35. I attempt a search for this energy without romanticizing it in my book *Remember the Poor*.

36. Bell addresses the question of desire when he reminds us that "savage capitalism . . . wages war against humanity on all fronts—at the level of ontology, desire—and not just at the level of political economy." As a response, Christianity is seen as an alternative "technology of desire" (*Liberation Theology*, 85). What is not clear, however, is how this technology of desire gets us in touch with desire formed through repression. Bell's therapeutic approach fails to move through the analytical tasks.

37. Elsa Tamez, *The Amnesty of Grace: Justification by Faith from a Latin American Perspective* (trans. Sharon Ringe; Nashville: Abingdon, 1993), 166.

38. He basically sees the irruption of the poor as "emergence of a demand for socio-economic rights," adding socioeconomic rights on top of civil and political rights (Bell, *Liberation Theology*, 113). Bell also acknowledges that for Latin American liberation theologians justice is partisan, which means taking sides (121). Nevertheless, he does away with the challenge quickly because this is seen as getting stuck in rights language. "Forming persons to respect rights is not enough to repel capitalism" (125). Worse yet, he misrepresents liberation theology's concern for the poor: "Liberationists face the poor and encourage them to become acquisitive; so, too, does capitalism" (129).

39. Bell also wants to move beyond distributive justice in favor of unitive justice—but this sounds like a move toward order rather than productivity (*Liberation Theology*, 127).

distributed tend to weld together people vastly different—including those white-collar employees (often white and male) who are now also experiencing the economic squeeze first hand. Theologians could be ahead of the game if we realized that the distortion of economic relations is a central issue in both Bible and Qur'an, once again not merely as a "social issue" but also in terms of the distortion of our relation to the divine.[40] Community needs to be rebuilt in light of the particular forms in which it has broken down and in terms of where the pressures weld us together—thus the need to pay close attention to economics as one of the primary matters of life and death, although this is obviously not the only reality that matters.

The preferential option for the poor of Latin American liberation theology has often been misunderstood as a special interest arrangement that is out to destroy community and that neglects the rich. Yet this was never the intention, since the problem can obviously not be resolved without the rich. In a situation that is marked by severe asymmetries, invoking principles of "fairness" or "order" will not suffice to rectify the problem. A preferential option for the poor includes those who distort relationships and who benefit most from asymmetries, but it reminds us that they are faced with a particular challenge; they are the ones who need not only a little push but all the help (grace) they can get. The energy and productivity that bubble up from the margins (God's own location in Christ's ministry, death, and resurrection) provide some help by pushing toward justice not in punitive or redistributive ways but by initiating the transformation of relationships. This changes the meaning of "love." Jesus' commandment to love the neighbor as oneself (Mark 12:31) appears in new light. Love of neighbor is no longer seen merely as a commandment (not even a *habitus*) but becomes a reminder of the deeper relations with our neighbors. With Frederick Herzog we might read Jesus' words as "love your neighbor as [being] yourself."[41] In the first case, where we seek to help out the neighbor (whether through alms or social programs), the relation depends on the will or formation of the self. In the second case, where the neighbor is not just part of the self but a part of the self (however repressed), the matter depends on becoming aware of our relationship and ceasing to maintain the other in a position of repression. Such a reshaped relation with our neighbor ("love") introduces a different note in our relationship with God ("love for God"; Mark 12:30) as well. In this sense, justice is indeed closely related to matters of reconciliation; but such reconciliation needs to ask questions like how this poses a challenge to those who marginalize others and how marginalization happens in the first place.[42]

Unlike the "unity" and "fairness" sought by the U.S. empire's proverbial melting pots, such solidarity and restoration of relationship does not seek to eradicate diversity. Solidarity is not uniformity or predetermined order of the sort that rightly worries postmodernists because it allows for the abuse of power. Nevertheless, the distortions of community, particularly when it comes to economics, point also to the need to overcome certain forms of severe difference and inequality that are often shrugged off as part of the "order of things." Both aspects, respect for some differences and the overcoming of other differences, are important in the formation of relationship and we

---

40. In Islam, economic injustice is also seen as a severe problem; see for instance Sura LXX.

41. Frederick Herzog, "Befreiung zu einem neuen Menschenbild," *Evangelische Kommentare* 5, no. 9 (1972): 518. See also my interpretation in *Remember the Poor*, 99.

42. Bell also argues for reconciliation but does not pay much attention to those questions.

must resist a common tendency in the United States to play them off against each other.[43] Unless we recognize the problem with certain forms of difference, the empire's notion of fairness can assimilate notions of difference without much of a challenge.

Finally, justice as preference throws new light on our vision of ultimate reality and, thus, on the doctrine of God. Without reverting to fixed metaphysical principles and the types of universals that are becoming more and more questionable because they monopolize power, we need to see whether there is some common thread emerging. The biblical sources, although not lacking in differences, converge in various important ways. What many of the biblical notions of justice have in common is their focus on relationship. The Hebrew verb *sdq* means to be faithful to the community established by the covenant.[44] The Greek term *dikaiosyne*, as used in the New Testament, has not eclipsed this emphasis on relationship. Although there is no uniform notion of justice in the New Testament, justice tends to include both the relations between human beings and the relation to God; here is a significant difference to the classical Greek notion of *dikaiosyne* that focuses exclusively on the relation between human beings.[45] More specifically, in the prophets of the Old Testament, the term justice addresses the distorted relationships between the rich and the poor, caused by oppressive actions of the rich, who "trample on the poor" (Amos 5:11).[46] In fact, this distortion of relationships by oppression is a concern in various parts of the Bible—the Psalms come to mind as another prominent example[47]—and can also be found in Jesus' message and other parts of the New Testament. Justice in all these cases aims at the restoration of relationships and at putting an end to oppression. The primary concern of justice is, thus, not so much helping those in need but overcoming oppressive relationships and learning how to relate differently—both to other human beings and to God. The apostle Paul's notion of justification needs to be seen in a similar light: not simply as a religious transaction but as a manifestation of God's justice, which resists injustice and reconstructs distorted relationships.[48] As a result, justice, as restoring broken relationships, needs to address the power differential between

---

43. For an extended argument about a distinction between the necessary recognition of difference (Iris Marion Young's "politics of difference") and the need to overcome socioeconomic differences, see Nancy Fraser, *Justice Interruptus: Critical Reflections on the "Postsocialist" Condition* (New York: Routledge, 1997), 189–205. Fraser sees a problem in the United States, where the two perspectives are often played off against each other: "Where else than in the United States does ethnicity so regularly eclipse class, nation, and party?" (197).

44. K. Koch, "sdq, gemeinschaftstreu/heilvoll sein," in *Theologisches Handwörterbuch zum Alten Testament* 2 (ed. Ernst Jenni and Claus Westermann; Munich: Christian Kaiser Verlag; Zurich: Theologischer Verlag Zurich, 1984), 507–30.

45. Dieter Lührmann, "Gerechtigkeit III," in *Theologische Realenzyklopädie* 12 (ed. Gerhard Krause and Gerhard Müller; Berlin: Walter de Gruyter, 1984), 419.

46. See the Jewish theologian Moshe Weinfeld, "'Justice and Righteousness': The Expression and Its Meaning," in *Justice and Righteousness: Biblical Themes and Their Influence* (ed. Henning Graf Reventlow and Yair Hoffman; Sheffield: Sheffield Academic Press, 1992), 238. If space would permit, a narrative approach to biblical stories about God's justice would further demonstrate God's struggle to establish relationship in the face of broken relationships. Karen Lebacqz, *Justice in an Unjust World*, works out such a narrative approach.

47. See the examples in Weinfeld, "'Justice and Righteousness,'" 242–43.

48. See Tamez, *The Amnesty of Grace*. Christopher Marshall describes what Paul and the writers of the gospels share in common: God's justice is "a redemptive power that breaks into situations of oppression or need in order to put right what is wrong and restore relationships to their proper condition" (*Beyond Retribution*, 93).

oppressor and oppressed and it is partisan insofar as God sides with those who are trampled underfoot. Gustavo Gutiérrez's reflections, published three decades ago, match these more recent reflections: "To deal with a poor man or woman as Yahweh dealt with his people—this is what it is to be just." And: "To be just is to be faithful to the covenant. . . . Justice in the Bible is what unites one's relationship with the poor to one's relationship with God."[49]

The image of God emerging here is dynamic. A God who opts for those whose relationships have been violated can never be pinned down in terms of an abstract notion of fairness or of predetermined order, once and for all. Those who want to know this God need to do so "on their feet," following God's creative resistance of oppressive relationships and the formation of alternative ways of relating.[50] Tenxwind of Andernach's claims that Christ had chosen his apostles from fishermen, the lowly, and the poor, not those who were "powerful and of noble birth" but the "low and despised" (cf. 1 Cor 1:26ff.), present an ongoing challenge to all. Following further along the lines of Paul's thought invoked by Tenxwind, it is part of God's justice to choose "what is foolish in the world to shame the wise . . . what is weak in the world to shame the strong, . . . what is low and despised in the world, things that are not, to reduce to nothing things that are" (1 Cor 1:27–28). This is God's own work of deconstruction, as it were. The question, then, is not whether "God is on our side" (whether in empire's claims of fairness or in some type of pre-ordered universe) but whether we are "on God's side," taking sides in the dynamic pursuit of God's justice with all the reversals and challenges that this justice entails.[51]

Conclusion

How are we supposed to make up our minds about justice? The fairness of the U.S. empire sees nothing wrong with equal treatment because it assumes a level playing field and equal access to the American pie. But where do such level playing fields exist? Anselm and Hildegard see nothing wrong with hierarchy and serfdom because they assume a higher order. More recent sentiments proclaim order in more egalitarian ways. But the postulation of such orders is problematic in itself because these orders miss the dynamic struggles of justice against injustice and the deeper levels of solidarity with those who experience injustice. Postmodernists see nothing wrong with diversity because they suspect that uniformity is invented by those in power. But some forms of diversity can lead to further stratification of society and can result in the neglect of life-threatening inequalities. Thus, the first step in reflecting on justice needs to be a question about our concepts.[52] A new perspective emerges when we dare to raise

---

49. Gustavo Gutiérrez, *The Power of the Poor in History* (trans. Robert R. Barr; Maryknoll, N.Y.: Orbis Books, 1983), 8, 10. In his critique of Latin American liberation theology, Bell is strangely silent about these biblical parallels.

50. Picking up an insight of Dietrich Bonhoeffer, we might say that we need to follow God where God is preceding us.

51. Are we talking about "spiritual" or "social" processes? If God is God, there is no way to separate those realms.

52. Marx and Engels raise similar questions, suspecting that "justice is but the ideologized, glorified expression of the existing economic relations, now from their conservative and now from the revolutionary angle" (quoted in Harvey, *Justice*, 331). Too many social movements in the twentieth century have assumed that they cannot behave unjustly because their cause is just. See ibid., 347.

questions, when we pay attention to the pressures of the current metamorphoses of empire of which we are a part, not in a moralizing way but in searching for alternative energies that push us in new directions. Keep in mind that the reversal of the justice of the empire is not first of all a matter of the will or of virtue but a matter of grace, which manifests itself in the unlikeliest of places.

7. "A Saint and a Church for Twenty Dollars"

Sending Radical Orthodoxy to Ayacucho

—Marcella María Althaus-Reid

I found this picture near a radio . . . [a voice in the background shouts: "it is yellow!"]. Well, it is pretty, nice. It has a house and a little virgin [a woman shouts: "Itatí!"] Yes! [laughs], it is the Virgin of Itatí. Well [confused] . . . what do I know . . . what else can I say . . .

> —José, a cartonero from Buenos Aires[1]

The question of how to speak of God in Ayacucho is related to Ayacucho as a symbol because etymologically, Ayacucho means "the corner of the dead."[2] This reminds us what has happened in Ayacucho, that is, the amount of suffering and pain experienced by people there. I believe that "how to speak of God in Ayacucho" is the most serious question that one can ask, and I am convinced that it is such a broad, big question that it is not always possible for us to provide a reply to it.

> —Gustavo Gutiérrez speaking in a radio interview, May 11, 2003[3]

Plateaus of Theology and Dispossession: What Is a House?

A small group of poor people talk about what they have found during the week in the bins in the streets of Buenos Aires. After a week of opening refuse bags, they have collected a group of things they would like to sell. The collection is an eclectic mixture of broken house adornments, discarded stamp books, and plastic jewelry. Among these, José has found a plastic bag with holiday photographs and a framed postcard of the cathedral from Itatí (located in northern Argentina) with the Virgin Mary. He describes the postcard as "a house beside the little virgin" (literally, "virgencita"), and

---

1. Online: http://liquidación.org/objetos/48.html, p. 1. *Cartonero* (literally, card collectors) is the name given to scavengers in Argentina. It is thought that more than one hundred thousand *cartoneros* travel every day to the capital city of Buenos Aires from the suburban areas to collect refuse that they can sell or eat. The Liquidación.org site also has the recorded voices of *cartoneros* who are telling their own stories.

2. Ayacucho is a very poor, largely indigenous city in Peru where, between 1980 and 1993, approximately thirty thousand people were killed and six hundred thousand made internal refugees in the war between the Shining Path guerrillas and government forces.

3. The interview with Father Gutiérrez is available online from Centro Bartolomé de la Casas, Perú. See *En sintonía con el P. Gutiérrez en vivo y en directo*. Online: http://www.bcasas.org.pe/GG.doc.

later on he will offer it for sale as "a saint and a church, for twenty dollars." José has not originally identified the cathedral as such but calls it "a house."

The same confusion about what is a "house" and what is not occurs when someone else comments on the bag of holiday photos that were found. A voice from the group describes them: "These are photographs from a holiday. . . . It is a house here. It is [a house in] a city, Mar del Plata [a beach resort near Argentina] . . . it is a house; this is a holiday at the beach with mountains."[4]

Mar del Plata is a holiday resort that does not have mountains, but the one who comments has never been there. Neither in all probability do any of the scavengers have any knowledge of a house, which could allow them to distinguish between a house and a cathedral, or between a house and a beach changing room in a holiday photograph. But what is a house for the homeless nomads of the city? What is a house in Ayacucho? The issue is important because much of theology depends on the answers to the question: What is a house, or a city, in theology?

I have taken the position of the scavengers as a starting point for considering some issues pertaining to the work of the theologians of radical orthodoxy from a material perspective. The Deleuze and Guattari concept of plateaus allows us to produce simultaneous epistemological exchanges among different theological living experiential sites or "organisms," as Deleuze would call them. Its aim is to produce an epistemology closely related to a *voicinage*[5] or a neighborhood of experiences and conflictive thinking that could enrich our reflections, not just by associations but by conceptual transgressions. Therefore to choose the plateaus of housing and scavenging becomes particularly important in relation to an English aesthetic theology such as radical orthodoxy.[6]

Radical orthodoxy represents a theology concerned with liturgy, truth, and beauty, in confrontation with what its proponents perceive as the presence of false "secular theologies" (basically, liberation theology from Latin America) that they see to be at the root of the decline of Christianity in the West. The question from our chosen plateau that starts this discussion is concerned with issues pertaining to the choice of theological subjects, themes, and class expectations in theological aesthetic inquiries. In other words, what would happen if radical orthodox theologians found scavengers searching in Cambridge refuse bags? What would happen if they went to Ayacucho?

What we have been contemplating here are scenes from postmodern life in Buenos Aires under the globalization processes that make the poor poorer and excluded from society. José happens to be a *cartonero* (a scavenger) who, together with a group, has decided to mount an exhibition of his collected objects, offering them for sale on the internet. So José has offered the framed postcard of the Virgin of Itatí for sale for twenty dollars on a website called Liquidación.Org (literally, Sale.Org)[7] in what is effectively a sudden and significant irruption of the poor in art and in the religious aesthetic

---

4. See "400 fotos de vacaciones $50." Online: http://www.liquidación.org/objetos/50.

5. Gilles Deleuze and Félix Guattari, *What Is Philosophy?* (New York: Verso, 1991), 21.

6. For an introduction to radical orthodoxy see, for instance, John Milbank, *Theology and Social Theory: Beyond Secular Reason* (Oxford: Blackwell, 1990).

7. The site Liquidacion.org has been produced by a Dutch artist (Matthijs de Bruijne), who, moved by compassion, joined the *cartoneros* to know them by working as one of them. Online: http:www.liquidación.org/información.html.

discourses on the streets of Buenos Aires. It is as if a chaotic aesthetics of the excluded has emerged in the market place as globalization processes advance.

Liquidación.Org is then a place of multiple signifiers. It is an art exhibition to be consumed by the public and at the same time the aesthetic product of a group of scavengers from Buenos Aires. Moreover, it is also a site of religious signification, as the sacred appears as a permanent horizon in the life and suffering of the poor in Latin America. It re-presents to us Ayacucho as a city of the Other God, where other kinds of *religare* experiences may occur in a community of scavengers recreating a different, strange, marginal Eucharist. That is, we are in the presence of an aesthetic theology gathered around the communion table of the excluded. Here we have the excluded from globalization processes gathered around a postcard from the cathedral of the Virgin of Itatí, which needs to be sold in order that more than one hunger can be satisfied.

Without real bread to be found in the bins there is no transubstantiation. God's eucharistic presence strangely depends on what can be found and sold in the streets, or even on the possibility of finding some stale bread in a bin. This is the Eucharist of the outcaste, where God sits as a scavenger among scavengers to share the grace of solidarity and some hope in the midst of much distress. And so it happens that this aesthetic theology from the excluded can inform us of a Eucharist in which Christ's transubstantiation depends on a discarded piece of rotten bread.

A theology from a plateau of dispossession takes us toward Christologies from Ayacucho and to Eucharists of homelessness aesthetics. The question, "What is a house?" leads us to enquire also about the house of God. What we are confronting here is a theology without housing. Houses and the "City of God" are theological issues not just untranslatable, but, more than that, diglottic for the destitute multitude of Christian people in the world. For any theologian who wants to consider a theology of the metaphorical two cities, she will need to reflect firstly on what is a house and even what is an *oikumene* (common house) for the millions of scavengers and children sleeping in the streets in Latin America.[8]

It so happens that from the issue of housing we have already started considering issues of class in aesthetic theologies. For that it is not necessary to discuss Marx, but simply to look around to find that there is no religious neutrality in aesthetic discourses of class, gender, sexuality, or racial assumptions. Therefore, if the scavengers from Buenos Aires can irrupt into the aesthetic canon of public exhibitions, selling a saint and a church for twenty dollars, could they also be taken seriously enough to irrupt into the canon of contemporary aesthetic Western theologies, such as radical orthodoxy?

Aristocratic Plateaus

Radical orthodoxy as a theological reflection has aims that are sometimes quite modest, if somehow aristocratic, in the sense of selective. At times radical orthodoxy seems to aim to return to the pre–Vatican II exclusive Latin mass and to the liturgical world so dear to some class-orientated Anglo-Saxon traditions. At other times its aims seem to be more contradictory. For instance, there is a call in radical orthodoxy to rethink

---

8. The only country in Latin American where there are not children sleeping in the streets is Cuba.

classical doctrines such as the Trinity, the incarnation, and the Eucharist by relating them to themes of forgiveness and social justice, while claiming a patristic aesthetics of goodness that only seems to produce metaphysical and not concrete (judicial) effects. Such is for instance Milbank's "socialism by grace" project, which advocates a transformation of capitalism from within, that is by the heart of the people and not by structural changes.[9] That is part of a very hierarchical cosmovision, where people at the top levels (the theological aristocracy) would like to have absolute control of Christianity as a dogmatic construction. This is not far from magical consciousness.

The reasoning behind this is that if Christian leaders are bad, everything tends to be very bad, but if they become good, everything may become very good. In any case radical orthodoxy's theological position derives from a chapter in pre-postcolonial mission studies. It aims to transform the heart of the natives while failing to exercise any hermeneutic of suspicion on the conditions of production (including intellectual production) that have been created around them. The conversion of hearts' theology is, of course, not a novelty, although biblically unsustainable. The prophets of the Hebrew Bible have clearly come to terms with structural sin, and one does not expect the Messiah to ignore the question of why it is that the scavengers of Buenos Aires suffer. They suffer, not because of the disposition of their hearts, but as a result of centuries of domination by a church that was unjustifiably rich and powerful, in alliance with imperial powers and colonial exploitation.

The disruption of these structures of sin in theology must be linked, as with many other things in Christianity, to the location of the theological subjects in terms of power and the urgency or desirability for supporting actions of social transformation. In a final analysis, what is at the core of this discussion is the repositioning of perspective taken from intransitive consciousness in theology, characterized by a general lack of ideological suspicion. Radical orthodoxy speaks from a plateau of privilege and lack of commitment to compassion and social justice.

We therefore return to the "saint and a church for twenty dollars"; in other words, to the communion that only can happen if some stale bread can be recovered from the bins. Here we have suspected that aesthetic theologies are by definition bourgeoisie theologies. Thus theologies from the underside of history carry disauthorized aesthetic claims, arising from the fact that the aesthetics of the dispossessed constitute also a social denunciation. Such theologies consider not only what happens to the consumers of theology but also those who are the producers of religious meaning. Or are liturgical acts independent of mundane things belonging to the sphere of production, such as a house, or the searching for stale bread in the bins? Radical orthodoxy misses these plateaus and these *voicinages* of exclusion because it is a class-constructed aesthetic theology. When it fails to take into account the epistemological plateau of the excluded (not only by class, but also by gender or sexuality, or even ethnicity) it is no wonder that its socialist projects cannot be conceived beyond discursive plots.

Radical orthodoxy still maintains a certain primitivization of the underprivileged,[10] which rejects thirty years of Base Christian Communities in Brazil, or the recent cooperative movements in Argentina, while searching for a relevant socialist

---

9. John Milbank, "Socialism of the Gift, Socialism by Grace," *New Black Friars* 77, no. 9 (1996): 545.

10. R. Chow, "Film as Ethnography; or, Translation between Cultures in the Postcolonial World," in *Literary Theory: A Reader and Guide* (ed. Julian Wolfreys; Edinburgh: Edinburgh University Press, 1999), 515.

model in the monasteries of medieval Europe.[11] But radical orthodoxy knows little of liberation theology. There is no sustained discussion in depth of liberation theology in its own proper context. Most of the criticism of liberation theology has been concocted by alienating liberation theology into a premodern, Western, medieval context, which produces serious omissions and inaccuracies. Anybody who takes liberation theology out of Ayacucho and pretends to argue against Gutiérrez from Spinoza or Machiavelli shows bad faith and lack of proper understanding.[12]

The point is that radical orthodoxy takes its archival theological options from what Segundo has called "the preservation of the monuments from the past" by avoiding the contemporary subject that emerges from the plateaus of exclusion. With all its faults this is not true of liberationist theology. Even when radical orthodoxy perceives that this archival theological option is necessary in order to avoid falling into what it calls "secular theologies," there is no justification for ignoring theological praxis outside a very limited understanding of how the concept of secularism should be understood. The problem is that radical orthodoxy fears for God, while liberation theology fears for the people of God in Ayacucho. The *voicinage* of these two theologies could not be more contrasting. The point is that for liberation theology, the *voicinage* of Christ is made up of many plateaus of failure and destitution. The real scandal of the cross is the magnitude of the failure of God in Jesus to intervene in the history of Israel's liberation. That proves that even gods need to address structural problems when dealing with imperial politics. Liberation theology takes account of the fragility of God in history, while radical orthodoxy seems to have a God-ideal, outside failures and plateaus of destitution.

Aesthetic Theology: Introducing Other Liturgical Plateaus

In reality, it is not that liberationists have difficulties with aesthetic theologies. I myself have been deeply moved by liturgical acts such as church demonstrations for human rights in my home country of Argentina. I still have a photograph taken at one of these demonstrations of a group of church leaders walking arm in arm toward a row of tanks in a street of Buenos Aires. They were the Methodist theologian José Míguez Bonino, Monsignor Nevares, the founder of an ecumenical human rights organization, and Bishop Federico Pagura, the founder of the first Protestant Base Communities in Central America. Behind them and in contrast are the faces of some young seminarians marked by fear. There is no such as thing as divine neutrality in aesthetics. Those leaders in clear defiance of the tanks provide us still with a sense of a fragile liturgical space, deeply moving and transcendental. It is a sacrificial and celebratory point of encounter between God and God's people.

What aesthetic should we use for the transcendental beauty in which God manifests Godself in solidarity with the marginalized? How often have aesthetics and ideology

---

11. For this point see John Milbank, "On Complex Space," in *The World Made Strange: Theology, Language, Culture* (Oxford: Basil Blackwell, 1977), 268–92.

12. Faithful to his colonial theological thinking, Milbank states that Gutierrez is Spinozist and Clodovis Boff, Machiavellian. Segundo's hermeneutical circle also comes from Spinoza according to Milbank. The Latin American thinkers cannot have originality because the natives can only repeat (and repeat badly according to Milbank) what their masters already thought. For this point see, for instance, Milbank, *Theology and Social Theory*, 242–43.

historically merged in alliances of power and control? The first plateau for a cross reading of a theology concerned with God's people is that of class analysis into notions of beauty and transcendence. The other plateaus are also contextual. For instance, "housing." The issue concerning homelessness with which we began has been developed by Pedro Trigo[13] from Caracas as part of a theological inquiry into the "obsessions" of the excluded. Thus Trigo asks: How does the obsessive behavior of the excluded contribute to an aesthetic theology? How can the ritualized acts from the lives of scavengers in their quasi-liturgical sense of loss give meaning to the mass?

The difficulty is not that liberation theology starts with the "secular" instead of with "God," as radical orthodoxy claims. The matter is more complex than that. The problem we need to confront is that neither theology nor God has an independent, stable identity. Theology always needs a second term in opposition to redefine itself. It needs its own stabilizing discourses, such as postmodernism, liberation, or neo-Platonism. However, the main stabilizer of a theological discourse is usually provided by the choice of its theological subject. The theological subject of radical orthodoxy is indifferent not just to the world's excluded masses, but to a British underclass whose "secularity" needs to be disputed. In Scotland, my adopted country, the experience of secularization among the poor is different from any other sector of society and tends to be pervaded with struggles around areas of spirituality.

In Latin America this is even more noticeable. There the poor are in general Christian people, living in societies that are not secular because they are legally dominated by a sometime pre-conciliar Catholicism ruling many aspects of their everyday lives. In some countries, even the names given to a newly born child must come from the Roman Catholic calendar of saints. People have been denied burial if they were not baptized in the Roman Catholic Church. And this is the paradox: if the excluded theological subject is still a religious one, in Latin America or somehow also in Scotland there is therefore no such thing as a homogenous secularism.[14]

Liberation theology cannot be criticized as a form of secular theology because the concept does not apply. In any case, the problem with historical liberation theology[15] is not, as radical orthodoxy suggests, that it is a theology that has lost the plot to secularism. Ironically liberation theology and radical orthodoxy both suffer from the same problem: both discourses lack a historical postcolonial consciousness, which should be manifested hermeneutically in interrogations on theological identity, structure, and language. Obviously there is a considerable degree of difference. Radical orthodoxy is a deeply colonial theology. It aims to represent the voice of the masters, restoring theology to its "queenly" (monarchic) role of sacralizing medieval European perspectives on culture, politics, even biology. That may be one of the reasons why radical orthodoxy is the only contemporary theology (apart from the preaching of Billy Graham) where God is still "he." There is no sense of exteriority in radical orthodoxy.

---

13. See, for instance, Pedro Trigo "La cultura en los arrios: Fundamentos," in *Irrupción del Pobre y Quehacer Filosófico* (ed. Juan Carlos Scannone and Marcelo Perine; Buenos Aires: Bonum, 1993).

14. The word "secularism" has no equivalent in a Latin American context. I personally have experienced difficulties using the term with Brazilian and even with Spanish theologians. Latin American societies cannot be considered secular, at least not in the sense used by radical orthodoxy.

15. By "historical" I refer to the liberation theology of the 1970s, but the term is sometimes used dogmatically without acknowledging current reflections pertaining to our present reality.

On Archives

The problem with colonial theologies such as radical orthodoxy is one of archival formation and legitimization of discourses. There is, of course, a lack of self-interrogation. Radical orthodoxy's aestheticism is made from a class option, but this needs to be understood in the pre-Freirean context of this theology. For a post-Freirean theology of dialogue, self-interrogation is the presupposition allowing us to find beauty and goodness among the destitute. Doctrines have to be rethought from sensuality outside class, sex, and cultural patterns. A self-interrogation hermeneutics makes theologies realize that theological genres carry in them identity struggles and, therefore, possibilities. That may constitute a first radical theological act, in the sense of going to some Christian "roots," as if it is from the realization of an unstable God unable to contain Godself, a messianic project out of which Christ needs to overflow. We could then say that the incarnation is a first rebellion that deprives theology of a sense of fixed identity in the past, as a contained divinity in Jesus. It may be this that makes theologies so restless. Far from a legitimate God or an originally contained God, Christ is an unstable, overflowing God and as such an outlawing of God occurs. In this outlawing, justice remains, but the law is deconstructed. Theology is a disputable law centered on a discourse of justice.

This restlessness in theology is both the source of a poiesis and subversion. That is to say, there is something in theology that tends to overthrow its own power settings. The main subversive forces that can be found in any theology, none of which are related to the actual content of theology, are those found in the particular dynamics of theological discourses. One of these disruptive forces lies in what we could call the archival movement of theology, which manifests the need that the theological genre has to organize and display its own genesis of authority. For every theology builds and displays its own archive of traditions and relevant sources.

The other disruptive force is of a different nature. I should call it the theological shadow or the supplement of discontent, which announces that somehow the coherence of a theological discourse cannot be seen as containable anymore. This "evangelical movement" is part of a theology's own messianism. Any theology (liberation theology or radical orthodoxy) must transgress its own boundaries and outlaw itself. This is the messianic movement from law to justice, which does not allow theological identities to settle.

The archival movement of theology is a dialectical one. However, a permanent legal movement tends to institutionalize theology. For that, the normalizing function of archives is important to return to the legal (or legalized) deposits of the past (traditions, scriptural texts). It is as if theology is permanently marred by a need for archives of origin. The archive functions as the ruling house, the site of the law or as I should say as an *oikumene* not of differences but more of Christian normalization processes.

The relationship of churches to archives is complex. Mechanisms of archive formation are heuristic procedures in themselves and should be reflected upon not only from the perspective of patterns of consumption but also from an analysis of production. Archives are more than inventions; they are dynamic sources of exploitation and silencing, of authority and the dismissal of ideas. They are also sites of nonrecognized, alienated knowledge as well as of knowledge illegitimately appropriated for different interests. Theological archival formation deserves attention, as it represents a theological, legal planning that is not immune to disarticulation. Behind every archive, behind, for instance, every patristic record or Latin mass response, there is an unrecorded story of illegal assemblies and counter-archival liturgies. The key to their disarticulation is to find what has disappeared from the files, which usually comes back in the discourse as a supplement to haunt and to judge a particular theology.

The question of the supplement (or shadows) in theology is related to how ideological formations in theology self-deconstruct. Every theology carries the seeds of its own outlawing linked to what I have called that first outlawing of "The Law of the Father"[16] in God who cannot contain Jesus. The supplemental shadows are linked with an unwanted dependency, a secret craving that theologies develop and without which they cannot gain access to coherence.

Which is then the counter-archive that haunts radical orthodoxy with threats of self-destruction? The counter-archive that haunts radical orthodoxy is constituted by the archives of liberation theologies in general (including feminist and black theologies) and of Latin American liberation theology in particular. However, it is the liberation theology archival production and not only its content that supplements radical orthodoxy as a permanent witness of the presence of a concrete Other that interrogates theology. The Other not only interrogates but also demands theological responsibility.

The illegal archives of theology are made of resurrections. The *testimonios* as narratives of contemporary martyrdom and Latin American popular religious culture resist obliteration and come to haunt and interrogate an aristocratic theology such as radical orthodoxy. Moreover, there is a different theological subject that, apart from constituting an archive, has become a theological para-authority that transgresses theological colonial rules. This self-legitimated theological subject now interrogates the legal archive of theology with the memories of her subjugated knowledge. What is more, it reclaims the right to have a dialogue, to share and transmit a theological praxis. Liberation theology, at its best, is a "Creole socialism" formed out of the traditional Latin American ethos of ancient economies of reciprocity and communities of solidarity.

Radical orthodoxy's logic of archives is different. It is a secretive, difficult to transmit, and privileged theology without any sense of self-reflection on its own process of archival formation. It is tempting to say that in the late twentieth century there has never been such a strong class issue between two theologies. Although given that the liberationists have been in existence for more than thirty years and the radical orthodox are relatively recent, comparisons are somehow disproportionate. But in any case the dependence of radical orthodoxy on liberation theology is clear to see: its identity comes by the way of negating liberation theology. Radical orthodoxy even appropriates a vocabulary that is identified with contextual, grounded theologies. This colonial way of redefining what has been defined by the natives would not be so important in itself, except that it is significant that after the dismantling of many Base Christian Communities by the Vatican and the withdrawal by the hierarchy of previous support for many community (eucharistic) Christian projects, radical orthodoxy continues rhetorically that same path of church power and interests, so painfully opposite to people's interest.

---

16. The "Law of the Father" (or "Name of the Father," or Phallus) is a concept from Lacan, referring to the submission to language rules governing the symbolic order. Jacques Lacan, "Seminar VII: The Ethics of Psychoanalysis," in Marcelle Marini, *Jacques Lacan: The French Context* (New Brunswick: Rutgers, 1992): cf. 173. It should be pointed out that this is also the origin of theology and monotheistic Christianity.

I still remember when the pope came to Chile during Pinochet's regime and to Nicaragua during the Sandinista revolution. In both contexts the pope ignored the people's political plea for peace and justice. Moreover, on both occasions the pope expressed his liturgical outrage. In Nicaragua, he rebuked people for asking for prayers for peace in the midst of the Contra War during his open air mass. In Santiago de Chile, when members of the group of Mothers of the Disappeared gathered at a short distance from the public mass, asking the church to pray for their children, the pope was outraged that the mass had been violated by such a "secular" interference. He even became vocal about it. Seconds later tanks and paramilitary forces intervened, beating those women and men standing in protest. The mass continued, without protest or interference.

My impression is that the sympathies of the radical orthodox would have been with the pope except that they would have criticized him for not saying the mass in Latin and turning his back to the people (which was what he was symbolically doing anyway). Masses are aesthetic acts manifesting a transcendental relation, or the lack of it. So Milbank says: "I realise that some of my conclusions . . . coincide with those of reactionaries in the Vatican."[17]

Radicalism

This dependency on liberation theology in radical orthodoxy as the "beloved enemy" can be traced back to the use of the term "radical." This term can be used in different ways, but the fact is that in theology, radical is a term associated with the theologies of the times of the cold war. They were radical in relation to their situation and their perceived association with the political "left." In Latin America, every attempt to oppose dictatorial local regimes or IMF (International Monetary Fund) policies has been catalogued as part of a "leftist" or communist agenda (which is not necessarily the case). A simple translation of the Scriptures, such as the Latin American translation, was considered "Marxist" simply because it made the biblical text clear to common readers in the way that contemporary Latin Americans speak. Such "radicalism" was the cause of persecution, which demanded a courage to be that Tillich did not envision. "Radical Christians" was also a term of scorn. Dictatorial regimes spoke with derision about "messianic projects" (meaning left wing/utopian) concerned with equality and peace, while "radicals" were those considered marginal to society.

However, in radical orthodoxy, radical means something different. "Radical" is here related to a movement that goes to the "roots" of archival Western theology. But the reappropriation of the term is paradoxical with respect to the safety of the term. No one will be identified with the excluded of society by being called a "radical orthodox," nor will academics who are called "radicals" in this sense have anything to fear. It may be that radical orthodoxy needs to define itself from the shadows of liberation theology. But using a term so characteristic of liberation theology is also a colonial gesture of redefining and making innocuous the terms of protest from the natives.

It could be argued that the cost implied in being seen a "radical" in Latin America could also be paid in Britain, in this case as theology is increasingly threatened by capitalism and as theologians are defined by the market. But radical orthodoxy may be able

---

17. Milbank, *Theology and Social Theory*, 208.

one day to claim the dubious glory of having depoliticized the "radical" in at least British theology. Its achievement will have been to realign "radicalism," which pertains to theologies identified with popular social challenges in history, with theological ineffectualism.

However, there is also a surplus of meaning to consider in radical orthodoxy. This is produced by juxtaposing the term "orthodoxy" with "liberation." At least, from the perspective of the established liberation theology term, that surplus should be orthopraxis. However, there is no orthopraxis in radical orthodoxy. Paraphrasing Gutiérrez, there is no one stopping at Ayacucho, at the location of human suffering and destitution, to ask how we can find the beauty and glory of God in the corner of the dead. Radical orthodoxy does not travel well, except on ancient Greek and medieval European tours. But this theology is not even done on the outskirts of Greek poverty or among the excommunicated wandering medieval populations that produced the compassion and rage in Martin Luther. Radical orthodoxy *oikumene* is one of privileged (legally protected) thinking.

For Whom Do We Do theology?
"The Next Train Is Not for Passengers"

In a suburban train station in Buenos Aires, everyday at a certain time there is a public announcement saying: "The next passenger train is not for passengers." It may seem as if part of a postmodern fictional plot. For whom are the passenger trains if they are not for passengers? In reality they are for passengers, but of another class. The announcement refers to the Tren Blanco (white train) that the scavengers take to go to the city to do their humble work of refuse collection. The contrast between trains in this station is curious. While passenger trains may leave the station at certain times almost empty, the Tren Blanco is always overcrowded. It is also recognizable for its broken windows and the fact that it does not have seats. In the chaotic life of a deteriorating world economy, not all the trains are for passengers, neither are all theologies for people. In the West there has been a tradition that announced "The next theology is not for people." In fact, this could become a further linking plateau between scavengers and radical orthodoxy.

This final plateau makes a link with Latin American martyrdom. Why? Because liberation theology is centered in martyrdom, but radical orthodoxy criticizes this feature as if martyrdom produces a secular start for thinking theology, instead of a divine one. However, I am not talking here about martyrdom as in the assassination of distinguished church leaders, although sadly thousands of them have died in the past thirty years in Latin America. I am linking martyrdoms to José, selling his postcard of the cathedral. I am thinking about the non-passengers from the Tren Blanco who are also non-subjects of theology. José, as a symbolic Christian worshipper in Ayacucho, extends the concept of martyrdom to the innocent victims of the system that has assassinated their present and their futures.

The Dutch artist Matthijs de Brijne describes everyday martyrdom in the city: "The country [Argentina] was bankrupt; unemployment reached unprecedented levels and poverty was so visible that it could be seen everywhere, and all sectors of the population faced poverty. The subways were full of unemployed artists, deaf people, blind people and incapacitated ex-soldiers. I even saw a child, a girl, whose body was completely burned. They all tried to sell you something. 'Do not marginalize me' they said to the onlookers."[18]

How do we respond theologically to this martyrdom? Stephen Long, who in his book *Divine Economy* ridicules this reality, writes that the "martyrdom principle" of liberation theology is "conflicting with the principle of economic scarcity."[19] Long has an unusual level of insensitivity even by Western theological standards. He makes comments in his book about the assassination of Archbishop Romero that reduce the enormity of the crime by transposing it onto the usual rhetorical level of radical orthodoxy's disaffection for anything that is not metaphysical. Long becomes offensive when claiming that liberation theology has been "demolished."[20] This violent language reflects a passionate desire for the downfall of what liberation theology has been for those who know it: the defense of human rights, the defense of the poor, and the participation in social projects from the movements for the landless to the organizations for free education initiated by Freire.

Radical orthodox language seems only befitting the military dictatorships under which my generation suffered, regimes that burned Bibles together with books from Freire and Foucault in the streets of my country. Radical orthodox theologians are the only group I know who can mention contemporary terms associated with the holocaust of thousands in Latin America with a disrespect arising from a depolitization of the obvious. This is illustrated in the following examples.

1. *The disappeared:* This word (which still produces shivers in me, as does the Jewish Holocaust, except that I lived through this one) is a highly political concept associated with torture, concentration camps, and barbaric murdering of people, including newly born children. In Milbank it becomes a rhetorical argument concerning the need of death to sustain morality, as the uncertainty of a disappeared creates a discursive problem on death as a (nonbeing) state.[21]

2. *Fortune:* Milbank uses this concept in relation to the givenness of good looks and good breeding in the Greek *polis* in an argument about happiness and Christian moral luck. Christians, he claims, need the fortune to belong to their communities.[22] However, "fortune" is a class concept that he never analyzes. Fortune relates to wealth and the construction of social status and power in church and society.

3. *Martyrs* (for instance of Central America): Long speaks of the killing of Oscar Romero and the six Jesuits in San Salvador with a casual tone, as if it were a dispute about a film's script. He starts with an act of colonial Anglocentrism by mentioning first the death of Becket in England. After the death of Becket, came the death of Romero,[23] as if Romero's death were

---

18. M. De Bruijne, "Información," 1. Online: http://www.Liquidación.org.
19. Stephen Long, *Divine Economy: Theology and the Market* (London: Routledge, 2000), 92.
20. Ibid., 115.
21. John Milbank, "The Midwinter Sacrifice," in *The Blackwell Companion to Postmodern Theology* (ed. Graham Ward; Oxford: Blackwell, 2001), 114.
22. Ibid., 110.
23. Long, *Divine Economy*, 91.

a literary account written after the model of the killing of an English bishop in other times, contexts, and circumstances. How he can do this is difficult to say except in relation to radical orthodoxy's claims of universalization. Moreover, he thinks that Becket was the only priest in history killed celebrating worship.

Unfortunately there have been many humble priests without glory or rich cathedrals who have been murdered in the slums while saying mass. Long goes as far as to mention the "defenders of capitalism" as the killers of Romero, who were "protect[ing] their people from their own archbishop."[24] The struggle and commitment of an archbishop for his people, a commitment that led him to his early death, is an issue treated almost with mockery. Long quotes Jon Sobrino (whom the paramilitaries intended to kill along with the other Jesuits), who saw in Romero's death the presence of the crucified God among the crucified people of El Salvador. To this Long simply retorts that the economic principle of "scarcity, substitution and marginal utility" are the true foundations of economy and not the death of Romero.[25] And he continues by saying that as liberation theologians do not understand mathematics they therefore use martyrdom to justify their economic theology. How does one who witnessed the effect of the death of Romero throughout the continent reply to such ignorance and lack of sensitivity?

All in all, radical orthodoxy lacks respect for the martyrs and the marginalized of yesterday and today. This was something that liberation theology knew very well: not to make easy theology with issues pertaining to the life and death of millions of Christians. The martyrdom of Latin Americans is the historical product of more than five hundred years of alliances between church and power. But "the church" is made of people with names and faces, and alliances of power and privilege too. European theologians have a long history of responsibility in the power games that demand the dehumanization of people disguised as a desire to put dogmatics and of course "God" first. In all this, the Other has become a depoliticized, metaphysical Other. So, "the next theology is not for people." But for whom do we think we do theology? For God?

Those of us who believe in the presence of God in history and specifically in the events of liberation also believe that history usually judges theologies. The overspiritualizing of people's suffering and depoliticizing of people's contexts of suffering produce theologies of indifference. Radical orthodoxy is not one of them though. Radical orthodoxy has taken a clear option for a discourse of privilege and class. But exteriority is not something they should look for only in Latin America. Britain also has its Ayacuchos. The council states of Britain, the situation of its ethnic minorities, and the reality of unemployment and degradation among its homeless would be enough plateaus to start a theology of passion and compassion aimed at transforming their lives, rather than a theology intent on producing medieval discourses.

But God Godself came in Jesus to Ayacucho, and God has not yet departed from there. The plateaus of destitution in theology are not simply optional, nor are they given up to secular gods. Christianity is a religion built around a destitute God who came for destitute people. This is why I should like to send radical orthodoxy to Ayacucho.

---

24. Ibid.
25. Ibid., 92.

8. Radical Transcendence?

Divine and Human Otherness in Radical Orthodoxy and Liberation Theology

—*Mayra Rivera Rivera*

For decades, "divine transcendence" has acquired a reputation for promoting social indifference. Its common associations with otherworldliness, immateriality, impassivity, and separation have lead most progressive theologians either to avoid the notion almost altogether or to use it as a pejorative shorthand for a long list of attributes that reinforce the disparagement of nonhuman nature, women, and subaltern groups.[1] Yet radical orthodoxy claims precisely the opposite: that transcendence grounds a Christian ethics adequate to support progressive political projects.[2] However, radical orthodoxy also distances itself from other socially concerned theologies on this issue. Indeed, John Milbank has explicitly accused liberation (and feminist) theologians of compromising divine transcendence, if not of simply avowing a fake one. Transcendence has nonetheless played a crucial role in liberation theologies and is arguably inextricable from other central liberationist themes, such as the reign of God. How then might we interpret radical orthodoxy's challenges to liberation theologies' notion of transcendence?

I am interested in this debate because I too have been drawn to the notion of divine transcendence; as a theological idiom alluding to God's otherness, transcendence suggests itself as a unique theological site for pondering questions of otherness. Yet, like feminist theologians, I am also mindful of how transcendence has worked to legitimize androcentric and hierarchical mindsets by establishing a metaphysical dualism where transcendence/immateriality/progress/independence/Man/God are set over against immanence/materiality/stagnation/dependence/Woman/Nature.[3] Might it be possible to rediscover the idea of transcendence, of God's irreducible otherness, without reinscribing the cosmological dualisms that it commonly evokes?

In this essay, I want to explore the possibility of such theological rearticulation by examining the proposals of the radical orthodoxy theologians John Milbank and Catherine Pickstock, which will eventually lead us to its specific challenges to liberation

---

1. I am grateful to Angel Méndez for his insightful and challenging comments to this essay.

2. Kathryn Tanner has consistently made this claim as well, without identifying herself either with radical orthodoxy or liberation theologies. Cf. Kathryn Tanner, *The Politics of God: Christian Theologies and Social Justice* (Minneapolis: Fortress Press, 1992).

3. Cf. Rosemary Radford Ruether, *Sexism and God-Talk: Towards a Feminist Theology* (Boston: Beacon Press, 1983), 269.

theology as lacking an acceptable concept of transcendence. My reading of radical orthodoxy will pay special attention to the metaphysical structure implicit in these depictions of transcendence—that is, to the image of God, the created world, and of human beings that they espouse. Having discussed the meaning and metaphysical basis of Milbank's transcendence I will proceed to assess his contentions against liberation theology.[4] I will then consider the proposals and critiques of the liberation theologians Ignacio Ellacuría and Marcella Althaus-Reid, among others, with an aim of uncovering not only the subtle ways in which liberation theology may in fact collude with a dualistic construction of transcendence, but most importantly, the not yet fully realized promise within liberation theology of a concept of *transcendence-in* creation and history.

Transcendence in Radical Orthodoxy

The idea of divine transcendence is inextricable from radical orthodoxy's definition of its own theological identity, indeed, of the very "truth" of theology itself. In the introduction to *Radical Orthodoxy*, the editors state: "[Radical orthodoxy] does not, like liberal theology, transcendentalist theology and even certain styles of neo-orthodoxy, seek in the face of [the nihilistic drift of postmodernism] to shore up [modern] universal accounts of *immanent human value* (humanism) nor defenses of supposedly objective reason." It also differs from those theologies that "indulge . . . in the pretence of a baptism of nihilism in the name of misconstrued 'negative theology'"—radical orthodoxy's typical characterization of postmodern theology. Instead, they argue that radical orthodoxy seeks to respond to "the secular demise of truth" by seeking "to reconfigure theological truth." The latter may seem surprisingly "close to nihilism" because "it, also, refuses a reduction of the indeterminate." Yet that theological truth differs from nihilism in "its proposal of the rational possibility, and the faithfully perceived actuality, of an indeterminacy that is not impersonal chaos but *infinite interpersonal harmonious order* in which time participates."[5]

The *radical* of radical orthodoxy means: (1) "return[ing] to patristic and medieval roots," (2) deploying the recovered vision of patristic and medieval sources for a critique of modern society, (3) rethinking tradition, and (4) espousing that "only *transcendence*, which suspends [embodied life, self-expression, sexuality, aesthetic experience, human political community] in the sense of interrupting them, 'suspends' them also in the other sense of upholding their relative worth *over-against the void*."[6] This is a basic pattern in radical orthodoxy's transcendence/human structure, the intricacies of which we will analyze in the following sections. This *over-against* is determinant as much for radical orthodoxy as a theological enterprise as for the model of transcendence that radical orthodoxy (re)formulates. Right from this moment of self-definition, radical orthodoxy sets itself off against liberal theology,

---

4. Unfortunately, Milbank does not offer the textual basis for most of his contentions, frequently not even referring to any particular theologian or text, and thus he precludes the reader from engaging him at specific points. Furthermore, for many of his points he refers to Karl Rahner, or to "Rahner and his followers," arguing that it is from him that liberation theology gets its problematic version of integralism.

5. John Milbank, Catherine Pickstock, and Graham Ward, *Radical Orthodoxy* (London and New York: Routledge, 1999), 2, emphasis mine.

6. Ibid., 3, emphasis mine.

modernity, humanism, and secularism. It is a movement sustained and mirrored by a divine transcendence set off against *the void*. Between these two poles—divine transcendence and the void—dangles human value.

The Problem of the Demise of Transcendence

Radical orthodoxy understands itself as a response to the concrete realities of the contemporary ("postmodern") world. Its defense of transcendence is aimed at rescuing theology from the grasp of *secular* modernity while rejecting postmodern options. More specifically, radical orthodoxy is posed as providing an alternative for *immanentist* modernity and its postmodern exacerbation, which, those theologians argue, leads only to nihilism. These characterizations of the contemporary world are inscribed in a fall narrative—a fall from a past society structured on the basis of an external transcendent realm (the legacy of Western Platonic philosophy). The fall is claimed to occur in two clearly defined historical steps: modernity and postmodernity.[7] In premodernity, it is argued, "everything had its appointed and relative value in relation to a *distant, transcendent* source."[8] The premodern teleology and hierarchy were lost in modernity, when "the world was . . . accorded full reality, meaning and value in itself," resulting in the emergence of a "spatial plane of immanence" where "fixed natures, especially human natures" were distributed and ranked across a "fixed spatial grid."[9] The ordering of the world no longer referred to anything outside; this gave way to the birth of humanism and secularism, which Milbank associates, as we will see through this discussion, with "immanence." The transcendence that modernity lost is thus imagined as an external source of value associated with vertical dimensionality itself: *highness*. A loss of height, it is assumed, is a loss of transcendence. Yet modernity is still not the lowest level of the fall, as Milbank describes it. In modernity, "Height was lost, but there was still *depth*," he claims.[10]

To depict modern social ordering as heightless is a simplification that risks occluding important aspects of a cultural imaginary (and its hierarchies) that still informs our thought. As postcolonial thinkers have shown, what Milbank describes as a "fixed spatial grid," which entailed the ordering of human beings in discrete races distributed geographically, was never devoid of a vertical dimension. The categorization of human beings was simultaneously hierarchical and temporal—each geographical area/race imagined as a different stage in evolution. North was high and contemporary; South was low and primitive.[11] Indeed, the North/ South division looms large in the mental

---

7. One would need to analyze the consequences of this historical depiction, not only for its reliance on a logic of fall—the inverted mirror of the myth of progress—but for the failure to problematize a basic assumption of the myth of progress: the primacy of the West as the gauge of world history.

8. John Milbank, *Being Reconciled: Ontology and Pardon*, Radical Orthodoxy (ed. John Milbank, Catherine Pickstock, and Graham Ward; London and New York: Routledge, 2003), 194, emphasis mine.

9. Ibid., emphasis mine. Milbank is referring to Gilles Deleuze and Félix Guattari's notion of the "plane of immanence": an "unlimited One-All" that gathers all philosophical concepts. They contrast the philosophers' plane of immanence with the religious "transcendent order imposed from the outside by a great despot or by one god higher than the others" (Gilles Deleuze and Félix Guattari, *What Is Philosophy?*, European Perspectives [ed. Lawrence D. Kritzman; trans. Hugh Tomlinson and Graham Burchell; New York: Columbia University, 1994], 43).

10. Milbank, *Being Reconciled*, 194, emphasis mine.

11. See Anne McClintock, *Imperial Leather: Race, Gender, and Sexuality in the Colonial Contest* (London and New York: Routledge, 1995).

cartographies of postmodern subjects, immersed as we are in the force fields of a glob-alized capitalist economy where that division coincides with the division of labor.

The fall from modernity to postmodernity—implicitly a step toward total immanence—is a further loss of spatial dimensions. In postmodernity, Milbank argues, "shifting surface flux" replaces any fixed grid, and even "depth is lost as 'imma-nence' comes to be conceived in terms of time, not space."[12] Time erases space. This demise of transcendence thus gives way to the "dissolution of limits," Milbank's main contention against postmodern culture (194). For all its talk of difference, "In the post-modern times, there is no longer any easy distinction to be made between nature and culture, private interior and public exterior, hierarchical summit and material depth; nor between idea and thing, message and means, production and exchange, product and delivery, the State and the market, humans and animals, image and reality—nor beginning, middle and end" (187). As a consequence, Milbank protests, humans no longer perceive their development as limited by nature nor moving toward a teleologi-cal goal. The distinction between men and women is blurred, and thus heterosexual-ity is being replaced by relation of multiples in a matrix of homosexual sameness (207). Human intervention with nature—an invasion of nature by culture—has pro-duced undesirable effects, from AIDS to global warming. Home has been invaded by public media, while the public spheres have become meaningless. The obliteration of political boundaries has supported the economic devastation of globalization. The cultural presupposition that underlies all these blurrings of boundaries, Milbank argues, is *immanence*.

Participation: Between Creation and the God Beyond

This account of the problem of contemporary culture as a fall from a past, when social structures referred to external and hierarchical transcendence, governs Milbank's proposed solution. To overcome the modern (heightless) spatially fixed categorizations or the postmodern (depthless) dissolution of limits, radical orthodoxy seeks to reassert stability of essences, and thus of boundaries necessary for real differ-ences to exist, by turning to premodern thought. Milbank provocatively calls for a *reappropriation* of "*our* Western legacy" expressed in "the creeds of transcendence in Judaism, Christianity and Islam" (175, emphasis mine).

We have already seen that in Milbank's depiction of premodernity, transcendence was a source—distant and high—in reference to which "everything had its appointed and relative value" (194, emphasis mine). Transcendence is a universal, "not as some-thing clearly grasped, spatially fixed and operable, but rather something eternally pres-ent yet not fully accessible"—always being given and deferred (174). How then does Milbank describe the process through which this source becomes inscribed as stable human essences? How does its *height* "suspend" embodied life, self-expression, sexual-ity, aesthetic experience, human political community?

Milbank's system is based on the interplay between an eternal and universal divine reality and the (human) dynamisms described through the platonic notion of *partici-pation*. Participation establishes the relation and balance between stability and change,

---

12. Milbank, *Being Reconciled*, 194 (consecutive references to this work are cited parenthetically in the text). Similarly, Pickstock mourns Western thought's departure from its ancient Athens roots, which has lead to a new version of immanentism, "immanentist modernity," with similar social consequences.

eternity and transience, old and new meanings, particularity and universality (171). Flux and permanence sustain each other. Thus Milbank's analysis poses two opposing poles, the relation between which constitutes the fabric of created existence. The relation between these poles is imagined, however, not as mutual intertwining of two distinct realities, one human, the other divine; for the divine is not only spatially distant and high, but it is also eminently "real." In the midst of the continuous change of our existence, "Only if reality itself is regarded as 'given' *from some beyond* does it become possible to *trust*" the seamless continuity between the old and the new (171, emphasis mine). What is *reality itself*? What is *not* reality itself? What can be said of that which can only receive *reality* from beyond? Is it something, or nothing? Is it the void?

And what about the *beyond* from which reality is given? Where or what is it? Is it an otherworldly realm of unchanging immateriality—more Platonic than biblical—the assumptions of which feminist theologies have challenged for decades? Not necessarily so, I believe—but I do so against Milbank's own contentions. Milbank's allusions to a beyond that is nonetheless a "pre-condition of justice," an elsewhere that invades our passing reality, evokes crucial liberationist moves (177, emphasis mine). Images of an elsewhere that irrupts in our daily life—of something beyond our selves, whose coming we experience as the irruption of the alien, the Other—have helped liberation thinkers reclaim and reformulate transcendence as an ethical opening of the self to the other. Welcoming that which comes from *elsewhere*, from *beyond* the self, is indeed a precondition of justice, liberation theologians would say.[13] However, as we will see, Milbank wards off such liberation (as well as Levinasian) moves. Milbank's notion of transcendence as always in a dynamic relation to participation—as a "horizon of *unknown* variation"—evokes a sense of openness that represents a promising move against the absolutization of an existing (or previously existing) state of affairs.[14] But Milbank also insists on locating this beyond *outside* of the world. He describes it as "*other-worldly*" (177).

Transcendence for Milbank means not just divine excess: the source of novelty, meaning, and unity of the created world. It also evokes discontinuity: the spatial separation and independence of that which resides beyond all "ontological heights" (211). In its relation to the transcendent God, the world's future, he argues, does not arrive through time (history) only, as this would imply the possibility of an organic development toward it. "It arises also from another space, or from a space forever constituted by externalities . . ." (180). It is God's absolute independence that *guarantees* "that the future contingency is super-added to the present, and not emergent from it by mere instrumental causality—whose absolute sway would demand that everything was given from the very first instance of time" (180). Keeping open the possibility of the coming of an unpredictable future is crucial for any discourse attempting to avoid foreclosing the coming of the Other. However, Milbank presents us here with two and

---

13. The Latin American liberation philosopher Enrique Dussel has consistently developed Levinas's model of transcendence encounters in the face of the other to propose a model of transcendence that supports an ethics of liberation. For an early exposition of his project see Enrique Dussel and Daniel E. Guillot, *Liberación Latinoamericana y Emmanuel Levinas* (Buenos Aires: Editorial Bonum, 1975). See also Marcella Althaus-Reid, *Indecent Theology: Theological Perversions in Sex, Gender, and Politics* (New York: Routledge, 2000), for a discussion that queers the liberation discussions on otherness.
14. Milbank, *Being Reconciled*, 171, emphasis mine.

only two alternatives: either the future emerges from "*mere*" *causality*, totally given from the beginning, or it comes from an *absolute exteriority*. He chooses the latter.

What does this contraposition of mere causality to absolute exteriority tell us about Milbank's notion of cosmological participation in the divine? A cosmos minus the externally constituted future would be *mere causality*—driven by whatever was *given from the very first instance of time*. Tellingly, his example of this type of causality is "a flower issuing forth from a shoot."[15] Are we to suppose then that this flowering takes place independently from participation in the divine? Or instead, if he is assuming that the blooming flower *does* participate in the divine, is he implying that such participation is not enough, that it must be supplemented? That something else must be *externally super-added* to, is lacking in, a cosmos participating in the divine? Something that must be unilaterally given from above?

Milbank argues that transcendence establishes the continuity between the old and the new. He also claims that transcendence guarantees (from the *outside*) the outcome: "we can, one day, be liberated" (211). But how would external intervention maintain the continuity between the new and the old? How can one then prevent the externality of this transcendence from overwhelming or rendering ultimately inconsequential the creatures' movement toward an ever deferred encounter with God and thus with their nature and essence? We are not told.

Let us try to resist the pull of that external space of ontological elevation and defer the talk of guaranteed futures to consider the complex space-time of a cosmos and the *indeterminacy* of its *infinite interpersonal* relations—the realm where social justice must be pursued. We are told that here in the cosmos access to the divine is "mediated throughout by an elusive participation." This vision of distributed rather than centralized power, which characterized Christian and Jewish descriptions of God until the end of the Middle Ages, represented a "revolt against *either* particularism *or* the cult of universalizable power" of its time (175). Through the concept of participation, Christians and Jews imagined a God who, being always beyond their grasp, was "only available as diversely mediated by local pathways" (174, emphasis mine). Through participation, humans relate to God, who is always beyond and always multiply, if elusively, present. "A recognition of transcendence," however, "requires not just the legitimizing . . . of infinitely many regional perspectives," each of them, "particular and ineffable," and thus, I presume, *uniquely* participating in the divine. It also requires an attempt at characterization, Milbank asserts.

How, then, does one judge between competing universals? Admitting the difficulty of this issue, Milbank proposes the following image: "A recognition of transcendence requires not just the legitimizing . . . of infinitely many regional perspectives, but also the constantly renewed attempt to characterize the one human 'region' in the cosmos, and to *erect*, as it were, the *universal totem*" (174). This totem is "tangible, and yet non-fetishistic," Milbank clarifies. That is, it is the product of the collective agreement, rather than the individual.[16] And yet, why is such a phallic image offered precisely at this point, where the discussion moves to the question of universals? Feminist theorists have shown the mutual implication between phallic images and Western culture's privilege

---

15. Milbank, *Being Reconciled*, 180.
16. I am grateful to Trish Sheffield for bringing Durkheim's distinction to my attention.

of sameness over difference, sight over sensation, man over woman.[17] Will Milbank's universal quietly drift toward a system based on masculine-defined parameters where woman is reduced to the one who lacks? We will return to this question in our discussion of the gender structure that Milbank explicitly delineates.

Milbank continues: "Catherine Pickstock . . . has provided us with an exemplary account of how one 'universal totem' . . . supremely operates in a fashion that is at once entirely tangible, and yet non-fetishistic and non-socially divisive"—"namely, the Catholic eucharist."[18] In Pickstock's rendering, the rite enacts the ceaseless reconstitution of a community "entirely from without," not mediated by human hierarchy. This kind of "collective and supra-rational devotion" is for Milbank a "pre-condition for collective solidarity and just redistribution," for which he argues (176f.). That is, this eucharistic totem is the kind of relation to transcendence that he would *erect*. Let us then turn to Pickstock's description of the eucharistic rite.

God in Language

In Pickstock's analysis, the relation between the linguistic sign and the referent in liturgy mirrors the relation between humans and the "transcendent" God. The worshipers, like the signs, stand in relation to something that transcends them. The Roman eucharistic rite, she proposes, enacts this asymmetrical relation between the worshipers and the "transcendent" God. Like Milbank, Pickstock associates transcendence with spatial distance and height; "the altar of God is an infinitely receding place, always *vertically beyond*."[19] However, her account of the rite gives special attention to the temporal element implicit in the notion of transcendence—that is, transcendence refers not only to those characteristics of God that place "him" at a distance, but also to the constant deferral of fulfillment. The I-Thou relationship established through the use of apostrophic language—the words addressed to an absent God as if God were present—is not completed "with the first utterance of an invocation, since the divine 'Thou' is not an object which our voice can stop at or appropriate. Rather, our utterance must give rise to further speaking" (197). Liturgical language must thus be ceaselessly repeated, striving for that which will always exceed it. The continuous repetitions and recommencements in the liturgy perform the deferral of the completion of liturgy until the eschatological time. Although Pickstock's emphasis here falls not on an insurmountable difference between God and the finite, but on the inexhaustibility of the divine, her interpretation of transcendence is intrinsically linked to the spatial distance. The "apophatic reserve" of language "betokens our constitutive, positive, and analogical distance from God" (173).

The incessant movements toward an ever receding transcendence are complemented by what can be described as movements in the opposite direction: from the referent toward the sign, from God to creature. Through what she calls "ontology of the gift," Pickstock claims to offer a model for the *reciprocal* exchange between God and

---

17. Luce Irigaray, *This Sex Which Is Not One* (trans. Catherine Porter and Carolyn Burke; Ithaca, N.Y.: Cornell University Press, 1977), 74.

18. Milbank, *Being Reconciled*, 176, emphasis mine.

19. Catherine Pickstock, *After Writing: On the Liturgical Consummation of Philosophy*, in *Challenges in Contemporary Theology* (ed. Gareth Jones and Lewis Ayres; Oxford and Madel, Mass.: Blackwell Publishers, 1998), 183, emphasis mine. Consecutive references to this work are cited parenthetically in the text.

creature, in contraposition to the unilateral flow that characterizes postmodern thinkers' depictions of "the gift." The possibility of the encounter between the transcendent God and the community is founded on a strong, even *essential*, link between the sign and the referent, exemplified in her descriptions of liturgical language and the Eucharist's bread and wine. The names Father, Son, and Holy Spirit "are really one name," she asserts (182). "This name is ... not a static name affixed outside being, but is an *essential name commensurate with the existential space of the Trinitarian journey*" (182, emphasis mine). Similarly, the "Amen" pronounced in the liturgy "is the *language in common between God and worshipper,* for it is at once the incarnational bodying forth of God and the true human response to God" (182). Pickstock argues that, by invoking the transcendent, apostrophic language establishes a "supreme dialogic relationship" between the celebrant and God, one that "shatters the protocols of all other relationships by taking place between the visible and invisible, the present and the absent" (197). Indeed she proposes an interpretation of the sign where they may be seen as "*leaping over the stage of indication or reference*" (262, emphasis mine). Given that languages are systems of relation between signs, this leap requires the liberation of the signs, as it were, so that their "character as *bounded things* become dislodged" (259, emphasis mine). Language is thus claimed not only to be more than it seems but also to exceed the limits of human relations and communication. While Pickstock's allusions to constant deferral, incompletion, and apophatic reserve emphasize the beyondness of a transcendent God, her descriptions of liturgical language move in the opposite direction by claiming instead the power of liturgical language to overcome its own limits.

In Pickstock's account of the encounter between God and creature, God's transcendence is desired, encountered, felt, enjoyed. In this reciprocal exchange, the simple chronology of call and response, gift and reception is destabilized. "The utterance of the apostrophe is, *by definition,* contemporaneous with God's entry, not simply as a subsequent response, but as that which enables the worshipper to call out in the first place" (194, emphasis mine). Participation appears as an endless and unrestrained flow where "it is impossible to desire God emptily, without that desire provoking and constituting its own *consummation*" (194, emphasis mine). That desire is never empty, never simply lack, but evidence of having had received, is perhaps an ancient insight, but one worth repeating to unsettle modern common sense.[20] But is *consummation* not the end of desire, grasping and thus completing the move toward the Other?

"At the same time," however, Pickstock asserts that the relationship established through the apostrophic utterance "reveals the *merely* (or empirically) '*present*' to be that which, without this relation with the apparent '*absent*,' constitutes the *ultimate absence*."[21] Surprisingly, creatures begin to lose "presence"—or their "solidity," as Milbank would say[22]—in comparison with the "transcendent subjectivity" of the God in which they are nonetheless "grounded," which makes them "more."[23] This relegation of humans to mere empirical presence might be hinted at in Milbank's references to

---

20. See Irigaray's discussion of this argument in Diotima's speech as recounted in Plato's *Symposium* (Luce Irigaray, *An Ethics of Sexual Difference* [Ithaca, N.Y.: Cornell University Press, 1993]).

21. Pickstock, *After Writing,* 197, emphasis mine.

22. Milbank, *Being Reconciled,* 210.

23. Pickstock, *After Writing,* 198. This might be a by-product of the Nicene definitions: "The father begets the Son out of his own essence, but makes the world out of nothing," in Virginia Burrus's succinct articulation. The world and its creatures fall on the side of (almost) nothing (Virginia Burrus, "The Sex

the reality itself as given from beyond, and in the statement that "only *transcendence*" "suspends" life "in the other sense of upholding their relative worth *over-against the void*," cited above.[24] Having examined the essential status that Pickstock grants to some signs only makes this assertion more startling.

Placing the constitutive source of subjectivity away from the self unto an *other*, radical orthodoxy refuses the idea of the priority and autonomy of the ego, which was central to modern constructions of subjectivity. However, this *other* at times seems to mirror the very model of modern subjectivity that arguably needs to be challenged. The transcendent other is described not only as eminent but also as absolutely autonomous. While compellingly warding off attempts to construe truth as an object to be apprehended and mastered, Pickstock's model still relies on a logic of mastery— in the opposite direction: from the divine other to the human subject. "Liturgical truth," she argues, is "a *prior seizure* of the subject by an overwhelming subjectivity."[25] To call out to God is to have already been, not merely called or touched, but *seized*.[26] I am encouraged by Pickstock's appeals to a reciprocal relation between the creator and creatures and by her questioning of the distinction between call and response. But can there be an authentic response when one is *seized* by an overwhelming subjectivity? Can a "reciprocal exchange which shatters all ordinary positions of agency and reception" take place in the context of a seizure, in the absence of real agency at both sides of the encounter?[27] In contrast with Pickstock's own promising proposals for a *reciprocal* relation, this portrayal of the encounter with God's overwhelming subjectivity hovers between two poles, as it were. On the one hand, the allusions to consummation, seizure, and commensurability evoke images of fusion, which is not reciprocity. On the other hand, we are offered a picture of humans as *mere presences* striving toward the "ultimate and elusive boundary . . . which surrounds *emptiness*."[28] This is a humanity that (being almost nothing?) strives for that union that will suffuse humanity with meaning and value. Neither one of these moments seems to keep the crucial balance between respecting the noninterchangeability of the subjects and the genuine but different contributions of each one.

In this model, we find a collection of selves (merely presences) turned toward the overwhelming subjectivity of a God that gives them whatever reality they have—from without. This relation reconstitutes the community "entirely from without," without the mediation of human hierarchy. Apart from the difficulties and dangers entailed in any claims to dislodge any human activity from its entanglement in its context, this scene of the human/divine encounter as a model for the constitution of a collectivity seems to occlude an essential element: other human beings.[29] Do human relations not

---

Life of God: Divine Begetting and Creativity in Ancient Christian Texts," paper presented at The Language of Body and Bodily Processes: Sensual and/or Metaphorical?, Oslo, Norway, 2004).

24. Milbank, Pickstock, and Ward, *Radical Orthodoxy*, 3, emphasis mine.

25. Pickstock, *After Writing*, 198, emphasis mine.

26. On the important distinction between grasp and touch, see Karmen MacKendrick, *Word Made Skin: Figuring Language at the Surface of Flesh* (New York: Fordham, 2004).

27. Pickstock, *After Writing*, 176.

28. Ibid., 198, emphasis mine.

29. Pickstock comments that "however much a particular finite relationship might seem to have the quality of destiny, it ultimately remains fortuitous and is at most transitory, since one I-Thou relationship can be followed by a second and a third, and in each case, the new 'Thou' will be endowed with a new and different name" (ibid., 197).

mediate the constitution of a collectivity? Do the selves in this scene ever look at or talk to each other? Do they give or receive from each other anything worthy of consideration for the constitution of the collectivity?

God's Transcendence and Human Otherness

Pickstock's account of the Eucharist evokes the image of a priestly God dispensing the elements to a congregation with no sense of each other. How then can it become a model for the universal that Milbank envisions as the "pre-condition of collective solidarity and just redistribution"?[30] What are the implications of this rite, which Milbank likens to a universal totem, for interhuman relations? What kind of collectivities does Milbank imagine it would foster?

In the Eucharist, Milbank observes, "symbolic power is not, primarily, mediated by a human hierarchy: on the contrary, it is in the first place mediated by the general ingestion of these symbols through time" (177). In Pickstock's view, the apophatic reserve of language, itself a sign of God's distance, leads to a constant deferral of the completion of liturgy. Thus, the "ruling principle" that this reading of liturgy evokes "is a deferral to a plenitudinous unknown Good which is always still awaited," Milbank explains; "liturgical rule is able to await on further capacities of the self as yet undisclosed or ungranted" (179). From this Milbank derives a principle for sociopolitical analysis: "Rule itself is (at least in principle) understood as the possibility of a self-critique through attention to what lies *beyond the self* (individual or collective)" and the "avoidance of absolutization of the self making this critique" (179). Observe that transcendence is here used to denote a *deferral of fulfillment*, the reality of something always beyond the self that prevents it from closing around itself. This openness to what lies *beyond* is sustained by what Milbank suggestively calls a "culturally imbued sense of transcendence" (180). Are other human beings about to appear on this scene? Although Milbank is quick to add the spatial otherworldly dimension of this *beyond*, in his chapter on culture he continues to develop the notion of transcendence as *deferral*. The deferral of God's presence implies a deferral of the fulfillment of human being's identity, which, as we saw, comes from God.

Thus Milbank proposes a reinterpretation of identity and difference, not as something given, a "natural law," but as something disclosed through time by repetition. It is in relation to this interpretation of the dynamics of identity formation that Milbank introduces the concept of "affinity." Affinity, as Milbank defines it, is "the arriving *gift* of something that we must partially discover in patient quest, active shaping and faithful pursuing" (204). The prime example of identity formed by *affinity* is Jesus. In agreement with Origen, Milbank explains that "Jesus was God because his affinity with God was so extreme as to constitute identity . . . not of substantial nature, but of character . . ." (203).[31] This bond of affinity—a "non-theorizable and almost ineffable

---

30. Milbank, *Being Reconciled*, 176f. Tellingly, Milbank's example of a collectivity constituted from without, as part of the body of Christ, is the "European collectivity"(ibid.).

31. Origen describes the incarnation as follows: "[The Son] granted invisibly to all rational creatures . . . a participation in himself. . . . each obtained a degree of participation proportionate to the loving affection with which he had clung to him. . . . [one soul] clinging to God from the beginning . . . in a union inseparable and indissoluble . . . was made with him in a pre-eminent degree one spirit. . . . This soul, then, acting as a medium between God and the flesh . . . there is born . . . the God-man, the medium being that existence to whose nature it was not contrary to assume a body" (*On First Principles* 2.6.3).

identity"[32]—is not exclusive to the God-Jesus relation. Jesus' community with his disciples is also established on the basis of affinity through their own repetition with difference of Jesus' character. And so also with subsequent Christian communities. Repetition continues—always with difference.

Milbank thus calls for a reinterpretation of identity, and thus of human nature and essence, not as givens but as "what may eventually be disclosed . . . with and through time" (201). In contrast to the modern notions of fixed and categorizable identities, Milbank proposes to think of identities as becoming. However, this openness toward transformation, expressed by the concept of affinity, is limited by his assertion of teleological ends. The two poles of this definition of identity mirror the two poles we have identified in Milbank's descriptions of transcendence: one emphasizes the inexhaustibility of the divine, while the other highlights its distance, autonomy, and power.

The tension between the two poles of identity becomes most visible in his treatment of gender difference. An idea of gender identity as disclosed through time rather than already given seems congruent with feminists' statements, from Simone de Beauvoir to Judith Butler, to the effect that "one is not born, but rather *becomes* a woman . . . *woman* itself is a term in process, a becoming."[33] But Milbank is not assenting to such "gender trouble." The becoming of identity is for him not open-ended, but guided toward a set teleological end. We may thus gain "true knowledge" about bodies only "when *we* share something of God's insight into how he wished them to be."[34] One can only hope not to be excluded from that "we"!

While Milbank begins by describing *affinity* as a "non-theorizable and almost ineffable identity," never fully present, he surprisingly proceeds to equate it to ontology (203). "Affinity or ontological kinship . . ." he says in passing, and moves on to describe sexual difference as "ontologically more *resistant* than people would suppose" (206, emphasis mine).[35] When the *ontological* nature of sexual difference is rejected, as was the case of Aristotle's philosophy, femininity is deemed a mere deficiency. Milbank's feminine-affirming gesture is nonetheless not followed by a welcome to the unpredictable challenges of women's views—that is, by openness to the other beyond masculinist discourse. Instead he attempts to categorize his sexual others. Despite disclaimers and even an encouraging nod to Luce Irigaray, the results are hardly *radical*: "men are more nomadic, direct, *abstractive* and forceful, women are more settled, subtle, particular and beautiful" (207). This restatement of "inherited generalizations" cannot but give a patronizing tone to the following: "both sexes are innovative, legislative, commanding and conservative *within* these different modes" (207, emphasis mine). Asserting the "equality of difference" supposedly implied in the gender depictions he has just offered, Milbank explains: "Without the feminine settled, male *abstraction* is not an abstraction but only another . . . settled view" (207). Indeed. But does this argument not pertain to the protection of a male ideal through the projection of its opposite onto woman? It is a male ideal imposed on women by men.[36] This

---

32. Milbank, *Being Reconciled*, 203.
33. Judith Butler, *Gender Trouble: Feminism and the Subversion of Identity* (New York and London: Routledge, 1999), 43.
34. Milbank, *Being Reconciled*, 210, emphasis mine.
35. Milbank claims that while race is a cultural construction, gender is not.
36. Luce Irigaray, "Each Transcendent to the Other," in *To Be Two*, trans. Monique M. Rhodes and Marco F. Cocito-Monoc (New York: Routledge, 2001).

mechanism has been deployed repeatedly to protect not only gender hierarchies but also racial and ethnic ones. To inscribe them in a narrative of divinely given identities occludes their historicity and, more dangerously, masks human hierarchies as divine telos. Rather than affirming a culturally imbued sense of transcendence, is this not a transcendentalizing of select cultural values?

Tellingly, we find the abstractive/settled dichotomy replayed in the very characterization of Christian identity. This time it is "Jewish specificity" that occupies the space of the settled to which "Christian *abstraction* is necessarily *betrothed*."[37] In another (related) statement of "inherited generalizations," Milbank characterizes Christianity as "the religion of the obliteration of boundaries," (196) and Judaism as "perhaps the very opposite" (197). Predictably, Christianity's *Other*, Judaism, occupies the space of the feminine, an association hardly upset by describing their relation as a betrothal—after all, for Milbank marriage is strictly heterosexual.

Milbank's invocation of Irigaray's thought in this discussion may at first glance seem appropriate. Irigaray, like Milbank, observes that our "masculine culture generally ignored the objectivity which exists in the pre-given: the body, bodies, the cosmic universe."[38] (The "culture" she refers to is a masculinist culture rather than postmodern culture.[39]) Irigaray further argues that ignoring the objectivity of the body has led to the loss of the transcendent potentials of the encounters across sexual *difference*. I would welcome a theological encounter between Irigaray's attention to transcendence as emerging across difference and Milbank's affinity as an ineffable bond between creatures as well as between creatures and God. But this betrothal seems, at this point, improbable. Whereas Milbank asserts the need to affirm a "supra-human power beyond" in order to provide society with a principle by which "it might be *measured* and *limited* . . . ,"[40] Irigaray, in contrast, sees the construction of a God as a transcendental subjectivity, not as a correction but as a symptom of the erasure of the objectivity of bodies, or, to use Pickstock's language, of their depiction as mere presences. The need to pose a supranatural limit to our subjectivity derives from the "erasure of the other as other," as a contiguous transcendent other always beyond the self.[41]

If male and Christian abstractions depend on a settled woman and Judaism, respectively, Milbank's depiction of transcendence seems to depend on a settled Other: *immanence*.[42] And vice versa. But the distance between the two poles of the transcendence/immanence dyad tends to infinity. Although the contraposition of transcendence to immanence is almost common sense in theology, it is important to notice its distinctive overtones for Milbank and Pickstock. Whereas many contemporary theologians attempt to hold together the "immanent" as much as the "transcendent" as aspects of God, evoking images of God's presence both *inside* and *outside* of creation, in radical orthodoxy writings we have considered, "immanent," "immanentist," or even "immanence" are frequently used to evoke the *rejection* or *absence* of God—that which denies

---

37. Milbank, *Being Reconciled*, 207.
38. Irigaray, "Each Transcendent to the Other," 90.
39. Irigaray also observes the anxiety that the givenness of the body and nature provokes in a capitalist society. Irigaray, *An Ethics of Sexual Difference*, 99.
40. Milbank, *Being Reconciled*, 5.
41. Irigaray, "Each Transcendent to the Other," 92.
42. Here I am referring to Milbank's sense of the term immanent, which I do not share.

the beyond. In general, one finds them associated with the terms secular, modern, *nihil*.[43] Indeed, Milbank is willing to attribute to "secular immanence" the horrors that contemporary criticism has credited to "totalitarianism."[44] "Secular immanence," Milbank writes, is "totalizing and terroristic because it acknowledges no supra-human power beyond itself by which it might be *measured* and *limited* . . ." (5).[45] This identification of immanence with godless totality is also apparent in Pickstock's *After Writing*. Platonic myths of transcendence, she argues, represent a radical challenge to "the immanentist city," "the beginnings of a technocratic, manipulative, dogmatically rationalist, anti-corporeal and homogenizing society undergirded by *secularity* and *pure immanence*."[46]

This setting off of a "purely immanent" realm is most evident in Milbank's engagement with other theologies. Milbank identifies two versions of "postmodern modes of religiosity." First, he identifies "new age religions," characterized by their assertion of "the sanctity of an empty mystical self able to transcend, identify with, and promote or else refuse the totality of process in the name of a truer 'life' which is invisible."[47] More relevant for my discussion is the second group, which he describes as the addition of a "Spinozistic twist" to "postmodern Marxist atheism," of which Deleuze, Negri, and Hart are given as examples. These he criticizes for seeing "*the plane of immanence* . . . as the sphere of active, productive forces, which manifest themselves in human terms as love and desire. . . ."[48] If posing a sphere of forces that manifest in human love, where "once oppression is surpassed, liberated nature-going-beyond-nature fully appears," is problematic for Milbank, it is because he assumes, or *implicitly* accepts, the assumption that such a plane of immanence is devoid of God (195).

Transcendence in Liberation Theology

The Debate with Radical Orthodoxy

A structurally similar critique is raised against Latin American liberation theology. In his essay "Founding the Supernatural: Political and Liberation Theology in the Context of Modern Catholic Thought," Milbank contends that liberation theology replaces transcendence with social processes.[49] He claims that the root of the problem is that liberation theology has "embraced" the "*immanent* principles of secularization and politics,"·as evidenced in its use of Marxism.[50] As a result of the alleged adoption

---

43. For example, "immanentist modernity," "spatialization [of modernity] constitutes a bizarre kind of immanentist ritual," and "the nihilism of immanent presence" (Pickstock, *After Writing*, 239, 198).

44. Milbank, *Being Reconciled*, 5.

45. For him, however, the term "secular immanence" might be tautology, as his definition of both "secular" and immanence emphasize their lack of reference to transcendence. Right after defining secular as, among other things, lacking reference to transcendence, he asserts that postmodernity is "not more open to religion than modernity," but indeed "more emphatically immanentist" (Milbank, *Being Reconciled*, 195).

46. Pickstock, *After Writing*, 48, emphasis mine.

47. Levinas would not equate visibility with graspability.

48. Milbank, *Being Reconciled*, 195.

49. John Milbank, "Founding the Supernatural: Political and Liberation Theology in the Context of Modern Catholic Thought," in *Theology and Social Theory: Beyond Secular Reason* (ed. John Milbank; Oxford and Cambridge, Mass.: Blackwell, 1993),

50. John Milbank, *Theology and Social Theory: Beyond Secular Reason* (Oxford and Cambridge, Mass.: Blackwell, 1993), 243, emphasis mine.

of immanent principles, liberation theology has posited an autonomous "profane sphere," which it has assumed can be understood outside of theology while, at the same time, claiming this space to be the site of God's grace. Milbank challenges the use of the social sciences to question theology; it is theology that should govern any description of and program for the transformation of society. Therefore, he asserts that liberation theology, guided as it has been by the social sciences, has mistaken "immanence" for transcendence. Liberation theology's praxis is, in his opinion, nothing but "political practice" "*outside* Christian tradition."[51] In the end, Milbank argues, "the social process is identified as the site of transcendence" (not a "culturally imbued sense of transcendence"?). Furthermore, "although the process is a purely human one, and although there are no human needs which cannot be immanently met, liberation can still be identified by theology as the anonymous site of all divine action."[52] A *purely* human process opposed to divine action? But who is assuming a *plane of pure immanence* here? Certainly not liberation theologians.

As a consequence, Milbank continues, liberation theology's concept of salvation has to do with an "empty, formless epistemological *transcendence*" while the social realm is "thought to possess its own *immanent* ethical principles."[53] Instead, Milbank argues, theology should be founded in its Christian "ethical distinctiveness."[54] A non-immanent Christianity? Indeed, the question of whether a particular theological assertion is conducive to social justice is somehow the wrong question for him in the context of this argument—for his starting point is the affirmation of the theological as the legitimate basis for judging the social.

Liberation theologies may be reluctant to subsume all ethics under the Christian understanding of the Christ event.[55] This circumspection, however, does not spring from an assumption of the autonomy of social ethics from the divine, as Milbank supposes. Instead, there is in liberation theologies a desire, indeed a commitment, to uphold all spheres of society—Christian or not—as potential sites of divine action. This is based, as we shall see, on a strong liberationist affirmation of all existence as *existence in God*. There is no region of "pure immanence," if that means the possibility of existing outside the divine. No *purely* human, if that means devoid of participation in the divine: "The very being of the human is constitutively a being in God."[56] As Michael Lee explains, for Latin American liberation theologian Ignacio Ellacuría, "Christian praxis, as the historicization of faith . . . which might employ social sciences

---

51. Ibid., 209, emphasis mine.

52. Ibid., 229. It is not clear whether the characterization of liberation as "purely human" or of the needs as "immanently met" are presented as Milbank's opinion or as his representation of liberation theology's stance. If the latter is assumed, one would have to contend that neither "purely human" (as opposed to divine) nor immanent (as opposed to transcendent) fit easily with the *historical* transcendence proposed by Ellacuría, Sobrino, or Dussel, for instance.

53. Ibid., 233, emphasis mine.

54. Ibid., 230. This ethical distinctiveness, however, is, he argues, "Platonic-Christian," as ethics begins with Plato and, in the end, all ethics is in some sense traceable to Judaism or Christianity (ibid.).

55. Milbank challenges liberation theology on a number of fronts, which, although not reducible to the question of divine transcendence, do seem to converge in a concern about its perceived failure to assert a theological foundation comprehensive enough to subordinate the social sciences.

56. Michael E. Lee, "Liberation Theology's Transcendent Moment: The Work of Xavier Zubiri and Ignacio Ellacuría as Noncontrastive Discourse," *Journal of Religion* 83, no. 2 (2003): 230.

in analysis of intramundane reality, still perceives reality's deeper theologal dimension, [its] rootedness in God."[57]

Paradoxically, Milbank's own contentions depend on an implicit—albeit explicitly denied—division between the profane and the sacred; that is, on the possibility of asserting the existence of "purely human" processes (devoid of transcendence), where human needs are met *immanently*. This is perhaps another side effect of the tendency to reduce humans to mere presences (almost nothing) over which future potentialities are externally super-added.[58] Is there still room for any significant (bodily) notion of participation where human needs are reduced to immanence—in Milbank's sense of the term? Conversely, Milbank seems also to assume the possibility of extracting the theological from all conscious or unconscious, past or present, sociopolitical assumptions and interests, in order to obtain Christian principles as the pure foundation for practices that would otherwise be purely human—*immanent*. This tendency to selectively "locate" certain things on either side of an assumed immanent/ transcendent line runs through Pickstock's and Milbank's works. We have seen, for instance, Pickstock's treatment of some liturgical language as essential and "commensurate with the existential space" of the Trinity, of some signs becoming dislodged of their "character as bounded things." The risk of the latter is to inadvertently cross the line between protecting God from appropriation and claiming a transcendent authority for one's own discourse.

The risk of appropriating divine transcendence to assert one's authority has been the main concern of liberation theologians, as Althaus-Reid summarizes: "Religion as the representation of an absolute essence is a Hegelian idea which has been disputed by the liberationist Marxist approach, through an understanding that the absolute essence is nothing more than a political ideology *homologizing itself with a God-like discourse* of sacred authority."[59] The challenge of the endowment of religious thought with divine authority is accompanied by a challenge of any notion of revelation that assumes it has *leaped over* the realm of human historical knowledge. Revelation, Althaus-Reid adds, "is not considered anymore as the almost mediumistic art of pulling down a Platonic idea of an abstract absolute idea of God." Instead, revelation is *enmeshed in* not only human language, but also in all aspects of human bodiliness. "In any case, revelation reveals (unveils, undresses) God in our historical circumstances, and assumes a materialist twist in our understanding."[60] "That is the point of doing theology from people's experiences, *and*"—adding her own zesty challenge to established liberation theology—"from their sexual stories, because they reveal the *falsity of the border limits* between the material and divine dimensions of our lives."[61] Rather than assuming it has leaped over boundaries, this theology questions them.

Thus, not only does liberation theology affirm the rootedness of all created reality in God (and thus would refuse to characterize humans as *merely* immanent), it also asserts the finitude of our own experiences of the divine. Like Milbank, liberation

---

57. Ibid., 241.

58. Milbank criticizes humanism because it "denies the inherent nothingness of things" (*Being Reconciled*, 179).

59. Althaus-Reid, *Indecent Theology*, 148.

60. Althaus-Reid, *Indecent Theology*, 148.

61. Ibid, emphasis mine.

theology attends both to the "infinitely many regional perspectives" and to the "constantly renewed attempts to characterize the one human 'region' in the cosmos." However, this would not lead liberation theologians to retrieve medieval Western universals, which after all supported the expulsion of the Moors, witch hunts, and other atrocities. Their view, indeed their experience, of history reveals complexities that challenge Milbank's appraisal of "universal values." Having been for centuries the receptors of externally imposed Western universals, having seen their own human value and needs subordinated to its principles, Latin Americans are keenly aware of the dangers involved in raising one set of values as predefined "universals."

Transcendence in History: Liberationist Voices

In his article "The Historicity of Christian Salvation," Ignacio Ellacuría explores the biblical basis and the theological importance of a liberationist interpretation of transcendence *in* history. Transcendence, he argues, "calls attention to a contextual structural difference without implying a duality;" it "enables us to speak of an intrinsic unity without implying a strict identity."[62] If for radical orthodoxy liturgical language (in its broadest sense) becomes a site of contact between a transcendent God and humanity, for liberation theology the point of connection is *history*. History is the "place of transcendence," where both God and human beings intervene.[63] Indeed, the unity of divine and human history "affirms the dual unity of God in humanity and humanity in God."[64] Ellacuría attributes to "pernicious philosophical influences" the fact that transcendence has been identified with *separateness*, which in turns leads to the assumption that "historical transcendence is separate from history."[65] In contrast, he argues that it is possible "to see transcendence as something that transcends in and not as something that transcends *away* from; as something that physically impels to more, but not by taking out of; as something that *pushes* forward, but at the same time *retains*."[66]

Ellacuría's incarnate notion of transcendence is coherent with his theological anthropology.[67] While radical orthodoxy's descriptions of creatures emphasize that their value derives from their dependence on their transcendent source, Ellacuría insists upon a certain innate worth, even divinity, in their finitude.[68] Rather than placing the value of human life outside of it, in something to which one may or may not relate or respond, Ellacuría places the value of human life *in* human life. Ellacuría asserts that God's creation is the "grafting *ad extra* of Trinitarian life itself," and thus "each thing, within its own limits, is a limited way of being God. This limited way is precisely the *nature* of each thing."[69] It is not "simply that God is in all things, as

---

62. Ignacio Ellacuría, "The Historicity of Christian Salvation, "in *Mysterium Liberationis: Fundamental Concepts of Liberation Theology* (ed. Ignacio Ellacuría and Jon Sobrino; Maryknoll, N.Y.: Orbis Books, 1993), 254.

63. Ibid., 259.

64. Ibid., 264.

65. Ibid., 254.

66. Ibid., 254, emphasis mine.

67. For a detailed analysis of the relation between Ellacuría and Zubiri, focusing on its impact on Ellacuría's notion of transcendence, see Lee, "Liberation Theology's Transcendent Moment."

68. This assumption of the intrinsic value of creation is shared by process theologies.

69. Ellacuría, "The Historicity of Christian Salvation, " 276, emphasis mine.

essence, presence, and potential," but that the Trinitarian life is "*intrinsic* to all things."[70] Thus, the human being is a "relative absolute," but one whose essence is also to lie open to the experience of the Trinitarian life—always dynamically open to God's "more."[71] This opening to God's "more" not only prevents each human person from closing around him- or herself, from absolutizing her or his own particularity, but also calls that person to turn toward creation and toward the human other. *Transcendence in* leads humans toward, not away from, creation.

This relation to transcendence requires a constant renewal of the received experience of God, a reception of "more than the God of the fathers" and the "historical repetition of what the scripture expresses as *theopraxy*."[72] Luis Segundo explains that the emphasis of revelation shall not be on the limited acquisition of knowledge about God but on the reception of a "difference that makes a difference."[73] Divine-human communication succeeds only inasmuch as the recipient succeeds in "transforming it into a humanizing difference within history."[74] According to Ellacuría, the historical repetition of theopraxy brings about a future that "invalidates negativity and recovers old experience in a new way."[75] The continuity between the old and the new is thus maintained through repetition with difference, through transformative practice, rather than through access to an external unchanging source. In history, "God and humanity collaborate," so that the future depends, although in a different way, on God's faithfulness and human response."[76] As discussed above, radical orthodoxy attributes similar functions to liturgical language. There are, however, significant differences. For instance, Ellacuría does not contrast transcendence with *immanence*. In fact, the term immanence does not play a significant role in Ellacuría's argument. The absence of this transcendence/immanence opposition results in an account of the Christ event quite different from that offered by radical orthodoxy theologians. For radical orthodoxy theologians "God's incarnational appearance is . . . a *condescension* to the conditions of finite, created perceivers,"[77] a downward movement from the heights of transcendence to the lowliness of creation. In contrast, Ellacuría interprets Jesus not as an instance of God's condescension toward *immanence*, but rather as "the supreme form of historical transcendence"—*transcendence-in*.[78] The theological potential of this notion of

---

70. Ibid., 277, emphasis mine.

71. Ibid. When the dynamic openness is limited there is a negation of Trinitarian life, there is sin.

72. Ibid., 259, 63, emphasis mine.

73. Juan Luis Segundo, "Revelation, Faith, Signs of the Times," in *Mysterium Liberationis: Fundamental Concepts of Liberation Theology* (ed. Ignacio Ellacuría and Jon Sobrino; New York: Oribs Books, 1993), 330.

74. Ibid., 332.

75. Ignacio Ellacuría, "The Historicity of Christian Salvation," 259.

76. Ibid.

77. James K. A. Smith, "Speech and Theology," in *Radical Orthodoxy* (ed. John Milbank, Catherine Pickstock, and Graham Ward; London and New York: Routledge, 2002), 126, emphasis mine. Marking his disagreement with Milbank's and Pickstock's readings of Plato, though not with their proposals, Smith argues that this condescension is not an *extension*, but an *inversion* of Platonic participation, as it implies not the finite participation in the infinite, but the infinite's participation in the finite.

78. Ellacuría, "The Historicity of Christian Salvation," 266. Ellacuría clarifies, however, that this does not imply the "subjection of profane history to the specificity of Christ as head of the church, and therefore to the church as continuation of the work of Christ," but to the "historical-cosmic Christ" (273).

transcendence-in—of a transcendence in creation and history, something that physically impels to more, but at the same time retains—is yet to be fully realized.

Despite the emphasis on the intrahistorical character of transcendence, Ellacuría's transcendence retains its independence from the created realm—a common feature of many (by no means all) Latin American liberation theologies. "In history," Ellacuría explains, "transcendence must be seen more in the relationship between necessity and freedom than between absence and presence. God is transcendent, among other reasons, not by being absent, but by being freely present. . . ."[79] In its freedom, transcendence retains its capacity to "break in the process," to cross a boundary, so that "something *more than history* becomes present in history."[80] Transcendence thus assures the possibility of unconditioned novelty. The depiction of a *transcendence-in* as that which retains as it impels forward—an image of development that evokes the cyclical rhythms of nature—is thus here overshadowed by the (more phallic) imagery of something "breaking in" from the "outside," in the present or at the end of history. These reassertions tend to reinscribe the idea of an external deity that liberation theologies have sought to challenge.

The idea of God who intervenes from outside the world becomes particularly problematic when theologians implicitly claim to have access, through God, to a criteria of judgment external to the realm of created existence—one of the most common traps into which theologies of transcendence have fallen. Feminist liberation theologians have been mindful of this risk and have tried to keep theology aware of its own limits. Arguing from within the force field of Latin American liberation movements, these feminist theologians do not follow Milbank's call to "replace theology mediated by social science" with "theology as 'metanarrative realism,'"[81] but quite to the contrary argue that liberation theology's questioning of the metanarratives—secular *and* Christian—has not gone far enough. These intimate *others* of liberation theology have urged liberation theologians to a "permanent exercise of serious doubting,"[82] or, as Milbank would say, of constant self-critique and avoidance of absolutization of the self (or one's theology, I add). This requires letting go of any illusions of *leaping over* contextual mediation. "Theological discourse about God gives God a historical substance, an image, and a role. But who are the people who give God a role?" asks Ivone Gebara—thus turning the critical gaze to the theologians themselves.[83]

"The point is," explains Althaus-Reid, "that Liberation Theology is not a self-contained entity or peculiar category of analysis related to God and a particular theological subject as the poor."[84] Even when liberation theology proclaimed to ground its experience of God in the encounter with the human other, it retained its claim (perhaps unavoidably, though not necessarily innocently) to discern which aspects of the other reflected God's image and God's calling. Althaus-Reid specifically observes that, in its relation both to secular and theological discourses, liberation theology has had

---

79. Ibid., 255.
80. Ibid., 258, emphasis mine.
81. Milbank, *Theology and Social Theory*, 251.
82. Althaus-Reid, *Indecent Theology*, 5.
83. Ivone Gebara, *Longing for Running Water: Ecofeminism and Liberation* (Minneapolis: Fortress Press, 1999), 35.
84. Althaus-Reid, *Indecent Theology*, 22.

problems accepting that "the simplistic confrontation between oppressive and liberative aspects of our lives" is "a farce." "In the end," she explains, "Liberation Theology
and structures of oppression both share a common epistemological field."[85] And so
does radical orthodoxy.

Final Thoughts

I agree with Milbank that transcendence offers unique resources to avoid the absolutization of the subjects or systems and promote ethical relations between human
beings. To unleash the potential of the notion of divine transcendence for social justice requires, as he insists as well, unrelenting openness to self-critique and avoidance
of self-absolutization. This, as Milbank argues, requires "attention to what lies *beyond*
the self (individual or collective). . . ."[86] But why, then, should one place this *beyond*
also *outside*?

Milbank argues that "if the immanent world is all there is, then it tends to reduce
to our abstract grasp of it" (209). I share this concern. However, I believe that the theological promise of transcendence lies not in proposing a reality other than the world,
but rather in its potential to help us overcome the habit of reducing the "immanent"
to the graspable, or more precisely to reduce the created to the *purely immanent*. This
is the strategy pursued by the liberation and feminist theologians I have engaged
herein; its full implications for theological anthropology are yet to be developed. It
does not necessarily mean, as Milbank suggests, a reduction of God "to a shadowy
hypostasized Other lurking just behind the human other"—a coded rejection of
Levinas's ethics, I suppose (154). To affirm *transcendence-in* is to proclaim the rootedness of all of creation in God and thus the participation of all creatures in God's
transcendence—a creation inherently related to God, not externally linked to God.

This theological model of divine transcendence in creation and history calls us to
seek divine transcendence within the *folds* of a divinely created reality, where things are
indeed "more than they appear" (Pickstock) and always exceed our most radical expectations. This entails a reinterpretation of the created others and of our relations to
them where others are not mere presences. Instead it would recognize the irreducibility of other human beings to any system as "ineffable likenesses of God" (203)—as
nonidentical repetitions of our relations to the intimate but ineffable God. This "culturally imbued sense of transcendence" would not think of human needs as only
"immanent needs" subordinated to some other (higher?) need. Instead, the processes
by which human needs are met—people are fed, sheltered, and loved, and societies
become mediators of such nurturing processes—are manifestations of transcendence,
which is always already taking place in creation.

To affirm *transcendence-in* is to accept that one cannot leap outside one's self. To
pretend to dislodge oneself from finitude to find a higher authority from which to
speak is the first step toward denying the transcendence of God and of the other. This
risk haunts discourses of transcendence. When liberation theology claims to be able to
discern the irruption of a transhistorical transcendent hand in particular historical

---

85. Ibid., 149.
86. Milbank, *Being Reconciled*, 179.

moments, or when radical orthodoxy claims to find a *commensurate* language with God, they are at risk of claiming to transcend the limits of creaturehood, of "homologizing themselves with a God-like discourse." These theologies might be better protected from these risks by integrating more consistently their own recognitions of the irreducibility of God to human systems, of the *agony of apostrophic striving*, of the *"failure to mean that haunts all theological claims,"*[87] of the *always beyond* of the reign of God—that is, divine transcendence.

---

87. Kathryn Tanner, "Creation as a Mixed Metaphor" (paper presented at the Drew Transdisciplinary Theology Colloquium, Madison, N.J., 2001), 2.

PART III

theology,
economics,
and politics

9. "We Must Give Ourselves to Voyaging"

Regifting the Theological Present

—Marion Grau

Today we must take up this project again and insist that the body of Christ is the true universality—against the taboos of tribes (even though the law of Christ extends as well as abolishes taboos[)] and the universality of enlightenment, whose dark gothic secret is *homo sacer*.... We must oppose also the sacrifice without return of individuals to the state, to globalization, to the future, to ethical duty, to pagan fatality.... Instead, beyond the medieval venture, we must give ourselves to voyaging, unto death if necessary, like English sailors John and Sebastian Cabot of Bristol ... and before them the Portuguese sailors Magellan, Vasco da Gama and Columbus.

      —John Milbank, *Being Reconciled: Ontology and Pardon*

Modernity, we would now argue, was not a western invention as such but itself a product of the west's interaction with the rest of the world, including the economic exploitation of colonialism which first provided the surplus gold that was the motor for modern capitalism.... The debate is not between modernity and its opponents, but rather between different versions of modernity, some of which offer alternatives to what is regarded, not always very accurately, as the western model.

      —Robert Young, *Postcolonialism: A Very Short Introduction*

In voyages across the seas, nothing ventured is nothing gained. John and Sebastian Cabot (Giovanni and Sebastiano Cabota) were Italian seafarers who relocated to the British Isles and sailed westward in the employ of Henry VII of England.[1] Through this voyage the English attempted to match the Spanish colonial effort and to find "an 'El Dorado' of their own, in the hope that England too could become rich on American metals."[2] In 1497, these mercantile mercenaries were the first Europeans to set foot on the North American Mainland (Columbus had never made it there) and "formally

---

1. This essay represents a first engagement with the history and theology of Anglican/Episcopal missionary ventures in the setting of British and U.S. imperialism and will be expanded in the future. As such these are preliminary thoughts toward a larger project.

2. Niall Ferguson, *Empire: The Rise and Demise of the British World Order and the Lessons for Global Power* (London: Penguin, 2002), 2.

annexed the region in the king's name."[3] During their imperial exploits, Northern Atlantic peoples encountered people whose ethnic and cultural otherness they constructed and described in ways that mirrored their own self-understanding. These colonial encounters continue to shape questions about our own postmodern context, especially where global warming and the swarming of financial capital across the planet suggest it might be very hard indeed to find a space untouched by "modernity."[4] Giving and taking, exchange of goods, religion and culture were at the core of these encounters. Gift exchange has become a staple of anthropological and philosophical academic discourse in the West since the beginning of colonial modernity and encounter and exchange between and among Europeans and peoples encountered through sea voyages. If postmodernity moves beyond modernity, what does this mean for gift exchange theories? Must exchange be "regifted"?

Interactions between colonizers and colonized were informed by and are being formed in part by theological structures, ancient and modern. This suggests the need for a postcolonial analysis of the gift as an economic, colonial, and a theological concept of exchange and human and divine encounters. What was exchanged, who were the agents, what ways of rationalizing and theologizing give and take in colonial encounters were employed? Where do those discourses leave theologians thinking about the 'gift' and gift exchange today? How might we assess these connections, and how might we 'regift'[5] theological presents in the present, and in resistance to continuing imperialist exchanges?

In the above passage, John Milbank invokes the colonial travels of the Cabots in a side trip from an otherwise consistent dedication to the pre-1300 medieval world, a trip that follows modernity's colonial travels to map and trade around the world.[6] If, as Milbank suggests, "we must give ourselves to voyaging," what is it that "we" give in the process of traveling, what do we receive, what is it we take? What happens to land, resources, culture, language, knowledge, religion in these exchanges? Who is on board these ships? Conquerors, speculators, deck hands, missionaries, anthropologists, bioprospectors, researchers? How did they perceive the "gift" and how might we "regift" it today in more reciprocal ways?

We can scarcely ignore the fact that such colonial journeys into modernity and their theological underpinnings and reverberations continue to be implied in the

---

3. See Lawrence James, *The Rise and Fall of the British Empire* (New York: St. Martin's Press, 1994), 15, and Ferguson, *Empire*, 3.

4. "Modernity," shorthand for many complex interacting developments, has produced far more than one mindset; it has also formed the present by way of the pervasive effects of imperial technologies, trade routes, and transfers of biomass across the globe that were enhanced, charted, and populated by North Atlantic peoples. I assume that "modernity," as well as "enlightenment," and "capitalism," are complex phenomena with multitudes of links to past and present. Consider, for example, that the British would not be the same nation without colonial interactions such as those that would present the gift of tea to a people for whom that herbal infusion now seems as characteristic as Stonehenge. Likewise, consider the "gift" of coffee, now, as some would say, the last unregulated drug and great obsession of millions as witnessed by coffee house, café, and coffee shop cultures across the globe.

5. The word 'regifting' has now reached the status of a new word that can be found at least in online dictionaries such as the *Macmillan English Dictionary*. There it is defined as "the activity of giving something as a gift that you yourself originally received as a gift." See http://www.macmillandictionary.com/New-Words/041220-regifting.htm.

6. John Milbank, *Being Reconciled: Ontology and Pardon* (London and New York: Routledge, 2003), 104.

formulation of "postmodern" theologies of any provenance, radical, orthodox, or not. As the postcolonial theorist Robert Young suggests, "the debate is not between modernity and its opponents, but rather between different versions of modernity"[7] that give the lie to rigid distinctions between the "West" and the "Rest." The risk of death involved in retracing these travels today may very well require a "dying to the Western self," or at least the death of imperially privileged notions of "Western theology" and claims to access and represent a privileged orthodoxy, radical or otherwise.[8]

This essay engages John Milbank's rendering of the gift while suggesting additional directions for thinking about theological economics in the context of contesting empire. While agreeing with Milbank's insistence on a need for reciprocity beyond mere givenness in human relations, I add considerations on how such reciprocity might be extended to human-divine relations and how reciprocity among humans might be engaged in thinking through colonial and neocolonial gift-giving and other forms of exchange. Hence I offer some considerations on the theological use of the concepts of giving and taking, pointing beyond the either/or of imperialist apologies of empire and a simplistic anti-imperialist rhetoric of the noble savage toward an ambivalent appreciation of hybrid transcultures[9] and transtheologies. It challenges notions of unilateral, unreciprocated giving, human and divine, and probes spaces of reciprocity intersecting in a variety of power scenarios.

I hope to begin to imagine a space beyond the false alternatives of a colonial imposition of a "white gospel" and an anti-colonial rejection of "Christianity" as "alien" or "foreign," one that encompasses a far wider spectrum of adaptive responses to the gospel. In order to concretize this imagination, I offer an exploration of gift exchange in a time and space that offers a *kairos* for coming to terms with Christian involvement in modern imperial enterprises, in this case, the Anglican Church's complicity with the expansionist "civilizing mission" of the British Empire. The history and present of British colonialism are inseparable from the present shape of the Anglican Communion.[10] As an Episcopalian living in a former British colony that has formed an empire of its own, I am trying to think beyond modernity as "beyond colonial

---

7. Robert Young, *Postcolonialism: An Very Short Introduction* (Oxford: Oxford University Press, 2003), 98. The epigraph is found on the same page.

8. Sea voyaging was so dangerous for the hired hands that Captain Cook calculated that he would lose at least 40 percent of his crew over the course of the journey. The crew was kept in line with large daily doses of alcohol (which lead to some alcohol poisoning and contributed to the number of people falling over board) and corporal punishment, an apparently inescapable naval disciplinary regime. See Tony Horvitz, *Blue Latitudes: Boldly Going Where Captain Cook Has Gone Before* (New York: Picador, 2002), 23–24.

9. I am borrowing this term from Chris Prentice, who created this analogue to Baudrillard's terms "transpolitical" and "transeconomic" and uses it to describe a cultural moment that connotes "freedom, fluidity and mobility," as well as "loss of specificity and contamination across terms." Chris Prentice, "Transcultures and the Right Use of Whales," in *Baudrillard West of the Dateline* (ed. Victoria Grace, Heather Worth, and Laurence Simmons; Palmerston North, New Zealand: Dunsmore Press, 2003), 83.

10. Ian T. Douglas, "Authority after Colonialism," *The Witness* 83, no.3 (March 2000): 10–14; and Ian T. Douglas, "The Exigency of Times and Occasions: Power and Identity in the Anglican Communion Today," in *Beyond Colonial Anglicanism: The Anglican Communion in the Twentyfirst Century* (ed. Ian T. Douglas and Pui-Lan Kwok; New York: Church Publishing, 2001), 25–46. The Anglican Communion is a curious, artificial construct trotted out for a variety of agendas, most recently in the Windsor report's suggestion to shore up the authority of the Archbishop of Canterbury to help control disputed issues of clerical leadership and relating contestations of ecclesial power.

Anglicanism"[11] in a way that is related to but also quite distinct from Milbank's Anglo-Catholic hearkening back to a vision of idealized conformity in matters of faith. Agreeing with Milbank that "we must oppose the sacrifice of individuals to the state, to globalization," I suggest that such opposition must include a critical appreciation of the colonial past and present. Hence, my question: What might postmodern theologies of "gift" and "regifting" beyond British coloniality and the U.S. empire look like?

Transculturation and the Ambivalence of the Gift

The answer depends in part on where and how one finds contributions for such theologies. I began working on this essay shortly after returning from a two-month research visit to Auckland, in Aotearoa/New Zealand,[12] during which a great number of whales beached themselves in the South Pacific, among them many on a remote part of that nation's North Island.[13] Many died, and some were pushed back into the sea and survived. The mysterious stranding of whales in what can seem like suicidal urgings captures people's imaginations across cultures, especially in a time when these animals have been decimated and brought near extinction.

There is something about whales, the largest mammals, creatures that sound the depths, stranding on shores. Mythical images of whales are inscribed in both sacred and secular literature: Job's Leviathan, Jonah's whale, Kahu/Paikea's guardian in Māori ancestral lore, and Moby Dick. Soon it seemed that the whales had beached themselves on the shores of this essay, too, and were making their presence felt. The larger context in which the whale strandings occurred began to interface with issues of gift economy, coloniality, and cultural encounter. My ruminations on gift economies in the work of Milbank and Marcel Mauss thus soon collided with James Cook's journeys on the *Endeavour*, Herman Melville's colonial male heroes, and Witi Ihimaera's 1987 Māori novel and source of the 2002 film *The Whale Rider*.[14]

These encounters between literature and life offer unexpected glimpses into the notions of gift, exchange, and trade as we negotiate ancestral worlds and the ambivalent gifts of modern Christendom's imperialism in the spaces of imagination spanning the North Atlantic and the South Pacific. These narratives are set on the faraway South Pacific shores of the British Empire and tell of encounters between two worlds in a give-and-take that had and has still many surprises. On the edges or in the center of these texts we find negotiations of women and natives as two incarnations of the Other to the self of North Atlantic colonial masculinity.[15] We encounter the ambivalence of

---

11. Ian T. Douglas and Kwok Pui-Lan, *Beyond Colonial Anglicanism: The Anglican Communion in the Twentyfirst Century* (New York: Church Publishing, 2001).

12. The term Aotearoa/New Zealand, a combination of the name given to the land by Polynesian marine migrants and the Anglo name given after settlement by Europeans, represents a transculture in its own way. Aotearoa is often rendered as "Land of the long white cloud" and, according to conflicting versions of Māori mythology, was named either by a principal Polynesian navigator or his wife. See Michael King, *The Penguin History of New Zealand* (Auckland: Penguin Books, 2003), 41.

13. Reuters, "Whale Strandings in New Zealand, Australia," CNN.Com, November 30, 2004. Online: http://www.cnn.com/2004/TECH/science/11/30/australia.whales.reut/.

14. Māori is the term indigenous inhabitants of New Zealand generally use to describe themselves, indicating a sense of belonging that goes beyond tribal and familial ties. The term means "ordinary person" in te reo, the language of the Māori.

15. On these exploratory travels of Western colonialism, the author can only come along as a stowaway. Women were able to be on such journeys only as stowaways, and so my perspective resembles somewhat

the gift as a transcultural resource for response and resistance to the impositions of colonial imperialism.

Resistance to the forces of imperial presence occurs in diverse modes and contexts. Elsewhere, I have proposed sacred tricksterdom or holy foolery as one possible form of agency for women and men who must resist oppression within circumstances often beyond their direct sphere of influence in their complex positioning within present global capitalist structures.[16] The gift also has some of the qualities of a trickster. Both are border crossers, and both represent the hopes and dangers of the borders/boundary lines.[17]

The gift can appear as a *pharmakon*, both "the remedy and the poison"[18] for a disease. The gift can enrich and impoverish, poison and heal, the communities it moves between.[19] While "traditional gift exchange is an agent of social cohesion," there are gifts that challenge the "demands of the collective" in such a way that roles become shifted, technologies are introduced, and silences become articulated, while exclusions are challenged.[20] Thus, in many cultures, the gift, like the trickster, can have the function of prodding a society or culture to come to terms with new circumstances. It often can introduce technologies and cultural innovations crucial for survival but with a dangerous side. Gift and *pharmakon* "can never be simply beneficial." Certainly this is the case for gift exchanges in encounters occurring within the reach of the British Empire.[21]

The status and economies of the gift in a colonial context are a complicated, nuanced, and notoriously messy affair. Postmodern philosophical and theological discussions of the gift often take place in an ideal theoretical location that urgently needs to be decolonized. Consider, for example, John Milbank's comment that "giving, therefore, is primarily a matter of shared expenditure and celebration. 'Primitive' societies know this, and group themselves around such ecstatic transition, not around accumulated illusions."[22] However, as the French sociologist and anthropologist Marcel Mauss stressed in his classic 1925 study *The Gift*, romantic notions of "native" gift economies reflect more the cultural context of the researcher than that of the people observed. He suggested that the European search for a pristine gift economy in fact revealed that "there has never existed, either in the past or in modern primitive societies, anything

---

an invisible presence with limited access vision, starved for light and air, for freedom of movement and speech. Apparently, large numbers of stowaways regularly were able to get on board on such ships, as demonstrated by New Zealand's first shipwreck, which uncovered the astonishing number of forty-six stowaways, including at least two women (King, *History of New Zealand*, 119).

16. Marion Grau, *Of Divine Economy: Refinancing Redemption* (New York and London: Continuum/T&T Clark, 2004), 174ff.

17. This trickster agency finds inspiration in images of Christ as the sacred trickster of redemption, of the divine acting as a wise, persuasive power, rather than as an omnipotent bully who will help Christians to "abolish capitalism" in some *deus ex machina* way.

18. The German word *Gift* is rendered as poison in English. See Jacques Derrida, *Dissemination* (trans. Barbara Johnson; Chicago: University of Chicago Press, 1981), 94. Hence one could say in Germlish *Das Gift vergiftet* (The gift poisons). See John D. Caputo, *The Prayers and Tears of Jacques Derrida: Religion without Religion* (Bloomington and Indianapolis: Indiana University Press, 1997), 166.

19. For an exploration of the various ways in which gifts can function, see Derrida's discussion of "Plato's Pharmacy" and especially some of the sections on the *pharmakon* in Derrida, *Dissemination*, 95–155.

20. Lewis Hyde, *Trickster Makes This World: Mischief, Myth, and Art* (New York: Farrar, Straus & Giroux, 1998), 133.

21. Derrida, *Dissemination*, 99.

22. Milbank, *Being Reconciled*, 181.

like a 'natural' economy."[23] The form of romantic orientalism unveiled by Mauss mirrors a matching occidentalism, as James Carrier has observed: the occidentalism of ascribing "impersonal commodity relations" as essential to the West "makes sense only when it is juxtaposed with its matching orientalism, the society of the gift. Compared to such societies, the West *is* the society of the commodity—these two essentializations defining and justifying each other dialectically."[24]

As European ethnographers such as Marcel Mauss considered Pacific regions in order to investigate the gift among indigenous peoples such as Melanesians, Polynesians, and Native Americans of the Pacific Northwest, the economies of both colonized and colonizer were beginning to be profoundly changed by those and other encounters—by trade between European and Pacific cultures.[25] Any accounting for postmodern as well as postcolonial exchanges must then occur in the context of those trading exchanges, economic, theological, and always inspirited and embodied. As we have seen, in the process of colonization, boundaries were crossed and relationships formed, while economies of goods, faith, and land changed hands. This suggests that essentializing distinctions are representative of only a small amount of the realities. James G. Carrier hence argues that there was and is more variety in both European and native societies, but that few anthropologists had studied the gift in the modern West and others are ignoring "commodity relationships in village societies."[26]

Milbank proposes "the recovery of mutual giving"[27] through a more fully lived reciprocity among humans. But what would such reciprocity look like in an imperial context where one of the tasks at hand may be to rethink how power, empire, and theology intersect? The absence of an encounter that actually could be described as close to reciprocal (where both sides engage in dialogue and where some mutual recognition and exchange can take place) in Milbank's dismissals of liberation theologians' critiques of capitalism and empire does not seem to be in tune with the proposed mutuality.[28]

Milbank's call to resistance against capitalism and globalization thus remains at odds with his continued investment in a hegemonic sense of "Western" orthodoxy that

---

23. However, Mauss's own fictions include that he was able to describe "the gift" in a way that has tended to universalize that notion across differences and hence potentially propagate "orthodox" notions about "the gift." Thus, his account has at least two effects: a reality check for Western notions of a "pure gift" and a tendency to claim a total description. See Marcel Mauss, *The Gift: Forms and Functions of Exchange in Archaic Societies* (New York and London: W. W. Norton, 1967), 3.

24. James G. Carrier, "Maussian Occidentalism: Gift and Commodity Systems," in *Occidentalism: Images of the West* (ed. James G. Carrier; Oxford: Clarendon Press, 1995), 94.

25. Cf. Derrida's *Given Time: I. Counterfeit Money* (Chicago: University of Chicago Press, 1992) and his account of the presence of tobacco in the European salon. On the effects of other colonial cargo such as sugar, coffee, and tea for European masculinity, femininity, and respectability, cf. also Woodruff D. Smith, *Consumption and the Making of Respectability, 1600–1800* (London and New York: Routledge, 2002), 161–69.

26. Carrier, "Maussian Occidentalism," 95.

27. Milbank, *Being Reconciled*, 155.

28. My concern in this exploration of colonial give-and-take is not so much to establish who "really gave" and who "really took," but rather to trace some of the instability of various degrees of exchange, reciprocal or not, and how they fluctuate across time and place. For Milbank's critique of liberation and political theology, focusing on the way in which these theologies have engaged enlightenment in a "mediating theology" that, so he claims, produces a "futile cycle," see John Milbank, *Theology and Social Theory*, 207, 233. Again, I do not so much disagree with some of his criticisms but with his unhelpful dismissals and apparent inability to appreciate these theologians' contributions.

is unthinkable without the forces of the British Empire, past and present. By the same token, his call for the "abolition of capitalism and the production of a socialist market,"[29] even if it were a realistic goal, might not represent the reciprocal action demanded by the present theological *kairos*. Rather, I suggest that a form of agency readily accessible to Christians who profess faith in redemptive and liberative relationality between God and creation, in a divine economy that explodes the oppressive potency of the brew of a divinized U.S. capitalism blended with a civil religion of manifest destiny, may best be found, as in pre-Constantinian times, in a variety of subversive strategies, witnessing words, and transgressive actions.[30]

Milbank assumes that ethical exchanges among human agents are reciprocal, in critical distance from an ethic of sacrifice that argues that a "true" gift must be without strings attached, and hence also from an impossible Derridean absolute gift.[31] However, he reserves redemption and forgiveness as a divine "true gift." God remains only a giver, yet is never a recipient in a gift exchange. Thus, the God-given gift is a "transcendental category"[32] in a way that structures theological discourse about creation, grace, incarnation, atonement, the church, and spirit, all of which have been described as a "gift." This gifting, and the related *methexis* as a "sharing of being and knowledge in the Divine,"[33] appear to flow only in one direction: From God to humans, and from there to other humans, but never toward "him."

Such sovereign lack of the need for reciprocity is echoed in representations of British colonial sovereignty.

> One of the most famous portraits of Queen Elizabeth I, the Ditchley portrait by Marcus Gheeraerts the Younger, shows her standing astride the globe. Written in Latin on the picture are three fragmentary statements describing Elizabeth, which stress a particular sort of power. They have been reconstructed and translated as "She gives and does not expect. She can, but does not take revenge. In giving back she increases." Also on the portrait are the remains of a sonnet on the sun, reflecting an established rhetorical tradition of comparison of the monarch's power with that of the sun, as the inexhaustible source of all that is good.[34]

Thus, there are certain echoes between theological and imperial language, including some troubling resonances in how such discourse represents and reflects the imperial male's relations (emissaries of the rare woman at the helm of a growing empire)

---

29. As paraphrased by Stephen Long in D. Stephen Long, *Divine Economy: Theology and the Market* (New York: Routledge, 2000), 260.

30. This is despite the fact that the current incarnation of U.S. imperialism has donned a vaguely Judeo-Christian garb plying an interpretation of Hebrew and Christian traditions that focuses in particular ways on reducing conflicts and complexities to choices between "good" and "evil," "dark" and "light," "right" and "wrong."

31. This move is critical toward notions of the absolute gift in Jacques Derrida and Jean-Luc Marion. These discussions generally refer to Marcel Mauss's influential study *The Gift*.

32. Milbank, *Being Reconciled*, ix.

33. Ibid.

34. David Murray, *Indian Giving: Economies of Power in Indian-White Exchanges* (Amherst: University of Massachusetts Press, 2000), 55.

with "Woman, Native, Other,"[35] reiterating "his" obsessions about power and fears for its loss.

The God image reiterated by Milbank builds upon a long but increasingly problematic tradition of casting God as a propertied male owner and humanity as an impoverished, lacking, feminized recipient. We are in our nothingness before "him,"[36] and yet the metaphor is unstable, and nothingness is gendered, a kind of "feminine lack" in giving.[37] Milbank thus reiterates classic tropes of divine economy such as the commerce of the *conubium*, whereby a "genuinely erotic body" is "restored" to humanity "in Christ, who offers it to his bride, the Church." In this image, however, redemption perpetuates a problematic gendering of the human-divine relationship where a masculinized, propertied divine bridegroom seeks to marry a feminized, unworthy whore-bride, giving "her" a new body.[38] God is here in the traditional husband, king, (and in more contemporary terms) CEO position in a structure that equates God with the good, abundance, and wealth, and juxtaposes it to evil, lack, and poverty.[39] But gender relations, relations between God and humanity, between colonizer and colonized, prove even more complex.

While Milbank might argue that the positioning of God as "ungiven giver" guarantees "his" sovereignty, might it not also isolate and drain the divine giver, not unlike a feminized emptying out? Can such talk of abundance in fact serve to subordinate the exploitation of God as well as the indigenous inhabitants when cast in the role of abundant givers? Is there a possibility that, not unlike the colonial dynamic of extracting more gifts from colonial cultures than are given, God's unilateral "givingness" is assumed while abused by the human assumption (and, in the case of prosperity theologies, the insistence) that the purpose of God's giving and promise is to fulfill human needs and desires?

Similarly, the "native" in colonial discourse is often imagined as the passive recipient of colonial culture and religion, while many indigenous peoples perceive themselves in the role of "givers" of land, resources, and culture, their often romanticized generosity continuously abused in the process of colonization. Hence, as we've seen in the actual ambivalences of the gift, the giver is not (always) the only person with power in a relationship. Might God's generosity, as imagined by much of Christian theology, be as problematic as the colonial view of the "Woman, Native, Other," either as idealized giver or as passive recipient of civilization and religion? Woman, native, and God (according to Barth "the wholly Other") alike would thus be open to exploitation in colonial theological accounts.

---

35. Trinh Minh-Ha, *Woman, Native, Other* (Bloomington: Indiana University Press, 1989).

36. Observe Milbank's insistent use of the male pronoun for God (Milbank, *Being Reconciled*, 46) and throughout the text.

37. I have explored the issue of the feminization of giving in strands of traditional interpretations of women in the Gospels and their excessive giving (which has also been read as foreshadowing Jesus' abundant giving of his life) in more detail in Grau, *Of Divine Economy*, 99–107.

38. John Milbank, "The Midwinter Sacrifice," in *The Blackwell Companion to Postmodern Theology* (ed. Graham Ward; Oxford: Blackwell, 2001), 128.

39. This gendered economy appears to be of one piece with Milbank's affirmation of the unilateral gifting of a *creatio ex nihilo*. See Milbank, *Being Reconciled*, 2, 4. For a critical investigation in the power and theodynamics of the creatio ex nihilo, see Catherine Keller, *Face of the Deep: A Theology of Becoming* (New York: Routledge, 2003). I am not here claiming that poverty is not often a form of evil and degradation; however, it therefore seems even more important to question the elevation of riches to the level of the divine and the problematic identification of the human condition as poverty.

The instability of colonial give and take is exemplified in accounts of "Indian giving" as leaving the status of the colonists undecided as taker, traders, or thieves, as a counterpoint to Europeans' long-standing presentation of themselves as bringers of gifts, specifically, the gifts of civilization and Christianity. . . . These were gifts so huge that they dwarfed any negative aspects that might come along with them and justified taking the bounty of the New World. So powerful and persistent has been the idea of Western civilization as the source of all that is important and valuable that recent emphasis on what "we" owe to Indians culturally as well as materially is felt to be claiming something new and controversial.[40]

Stephen Greenblatt's lucid investigation of the theological underpinnings of such gift rhetoric suggests it was supported by "an ancient Christian rhetoric that has its most famous Renaissance English expression in the Holy Sonnets of John Donne:

That I may rise, and stand, o'erthrow mee, and bend
Your force, to break, blowe, burn, and make me new. . . .
Take me to you, imprison me, for I
Except you'enthrall mee, never shall be free
Nor ever chast, except you ravish me.[41]

Here, Christian imperialism blends a discourse of "commodity conversion and spiritual conversion"[42] with strong undertones of erotic violence. Melville's 1851 *Moby Dick*, an overloaded economic parable by any accounts, likewise exposes the complexity of exchanges that blur boundaries between colonizer and colonized, gift economy and consumer capitalism. After all, the initial purpose of the whaler *Pequod*'s trip is to provide a rare and much demanded source of energy for the U.S. economy, sperm whale oil, which in Melville's time was still a major source of fuel for lamps and candles.[43] Roaming the seas of the world for this precious substance, the floating cosmopolitany converts the whale and everything on the ship into what it translates into on the money market back in port: "Don't ye love sperm? There goes three thousand dollars, men!—a bank! a whole bank! The bank of England."[44]

The whale's wondrous body and the currencies it can be converted into dwarf the worth of a human being, especially that of a slave. Thus, when the black crewmember Pip falls overboard and the crew has to let a whale get away in order to pull him back in, the overseer Stubb retorts: "We can't afford to lose whales by the likes of you; a whale would sell for thirty times what you would, Pip, in Alabama."[45] Colonizer and colonized are uncomfortably united in situations where race and class dynamics constantly destabilize the common quest for fuel, adventure, and riches.

---

40. Murray, *Indian Giving*, 18.
41. Stephen Greenblatt, *Marvelous Possessions: The Wonder of the New World* (Chicago: University of Chicago Press, 1991), 70.
42. Murray, *Indian Giving*, 5.
43. Herman Melville, *Moby Dick* (New York: Signet, 1955), 340.
44. Ibid.
45. Ibid., 395.

There are three colonized subjects among the harpooners of the *Pequod*, representing three areas of the globe colonized by Britain. In this racist economy, these harpooners perform the most physically enormous, most important, and most dangerous job on the whaler. Melville bluntly writes of a Protestant work ethic outsourced: "Be it said, that at the present day not one in two of the many thousand men before the mast employed" are born American, but rather that the "American liberally provides the brains, the rest of the world is generously supplying the muscle."[46] The harpooners are Tashtego, a Native American from Martha's Vineyard, Daggoo, from Africa, and Queequeg from "Kokovoko, an island far away to the West and South." Melville further comments: "It is not down in any map; true places never are."[47] And yet, there are clues that might help us find it on a map:

> Having come themselves from a highly maritime culture, even though they had long since ceased to make ocean voyages by canoe, Maori turned out to be excellent crew members on European ships. They began to join ships' companies in the 1790s. . . . By the first decade of the nineteenth century Maori were visiting Sydney regularly, and from the following decade travelling on vessels around the Pacific—Herman Melville's tattooed harpooner Queequeg in *Moby Dick* was in all probability based on a Maori crew member whom the author had met on the whaling ship *Lucy Ann*—and on to North America and England.[48]

In his reading of *Moby Dick*, Graham Ward comments that "Queequeg only has a voice so far as the narrator (and the author) gives it to him."[49] However, in Queequeg's actions, even as seen through Ishmael's eyes, we can glean facets of a complex character pointing beyond the limits of the page. I cannot, nor do I want to try give voice to Queequeg beyond attempting a small midrash, but there are a few things that might suggest Queequeg was more than a device used by Melville. We learn from Queequeg's own narrative that he was on board by his own will, stealing on board at night. Having descended from ancestors who were formidable sailors, Queequeg participates in this voyage of discovery and exploitation and participates in the merciless hunt after the white whale. His spear skills translate nicely into harpooning skills, making him thus one of the most important men on board, but also one of the most dangerously employed.[50] His presence on the ship causes deep reactions in Ishmael: His initial fear and repulsion and his ensuing intimate physical and emotional connection to Queequeg profoundly change and challenge Ishmael, culturally, erotically, religiously, economically.

For Ishmael it may be what he sees as Queequeg's exotic beingness and masculinity that "allows" the eroticism of the "marriage bed" of the two men to unfurl. Although it is Ishmael who admits that he was "bent upon narrowly observing so curious a creature," though "he treated me with so much civility and consideration, while I was

---

46. Ibid., 127. This may indicate a self-consciousness of Americans as inheritors of the British Empire.
47. Ibid., 70.
48. King, *History of New Zealand*, 128–29.
49. Graham Ward, *True Religion* (Malden, Mass.: Blackwell, 2003), 107.
50. Anne Salmond, *Between Worlds: Early Exchanges Between Maori and Europeans 1773–1815* (Honolulu: University of Hawaii Press, 1997), 320.

guilty of great rudeness; staring at him from the bed, and watching all his toilette motions," we wonder whose subtly orientalist reading of the Other fuels this homo-erotic encounter.[51] Despite the power differential of Ishmael's voyeuristic gaze, consider the hybridic transformations that his visual encounters occasion. Who is transforming whom, who is "colonizing" whom?

The equivocal nature of the gift also can be seen in the "gifts" Captain James Cook brought to the natives of Aotearoa/New Zealand. Cook and his fellow travelers tried to induce Māori interest in the tools and goods they had with them, partly to divert them from possible hostile actions, but partly also, surely, to civilize them by trade. The "civilization" thus acquired brought with it an ideological opposition between capitalism and communism: Later, the Native Land Act aimed to give settlers easier access to Māori land that was communally owned in order to "break down the beastly communism of the tribe."[52] The forcible transition from communal guardianship and usage rights of *whenua* (land) to capitalist ownership of real estate in Aotearoa/New Zealand was brought about by a particular version of commerce by deception, or what Māori have called land "taken by sale."

Ambivalent dynamics also obtain in missionary acts of translation. The Ghambian missionologist Lamin Sanneh has argued that while it may look like the missionary is in control of the dynamics of cultural transmission, in fact he (and for the most part it was a "he") has to submit himself and his language, theology, and culture to the language, theology, and culture of the location in which he is working: "If people are trying to learn your language, then they can hardly avoid striking up a relationship with you however much they might wish to dominate you."[53] The relationship between missionaries and Africans, he argues, then would in fact constitute a form of "reciprocity" that goes beyond the assumptions that "Africans" are merely "victims of missionary oppression, either because they were forcibly converted or because missionary contact proved fatal to indigenous originality."[54] Although Sanneh claims that translation breaks the stranglehold of Western culture,[55] it would seem that such hybridity remains ambivalent in its particular economies of exchange, especially since the biblical text comes loaded with many cultural assumptions as well, and is not, as Sanneh claims, somehow free of culture. Hence, power, most likely, flows in multiple directions.

Under these ambivalent conditions, colonial encounters have caused culture clashes that find indigenous peoples struggling to find constructive ways to survive and thrive under colonial hegemony. When one of Witi Ihimaera's characters wonders whether adaptation to new technologies and mindsets will allow Māori to still be Māori,[56] he is asking a crucial question: What makes or breaks identity, personal and

---

51. Melville, *Moby Dick*, 45.

52. M. P. K. Sorrenson, "How to Civilize Savages: Some 'Answers' from Nineteenth-Century New Zealand," *The New Zealand Journal of History* 9, no. 2 (October 1975): 107.

53. Lamin Sanneh, *Translating the Message: The Missionary Impact on Culture* (Maryknoll, N.Y.: Orbis, 1989), 173.

54. Ibid.

55. Lamin Sanneh, *Whose Religion Is Christianity? The Gospel beyond the West* (Grand Rapids, Mich.: Eerdmanns, 2003), 130.

56. "Will we have prepared the people to cope with the new challenges and the new technology? And will they still be Maori?" (Witi Ihimaera, *The Whale Rider* [Orlando: Harcourt, 1987], 71.

tribal? Colonial encounters confronted the people of the land with severe challenges to their values, economies, and way of life before the term "postmodern" ever crossed the North Atlantic. Hence, according to Michel-Rolph Trouillot,

> if the collapse of metanarratives alone characterized the postmodern condition, then some of those populations outside of the North Atlantic that have been busily deconstructing theirs for centuries, or that have gone through mega-collapses of their own, have long been "postmodern," and there is nothing new under the sun.... [But] even if we concede, for the sake of argument, that metanarratives once were a prerequisite of humankind and are now collapsing everywhere at equal rates (two major assumptions indeed), we cannot infer identical reactive strategies to this collapse.[57]

While Māori were still in charge of their resources and offered needed protection to traders and whalers, they also had some control over trades and exchanges. Queequeg, for example, engages in his own informal economy: He is trying to find buyers for his *moko mai*, his preserved head, but, as the landlord in Ishmael's Nantucket inn notes, the market is saturated: "I told him he couldn't sell it here, the market's overstocked."[58]

Commerce was seen, by some of the British, as a means of "civilizing" the Māori, and indeed some Māori appear to have been quick studies (Queequeg perhaps one of them) in bartering and trading, so much so that some British observers observed with regret that a form of consumerism became apparent. Others, such as Samuel Marsden, the founder of the Anglican mission in Aotearoa/New Zealand, participated in trade "for his personal profit," believing that distribution of tools and goods would lead to an inevitable "very rapid progress in the attainment of the necessary comforts of civil life."[59] The hope was that commerce would turn the Māori away from the pursuit of intertribal warfare and would advance "their civilization."[60] Others seem to have been saddened by what they felt was a corruption of the Māori into consumers, as they became "irrevocably enslaved by wants which were unfelt by their ancestors."[61] Here, as so often, the gospel traveled in close companionship with European modes of capitalism and commerce, and some of the empire's agents, such as Marsden, saw in "agriculture and trade the first steps in civilization, and in turn, the adoption of Christianity." Other local missionaries reversed the order and proceeded to focus on the propagation of the gospel first.[62] But this change of strategy did little to challenge

---

57. Michel-Rolph Trouillot, *Global Transformations: Anthropology and the Modern World* (New York: Palgrave, 2003), 11. Trouillot's phrasing about a "collapse" of metanarratives may be so strong as to seem untenable. The questioning of metanarratives seems a more appropriate term given that the discourse and practices of empire and capitalism are alive and well in the world today.

58. Melville, *Moby Dick*, 36. Many items were traded between the residents of Aotearoa and European and American visitors and traders, too many to lay out in detail here. Some of them were flax, muskets, heads, agriculture, livestock, sexual partners, language, writing, spiritual knowledge, the gospel, marine skills (harpooning), tattoos, and various other items of "curiosity."

59. As quoted in Sorrenson, "How to Civilize Savages," 99.

60. Ibid., 100.

61. Ibid.

62. Ibid., 99–101.

the naive assumption by the British that they would be able to control how their goods—and their religion—would be received, interpreted, and adapted by these tribal societies. This fantasy was to be undeceived many times in the coming years.[63]

In fact, the transmission of Christian theological traits proved far from under the control of the missionaries, of Western theological or cultural orthodoxies. The evangelicals' millennialist eschatologies, for example, morphed into Māori prophetic movements resistant to British settlement and expansion while adapting "the gospel" to the purpose of survival and resistance:[64] "Māori did not so much convert to Christianity as *convert Christianity*, like so much else that Pakeha"—people of non-Māori descent—"had brought, to their own purposes."[65] The gift of religion here was received in a manner that was in many ways as much if not more on the terms of the recipients than of the givers.

Postcolonial Reciprocity

In such colonial economies, it may seem that God is in the "market slot"—and the market is in the God slot. But what if, in a postcolonial world, it were necessary to abandon the God slot—as it might be in contemporary anthropology to abandon the "savage slot"[66]—so as to decolonize God, woman, and native? In fact, in a postcolonial, transcultural world, there are multiple possibilities for thinking reciprocity between humans in terms of time, degree, location, and differences in power, age, and knowledge, as well as for thinking the divine-human-world relationship in terms of various degrees of reciprocity. A variety of exchanges partake in the formation of the hybrid identities of transcultures.

---

63. The CMS (Church Missionary Society) missionaries, for example, propagated a relatively specific Victorian evangelical theology that became spread within the confines of the denominational churches. It would appear that traditional Eurocentric theology remained fairly stable, as can be seen in the theological conversion strategies outlined by Judith Binney: The missionaries argued that Christian society was a result of God's favor and that with it came material prosperity (Judith Binney, "Christianity and the Maoris to 1840: A Comment," *New Zealand Journal of History* 3, no. 1 [April 1969]: 152). They further emphasized, true to Puritan form, a strong Augustinian notion of sin (Robert Glen, "Those Odious Evangelicals: The Origins and Background of CMS Missionaries in New Zealand," in *Mission and Moko: The Church Missionary Society in New Zealand, 1814–1882* [ed. Robert Glen; Christchurch: Latimer Fellowship of New Zealand, 1992], 20). Thus having talked up human depravity, which was not a concept familiar or obvious to Māori, they attempted to convey the notion of redemption via the cross. While the missionaries found the *tapu* restrictions of Māori society a great hindrance to conversion, they ironically claimed sickness is a result of sin (which one could in some sense compare to the breaking of a *tapu* restriction). Māori fear of imported diseases came in handy in stressing that the British had better medicine (ironically not a better form of faith healing) and was problematically merged with a "European religion of rewards (and punishments)" (Binney, "Christianity and the Maoris," 153–54). Ironically, the missionaries' efforts were hampered by their own emphasis on keeping themselves separate from the Māori, as well as on isolating converts from the villages, and often proved the wrong strategy for propagating the gospel. Owens argues that the missionaries transferred British class divisions onto interrace relationships, treating Māori as lower-class people with whom they would not intermarry or socialize. Not surprisingly, then, native catechists were far more effective, being able to express the gospel as they understood it in Māori terms (John Morley R. Owens, "Christianity and the Maoris to 1840," *The New Zealand Journal of History* 2, no.1 [April 1968]: 29; and Binney, "Christianity and the Maoris," 163).

64. Bronwyn Elsmore, *Mana from Heaven: A Century of Maori Prophets in New Zealand* (Auckland: Reed, 1989).

65. King, *History of New Zealand*, 144, emphasis mine.

As has been observed by many, the hierarchical gender dynamic often overlaps with the structural economy of colonizer-colonized. Consider the rhetoric of the British colonial propagandist and Anglican cleric Samuel Purchas, who argued that the "Virgin Portion" of North America had been divinely allocated to his countrymen, "God in wisdom having enriched the savage countries, that those riches be attractive for Christian suitors."[67] In colonial travel and propaganda literature, the trope that "the American continent was a richly endowed virgin bride awaiting a husband enjoyed considerable usage" in early colonial times.[68]

Other instances equally revealed the dangerous side of the gift as gendered exchange. Cook's journal often mentions that a canoe with "people" came by his ship. This may indicate the presence of women in Māori war canoes. However, Māori women, in these encounters narrated by Cook and company, are even more silenced, perhaps doubly so, by the hypermasculine world of a floating homosocial imperial naval society that often overlaid its particular sexist assumptions and needs on native communities. Some Māori women became sexual partners of the erotically starved male ship population and often the first recipients of sexually transmitted viruses introduced by sailors. Soon they would also be mothers, and hence the main producers of intercultural genetic exchanges, harnessed in the cause of assimilation through the "amalgamation of races" policy as pursued by the British in New Zealand.[69]

Early accounts of travels to North America were "characterized by promises of abundance, even excess,"[70] even as the early settlers were dependent on credit from home. Furthermore, the "New World" was considered to be possessed of "an abundance that was permanent and natural and therefore needed none of the hierarchies and hoardings that followed from a scarcity economics,"[71] although the lust for gold soon did away with such romantic ideas. Assumptions of divine and natural abundance merged with other constructions to form the dissonant, mixed messages of colonial imagery: "What we have is a persistent presentation of Europeans as the givers, and a stress on the power of giving, *alongside* the counteridea of the New World as a bountiful, fecund place from which to take."[72] The double resonance of the theological troping in these inherently ambivalent and unstable exchanges serves as an apology for empire as royal and divine sovereignty are merged together in order to subordinate humans.

In colonial exchanges, the trope of the gift actually can function in several ways as power fluctuates across boundaries of giving and receiving. Colonial explorers often

---

66. Trouillot, *Global Transformations*, 25.

67. James, *British Empire*, 12.

68. Ibid., 12. On Columbus's use of the same trope, see also Catherine Keller, *Apocalypse Now and Then: A Feminist Guide to the End of the World* (Boston: Beacon, 1996), 154–56.

69. Sorrenson, "How to Civilize Savages," 103. This policy remains unsuccessful in many ways in part because many indigenous peoples, among them Māori, resist the Western notion of identification of blood/race/ethnicity with cultural, communal belonging. Hence, in contemporary Aotearoa/New Zealand, while there is a great degree of intermarriage, there is increased resistance to assimilation when it means the erasure of Māori culture, and great resistance to identifying as Māori as having to do with the person's blood content (cf. http://maaori.com/whakapapa/fullblood.htm).

70. Murray, *Indian Giving*, 49.

71. Ibid., 51.

72. Ibid., 60, emphasis mine.

remarked upon the abundant nature of resources they encountered on their travels. Hence, James Cook, who served, in many ways, as a bioprospector for the merchants of empire, drew tidy and accurate maps to many "treasure islands" later visited by seal-hunting and whale-hunting ships (such as the *Essex*, the factual antecedent of the fictional *Pequod*) and finally by European settlers in South Pacific Islands.[73] It took only forty years of exploiting the "abundance of the New Zealand fur seal" reported by Cook for that population to crash, and the whaling industry in pursuit of whale oil as fuel for industry and lamps peaked not long after.[74]

Today, however, Cook's journals are used by Māori as a source for lands and resources claims staked in the Waitangi tribunal.[75] In reclaiming some of the land and resources disenfranchised during the process of colonization, Māori have taken advantage of Cook's detailed prospecting:

"We've survived colonial oppression by being proactive," Tracey [Tangihere] said, "and by adapting Western skills to our own ends."

To illustrate this, she showed me a three-hundred-page "working paper" for a land claim one local tribe had filed with the government. To prove such claims, tribes had to demonstrate a long-term pattern of use and settlement. "Cook's one of our best sources," Tracey said. With a surveyor's eye, Cook had carefully delineated the boundaries of villages, the location of shell mounds, the use of fishing nets. At one point, the *Endeavour*'s men saw fishing canoes more than twelve miles offshore—evidence the Māori now use to determine the extent of their traditional fishing ground. . . . "It's come full circle, eh?" Tracey said. "Cook led to the destruction of our world, and now we're using him to put it back together again."[76]

This is not a simple act of resistance by a colonized culture against the culture of the colonizer. It is a transcultural act, the unexpected product of the "gift of civilization" in all its ambivalence.[77]

---

73. Cf. Londa Schiebinger, *Plants and Empire: Colonial Bioprospecting in the Atlantic World* (Cambridge, Mass.: Harvard University Press, 2004).

74. The depletion of fur seals was intimately connected with a new addiction the British had picked up during their imperial adventures: sealskins functioned as payment for tea from China (King, *History of New Zealand*, 118, 121).

75. "The Tribunal is a permanent commission of inquiry charged with making recommendations on claims brought by Maori relating to actions or omissions of the Crown, which breach the promises made in the Treaty of Waitangi." See online: http://www.waitangi-tribunal.govt.nz/about/waitangitribunal/.

76. Horvitz, *Blue Latitudes*, 130. This should not give the impression, however, that resources in the pre-European settlement of Aotearoa/New Zealand were uncontested. Much of intertribal warfare concerned contested resources.

77. In contemporary Aotearoa/New Zealand, Māori continue to struggle to deal with the gifts/poisons received from British and now American civilizations. In the wake of the North Atlantic merchants and missionaries came the social scientists. Māori were somewhat of a favorite with anthropologists, since at one time race and diffusionist theories harbored by European scientists ranked the South Polynesian Māori above Africans and Australian "sons of Ham," and they were at times identified as the "lost tribes of Israel." "Indeed the Maori had the good fortune to be ranked higher than most other 'savages.' Exponents of the Great Chain of Being invariably put the Maori somewhat above the unfortunate Hottentots or the Australian Aborigenes who were usually placed in the last links in the chain between man and the apes. [Similarly,] the Maori, with their sedentary agriculture and skilled arts, were usually

Recognizing transcultural creativity through resistant adaptations such as this, which is likewise far from giving in to the pressure for assimilation, is the best way to respect the agency and contribution of colonized peoples. It is the way to move beyond the liberal "bleeding heart" depiction of natives only as victims of merchants and missionaries.[78] Indeed, acts such as these are places where transcultures emerge, the places of creative hybridity, places on the "edge of chaos" where divine *dynamis* offers a space for healing transformation to all involved.[79] In transcultures, the lines run less and less along ethnic, gender, and even class boundaries and are increasingly being redrawn around issues such as justice, peace, ecological sustainability, and the desire to form societies built on more equitable exchanges with indigenous peoples. A transcultural encounter under less hegemonic terms, if such a thing is possible, would sound the depths of questions that lie much deeper than just references to exotic observations that in the end are self-mirroring, because they are aimed as a criticism at the writer's own context.[80]

This self-mirroring has long ceased to be a secret.[81] In it, one claimed difference between Western modern capitalist cultures and many indigenous cultures is that in many indigenous cultures, generous giving (which of course is predicated by the acquisition of enough resources to be generous) enhances status as "the giver gains rank."[82] Giving is then the marker of social status, whereas often within capitalist cultures, taking and owning have been the primary indicators of social status.[83] Where

---

placed on the border between savagery and barbarism and assumed to be capable with proper guidance, of graduating to civilization" (Sorrenson, "How to Civilize Savages," 97, 98). James Cook considered them a "warlike people" (Horvitz, *Blue Latitudes*, 117) and commented on their sedentary agricultural economy, something that indicated a level of "culture" to imperialist Englishmen. It seemed, however, that for the most part, the Māori remained a very ambivalent encounter for European visitors to Aotearoa because they defied the labels of both "barbaric" peoples and "noble savage."

78. Assimilation here appears as the pressure to conform to a hegemonic culture, something that was asked of Jews in Germany, for example. The psychological costs of assimilation are, however, immense.

79. For a theological exploration of chaos theory and the dynamics of systems oscillating between versions of chaos and order, see Keller, *Face of the Deep*.

80. I am aware that this essay is implicated in this very problem.

81. Thus, Christopher Bracken contends that the Canadian legislation to forbid the potlatch and the controversy around it implied that "when Canada finally delivered itself to its western border, it found Europe already embodied in a group of cultures that white Canadians wished to define themselves against. Europe was already there among the very First Nations that European Canada, Europe-in-Canada, considered absolutely different from itself" (Christopher Bracken, *The Potlatch Papers: A Colonial Case History* [Chicago: University of Chicago Press, 1997], 2). Hence, it is no surprise that, as Bracken further contends, Mauss's investigations were conditioned not so much by his romanticism about "primitive peoples" but by his culture's unconscious. Bracken contends that the notion that there had once been societies that practiced a "true gift" was a quite recent invention: "for Mauss the distinction between a gift, conceived as an event that brings nothing back to the giver, and an exchange, understood as a reciprocal circulation of goods and services between two or more parties," is a "fairly recent" development, "peculiar to Western European societies" (155).

82. Carl Olson, "Excess, Time, and the Pure Gift: Postmodern Transformations of Marcel Mauss," *Method and Theory in the Study of Religion* 14 (2002): 357.

83. That such taking and owning have been the main indicators of status is evidenced in many detailed accounts of extreme capitalism, such as the following: Juliet B. Schor, *The Overspent American: Upscaling, Downshifting, and the New Consumer* (New York: Basic Books, 1998); Dell deChant, *The Sacred Santa: Religious Dimensions of Consumer Culture* (Cleveland: Pilgrim Press, 2002); and Thomas Frank, *One Market under God* (New York: Anchor Books, 2000). This does not exclude the existence of strong expectations of charitable giving or of "giving back" to one's alma mater. However, these, too, are not simply "gifts" but expectations of reciprocity.

these different value preferences are maintained, they function to enhance the power of one side at the expense of the other. Between certain cultures, then, one prioritizing giving, the other taking, the flow of power will tend to impoverish the culture prioritizing giving if the receiving culture does not keep up in kind.

For the Māori, there exists a strong sense of reciprocity and obligation in economies of exchange. Anne Salmond comments that "it has often been remarked by European scholars that there is no precise word for 'gratitude' in Māori. This is probably because words are an inadequate return for kindness, or help in time of need."[84] And Mauss observes about the *hau*,[85] the "spirit of a thing given," that *taonga* ("treasures")[86] have a form of "mana," which Mauss defines as "magical, religious and spiritual power" that can destroy a recipient if "the law, or rather the obligation, about making a return gift is not observed."[87] "The taonga and all strictly personal possessions have a hau, a spiritual power. You give me taonga, I give it to another, the latter gives me taonga back, since he is forced to do so by the hau of my gift; and I am obliged to give this one to you since I must return to you what is in fact the product of the hau of your taonga."[88] Likewise, "The obligation attached to a gift itself is not inert. Even when abandoned by the giver, it still forms a part of him [*sic*]."[89] Hence, even though giving may convey high status, it is part of a cycle of reciprocity.

Does becoming assimilated to capitalist forms of economic and social interaction then also mean not being so "naive" (as defined in Western culture) as to "always give," foolishly expecting reciprocity in giving? Does becoming assimilated, becoming a capitalist, then also mean prioritizing taking and abandoning giving? This notion of the gift without any concomitant reciprocal obligation also bolsters the theological notion of God as boundless giver and makes people who have been reared in the societies that assume such a gift is possible feel less "obliged" to reciprocate in their relations.

In fact, one anti-imperialist argument raised both by peoples within and without North Atlantic colonizing cultures has been that "it is a problem of whites, and therefore of the entire earth, that they always take and never give,"[90] especially where land and resources are concerned. Some of the more ambivalent "gifts" of Euro-American culture

---

84. Thus Anne Salmond begins her acknowledgments in Anne Salmond, *Two Worlds: First Meetings Between Maori and Europeans 1642–1772* (Honolulu: University of Hawaii Press, 1991), 9.

85. Williams gives several meanings, among them "wind, air," "property, spoils," and "return gift" in Herbert William Williams, *Dictionary of the Maori Language* (7th ed.; Wellington: Legislation Direct, 2003), 38–39.

86. While Mauss concentrates on taonga relations between people, the term includes the "treasure" of the land that Māori are set over as guardians (see King, *History of New Zealand*, 160; and Hirini Moko Mead, *Tikanga Maori: Living by Maori Values* [Wellington: Huia, 2003], 186–87). Land was regarded as the ultimate gift and could be something given in return for help in armed conflicts or to entice a future husband to live with the bride's family. Hence, Māori *taonga* are mentioned in the Treaty of Waitangi, often considered the "founding document" of New Zealand. (On the history and terms of the treaty, see Claudia Orange, *The Treaty of Waitangi* [Wellington: Allen & Unwin, 1987].) The treaty, a highly contested document owing to its problematic genesis and differing versions in two languages, guarantees unequivocally that Māori will enjoy full power over their *taonga*. This includes *whenua* (land), though later the treaty was soon used in ways that justified the phrase that land was "taken by sale," confiscated or otherwise alienated.

87. Mauss, *The Gift*, 8–9.

88. Ibid., 9.

89. Ibid.

90. Heiner Uber, "Die Aktivistin: Amerikas Farmer Wollen Wieder auf Büffeljagd Gehen—die Indianerin Winona LaDuke Will es Verhindern," *Die Zeit* 2 (January 7, 1999): 54, translation mine.

(technology, literacy, culture, monetary capitalism) that are sometimes unacknowledged in anti-colonial discourse, however, can and should be used, Winona LaDuke argues, for the survival of her people.[91] But the gifts that Western cultures claim to have brought also have poisonous uses. Some cultures affected by colonialism have sustained more toxic buildups than others. Resistant agency occurs in adapting the gifts/poisons of the colonizer to survival.[92]

Toward Theological Regifting:
Depth Charges for Christian Theology

Milbank, who seeks to "outwit nihilism" through the proclamation of a radical orthodoxy, appears to find support for his project in those "radical pietists" who realized that "to be human means to reckon with an immense depth behind things."[93] The only possibility for escaping "nihilism," according to Milbank, is to "trust the depth, and appearance as the gift of depth, and history as the restoration of the loss of this depth in Christ."[94] What then would it mean to "trust the depth," as Milbank suggests? Investigating the deep means paying a depth charge.

Let us consider Milbank's suggestion that the only thing required of humans in response to forgiveness is acceptance and penance: "Christ's atonement is without measure and without price, and the only penance demanded of us in return" is the "non-price of acceptance."[95] Milbank here seems cryptically both to concede and deny reciprocity, exemplifying the paradoxical non-reciprocity of his approach. His claim that forgiveness either is a totally "aneconomic economy of pardon" (without strings attached) or does not exist thus exemplifies a false alternative that breaks down even within the limits of his own text. Catherine Keller's theological analysis of depth in the first verses of Genesis and their afterlives, biblically and otherwise suggests that "the deep" emerges as neither simply trustworthy, or scarily abysmal, but as a site of complexity, of "chaosmos," that we may need to face in order live honestly and faithfully within the fullness of the created world.[96] Similarly, our Christian traditions—and the gift of them—are only simplistically seen as either trustworthy or untrustworthy. If we want to carve out possibilities of living faithfully with them then it is crucial to acknowledge them in their complexity and wrestle with them in their depth.

Yet one may doubt whether such a regifting needs to fit neatly into creedal orthodoxy, and thereby lose too many things in retranslating the complex compromises of conciliar language into a problematically unified one-voicedness that feels imperial in its neglect to absorb more deeply the issues of gender, class, race, ethnicity, and the

---

91. Ibid.

92. This adaptation would be distinct from the policy of the "amalgamation of the races" pursued by the British settlers, the goal of which would have been assimilation rather than creative, flexible adaptation and a truly bicultural society—something that is still a hope rather than a reality in Aotearoa/New Zealand.

93. John Milbank, "Knowledge: The Theological Critique of Philosophy in Hamann and Jacobi," in *Radical Orthodoxy: A New Theology* (ed. John Milbank, Catherine Pickstock, and Graham Ward; London: Routledge, 1999), 32.

94. Ibid.

95. Ibid., 47.

96. Keller borrows this term from Joyce's *Finnegan's Wake* and suggests that the deep hosts a matrix of possibilities (Keller, *Face of the Deep*, 12).

need to decolonize creedal formulations. This is especially problematic because creedal orthodoxy was formulated under the eyes of the newly Christian empire, under imperial duress, and, as has often been remarked, history is written by the winners. All these factors need to be taken into consideration in a theology that wants to decolonize Christian faith and tradition to allow for a more equitable economic and social world without discarding or uncritically affirming problematic dogmatic decisions made on the basis of some very particular contingencies that are not necessarily the eternal and final enunciation of a cultural interaction between Jewish, Christian and Hellenistic, Platonic ideas.[97]

Beyond Milbank's claims that modernity can be reduced to "nihilism" and "secularism," some of the subplots of modernity—the Reformation, colonialism, the Enlightenment—likewise witnessed explosions of new forms of religiosity (such as romanticism, pietism, awakenings in the United States, missionary cultures, and so forth). It is crucial to recognize the ambivalence resident in the Christian tradition, as in any other tradition—that there is no access to a "pure," uncontaminated past, no access to radicals, roots (*radius*) that would be somehow representative of an "originary" sense of Christianity. Rather, the "roots" and hence the radicality of Christian traditions may function more like a rhizome, the root network of plants such as potatoes and mushrooms, which are multiple and remain invisible to the eye, though the way this structure fuses "connection and heterogeneity" is crucial for the formation and survival of the plant system.[98] As concerns reciprocity between God and creation, God and humans, it would seem to me that there is at least a reciprocity through which our responses to divine energy, matter, *dynamis*—how we understand it, relate to it, act out of it—help shape the world we live in, for better and for worse.

---

97. Among many Pakeha, a pretense continues to be upheld, in universalist language, that "we are all the same," echoing Busby's pronouncement after the signing of the Treaty of Waitangi by a delegation of Māori leaders that "we are now one people." There should be "no special treatment" for Māori, which, of course, means all citizens should be assimilated in the Pakeha way of doing things and cease to be "different." As Trinh Minh-Ha has accurately analyzed: "Gone out of date, then revitalized, the mission of civilizing the savage mutates into the imperative of 'making equal.'" Again, the colonizers speak: "*They* decide who is 'racism-free or anti-colonial' and they seriously think they can go on formulating criteria for us, telling us where and how to detect what they seem to know better than us: racism and colonialism. Natives must be taught in order to be anti-colonialist and de-westernized; they are, indeed, in this world of inequity, the handicapped who cannot represent themselves and have to either be represented or learn to represent themselves" (Minh-Ha, *Woman, Native, Other*, 59). The danger and constant temptation is to repeat the scripts of the North Atlantic "geography of imagination" and to use differences as devices in rhetoric to reinscribe "the West" as the "better savage" ("better" or "more authentic" than the actual native person, a dynamic based on a strong binary division between self and Other/Native). Trouillot recommends: "The "us and all of them" binary, implicit in the symbolic order that creates the West, is an ideological construct and the many forms of Third-World-ism that reverse its terms are its mirror images. There is no Other, but multitudes of others who are all others for different reasons, in spite of totalizing narratives, including that of capital" (Trouillot, *Global Transformations*, 27). Theologians in transcultures would do well to defer the rhetoric of otherness in a way that is neither assimilationist nor nationalist, but that writes and preaches new possibilities for intertextuality and the adaptation (as distinct from the assimilation) of ancient tribal narratives and contemporary transcultures.

98. The writers discuss the rhizome in the introduction (Gilles Deleuze and Felix Guattari, *A Thousand Plateaus: Capitalism and Schizophrenia* [trans. Brian Massumi; Minneapolis: University of Minnesota Press, 1987], 7).

Forgiveness may be unachievable in human understanding, as Milbank claims, even when "inaugurated" by the "divine humanity"[99] of Christ, but acts of restorative justice can at least begin to cease some of the abuse, whether physical, structural, or epistemological, even as imperialism's effects continue. For colonized peoples (and colonizers, as well), an easy time warp skipping modernity would instantiate a form of dangerous amnesia on the part of the colonizer and make a mockery of the lives of those under the influence of imperialism. Restorative justice in theological discourse, then, must strive to come to terms with colonial theologies of give-and-take.

Since there is no pure space in Christianity (or any other culture for that matter) that allows a retreat before a certain time of "spoilage," the task at hand might be to come to terms not only with the hybridities that have existed in all cultures, but with those new ones generated by new phases of imperialism and colonialism. How might human beings find a sense of culture and identity that is neither impermeable nor completely assimilated? How might we trade in economies that allow most people to satisfy their basic needs and be able to live in relative comfort while restoring much of the integrity of colonized lands? How might we construct Christian theologies that neither simply repeat the cultural expressions of the missionaries nor are searching for some pure lost expression of indigenous religion? These seem to be some of the challenges of the future.

Such theologies need to see beyond an "either/or"[100] approach to theological loci, periods, and discourses and instead come to theological terms with the ambivalent exchanges inherent in colonial trades, theological and economic. Accounting for our complex history allows for the repentance of the Christian complicity with exploitation and empire and searches for ways to embody restorative justice and less antagonistic, more cooperative, and conciliatory relationships among humans. The challenge is to find clear-sighted, hopeful, and creative responses to the divine spirit calling us beyond guilt-ridden despair and disengagement or forgetful denial and resentment toward new iterations of divine economies. To accept the "gift of depth" would then mean to bring into our presen/ce/ts the extensive ties that have been formed between cultures since modern anthropologists (and colonists and missionaries before them) set out to describe "gifts" among "natives." We also might then have to learn to live in the presence of unstable economies of giving. We ignore their ambivalent locations at the peril of being unable to discern God's agency in a way that may help heal the abuses of imperial theologies and economies of exchange.

---

99. Milbank, *Being Reconciled*, 61.
100. Milbank, "Knowledge," 32.

10. Embodying and Emboldening Our Desires

—Lisa Isherwood

This essay will engage with Daniel M. Bell Jr.'s book *Liberation Theology after the End of History: The Refusal to Cease Suffering,*[1] which is part of the Radical Orthodoxy Series. Bell's book captures what appears to have become the essence of the radical orthodoxy movement, that is, the apparent promise of truly radical theology and the reality of fairly conservative theology being reinterpreted with a contemporary and alluring feel. Bell's book is indeed alluring, engaging as it does with a radical analysis of how capitalism has put Christianity in captivity, even if it does by extension claim that liberation theology with its preferential option for the poor has failed. Bell engages with Fukiyama's thesis that we are at the end of history,[2] that savage capitalism is the only reality left to us, and that there is no room for change and alternative ways. Bell argues that our desires may have been imprisoned by capitalism, but Christianity can free us from this end-of-history scenario by finding answers that appear to have eluded liberation theology. This is all very appealing to an old dyed-in-the-wool feminist liberation theologian such as me and I found myself responding quite positively, despite the apparent dismissal of liberation theology as a bygone dream of utopia. It was in this spirit that I read the book and what follows is the reaction to what I understand as dangerously seductive conservative theology—a theology that, while appearing radical through an understanding of how Christianity has become co-opted into the service of the Monster of savage capitalism and all the ills it generates, does not for one minute consider its own part in the creation of the secular system that now reigns. Further, Bell does not seem to find it necessary to reformulate that same co-optable theology but rather as I have said restates traditional, indeed, conservative theology. I will be using September 11th to illustrate why Bell may be right about the captivity of desire by capitalism but why I think he is way off course with his solution of restating the conservative tradition. By September 11th I, like many of us in Britain, mean much more than the events of the day that has come to symbolize the imperialistic aspirations and maneuvers of the United States before the events and the breaking of international law through preemptive military action since the events. My use of this example may not seem fair as Bell himself concentrates on Latin America, but as we all know liberation

---

1. London: Routledge, 2001.
2. Francis Fukuyama, *The End of History and the Last Man* (New York: Free Press, 1992).

theologies have for a long time reached far beyond the borders and particularities of Latin America; whether they are still viable or not should therefore in my opinion also be judged in the broader context and within one where violent resistance is possible.

And the Walls Came Tumbling Down

Now that we have had time to reflect and to see what happened next it has become all too apparent that September 11th has come to represent a series of aspirations and actions that were truly shocking. The images of falling masonry and falling bodies played over and over again are meant to obliterate the events that led to such a seismic eruption and to justify the horrors since. These horrors take many forms, from the devastation of lives, homes, and countries to the strengthening of the imperial Monster and the rallying of theology to the assistance of that unleashed beast. These are crucial times yet so many in the world seem to be inert. Why? We are not heartless people, we wept as we watched the pitiful events of September 11th unfold. Some of us even expressed concern about the international politics that were bound to lead to such catastrophic events in the course of time! I do not think that we felt unconcerned or even hardened to the plight of others before and after the events of September 11th— most of us felt and feel powerless. We are caught up in a web, not entirely of our making, of politics, economics, imperialism, and the racism that underpins many of these movements. Contrary to imperialist political mythology, September 11th did not change everything, it merely accelerated global agendas and events and provided a pretext for the destruction of social democracy through the projection of an exaggerated enemy, protection from which meant that civil and human rights could be suspended (through for example the Patriot Act) and large numbers of people demonized.[3] September 11th does indeed illustrate very well Bell's contention that we have lost our desire, we have been captured by forces beyond our control—forces that are not isolated incidents of oppression but rather stem from a web, technologies, of oppression and power.

The events of September 11th and those that have followed therefore act as a hermeneutic for Christian theology; these events seem to me to be central in any theology that can be proclaimed from now on. They encapsulate the world we are in, the global economic and imperialist mess that we are drowning in and the ways that Christian theology has become an ally (sometimes unwittingly) rather than a judge of this destructive praxis. September 11th was a wake-up call not least to theology—like the Holocaust before it, September 11th asks profound questions of the Christian God and his church. For those of us who explore the reality of enfleshed redemption, we are asked in a deep and disturbing way what incarnation can offer in these times of terror. Let me be clear here, the terror is not that unleashed by disparate groups of disaffected "terrorists" but rather that perpetuated by the well-organized, dug in, and ruthless terrorist advocates of advanced capitalism and its global agenda of greed based on the insistence that all that is distinctive in human culture be reduced to nothingness[4] by the global people and value crusher of savage capitalism. The acts of violent resistance

---

3. "The Power of Fear," BBC documentary, 2004; and John Pilger, *The New Rulers of the World* (London: Verso, 2002).

4. See George Ritzer, *The Globalisation of Nothing* (London: Pine Forge, 2004).

that such a mindset breeds are, in my opinion, almost glimpses of redemption as we intuit that the spirit is not dead, that some people are not so crushed by the hand of the imperialist Monster that they have no cause, no culture, no desire to be who they are—they have not been McDonaldized[5] into oblivion! Large numbers of people throughout the world have, however, been robbed of a voice and imaginative and creative ways to express their personhood—they are reduced to violence and we (the rest who have no power but live in the privileged part of the world) are reduced to stunned silence and impotent witnessing. Carter Heyward remarks that many of the American people are grieving—grieving deeply for lost illusions as well as for lost loved ones. September 11th shook many core beliefs about the security of the United States and the way in which it was viewed around the world. Many people fled to churches, into the presence of icons of patriarchal power, in order to try to regain a sense of security and belonging.[6] What this actually did was restate some of the existing problems, that is, set the circle in motion again by rooting itself deep in abstract power and the metaphysics that such a power requires and in so doing contributing to the division of the world into good/bad, us/them, the righteous/the infidel. Some security returned, but the people projected many demons and left the root causes of the violence untouched. Indeed, those neoconservatives who had for many years been attempting to regain control of the public mind felt that a door had been opened into the American psyche through fear, disbelief, and a search for ultimate security. The re-election of George Bush seems to suggest that they have regained some of the control they so desired.

We are to one degree or another a divided people—divided between us and within our own skins. This I see as the root cause of our stunned silence, impotent witnessing, and inability to resist—we are removed from the source of our imagination, we do not trust our embodied selves, and we are cast adrift in the world of the market and its military servicing. In short our theology has failed us—it enables us to be delivered up to the imperialist Monster through its service industries. So, unlike Bell, I am not saying that liberation theologies have failed us but rather that the basic technologies of traditional theology have delivered us up through their assumptions of hierarchical power and their fleeing from passion. Traditional theology has boxed us into a very narrow paradise, tightly controlled and free from risk, but the price has been a removal of ourselves from our own desires and a disconnection from others, except in some ethereal and heady way. In short, we have lost our passions and our vision—the over emphasis on personal salvation has made us self-absorbed and ripe for the picking by an economic system that depends on isolation, inward thinking, and the desire for material security. The radical message of Jesus has been reduced to the self-seeking personal salvation narrative of those who would prefer the security of ultimate salvation to the risk and vulnerability of radical and mutual living. People are being fossilized by static systems, political and economic, that declare themselves to be in line with ultimate and already declared ends. I hope my argument will become clearer as this essay progresses.

---

5. Barry Smart, *Resisting McDonaldization* (Thousand Oaks, Calif.: Sage, 1999).

6. Carter Heyward, *God in the Balance: Christian Spirituality in Times of Terror* (Cleveland: Pilgrim, 2002), 53.

Rebuilding the Promised Land

The challenges of September 11th as John Pilger has framed the question are then: "Who will put aside the chessboard and explain that only when great grievances, injustice and insecurity are lifted from nations will terrorism recede"?[7]

He states plainly that economics underpin the actions of the United States and its allies and that when the globalization agenda is mentioned the reality is the globalization of poverty where the majority never have access to all that we call normal in a "civilized society." There is no desire to include all in "developed standards of living," indeed such an idea is almost seen as a threat. The first world still needs the *rest*—but only the sea, air, nature, materials, and space in which to dispose of its waste; it does not need the people, indeed people just require that resources be distributed more thinly—their continued presence is not required! Pilger claims that the response to September 11th was really about the advancement of savage capitalism and not the overcoming of a threat through the containment of terror. Indeed, the illusion of dire consequences and the ever lurking terrorist are very effective tools in the hands of those who wish to pulp real politics even further through the reduction of democracy to a mere election ritual where indistinguishable parties manage single ideology states[8] in the interests of the increase of wealth for the few at the expense of the many. When faced with this reality we have to dig deep to find a Christian theology that goes beyond the call to love each other more and to forgive our enemies, even if we are engaging in the "therapy of forgiveness." I believe the events surrounding that day call for a reappraisal of the core of our belief because silence on these matters is no longer simply holding fast to time honored and divine truths but is rather betrayal of Christ incarnate. We have to be equipped to overcome the political chessboard by putting aside the theological one. That is to say, we can no longer create theological worlds that are hierarchical, power laden, and lacking in mutuality and claim to be surprised that the secular world mirrors this world but of course with much more power and therefore the ability to damage cultures, environments, and peoples. We have to offer radically alternative mindsets if we are to challenge the worst excesses of savage capitalism and its imperialistic agendas and not simply sit in the same ruts while claiming that we are better because our theological motivation is good.

Bell's insistence that we put aside calls for justice—"forgiveness overcomes the conflict of claims to rights[:] The terror of justice is warded off by the refusal to assert rights—"[9] seems strange in a world where the causes of violence seem so clearly rooted in lack of justice in the past and present histories of people, communities, and countries. However, Christianity is a way of life that right from the beginning appeared to fly in the face of received wisdom and so Bell may have a case. What is his argument about justice? His main contention is that Catholic social teaching by concentrating on justice has adopted the secular idea of rights and so has prioritized the individual over the whole (105). This striving for societal equilibrium through the upholding of rights and duties is, Bell suggests, far removed from the shared love of the common good

---

7. Pilger, *The New Rulers*, 157.
8. Ibid., 2.
9. Bell, *Liberation Theology*, 150. Consecutive references to this work are cited parenthetically in the text.

advocated by Aquinas. Bell claims that the concept of justice is what is necessary to hold a society together when that society is based on the idea of competition. In this way then he claims that liberation theology is playing by the rules of the capitalist system, which he has agreed is not in the interests of the majority or in complete accordance with Christian teaching. He says that "liberation theologians have embraced civil society seeing politics as state craft" but "the state and civil society are unmasked as servants of regnant capitalist order, extending its hegemonic rule either by incorporating or crushing resistance. Politics as state craft is futile (70)." He suggests that forcing people to respect rights is not enough to repel capitalism (125) since the capitalist system is compatible with the discourse of rights. Furthermore, he claims that justice viewed as rights perpetuates the violence and prolongs the conflict as it keeps people trapped in antagonistic logic (128). Bell seems to assume that liberation theology, in being in part a theory of distribution, can not free itself from the acquisitive discipline of capitalism. This seems to ignore completely the work of many liberation theologians in the area of alternative forms of economics—Bell in my opinion is making a fundamental error in seeing liberation theology as static. It may well be the case, as it seems to be, that liberation theologians have not yet managed to replace the savage capitalist system, but that is far removed from saying that they are content to accept it. Theories of just distribution may not be the end in themselves but would be a large step on the way. In these postmodern days we may have to look again at Marxist views of the production of wealth, but it seems to me that capital based on sensuous labor, that is, the involvement of the people in both production and distribution and not capital for its own sake and the comfort of the few at the expense of the many is still a good place to start.

A larger part of Bell's argument deals with desire and the fact that he believes it has been captured by the forces of capitalism. I will deal with this in more detail later, but for now it is sufficient to emphasize that Bell believes forgiveness and not justice to lie at the center of any "therapy of desire" (143). Through returning God's gift of forgiveness for us to others we are liberated from the hold of capitalism. God did not demand what was due to him; rather he forgave us and gave up on the terror of justice as Bell sees it. Bell states, "The claim that forgiveness more faithfully characterises the way God overcomes sin than does the liberationists' account of justice rests upon an interpretation of the atonement" (146). This interpretation is of course that of substitution atonement, which has certain problems attached to it. We may not have paid but an innocent did, an interpretation that sits well with savage capitalism since Christ's sacrifice is interpreted as belonging to an economy of credit and exchange that is reimaged as a gift of love, a point that Bell seems to overlook entirely. Bell sees those events as Jesus returning the gift of love and obedience to God (150)—the fact is that there was a crucifixion and this should not be overlooked, even in the light of a resurrection, in the world in which we live today. Bell in fact does not overlook it, but he states that crucified people are bearers of salvation in the world—that is, of course, as long as they do not complain about their crucifixion and their communities remain open and hospitable to those who have oppressed and crucified their compatriots (168). Bell finds it amazing that despite the fact that the blood and tears of the poor make capitalism grind on, they do not lash out; instead they forgive, they open their doors and share what they have. This I think is a very sentimentalized view that can only spring from the sanitized version of the crucifixion that is so popular among certain kinds of

Christians—the kind that allows us to place the blood and pain within a greater scheme that has the effect of neutralizing it through an argument about greater goods. This version is not based in much reality either except perhaps the kinds that have the resolution required of the powerless, not reconciliation of equals, at their heart. It is also a little off the mark in terms of what actually has happened in Latin America. There has been resistance and it has been mostly met with U.S.-backed defeat. The United States has not been slow to bomb countries that do not fall into line, to train torturers of regimes that hold the people in bondage, and to provide money to governments that fulfill its global aspirations. As we see if we transfer his argument to the Middle East, there are outcomes other than forgiveness, which, despite the devastation that has occurred, do seem to be shifting international politics and in time perhaps the savage capitalism that now everywhere underpins them. Bell is, however, insistent that forgiveness is the first step and that once people receive that grace they will change their ways. He states boldly that capitalism can't handle forgiveness. This seems the most outrageous claim as capitalism does not seem to be dwindling in the face of forgiveness even among the Latin American communities that Bell places before us as examples of forgiving Christian praxis. This is the male theology that feminists have been critiquing for decades. It is the kind that valorizes suffering, seeing it as an ontological way to change reality. Children continue to die and women continue to sell their bodies to feed their dying children (a reality that is now in Iraq as well as many other parts of the world), but if these sufferings are aligned with the suffering and obedience of Christ all will be ultimately well. This seems to me to be a green light for savage capitalism, which does not have to worry about suffering but can console itself that it gives people the opportunity to be noble, heroic, and salvific for themselves and others under its crushing weight. As feminist liberation theologians have endlessly pointed out, this is a narrative that only works in theory. When placed against the lived experience of women and men, new stories emerge that are less reassuring to the supporters of this slightly warped theology. Suffering and oppression take their toll in the lives of people who do not necessarily become ennobled by it; they simply become reduced and worn down, dehumanized and marginalized. Substitution atonement does not work in the lives of real people as has been skillfully demonstrated by many of my womanist colleagues![10] (The constraints of this essay do not allow for a further rehearsal of those already solidly made arguments.)

Further, we are told that reparation is never possible and so for liberation theology to look for it is futile. Unjust suffering, according to Bell, is not overcome by looking for justice but by being borne, just as Christ bore his own unjust suffering. It is then willingness to cease suffering that is the great act of hope in God, following the example of Christ, and this is the only solution to savage capitalism. Forgiveness in addition is a wager on God and how Christians must live in the absence of reconciliation.[11] All of this has to be linked to crucified power, that is the community of the crucified gathering together, in which God empowers them and delivers them from being disempowered victims (192). (Do we hear from the distance the cries of Nietzsche that

---

10. See for example, Delores Williams, *Sisters in the Wilderness: The Challenge of Womanist God-Talk* (New York: Orbis, 1993); Ivone Gebara, *Longing for Running Water: Ecofeminism and Liberation* (Philadelphia: Fortress, 1999).

11. Bell, *Liberation Theology*, 195.

Christianity develops in people this slave morality that never allows them to get off their knees but allows them the moral high ground at the same time? Is Bell espousing this kind of weakness that Nietzsche so rightly despised?) These are extraordinary claims from an author who early in his work called for religion and politics to be closer bedfellows and criticized even liberation theology for not being radical enough. This illustrates the way in which many of those who espouse radical orthodoxy seem to double back on themselves to restate traditional formulas as though they were newly discovered truths teased from dusty tomes. What exactly is new here and how does it indeed link theology and politics in a new and empowering way? Is it not the case that the poor and oppressed are being asked once again to align their suffering with Christ and in that find power, a power that is more ethereal than real and liberating? Bell does admit that forgiveness has yet to be tried as a sure tactic against capitalism, but he does place his faith in it, believing that through it the Spirit opens up paths of reconciliation. This may, in some cases, be true on the individual level where people look each other in the eye. However, when we are considering multinationals other means may be necessary.

To his credit Bell does wonder if forgiveness makes people more vulnerable. This in my opinion would be a good opportunity to look again at what vulnerability may mean in this context, an opportunity he does not take. Carter Heyward was one of the first theologians to reflect on the events of September 11th and she suggests that our response to the fear and uncertainty that we feel in this world of terror should be an embrace of vulnerability. This vulnerability is, for her, Christic in nature. In other words, it is one that truly opens us to mutuality in relation and offers redemptive possibilities, which is how she understands the mission of Jesus. Within the context of current world politics this translates as much more than letting down the psychological barriers. Waging peace through vulnerability involves engaging with social and economic injustice.[12] Heyward has a point here when she suggests that we embrace vulnerability rather than look for assured safety through bombs and the enforcement of Western economic systems. After all, it was the desire by the United States for security through the acquisition of great wealth and control of resources that led to September 11th. Giving this up is surely a way ahead. For Heyward then one of the questions raised by September 11th is that of the pervasive problem of the greed that underpins savage capitalism and its politics of power and conquest. Her answer is not that those who are oppressed should become vulnerable through the practice of forgiveness but rather that those who perpetuate the world politics that exclude should try a little economic vulnerability for size. Not the oppressed but the oppressor should walk in the paths of vulnerability and embrace it as one of justice seeking. Her answer is quite the opposite from Bell, yet it is a solution based as deeply in the heart of Christology as his suggestions seem to be—albeit, one feels, with a different Christ! Mary Grey, although not addressing the aftermath of September 11th, has much to say about conversion to the neighbor as a way of overcoming the greed of advanced capitalism. Remembering Gandhi, she asks us to think of the most marginalized and the poorest before we act, considering the effect of our actions in their lives.[13] This she suggests will lead to just relating. Of course she realizes that this approach does not seem to have mass appeal.

---

12. Heyward, *God in the Balance*, 79.
13. Mary Grey, *Sacred Longings: Ecofeminist Theology and Globalisation* (London: SCM, 2003), 199.

Grey moves her analysis further by suggesting that we are not in fact innately bad people but rather people who have been worked on by the markets and their advertising gurus—we are an addictive society trapped by the seduction of the markets. She is in agreement with Deleuze, who explains that capitalism does not just exert power by extracting labor and production but by capturing and distorting the fundamental human power of desire. Grey suggests that once this has happened we have no way to think beyond, no dreams that propel us beyond the mundanely material and so no ability to resist the market. Indeed we have an almost obsessive need for the market to keep feeding us. Anthony Giddens has reminded us in a parody of Marx that we have nothing to lose but our mock Rolex watches. I suggest that we do not even wish to lose them for they proclaim our nonidentity and we are addicted to our oblivion, believing it to signal something of significance about a self we have trouble articulating. Our chains may continue to bind us, but we stagger under their weight with joy once we have the tat of dreams adorning our increasingly indistinguishable bodies.

Grey, like Bell, argues for the urgent recovery of desire. She wants us to know what we are for as much as what we are against. Further, she puts forward as a theological task of great significance the reclaiming of the language of desire by theologians from the high priests of the market. While we continue to long and yearn for the new car, the new house, and all the goods that shine so brightly in them, we silence God. God too is turned into a commodity and salvation becomes an exchange economy with the blessed showered with gifts in the super cathedrals of capitalism. I believe this exchange economy is evident in some of the more bloody notions of substitution atonement, where the exchange is seen as fair and the sacrifice sufficient in order that the gift of salvation may be bestowed—the price has been paid and the wages of sin satisfied. It is no accident therefore that it tends to be fundamentalist Protestants who make the links between financial prosperity and salvation, totally encompassing the suffering of others into their blessed life. Bell had an opportunity to deal with these issues but instead preferred to restate theology that can, in reality, underpin the position he appears to critique.

Grey, despite sharing Bell's concern, is critical of him for suggesting that desire is restless in consumerism because its true end is God. This is not a new suggestion, and it is one that, in my opinion, shows its limits within the present world in one of Bell's more questionable assumptions, which is that, in order to achieve this fulfillment of desire, we should examine the world of the twelfth-century monastery. Grey thinks that Bell ducks the question of how desires are related to God and so considerably weakens his argument.[14] Bell assumes that all genuine desire is directed toward God, an assumption that can not be made in our secular world. Most contemporary theologians would be careful with such assumptions, noting as they do the genuine and passionate commitment to a better world by those who have never been connected with religion or who have fled the churches and are looking for more genuine and deep commitment to causes outside their walls. Bell seems undeterred by this knowledge and asserts that we are constituted by desire for God, a desire that has been corrupted through sin, which bends desire toward unnatural ends. Capitalism is one such sin that disciplines and enslaves desire and Christianity "is a therapy, a way of life that releases desire from its bondage"[15] in order that desire may flow again.

---

14. Ibid., 110.
15. Bell, *Liberation Theology*, 3.

Relying heavily on Deleuze and Foucault, Bell argues that the subject is an assemblage of desires in varying intensities captured as it is by particular regimes. The state and also capitalism include a host of what Foucault calls technologies of the self, but, says Bell, so does Christianity. It works with technologies of desire and this is its great strength in overcoming capitalism. Liberation theology, with its appeal to justice, has failed precisely because it does not work at this level of desires, it does not have a therapy for desire. Of course the big assumption that Bell is making here, which I wish to challenge, is that desire for justice is itself misguided and so not real and correctly aimed desire. Bell seems unable to understand God as justice, a concept that is biblical in origin, and so he is able to relegate the desire for justice to some second-rate position. It is also necessary to understand human desire as distorted if he is to do this. Feminist liberation theologies certainly have what Bell would wish to call a therapy for desire and it is christological in nature, understanding our very passions and desires, our dunamis, to be the very stuff of Christ. The therapy for desire in this case is to embrace and develop the passion that draws us into mutuality with one another and not just with an abstract God. I hope to show that this is the case in the final section.

Bell considers Fukuyama's work and his assertion that we are at the end of history as signaled by the grip of savage capitalism. There is no space for development, only repetition and the spread of one ideology. Capitalism has won the day. However, he sides with Deleuze in claiming that another reality is possible because desire will never rest because it can not accept endings. This claim is based in the theology of Bernard of Clairvaux, who, in dealing positively with desire in Bell's view, imaged it as movement because humanity was created in motion. It is through a re-evaluation of Cistercian monasticism that Bell believes we can rehabilitate desire, understanding it as something that springs from God and in its true form is full of God. Desire that has not been tainted is not to be seen as an absence but rather as a consequence of God's presence. Owing to the fall, desire is now fuelled by what debases it and it lacks direction, but this is an ethical and not an ontological state. Jesus and spiritual growth are the starting point for the healing of desire, which always takes place in the midst of the world. Bell attempts to put forward a very appealing picture of the monastery under Cistercian rule as a school of charity where distorted impulses "were sublimated, redirected or rechannelled into a spiritual engagement: doing battle and winning glory for the sake of divine love and the Divine Lover" (93). Taking into account that the early Cistercians were recruited from knights and nobles we can perhaps understand this very military language and confrontational attitude, but to be encouraged to engage with that kind of theology in a world plagued as it is by that mindset, which has of course sprung from just this cultural heritage, seems rather naive at best. At first glance Bell appears to be reassessing desire, which he says has had a poor press in Christian theology, but when we look deeper we see that what he is understanding as desire and his suggestion for an engagement with it are far from positive. Here lurks the same basic assumption that desire even if it was good once is not so anymore owing to the fall. It needs monastic discipline to rehabilitate it through battle and the winning of glory for the divine, who is clearly imaged as external to our being. It is as if thirty years of feminist liberation theology need not have happened and all that is necessary is to snuggle up to Bernard and be a lover of God. There is no engagement with feminist work on desire and the idea that it is the force that draws us out toward others and the planet and in so doing spurs us on to find answers to all that divides and cripples us.[16] Bell still places at the center of our being alienation, competition, and overcoming/ subduing, all of which deliver us into the system he speaks so vehemently against. He appears to go in for the patriarchal view that desire was good originally, but now no longer is. There is no acknowledgment that life is process and that such black and white statements are less than helpful and less than true, only making sense in a tight, theologically constructed narrative that has long since been questioned. The notion that life is unfolding, drawn out by desire and fuelled by that erotic energy that is the raw stuff of the divine, seems to have passed him by, which suggests that when he is speaking of liberation theology he really means male liberation theology. Bell continues with his monastic theme and asserts that liturgy is a splendid technology of desire as witnessed by the engagement with it of the Cistercians, whose whole day was thus given over to "therapy." While this may be true, Bell does not acknowledge that very few people partake of liturgical exercises, let alone in a strict monastic environment, yet capitalism remains the problem for us.

Bell is in agreement with Hinkelammert's assertion that we are in the grip of a "mysticism of death,"[17] a madness that in its destruction of people and nature amounts to collective suicide—seeing this as quite the opposite of the true and well-directed mysticism of the monastery. He would do well to consider the requirements of much male mysticism, a death of the self that when held up as a spiritual goal actually kills, rather than redirects, genuine desire and any sense of self-determination. Traditional Christianity, I wish to argue, had a role to play in our present predicament through precisely this negating theology and the great vacuum it leaves when it claims that one has been filled by an external colonizing, yet benevolent God. How similar this sounds to the descriptions one hears from those who have been abused by an authority figure or an object of love. Just as people who have been repeatedly abused can find it hard to identify their edges and their own desires, so too the Christian who gives herself over to a battering by the "three-personed God" (John Donne) in the name of love is offering herself to the world in a very wounded state and one that can make decisive action difficult.

Grey, in having reservations about Bell's approach, wishes to suggest that it is the Spirit that, as she puts it, "finds cracks in culture in order to give birth to alternative cultural expressions."[18] The Spirit, she argues, finds a home at the edges of the personal and the nonpersonal from where it reawakens the power of dreaming and imagining— the Spirit is the power of life and space for living. The Spirit is vitality and energy and connects us to all living systems. It draws us out into the unknown and sustains us in it. Grey echoes Heyward, only the latter is describing the role and power of eros and the desire for erotic connection with all of creation that is our driving force and our birthright. For Grey, then, the Spirit appears to enter the world and us, while for Heyward the erotic lies within us and is called forth through the presence of others and the recognition of their raw dynamic erotic natures. Both, as we see, have questions to pose to Bell, who in reclaiming desire still manages to keep it at arms' length and under military discipline.

---

16. See Carter Heyward, *Touching Our Strength: The Erotic as Power and the Love of God* (New York: Harper Collins, 1989); Rita Brock, *Journeys by Heart: A Christology of Erotic Power* (New York: Crossroad, 1988); or Lisa Isherwood, *Liberating Christ* (Cleveland: Pilgrim, 1999).

17. Grey, *Sacred Longings*, 12.

18. Ibid., 110.

Expanding the Walls of Paradise

So how do we expand the walls of paradise; that is, how do we infuse theology once again with its pilgrim spirit and encourage it beyond the narrow walls of its tight systems and worked-out heavens, which have played so neatly into the imperialist agendas of the present day? Michael Ignatieff has said, "It is not a sense of radical difference that leads to conflict with others but the refusal to admit a moment of recognition. Violence must be done to the self before it can be done to others. Living tissue of connection and difference must be cauterised before a neighbour is reinvented as an enemy."[19]

I wish to suggest that most traditional Christian theology, with its insistence on dualism, encourages us to do the necessary damage to ourselves, through a fundamental removal of ourselves from our passion, and by extension enables us to make enemies and learn to hate through that same fundamental distrust that dualistic thinking fosters. I am unconvinced that a theology of desire as Bell envisages it can provide the required healing as this too remains one step removed from our very essence. Indeed Bell's valorization of military discipline when considering desire does nothing but continue the alienation from self that is so destructive of our desires and passions and allows us to destroy others in the name of this alienation from self. What is needed in my opinion is engagement with raw/radical incarnation, the vulnerability and bravery to feel and to touch. We need skin on skin, not simply schools of charity and circles of forgiving friends. Dualistic theology and the "one step removed" mentality that it produces rips us from ourselves and cauterizes us, enfeebling our judgment, our hearts, our passion.

When we look at savage capitalism and what it leads to, that is, the violence and alienation between peoples, we as theologians have to look again at our systems of thought that are not as removed from the basis of the problem as we may hope. Along with Heyward I do think that radical vulnerability, rather than a barrage of bombs and a renewal of imperial aspirations, should be embraced if we are ever to live in right relation with others. I also agree with Grey that desire has been misled and that if the market is to be contained it has to be confronted by people who are firmly rooted in other ways of desiring—the market does not listen to reason; it is led by consumer desire, which it in turn leads through media and social pressure. A new Christian self-worth and self-direction is needed to stand unperturbed before that savage beast and pinion it with the passionate spears of unrefined and uncluttered desires—desires that spring from the raw and mutual relationality of all living things. I still wonder how we can transform desire when we have theologies, such as Bell's, that do not allow for it beyond a rather ethereal and self-indulgent longing after God, a romantic and slightly sadomasochistic notion that we find no rest until we find it outside ourselves in the perfect divine. I want bolder, more embodied passionate desire! For me then the question is again and unsurprisingly a christological one revolving around what we claim about our incarnate God. How does incarnation, our ground of passion and connection, stand in the face of the raging beast of savage capitalism? Does it cauterize and deliver us or does it root us in who we are and make us resisters?

I, along with Joan Casanas, understand Jesus to be a comrade who through transgressive praxis, not through a "school of charity," made a hole—created a space,

---

19. Quoted in ibid., 115.

opened up a gap—in what was hitherto understood as reality and invited others to make it bigger. There is no better time than now to make it even bigger, to root deep in one's own divine/human nature and find a way through the maze of misinformation and the temptations to rise above all the problems through consumption of the right products and possession of the right body on which and through which to show them off. I have argued in the past[20] for an understanding of incarnation as the flesh becoming word, that is the drawing out through engaged praxis, skin on skin, of our Christic natures and the living of what it is we prefer to project into the realm of metaphysics. The flesh made word enables us to find a voice and to make our desires known—we do not have to conform to agreed absolutes but rather discover where dunamis leads us. Further, our bodies and the bodies of others—far from being aliens to us through the basis disassociation that much Christian doctrine has required, and thus being prime targets for the market—become sites of moral imperatives. Those who are starving present themselves as challenges to redress the imbalances in food distribution, those who are poisoned by toxic waste challenge the ethics of business and profit and call into focus the integrity of the planet as well as people. Meanwhile those who labor under the genocidal reality of advanced capitalism present their bodies as a moral challenge to find alternative economic systems. When the flesh is word these questions cannot be delayed or avoided by talk of reward in heaven. Those who have only violence left as a way to be heard shake us to the core and challenge our faith and courage—we are frightened and frightened people shrink within their skins, wishing to be invisible and protected. Incarnation demands that we flee from the temptation to hide in the comfort of metaphysics and commit to our flesh and the flesh of others as the sites through which redemptive praxis unfolds. This rooting of the divine within and between us is a foundational act of resistance to markets that take advantage of our uprooted desires. When Christ is in heaven we are removed from ourselves and uprooted enough to be vulnerable to manipulation through an engagement with delayed eschatons, borne through forgiveness, and present partial satisfactions fuelled by capitalism.

Committing to flesh is a risky business and a very frightening thought in these unstable times. However, risking embodiment is perfectly in line with a religion that has incarnation at the heart. Incarnation acknowledged as risk means that the kingdom, our visions, are always on a knife edge between the gloriously successful empowerment of ourselves and others and the devastatingly wrong and the mundanely unimaginative. If we are to break out of the hold that oppressive systems increasingly seem to have on the world, then vision empowered by imagination is crucial. Our second act of resistance is then to be alive to countercultural possibilities, to living transgressively. Such an act affects all areas of our lives, from the choices we make in the consumer market to the choices we make over patterns of relationship and the very theologies we dare to support. Indeed, we have to incarnate transgression, that is, we have to play with existing categories and break boundaries. Living transgressively spurs us on to be limitless and without boundary; it requires that we face imaginatively those limits erected in our own minds, cultures, religious systems, and environments and overcome them through the power of intimate connection. We have to think beyond

20. Isherwood, *Liberating Christ*.

boundaries and can do this best when we have also destabilized the Christ of ultimates and absolutes, the Christ who only leads to already decided answers which fail us. It is this Christ of hierarchies, ultimate power, and metaphysical magic that Bell and others of the radical orthodoxy movement are not willing to let go. Indeed, I am not sure that they feel it is even in question that they should.

Some may feel that I am making a crucial mistake by plunging into flesh and sidelining metaphysics. They argue that metaphysics gives the space required to see things differently, to have another perspective. However, it seems to me that using the same old system will lead to the same old answers. I believe that Bell illustrates this through his insistence that we are forgiven by God and so have to forgive others as a form of resistance. This clearly only makes sense when there is an overemphasis on the metaphysical and a downplaying of the material. As I have shown, a religion of incarnation such as Christianity can not downplay the material without dire consequences. The suggestion that we refuse to cease suffering is just one of those peculiar suggestions that will lead to dire consequences, although strangely, not for the one who suggests it. It may be a sign of Christian hope, but it flies in the face of the God who left the heavens and dwells in flesh that we may have life and have it abundantly. I do not wish to do away with the utopian vision that the distance of metaphysics has traditionally supplied; rather I wish to see it incarnated here and now, among us—I wish to see it enfleshed because in that way the nuts and bolts of what it means have to be worked out in the skin of people, not left as an intellectual exercise.

We have to enflesh incarnation deep in the marrow of who we are, stripped of the trappings of false and created identities, be they commercial or theological. The Christian right is finding influence in places of power and they are not kidding[21]—they wish to reassert the imperial Christ, who we all know had such devastating effects throughout history. This Christ was a destroyer of cultures and an obliterator of peoples—he is not dead in their hands. Along with many theologians I am determined not to hand this powerful narrative of ours, that of mutuality and vulnerability as redemptive praxis, over into the hands of Christo-fascists who would rip the guts from the world and impose a single and deadening ideology, advanced capitalism, on all cultures for all times. I am concerned that Bell and many of those involved in the radical orthodoxy movement are allies in this Christo-fascist agenda. This in itself is an irony and goes to show how very careful we have to be with our theological constructs since many of the founders of the movement would find no home in right-wing theology and politics.[22] I am, however, unconvinced that this can be done without deeply examining the roots of our own thinking—our Christian heritage—and I am equally unconvinced that reasserting theology from the past is the way to move into a future of resistance and creative incarnation. While I applaud Bell's critique of savage capitalism, I do not feel that he has taken enough notice of the part that Christian ideology, and the mindsets that it put in place in secular politics and economics, has played in bringing us to where we are. We have not just arrived at this point without some

---

21. See, for example, Doris Buss and Didi Herman, *Globalising Family Values: The Christian Right in International Politics* (Minneapolis: University of Minnesota Press, 2003).

22. I know both Graham Ward and Gerald Loughlin and it could not be remotely claimed that either of them are arch theological conservatives.

interplay between theology, religion, politics, and economics. As we see with the Christian right, a group that prides itself on conveying an unsullied tradition, its adherents have a political/economic agenda that they see as an extension of their Christian faith. Acts of terror, which may not be easy to justify but are made necessary by global economics and politics, should sharpen the theological mind. This must happen, not through glib and ethereal theo-speak, but through real resistance to the Western mindset that generates imperialistic actions and economics that was, and in part still is, underpinned by a theological heritage.

Bell draws us into an analysis of economics and politics, at the same time asserting that Christianity has lost its edge to critique the worst excesses of both systems. Yet, in my view, he simply restates the problem. It is as though by acknowledging it, and attempting to ground the reader in traditional theology and a certain monastic understanding, the problems will go away and Christianity will have risen once again as a world-transforming power. I fear it is not as easy as that and we theologians really have to find the faith to examine where our theological mindsets feed the worst excesses of savage capitalism and, far from excusing them, root them out. As I hope I have shown, the world of terror in which we now live requires that we radically rethink our christological understandings as much as our economics.

11. "My Yearning Is for Justice"

Moving Beyond Praxis in Feminist Theology

—Mary Grey

Liberation theology, including feminist liberation theology, often regarded by the academy as having had its day, after criticism from the Vatican and the failure of revolutionary movements, has been critiqued for a number of reasons. One of the most consistent criticisms is on the grounds that it reduces theology to politics;[1] another is on the grounds that it is not being political enough.[2] This essay grapples with critiques of liberation theology from several angles: it explores feminist theology's own anxieties over "praxis" as a theological basis, arguing that this was never a narrow sociological concept but rather a deep theological spirituality from which concrete social engagement emerged. This is true of earlier religious movements against affluence and extravagant luxury, such as the Franciscans, as well as of contemporary communities such as the Iona community in Scotland, that combines anti-poverty action with a vibrant liturgical life. Some Christian feminist liberation theologians have further developed this as mystical theology that never loses its grounding in concrete engagement with the world. But it is a mystical theology of desire and yearning of a totally different character from any neo-Augustinian theology that longs for a God transcendent to and beyond this world. Engaging with two contemporary figures, Dorothy Day and Dorothee Soelle, this essay explores a two-pronged mysticism: on the one hand, a mysticism of resistance to injustice in all shapes and forms; and on the other, an experience of the joy and fullness of presence of the sacred in the embodied life of all creation. Both dimensions are experienced as participation in the *divine praxis* of bringing to birth the kingdom of justice and peace. So, whereas for radical orthodoxy participation in the life of the divine is a key feature, for feminist liberation theology, participation means sharing God's suffering (pathos) in the affliction of oppressed peoples and earth, in the hope of a transformed world.

Introduction

It is ironic that feminist theology shares some of the agenda of radical orthodoxy: both are critical of the Enlightenment and the subsequent privileging of an excessive

---

1. Joseph Ratzinger (now Pope Benedict XVI), "Central Problem for Faith," in *Briefing* 27 (January 16, 1997).
2. John Milbank, *Theology and Social Theory* (Oxford: Blackwell, 1990); Nicholas Lash, "Not Exactly Politics or Power," in *Modern Theology* (8/92): 353, 364.

rationality. This is not only because of the inferior place given by Enlightenment thinking to emotion and a non-dualistic form of human personhood, but because by this—
together with the progressive autonomy of the secular world—the way was paved for
that form of competitive individualism so characteristic of the contemporary age of
"capitalism triumphant." Further, there is something very compelling about radical
orthodoxy's repudiation of "bastard dualisms" such as faith/reason, grace/nature[3]—a
repudiation that feminist theology shares, if for different motives. But it is the unitary
scheme that replaces them that fails to convince: Milbank's statement that "once one
has realised . . . that sexual Puritanism, political disciplinarianism and *abuse of the poor*
are the result of a *refusal* of true Christianity . . . one is led to articulate a more incarnate, more participatory, more aesthetic, more erotic, more socialised, even more 'platonic' Christianity" immediately raises the question as to how we are to recognize *true
Christianiy.*[4] What are the criteria for recognition? A fundamental stumbling block is
the tension between radical orthodoxy's leanings toward some form of Christian
socialism and its refusal to enter into dialogue with secular readings of history, or to
give weight to disciplines such as sociology and anthropology. John Milbank openly
espouses a theology without *any* mediation of the social sciences.[5] Richard Roberts
accuses him of paralyzing *both* theology and sociology—theology as a grace-driven
reflection and sociology as a discipline of clarification and critical representation of
patterns of social order: "his attempt to resolve global history through a post-modern
rehabilitation of a Christian 'meta-discourse' and its triumph over secular reason may
well in the final analysis encourage a form of 'hibernation' that sanctions the masquerade of eschatological-political impossibilisms in the guise of 'praxis.'"[6] A brief look at
some of the criticisms of liberation theology is a necessary stepping stone before
addressing the central focus here, namely, that some feminist liberation theologians
have creatively developed liberation theology as a mysticism of liberation that is at the
same time political.

John Milbank's Dismissal of Liberation Theology

I begin with a focus on Milbank, because he alone has developed a detailed critique.
Others—such as William Cavanaugh and Daniel Bell—share Milbank's metaphysical
approach but show greater sympathy and a more nuanced approach to liberation
theology.[7] If the mediation of the social sciences is the issue, then liberation theologians fail the first hurdle: they make no secret of the importance placed on dialogue
with sociology, anthropology, and Marxist philosophy. The grounding for this move in
the Roman Catholic world lay in the cautious statement of the Constitution of the
Second Vatican Council, *The Church in the Modern World (Gaudium et Spes)*, that
there is a rightful autonomy of earthly affairs, including the sciences, but within an

3. John Milbank, Catherine Pickstock, Graham Ward, eds., *Radical Orthodoxy: A New Theology*
(London and New York: Routledge, 1999), 2.

4. Ibid., 3, emphasis mine.

5. John Milbank, *Theology and Social Theory* (Oxford: Blackwell, 1990), 246.

6. Richard Roberts, "Transcendental Sociology: Critique of John Milbank's *Theology and Social Theory
beyond Secular Reason,*" *Scottish Journal of Theology* 46 (1993): 527–35.

7. See Cavanaugh, *Torture and the Eucharist: Theology, Politics, and the Body of Christ* (Oxford: Blackwell,
1998); Bell, *Liberation Theology after the End of History* (London and New York: Routledge, 2001).

overall dependence on God.[8] As will be pointed out, Milbank thinks this statement has been wrongly interpreted.

His main critique is that liberation theology "has been simply another attempt to reinterpret Christianity in terms of a dominant secular discourse of our day."[9] The question for Milbank is precisely what kind of mediation—if any—with the secular world is acceptable. Second, he accuses liberation theology of a reductionist view of salvation: ethics is placed firmly in the social sphere, which is separate from the religious. Third, as Ian Linden writes, in an insightful book defending liberation theology, liberation theology is charged with taking over an uncritical Nietzschean view of power as domination and violence, and with it a form of rationality that imprisons and turns persons into instruments of a universal "will to power."[10] In addition, liberation theologians are accused of simply stating an algebraic, reductionist formula "salvation = liberation." A natural morality that is essentially unaffected by religious belief, "and shared in common with all humanity, goes along with a thoroughly unhistorical view of ethics, which can even survive the encounter with Marxism."[11] Further, Milbank accuses this limited notion of salvation as being a-historical, individualistic, and only *expressed*—as opposed to being sacramentally offered by the social institutions of the church.[12] These are strong words, underpinned by careful argument. How is feminist theology to react?

The Ambiguity of the Stance of Feminist Theory

Feminist philosophical thinking is in an ambiguous position: it could itself be called a child of the Enlightenment, since the (most recent) focus on the rights of women certainly dates from the political movement set in motion by it.[13] Yet feminist philosophy and theology cannot be limited to liberal feminism and the struggle for equal rights that still necessarily continues in many contexts of oppression. Important though this is, its focus obscures other strands that offer a more radical agenda of social transformation—an agenda that also exerts appeal for radical orthodoxy. More importantly, feminist theologies, sharing the suspicion of many facets of the modernist agenda, especially its encouragement of competitive individualism, do not limit criticism only to this period: feminist theory has demonstrated that the subordination of women is constant throughout patriarchal history with a diversity of contextual expressions. Gerda Lerner has suggested that patriarchy emerged at least two thousand years before the Common Era owing to a complex combination of agricultural techniques, invasions, the stealing of wealth and war spoils, the solidifying of class power and political elites, and the realization that strength and domination are effective tools and weapons.[14] To plead, as radical orthodoxy does, for a return to an idealized,

---

8. Austin Flannery, ed., *Vatican Council II: The Conciliar and Post-Conciliar Documents* (New York: Costello, 1975), 935.

9. Milbank, *Theology and Social Theory*, 208.

10. Ian Linden, *Liberation Theology: Coming of Age?* (London: CIIR, 1997), 33.

11. Milbank, *Theology and Social Theory*, 230.

12. Ibid., 240.

13. Mary Wollstonecraft, *The Vindication of the Rights of Woman* (Hardmondsworth: Pelican, [1790] 1975).

14. Gerda Lerner, *The Creation of Patriarchy* (New York: Oxford University Press, 1986). A useful summary of theories as to the rise of patriarchy is found in Heather Eaton, *Introducing Ecofeminist Theologies* (London: T & T Clark International, 2005), 41–45.

patristic, and medieval period without acknowledging the subordination and misogynistic dimensions that controlled women's lives in this period—as well as before and after—raises questions as to the claim that this is the location of true Christianity.

The next step in the discussion is to engage with radical orthodoxy's critique of liberation theology and its rejection of praxis as a privileged tool, and then to engage briefly with feminist theology's own consideration of the limits of praxis. The aim is to explore the nature of the mystical and prophetic spirituality emerging from liberation theology, which is profoundly underrated by radical orthodoxy. By engaging in a "conversation" with two deeply spiritual and *political* persons, Dorothy Day (1897–1980) and Dorothee Soelle (1929–2003), figures who between them mirror the political tapestry of the entire last century, I will show that the mystical dimension inherent in liberation and political spiritualities and inseparable from their very heart is one of the richest resources of Christianity, congruent with any Augustinian yearning for the divine, yet refusing to separate this from a passion for justice on this earth.

Radical Orthodoxy's Dismissal of Praxis

An anecdote illustrates the perception of the academy that liberation theology is passé, a passing fashion of the 1970s and 1980s. In 1990, the journal *Concilium* held a conference at the University of Louvain, Belgium. In the morning well-known theologians from Europe and North America held the floor while discussing paradigm shifts and postmodernism. They were interrupted by *cris-de-coeur* from liberation theologians from different contexts, pleading that their voices of suffering be given space in the discussion and in the academy. The theologians who were dominating the discussion listened to them politely and then immediately resumed the discussion as if they had never spoken.[15]

Liberation theology has been criticized as reducing theology to politics and a Marxist view at that: the Vatican's critique is a classic of this approach.[16] It is also seen to be diminished by the failure of popular movements or the crushing of promising democratic regimes (for example, in Chile and Nicaragua).

Radical orthodoxy's critique centers on the liberation theologians' "uncritical" reading of the secular world and politics. As hinted earlier, radical orthodoxy repudiates the autonomy of the "profane" world acknowledged by the Vatican Council document *The Church in the Modern World* and the centrality of praxis as privileged tool. Instead of the priority of praxis, Milbank proposes "a singular, seamless, theory/practice, which

---

15. Another incident occurred at the American Academy of Religion, Chicago, 1993, on the occasion of the publication of Gutiérrez's biography of Bartolomé de las Casas. When, as "founding father," he was asked how liberation theology had changed over the years, his reply was: "The poor are even poorer and the world cares even less." Courses in liberation theology are rare in the United Kingdom—the church colleges forming an exception. My own master's program in liberation theology and globalization at the University of Wales, Lampeter, was always undersubscribed, when at the same time Celtic spirituality was bursting at the seams!

16. As expressed in the Vatican document *Instruction on Certain Aspects of the Theology of Liberation* (Vatican City: 1984). This document is always assumed to be the work of the former Cardinal Joseph Ratzinger (now Pope Benedict XVI).

has one privileged canonical moment, one canonical binding in words, and many less normative points of reference."[17]

In response to the dismissal of praxis, it has to be admitted that the charge is not without substance: Gutiérrez's earliest work certainly engages closely with key foundational thinkers of European rationalism;[18] his—and others'—work is deeply influenced by the thought of Karl Rahner, rather than by the French version of *integralism* preferred by Milbank and his colleagues, who admit some continuity with La Nouvelle Théologie. The grace/nature synthesis that so inspired many in Rahner's thought is seen by Milbank as reducing revelation to the status of making explicit the universal availability of grace and as "naturalising the supernatural." This unnuanced, unsympathetic reading of Rahner—who was able to distinguish between the possibility of grace offered throughout the whole of creation and the actual experience of receiving grace in the existential encounter—lies behind Milbank's rejection of the methodology of liberation theology.

For radical orthodoxy there appears to be no *both-and* possibility, only an *either-or* (despite the fact that Milbank abhors any involvement in Hegelian synthesis). Rahner's position is indeed crucial for feminist theology, as Anne Carr mentions in her influential study: "Rahner points, rather, to the importance to the creativity of human freedom, decision, and praxis as these play back into the elaboration of a never-finished project of human nature."[19]

Certainly the aspects of Rahner's thought that Carr selects are hardly germane to radical orthodoxy! "Human self-creation," "human freedom," and decision making in the determination of what human being is and will become are vulnerable to the criticism that they may overemphasize the autonomy of the secular and encourage a semi-Pelagianism. They are also the very aspects of Rahnerian thought selected by liberation theologians, stressing not only the persuasiveness of societal conditioning but as providing the basis and precondition for human and religious response to God. Yet according to Carr, Rahner also delivers a salutary warning to the privileging of any position on God or theology: "He maintained that in the Christian perspective, any knowledge or way of understanding of God which absolutizes a particular mode of approach must 'come under the hammer of its own principle of "destruction." ' "[20]

So Rahner is a strong support that there is no compelling argument to privilege a specific period of Christian history as a golden age before so-called pernicious influences set in. My own hunch is that radical orthodoxy has underestimated the strength of Christian faith that underpins the use of praxis as method by the liberation theologians. In its anxiety to critique the stress on human action and social analysis, it is insensitive to the stress on the mystery of divine grace and its role in achieving human freedom and liberation. In the last few weeks, rereading the works of Gustavo Gutiérrez, I have been overwhelmed by this fact. What I reverence—and this is precisely what I miss in radical orthodoxy—is the deep level of engagement with the anguish of human

---

17. Milbank, *Theology and Social Theory*, 251.
18. Gustavo Gutiérrez, *A Theology of Liberation* (London: SCM, 1974), 27–33.
19. Anne Carr, *Transforming Grace: Christian Tradition and Women's Experience* (San Francisco: HarperSanFrancisco, 1988), 132.
20. Ibid., 141.

suffering. Gutiérrez's commentary on the book of Job is a poignant cry for the kind of theology that can offer an authentic response to the level of mounting global oppression.[21] This cry itself indicates that what is not needed is a return to some imagined golden age but a recognition that new situations demand new responses.

If political theology responded to the question, "How can we do theology after Auschwitz?," liberation theology has had to move on (and continues to move on), because what happened in the death camps and ghettos still continues in Latin America (and elsewhere):

> Our task here is to find the words with which to talk about God in the midst of starvation of millions, the humiliation of races regarded as inferior, discrimination against women, especially women who are poor, systematic social injustice, a persistent rate of infant immortality, . . . terrorism of every kind and the corpse-filled common graves of Ayacucho (Gutiérrez, *A Theology of Liberation*, 102).

It is here that we should locate the discussion of praxis: how to do theology when the reality of Ayacucho still exists was the burning issue for Gutiérrez. (And we should add: the reality of Palestine, of the Dalit people [former Untouchables] in India, the refugees in the Sudanese camps of Darfur, the destruction of Afghanistan and Iraq.)

And finally, the context from which praxis arises is a faith context. Gutiérrez in a recent text has pointed out that the scriptural and medieval attitudes toward poverty, of "helping the poor," are inadequate in this contemporary context,[22] where poverty is on a massive scale, globalized, with multidimensional structural causes, and where economic factors determine even who shall be counted as a human being. This is the context of the "preferential option for the poor": it is a *theological* not a sociological category. It has nothing to do with any assumed moral superiority of the poor, but with the universality and profundity of the love of God: "The poor are loved by God preferentially because they are poor. All the better if they are good! . . . But it is not about loving the poor man because he's good. No! . . . Love of the poor is not necessarily because they are good but because there is an original gratuitous divine goodness to be seen right through the Bible."[23]

Gutiérrez's message is very simple: solidarity with the poor is the concrete meaning of Christian discipleship today. What I understand here is that at the heart of Christian community is not a seamless metanarrative but many interlocking concrete narratives, narratives of solidarity, resistance, and hope. For liberation theologians, faith experience grounds the experience of the praxis of liberation: these are the narratives that could form the basis of a renewed ecclesiology, an agenda that is also dear to radical orthodoxy.

Feminist Perspectives on Praxis

The first link between radical orthodoxy and feminist theology is the admission that we live in a violent culture. Yet the former's analysis of this violence is woefully

---

21. Gutiérrez, *A Theology of Liberation*.
22. Gustavo Gutiérrez, "La Pauvreté," in *Parole sans Frontières*, September 19, 2001 (text of lecture).
23. Ibid., translation mine.

inadequate. As I indicated above, patriarchal violence is not factored into the analysis: in reality what is offered is more an assertion of this violence, which is then contrasted with Christianity's culture of peace, a peace that is offered initially with the vision of *creatio ex nihilo*. But where is the admission that in the very age that Milbank would bring us back to Christianity was imposed through the slaughter of the Crusades? Furthermore, Milbank's rejection of a culture of violence lacks, for example, the explicit naming of sexual violence, torture, child abuse, or violence inflicted on the earth.[24] As critics have pointed out, violence is equated with the Nietzschean account of power, power that is itself to be rejected.[25] Recent feminist theology has offered careful analyses of both violence and power—in fact there is scarcely a serious work of feminist theology that does not critique power as understood within traditional theological and secular discourse, an interpretation of power that is coherent with what Elizabeth Schüssler Fiorenza calls the logic of domination or *kyriarchy*.[26]

Furthermore, in her ground-breaking works, Grace Jantzen has explored the entire Western symbolic as both violent and death dealing.[27] Instead of a symbolic imaginary based on death, mortality, and violence, she proposed an alternative based on *natality* (from French: *natalité*), on birth and life: this is not an abstract proposal but based on concrete realities.

The liberation theologians' understanding of praxis has been criticized from two main axes within feminist theology. (This critique is on the basis of feminist theology operating from the priority of *experience* rather than praxis, yet concurrently realizing the importance of concrete action for justice as central.) First, Rebecca Chopp has given a critical appreciation of both Johann Baptist Metz's and Gutiérrez's account of praxis.[28] Within an overall appreciation of liberation theology as a new paradigm for theology, as well as appreciating the different sociological tools of the two theologians, she criticizes them both for locating the "social" subject within a philosophy of history that ignores the related structures of situated societies: "To ignore these interrelations dictates that the critique will be inadequate and impotent, and that models of transformation will have to be content to envision new forms of consciousness and not new forms of socio-political existence."[29]

The focus on "situated practices" is now at the heart of feminist postmodern theological method, having now distanced itself from false pretensions of universalism. It brings into the foreground conflicts and tensions of real historical cross-cultural engagement, as well as the need for continual reinterpretation, if the goal of social transformation is to be more than ideology.

---

24. This is not true of Cavanaugh, *Torture and the Eucharist*, who writes poignantly from the context of torture in Chile.

25. Linden, *Liberation Theology*; Nicholas Lash, "Not Exactly Politics or Power," *Modern Theology* (8/04/1992): 353–64.

26. Elizabeth Schüssler Fiorenza, *But She Said: Feminist Practices of Biblical Interpretation* (Boston: Beacon, 1992).

27. Grace M. Jantzen, *Becoming Divine: Towards a Feminist Philosophy of Religion* (Manchester: Manchester University Press, 1998); Jantzen, *Foundations of Violence* (London and New York: Routledge, 2004).

28. Rebecca Chopp, *The Praxis of Suffering: An Interpretation of Liberation and Political Theologies* (Maryknoll, N.Y.: Orbis, 1986), 146–48.

29. Ibid., 147.

Second, the most thoroughgoing critique of praxis as privileged tool for liberation theology has been made by Elina Vuola.[30] Both Vuola and Althaus-Reid[31] criticize liberation theology for its limited notion of praxis—often empty and vacuous—that does not comprehend the deepest level of poor women's suffering, namely through their sexuality. Vuola's important study therefore focuses on women's reproductive rights in the concrete reality of daily life. As she concludes: "The perspective of *vida cotidiana* (daily life), if it is further concretised, could be a corrective for these tensions of LT (Liberation Theology). If too abstract theorising on 'femininity' and 'masculinity'— instead of concrete women and men and their life situations—seems to make it impossible to speak of sexual ethics in new terms, holding up the *vida cotidiana* merely as a theoretical tool may have the same result."[32]

Vuola argues that the holding up of the realities of *la vida cotidiana* of poor women is the task of feminist liberation theologians—in dialogue with feminist theology and theory. A focus on life in its fullness is characteristic of feminist liberation theologies. In the intercontinental dialogue on violence against women in Costa Rica in 1994, the critique against violence—sexual, military, ecological, economic, and racist—was placed within a deep affirmation of a spirituality for life.[33] Significantly, Maria Pilar Aquino's liberation theology for Latin American women is titled *Our Cry for Life*.[34]

In the inseparable connection between the affirmation of life on the basis of suffering and anguish and the contextual political struggle lie the seeds of a liberation spirituality: it is to this that I now turn.

Features of a Political and Liberationist Spirituality

Liberation, feminist, and mystical spiritualities have been claimed to be among the most significant currents of our age, and feminist theology as the source of the most notable cultural change.[35] Liberation spirituality focuses on the encounter with Christ in the persons of poor people. Usually seen as originating in Latin America, it is also rooted in the Catholic Church's commitment to justice and peace, as seen both in the social justice encyclicals and documents following the Second Vatican Council. From many angles political spirituality has brought together prayer within action for justice. Liberation spirituality strives for a deeper unity of prayer and action than had been found earlier in Christianity, for example within the Benedictine tradition. As Segundo Galilea wrote, "It is not a question of keeping prayer and action in separate compartments,

---

30. Elina Vuola, *Limits of Liberation: Praxis as Method in Latin American Liberation Theology and Feminist Theology* (Helsinki: Suomalainen Tiedeakatemia, 1997). See also her contribution to this volume— although the criticism that liberation theology forgot about the situation of women predates her work. Liberation theologians often speak of "a theology of life"—but this, until more recently, did not include the lives of women.

31. Marcella Althaus-Reid, 2000.

32. Vuola, *Limits of Liberation*, 213–14.

33. Mary John Mananzan, Mercy Amba Oduyoye, Elsa Tamez, J. Shannon Clarkson, Mary C. Grey, and Letty M. Russell, *Women Resisting Violence: Spirituality for Life* (Maryknoll, N.Y.: Orbis, 1996).

34. Maryknoll, N.Y.: Orbis, 1993.

35. Otto Steggink, "Spiritualiteit-wat is dat eigenlijk? *Verbum* 47, no. 4 (1980): 232–42; Timothy J. Gorringe, *Furthering Humanity: A Theology of Culture* (Aldershot, U.K.: Ashgate, 2004).

nor prayer outside a concrete commitment to the liberation of the oppressed, but rather prayer inserted in the process of liberation, living out an encounter with God 'in the encounter with our brothers and sisters.'"[36]

To criticize liberation and political theology as reducing theology to political action[37] also fails to recognize its rootedness within sacraments and liturgy.[38] William Cavanaugh is one of the few theologians of radical orthodoxy who has developed a eucharistic ecclesiology in the context of violence in Chile: there is much that is inspiring about Cavanaugh's exploration.[39] But, like Daniel Bell,[40] whose chosen embodiment of *ecclesia* is the twelfth-century monastery of Bernard of Clairvaux, he fails to engage with the realities of the contemporary church—corruption, betrayal of trust though widespread sexual abuse, clerical elitism, and absolutist forms of governance— that are estranging thousands of loyal believers today.

What political spirituality explores is not merely the prophetic dimension of protest, denunciation, and resistance, but a new form of asceticism and renunciation, and a new way of seeing: these lead to the dimension of mysticism. One dimension of Rahner's thought that attracts no attention from radical orthodoxy is his insistence that the Christian of the future will be a mystic: spiritual life would be rooted in *mystagogia*, or the absolute mystery of God, and that mystical experience would determine the very identity of the "Christian": "Der Fromme von Morgen wird ein 'Mystiker' sein, einer, der etwas 'erfahren' hat, oder er wird nicht mehr sein."[41]

Seeking a way through the varieties, definitions, and interpretations of mysticism through the ages, in the context of liberation spirituality, Grace Jantzen's criticism of William James is helpful: in his restriction of mystical experience to the private world of the individual he obscures a more profound theological dimension of mysticism that is not focused primarily on states of feeling or emotion. In addition, she makes us aware of a gendered dimension in the way mystical experiences are frequently described: the "ladder" motif, for example, is never found in the female mystics' descriptions of their visions. "The privatised, subjectivised, ineffable mysticism of William James," Jantzen writes, "keeps God (and women) safely out of politics and the public realm; it allows mysticism to flourish as a secret inner life, while those who nurture such an inner life can generally be counted on to prop up rather than challenge the status quo of their workplaces, their gender roles and the political systems by which they are governed, since their anxieties and angers will be allayed in the privacy of their own hearts' search for peace and tranquillity."[42]

Jantzen and others alert us to the power and vested interests frequently hidden by the expressions of visionaries. This is not to invalidate their content but to place it in

---

36. Segundo Galilea, "The Spirituality of Liberation," *The Way* 25, no. 3 (1985): 193.

37. See the Vatican criticism referred to earlier.

38. Rafael Avila, 1981; Tissa Balasuriya, *The Eucharist and Human Liberation* (London: SCM, 1979).

39. Cavanaugh, *Torture and the Eucharist.*

40. Bell, *Liberation Theology.*

41. "The believer of tomorrow will be a mystic, a person who experiences something, or he/she will cease to exist" (Karl Rahner, "Frömmigkeit Früher und Heute," in *Schriften zur Theologie 7* [Einsiedeln, Zurich, and Cologne: Verlaganstalt Benziger, 1966], 22).

42. Grace M. Jantzen, *Power, Gender, and Christian Mysticism* (Cambridge: Cambridge University Press, 1995), 346.

the wider setting of their contemporary religious and political communities. For example, it is no accident that the great twelfth-century abbesses Hildegard of Bingen and Gertrude of Helfta appealed to their visions of God as a source of authority at a time when women's authority was diminished.[43]

For the liberation theologians, the notion of vested interests is turned upside down, as, paradoxically, the direct, intense encounter with God is discovered through solidarity and commitment with the powerless. It is precisely through resistance to oppressive powers that a different experience of God's mystery is discovered. So Gutiérrez speaks of the revelation granted to Job when he surrendered to the wisdom of God: "What is it that Job understood? That justice does not reign in the world God has created? No. The truth that he has grasped and that has lifted him to the level of contemplation is that justice alone does not have the final say about how we are to speak of God. Only when we have come to realise that God's love is freely bestowed do we enter fully and definitively into the presence of the God of faith."[44]

This is a mystical faith, lighting the way through anguish and despair, and, as the murdered Bolivian priest Louis Espinal cried, calling us to

> fling ourselves upon the impossible for behind the impossible is your grace and your presence; we cannot fall into emptiness. The future is an enigma, our road is covered by mist, but we want to go on giving ourselves because you continue hoping amid the night and weeping tears through a thousand eyes (Gutiérrez, *A Theology of Liberation*, 91, 92).

This is the mystic hope glimpsed in the lives and deaths of the murdered Jesuit Ignacio Ellacuría and his companions, as well as of the beloved archbishop of El Salvador, Oscar Romero. What is remarkable in the lives of these contemporary martyrs is that this intense experience of mystical hope does not merely emanate from an individual but is shared by the community. Since the days of the death squads and wars of the 1980s and early 1990s, the cry of *Presente!* in the ecclesial gatherings witnessed to the living communion with murdered loved ones. Even today it is reported that poor people of El Salvador gather round the tomb of Romero with prayers, tears, and hopes, remembering his words: "If I am killed, I will arise again in the poor of El Salvador." As Jon Sobrino has written in the context of the murder of his colleagues but linking this with all martyrs for justice,

> "All martyrs will rise again in history, each in their own way."[45]

Turning now to the lives of Dorothy Day and Dorothee Soelle, the hope is to discover what light they bring to political and mystical spirituality, with special attention to the concrete realities of *la vida cotidiana*, the daily lives of poor people, especially poor women.

---

43. Barbara Newman, *Sister of Wisdom: St. Hildegard's Theology of the Feminine* (San Francisco: University of California Press, 1987).

44. Gutiérrez, *On Job*, 87.

45. Jon Sobrino, *Companions of Jesus: The Murder and Martyrdom of the Salvadorean Jesuits* (London: CAFOD, 1990), 55.

Political Spirituality and Mysticism—
Dorothy Day: *The Long Loneliness*

The Long Loneliness is Day's autobiography as well as a metaphor for her journey of faith.[46] Indeed, renunciation and loneliness haunted her from adolescence to adulthood, in her penurious years as a journalist following protests, rallies, and strikes, to her struggles as a single parent to bring up her daughter Tamar, and throughout the whole Catholic Worker period up until her old age. Not only does loneliness describe her financial situation, it also speaks to her spiritual search as well as to her personal struggle and isolation after she renounced her common-law husband, Forster, whom she dearly loved, on conversion to Catholicism.[47]

Dorothy Day, like Dorothee Soelle, was haunted by God and the search for God all her life: "'All my life I have been haunted by God,' a character in one of Dostoevsky's books says. And so it was with me."[48]

The striking point about this yearning for God that haunted her is that it was never separated from commitment to poor people from whom she was never separated: "I wanted the abundant life. I wanted it for others too. I did not want just the few, the missionary-minded people like the Salvation Army, to be kind to the poor, as the poor. I wanted everyone to be kind. I wanted every home to be open to the lame, the halt and the blind, the way it had been after the San Francisco earthquake. Only then did people really live, really love their brothers. In such love was the abundant life and I did not have the slightest idea how to find it."[49]

This search for the life abundant led her through socialism and communism into Catholicism and the founding of the Catholic Worker movement, with its astonishing achievement of numerous houses of hospitality and its thousands of daily battles against poverty, addictions of every sort, violence of all kinds, and the attempt to live in genuine community with rejected people. *The Catholic Worker*—still in print— carried the stories of struggles every month: its pages and the pages of Day's writings are alive with names and stories of desperate people. She presents a challenge to abstract theology with its talk of "the poor." For her poor people have names, families, hopes, and dreams, which she shares. The struggle to find enough money to cook the daily soup for the community is told in gritty reality. Within the honesty and admission of failure, there is also a revolutionary sense of hope.

But what gives this a claim to be mystical and political holiness? To answer this question we plunge deeper into her spirituality.[50] Day was largely self-educated, leaving university early to plunge into journalism. As we shall find with Dorothee Soelle, she loved literary texts and was particularly influenced by Dostoevksy, to whom she frequently returned. After her conversion she became immersed in the mystical texts

---

46. San Francisco: Harper & Row, 1952.

47. This was because Forster would have nothing to do with religion or the church, to the extent of refusing all conversations on the subject. The crisis and separation came over the baptism of their daughter Tamar Teresa. Day makes frequent reference to a subsequent loneliness that persisted all her life.

48. Robert Ellsberg, ed., *Dorothy Day: Selected Writings* (Maryknoll, N.Y.: Orbis, 2001), 9.

49. Day, *The Long Loneliness*, 39.

50. I first admit that unlike contemporary feminist theologians Day used the language of her day, which was not gender sensitive. This does not prevent her from being close to the sorrows of poor women, by which she herself was personally affected.

of Teresa of Avila and John of the Cross. But the deepest influence on her spiritual and philosophical education was the French thinker Peter Maurin, who became her teacher and mentor for many years until she caught up with him and was able to take more of a leadership role. Through Peter Maurin she discovered Catholic social teaching (of which she had never heard), but also many of the French thinkers such as Maritain and De Lubac. Maurin was steeped in Aquinas and his aim was to make a new synthesis of faith and culture, just as Aquinas had done. This was to be a revolution comprising cult, culture, and cultivation.[51] It is this synthesis of Aquinas, fashioning social transformation, that stimulated the political dimensions of Day's and Maurin's thought. It was this that inspired houses of hospitality, Catholic Worker farms, and what Peter Maurin termed "agronomic universities." People who reduce Day's achievements to schemes for the urban poor underestimate how her thought and that of Maurin anticipated much of "green thinking" today. Life abundant meant the possibility for the very poorest people of enjoying fresh air and eating nourishing food in surroundings that nurtured soul and spirit as well as body.

The point at issue here is that Maurin and Day concur with Milbank as to the inspiration of Maritain, De Lubac, and others who were the architects of the version of integralism of which he approves. Yet they are closer to the approach of liberation theology in that the chosen starting point is not a pre-elaborated theology of grace but the experience of poverty and degradation in the lives of the poor: this summons the praxis of evangelical discipleship that is the only authentic way to live out Christianity.

Praxis for Day was a rich concept: through it she came to appreciate the "sacramentality of life" and all that made it possible. Both Day and Maurin seem to have been influenced by Gandhi's ideas, especially in their dedication to nonviolence and peace making.[52] Day's mysticism primarily lay in discovering God in these poor communities (although she does admit to some experiences when alone): "A mystic may be called a man in love with God. Not one who loves God, but who is *in love with God*. And this mystical love, which is an exalted emotion, leads one to love the things of Christ. His footsteps are sacred."[53]

Identification with the sufferings of Christ brings her to a mystical element in the love of a radical for his brother (and sister), so that this extended—as it did with Romero and the murdered Jesuits—to the scene of sufferings, so that the places of struggle and death became hallowed: "You know this feeling, as does every other radical in the country. Through ignorance, perhaps, you do not acknowledge Christ's name. Yet I believe you are trying to love Christ in His poor, in His persecuted ones."[54]

It would also be false to limit Day's attitude to practical charity on an individual basis. Though she did insist on beginning with a revolution of the heart, her achievement was

---

51. Day, *The Long Loneliness*, 170–72.

52. I have to admit that I have found very few explicit references to Gandhi. But his imprint is there in what Peter Maurin tried to achieve. Sharing the humblest of household tasks was a principle, for example. But Maurin also aimed in the Catholic Worker farms for self-sufficiency with vegetables and keeping poultry. As well as baking their own bread the farms attempted to look for ethical sources of food. Day's daughter Tamar chose an unusual education, learning crafts such as spinning and weaving, and how to budget for a poor family, at the same time ensuring that they were able to eat nourishing food. Life with Tamar and her family on their farm would become one of the joys of Day's later life.

53. Ellsberg, *Dorothy Day*, 7.

54. Ibid.

to unite the personal with the political, the inner and outer expressions of mystical love. Until the end of her life the prophetic and mystical dimensions were held together by that indivisible love. Daniel Berrigan paid tribute to this after her death, while still on trial, as one of eight Christians, for having destroyed two nuclear warheads: "Without Dorothy, without that exemplary patience, courage, moral modesty, without this woman pounding on the locked door behind which the powerful mock the powerless . . . the resistance we offered would have been simply unthinkable. She urged our consciences off the beaten track; she made the impossible . . . probable, and then actual. She did this, first of all, by living as though the truth were true."[55]

Mysticism of resistance is a profound concept and one that is also a crucial feature in the life of Dorothee Soelle, to whom I now turn.

Political Spirituality and Mysticism—Dorothee Soelle

One of the elements that links Dorothy Day with Dorothee Soelle is the search for God, and in Soelle's case, the struggle to find a way to speak about God. When I met Dorothee Soelle at a conference in 1991 I was immediately struck by her argument that the only place to find God today is in the political struggle. She had discovered this painfully at a demonstration in Bonn in 1983 when the police turned water cannons against those protesting against the U.S. nuclear weapons stationed in Germany. Somehow she had to find the courage to speak to the bedraggled protesters and she found herself screaming to God—"Why have you forsaken us?" But then she found the answer coming from deep within, "The God to whom this prayer was addressed was as grieved as we were, small like us, with no bank account or bombs in the background. . . . And yet God was with us that night."[56]

Seeking a language to speak about God was a lifelong quest for Dorothee Soelle. Its roots lay in her deep shame over the Nazi responsibility for the horror of the Holocaust. Born in 1929 in Cologne, Soelle lived through World War II, with its bombings and the Holocaust, which formed the contours of her early life. (Her parents were opposed to the Nazi regime in private but made it clear that Dorothee had to keep her thoughts to herself or she would end up in a concentration camp.) She found an outlet in a diary, and, like Day, in her love of literature and poetry, where she found a Germany other than the fascist regime that surrounded her. Her initial studies were in literary criticism, and as she pursued higher study she found herself in conflict with the severely traditional and patriarchal system of German universities: having a baby while engaged in completing her *habilitation*[57] was definitely disapproved of. So when Soelle was offered a teaching position at Union Theological Seminary in New York in 1975, she accepted and speedily adapted to the new situation in the United States, discovering politically active Christians and a receptivity to her developing theology.

The first key point about her work is that, again like Day, whose work she knew, Soelle was an *activist* theologian. Like Metz, she was a political theologian (indeed, she

---

55. Day, *The Long Loneliness*, xxiii.
56. Dorothee Soelle, "Liberating Our God-Talk: From Authoritarian Otherness to Mystical Inwardness," in Ursula King, ed., *Liberating Women: New Theological Directions* (Bristol: Bristol University Press, 1991), 40–52.
57. The German university system requires a second doctoral thesis before granting permission to teach in the academy.

could almost be considered a cofounder of political theology) but soon changed to be fully identified with liberation theology and its different struggles. But more than this, Soelle was a genuine theologian of the struggle and was never at home in the abstractions of systematic theology. Again like Day her theology was based on involvement with real people and experiences in the struggle. Keeping open a *"window of vulnerability"* to people and their suffering was always crucial to her. The German liberation theologian Luise Schottroff—Soelle's closest friend—remembers how she initiated "political evensongs" in Cologne from 1968 to 1972. Here forty people—from both Roman Catholic and Protestant traditions—came together in a new church community unconnected with parish structures. Through analysis, meditation, and guidance toward praxis, they confronted the political scene—for example the Soviet invasion of Czechoslovakia and the Vietnam War. Luise Schottroff thinks that this was the hour when liberation theology was born in a German—even a European—context.[58]

The move to the United States brought Soelle in touch with the women's movement. Immediately she saw the relevance of patriarchy to the death-dealing systems of dominance. Some have criticized her lack of explicit attention to feminist theory, but Rosemary Ruether argues that she integrated successfully a gender analysis into "what remained a liberation theology steeped in Marxist critique."[59] Others have been more critical that she did not theorize at all about gender or consider the significance of sex/gender in liberation theology. But Soelle, again like Day, was far more interested in *what we do* than in theorizing on *who we are*. Here she stands in polar opposition to radical orthodoxy with its metaphysical superstructure of God, Christ, and church. With a profound distrust of doctrinal formulation and superstructure, Soelle seeks God through clouds of unknowing.

Given the rigidity of systems of some of the German theologians—Barth and Bultmann, for example—who formed her original formal theological horizons, Soelle moved through radical questioning to discover her own path.[60] The German experience of complicity in the structures in an evil regime was initially a dominating theme for her. She saw how the issue of identity became linked with this supremacy of dominating powers. (It is significant that one of her earliest books, *Beyond Mere Obedience*, explored the possibility of another identity beyond compliance with fascism.) Far more than Dorothy Day, she was able to develop an analysis of structural sin as a demonic counterworld to God's creation. A straight line can be drawn from Soelle's opposition to fascist domination in Germany, to opposing the U.S. government's action in Vietnam and in Latin America, to her resistance to the economic domination of global capitalism. The most important dualism that she unmasked was that between death-dealing dominating powers and life-giving love. For Dorothy Day, as with feminist theologians cited earlier, *choose life* was a leitmotiv. If radical orthodoxy saw the goal of Christianity as life as lived in the presence of the divine, for both Day and Soelle this could not be separated from the priority of transforming the lives of the most humiliated people of the world.

---

58. Sarah A. Pinnock, ed., *The Theology of Dorothee Soelle* (London and New York: Trinity Press International, 2003), 45–53.

59. Ibid., 205–17.

60. It was these German Protestant thinkers rather than Karl Rahner and French theology who influenced her.

An important part of this was the struggle to create an appropriate language for the project of liberation. Abstract and systematic argument does not feed the soul. Soelle gravitated to myth and poetry from many sources but was also sensitive to where they were offered in the Bible. To say she loved the psalms—also a source of nourishment for Dorothy Day—is an understatement. She even spoke of "eating the psalms":

> For me the psalms are one of the most important foods. I eat them, I drink them, I chew on them. Sometimes I spit them out and sometimes I repeat one to myself in the middle of the night. They are bread for me. Without them the spiritual anorexia that is so widespread among us sets in and often leads to a deadly impoverishment of the spirit and of the heart. (Soelle and Schottroff, 31)[61]

Very early on in her search she visited Martin Buber in Jerusalem. (Buber had been a great influence on Day mostly through his ideas on social change in *Paths in Utopia*.[62]) On her telling him that she was a theologian, he disconcerted her by replying, "Theo-logy—how do you do that? There is no logos of God." This disconcerting answer prompted her life-long exploration in poetry and myth, culminating in what would be recognized as a full-blown mystical theology. Her last book, *The Silent Cry: Mysticism and Resistance*,[63] is her most explicit expression of this yearning for God that fuels resistance to injustice and eludes complete rational expression, a theme common to many faiths. In a way, she embodies the old adage: *all things begin in mysticism and end in politics, only to begin again.*

In an early essay, "Breaking the Ice of the Soul," Soelle, complaining about the inadequacy of most theological language, rediscovers the old meaning of poetry as *remaking*[64] *the world*, and at the same time recreating a different world, on the basis of memory: "We always live in a house of language, built by previous generations. That is why the memory of a different life and the hope for less destructive ways of living can hardly be rooted out. Poetic, transforming, ice-melting speech is structured into language itself."[65]

Soelle situates her search in the context of global capitalism, where language has been corrupted, where a word like "love" refers to a car, and the word "purity" to laundry. Because the idols of money and power are marketing language in terms of ownership and commodification, the language of consumer capitalism based on acquisition leaves little space for the articulation of a different value system. In despair Soelle comes to the biblical mythic poetic language as a tool of resistance to the domination of consumerist values, to a rediscovery of prayer as poetry, to the challenge to sing different songs and to dance to a different tune: "'If there is any verb for the language of mysticism, it is praying,' she wrote."[66]

---

61. *Den Himmel Eden: Ein ökofeministische Annährung an die Bibel* (Munich: Deutscher Taschenbuch Verlag, 1966).

62. Boston: Beacon, 1958.

63. Minneapolis: Fortress, 2001.

64. The old Greek word for poet, ποιητής, means "the Maker." In parts of Scotland the local poet is referred to as "the Maker."

65. Pinnock, *Dorothee Soelle*, 37.

66. Dorothee Soelle, *The Silent City: Mysticism and Resistance* (Minneapolis: Fortress, 2001), 292–93.

With the language of prayer she discovered hope of penetrating beyond domination and control. The language of prayer draws us into paradox and silence. To pray is also not to give way to despair. But it should not be thought that Soelle draws on biblical mytho-poetry uncritically. She revisits texts in a subversive way, in full awareness of centuries of misinterpretation. For example, she writes poetically of resurrection:

O don't ask about resurrection
A tale of ages long ago
That will soon skip your mind
I listen to those
Who dry me out and diminish me
I accustom myself
To the creeping accommodation to being dead
In my well-heated abode
The big stone at my door.[67]

But later on in the poem, she cries,

O do ask me about resurrection;
O don't stop asking me.

This is poetry as theology, a method that continues to offer a way to express yearning for God that breaks out of the tired categories of abstract theology.

Christology—along with the quest to speak about God—was Soelle's life-long passion. Based in praxis, in relation, and in human experience, her Christ is a political Christ, because historically Jesus of Nazareth took a stance against institutional power; his presence evokes imagination, freedom to risk, and brings liberation—the unchaining of all powers which lie imprisoned in all of us.[68]

Christ symbolizes truth, the concrete truth of right relation where the blind see, the hunger of the poor is satisfied, and the mighty are dethroned. This concreteness, cutting through abstractions, blazed a trail for a transformed future.

This emphasis on praxis and right (just) relation also offers one solution out of the dilemma of feminist Christology, enunciated by Rosemary Ruether much earlier in the challenging question, "Can a Male savior save women?"[69] All traditional salvation/redemption/liberation trajectories fall back on a central male figure, but Soelle suggested one way out of the quandary by seeing Christ as *enabling* liberating praxis. *Christopraxis* but not *Christolatry*[70] lifted the weight from the man Jesus, solving the problem of what Carter Heyward would name later as "Christ stops history" and paving the way for a relational Christology.[71] This in turn evoked and enabled the

---

67. Dorothee Soelle, "Über auferstehung," in *Fliegen Lernen* (Kleinmachnow: Wolfgang Fietkau Verlag, 1979), 21.

68. Rosemary Ruether in Pinnock, *Dorothee Soelle*, 214–15.

69. Rosemary Radford Ruether, *To Change the World* (New York: Crossroad, 1989), 45–56.

70. "The idolising" of Christ the man.

71. "Christ stops history" is Heyward's dramatic way of indicating that an overemphasis on the once-for-all actions of Jesus can, in effect, remove the necessity for human beings' own redemptive efforts.

development of diverse liberation Christologies within different discourses, such as African American and *mujerista* (Hispanic American Women). These continued the process of interpreting Christopraxis from the context of concrete social engagement with the suffering of the specific community. As time progressed, although Soelle's passionate social engagement did not falter, the incarnational project seemed to have faded from central place, as her focus shifted from Christ to the God of mysticism. There is barely a mention of Christ in *The Silent Cry.*[72]

The search for God against the backcloth of growing social injustice remained the context for Soelle's approach to creation theology. It offered an exciting way to privilege justice and liberation in a mystical affirmation of creation. In *To Work and to Love: A Theology of Creation*, written by Soelle with Shirley A. Cloyes, Soelle stated firmly, in a most surprising move, that—to paraphrase Buber—"In the beginning was Liberation."[73] By this she meant that we need liberation before we can affirm creation: "At the very least, oppressed people need a God who sides with them against the oppressor. The cosmic order as such, without a liberation tradition, does not reconcile slaves and other oppressed peoples, because it cannot empower them to free themselves."[74]

The context for her writing this was the controversy with the creationists—who ignored history, God's action in history, and the exodus experience. She referred to the exodus as "the second creation" because it was the paradigmatic historical moment of escaping the oppressor. Beginning with broken creation it would anticipate the frequently expressed feminist view that we always begin from "the broken web."[75] Rather than an imagined primeval state of perfection, from which humanity "fell," (with the attendant problems of sin/punishment/restoration), "the broken web" metaphor succinctly captures not only the ravaged state of creation but the existential separation of all forms of life from nurturing relations with each other.

For Soelle, the third moment of creation was a rebirth into the resurrection of Christ, into commitment to the renewal of the earth, to resistance against all forms of bondage. This is the creation that lies in the future, in human hands. But the three strands[76] have to be held in tension. It is in the recurrence of the theme of resistance within the context of mysticism that could make a permanent impact on theology.

The Silent Cry pulled together the two strands that inspired her life, God and justice.[77] Written when she emerged out of a coma from which few thought she would survive, the book brings together all her familiar themes—nature, suffering, community, politics, relation, justice, joy, eros—all finding meaning in the yearning for God, a God sought in a diversity of traditions. Resistance returns, in the need to resist the seductions

---

72. Nor was she very interested in the Holy Spirit. Many of us in feminist theology have focused on the Spirit, or preferably *Spirit-Sophia*, as a way not only of shifting emphasis from Jesus the Man-hero, but of opening up Christianity to engage in dialogue with Goddess and indigenous religions and the world of other faiths.

73. Philadelphia: Fortress, 1984. Several feminist theologians would creatively appropriate Buber's phrase, "In the beginning was relation" (Buber, *Paths in Utopia*, 18). Isabel Carter Heyward (*The Redemption of God: A Theology of Mutuality* [Washington, D.C.: University of America Press, 1982]) had just predated Soelle with this expression.

74. Soelle and Cloyes, *To Work and to Love*, 10.

75. Catherine Keller, *From a Broken Web* (Boston: Beacon, 1986).

76. God's initial creation, exodus as escape from oppression, and resurrection as commitment to renewal.

77. Pinnock, *Dorothee Soelle*, 235.

of globalization. *We have to live as if we lived in a liberated world*, and only by letting go of these seductions can we see with other eyes. This is the mystical *via negativa*, the apophatic way, reclaimed as resource against global capitalism, sustaining our energy for social change. We have to keep resistance alive in an age that believes it is finished—in an age *when the default spirituality is a capitalist one*. We have to recover the passion for resistance when everywhere there seems to be apathy and acquiescence in the inevitability of global capitalism. Catherine Keller suggests that Soelle hears the silent cry of mysticism as a call to resistance and that its "*topos* of ineffability" nurtures a language without dominance.[78] In the context of action for justice this mystical alternative language is expressed not only in silence, in paradox, and in poetry, not only in seeing and imagining a different world—as for example when the World Social Forum, Mumbai 2004, chose as its title "Another World Is possible." It is also experienced as joy—"Resistance is the Secret of Joy"[79]—and as the spur to the formation of alternative communities.[80] But, unlike the insistence of radical orthodoxy on theological metadiscourse, coalitions are formed between disparate groups that share this "passion for justice" without its theological underpinnings.

But Soelle did not always take this stance: in an early book Soelle tells the old Grimm brothers story, "The Golden Bird."[81] In her early interpretation Soelle explored the meaning of the mystical quest. The golden bird symbolizes our yearning for something beyond the ordinary. Nothing that is fabricated or manufactured can satisfy this yearning—or compare with *the golden bird*, or *water of life*, or *the red flower*. The yearning for the absolute is the yearning for transcendence, the desire for the whole. This world is not enough. Working and consuming, we destroy our souls: "The bird is the great *no* spoken to this world and all its fulfilments, and the refusal to be fed by them, the refusal to be fed by bread alone. The bird is nothing extraordinary but is the wish of ordinary people that has been muted. . . ."[82]

In a sense her position was not unlike that of John Milbank: nothing in this world suffices—only God fully answers human desires.[83] But, nearly thirty years later, how changed her orientation became. Transcendence is not longed for beyond all earthly life. Joy, eros, justice, relation, resistance, are all to be embodied *here* on this earth. As Carter Heyward wrote, "She does not accept mysticism as an 'inward' journey taken by and on behalf of the self. The mystical journey 'leads into a healing that is at the same time resistance.'"[84]

This is the same problem I explored in *Sacred Longings* when I sought a way of resisting the language of consumer capitalism in order to set free a more profound

---

78. Catherine Keller, *The Face of the Deep: A Theology of Becoming* (New York: Routledge, 2004), 203.

79. *Possession is the Secret of Joy* is the title of Alice Walker's novel on female circumcision (London: Vintage, 1993). This book inspired several feminist theologians to alter the phrase to "Resistance is the Secret of Joy," for example, the PhD thesis of Dr. Lieve Troch, University of Nijmegen, the Netherlands (1999).

80. In Britain in the 1980s many of us experienced this in the resistance to the presence of cruise missiles at the Peace Camps. There was resistance to the army and police: but there was joy in the tangible presence of an emerging alternative world.

81. Dorothee Soelle, *The Inward Road and the Way Back* (London: Darton, Longman & Todd, 1979), 41–48.

82. Ibid., 51.

83. Milbank, *Theology and Social Theory*.

84. Pinnock, *Dorothee Soelle*, 235.

level of human longing.[85] All turns on being able to discover what humanity truly yearns for and desires: we engage resistance to the seductions of the market, not because of any mistrust of physical goods or pleasure, but because in contemporary society they are pursued to an extent that blocks the real object of desire, the golden bird that truly brings joy, as well as preventing two-thirds of the world from enjoying even a modest standard of living. This is the crux of the different approaches of Milbank and Soelle: it is not a pure opposition between "theology as metanarrative realism"[86] or theology as mediated by social science but the capacity to see in the pathos of poor communities the presence of the suffering God. It is here that there have been crucial developments in some liberation theologies, notably Dalit. I suggest that before praxis comes pathos, and that this is a deeply theological category. It arises from the situation of many communities in the world, of trafficked women, of Dalits, of people afflicted to such a degree that hope of liberation is almost extinguished. It is not poverty that is the primary category, but affliction, pathos, from which poverty and other forms of oppression emerge.

What do we really want? is the issue. Desire for God takes the form of an embodied hope for the well-being of ourselves, of others, and of the global community: in hospitality and commitment to the flourishing of the other lies the hope of recovery of our interconnected selves. This is earthed grace, the project of Dorothee Soelle, shared by many liberation and feminist theologians alike.

Out of the wreck of society's idolatrous perspective our longing is also for a new sense of the sacred to emerge. A mystical and political spirituality—analogous to but not identifiable with the medieval asceticism idealized by radical orthodoxy—brings its own demands for renunciation and simplicity of life-style. A language of voluntary simplicity emerging from solidarity with poor and oppressed communities leads to recognizing and engaging with vulnerability, God's vulnerability, and compassionate suffering shared with numerous vulnerable communities around the world. Both Soelle and Day in their resistance to the arms race and work for peace pleaded for keeping open this place of vulnerability:

> The window of vulnerability
> Must be closed—
> So the military say
> To justify the arms race.
>
> My skin is a window of vulnerability
> Without moisture, without touching
> I must die
>
> The window of vulnerability
> Is being walled up
> My land
> Cannot live

---

85. London: SCM; Minneapolis: Fortress, 2003.
86. Milbank, *Theology and Social Theory*, 251.

We need light
So we can think
We need air
So we can breathe
We need a window
Open toward heaven.[87]

Along with radical orthodoxy we can affirm that divine generosity created *the very possibility of the incarnation of Christ*. Along with liberation theology we affirm the challenge of *Christlike liberating praxis*. Along with Milbank, Christians affirm the mystical vital force of the peaceableness offered by Christ[88] amid the overwhelming sense of bereavement that globalization has caused. But liberation theologians see globalization as challenge to a mysticism of resistance. *Choosing life* even where liberating praxis is impossible and engaging with social movements that work to keep hope alive[89] remain the path to be trodden. In this process of outrageously hoping, it is enough that there is sometimes a glimpse of the golden bird for our courage to be rekindled and desires to be reawakened that redeemed creation will be a reality.

---

87. Soelle, *Window*, 7.
88. Milbank, *Theology and Social Theory*.
89. For example, Jubilee 2000, trade justice movements, and cancellation of debt campaigns.

PART IV

pushing the margins of radical orthodoxy

12. Standing at a Demythologized Sinai?

Reading Jewish Feminist Theology Through the Critical Lens of Radical Orthodoxy

—Melissa Raphael

Radical orthodoxy's project has been to return Christian theology to its patristic and Augustinian roots in order both to criticize theology's accommodation with secular modernity and to rethink the tradition in the light of selective reference to the post-modern turn. Although radical orthodoxy has encouraged a regressive neoconservatism in some Christian quarters and seems to give permission for an exclusivism that would ignore or deny the worth of theologies articulated by other communities of faith, it is arguable that contemporary Jewish feminist religious thought might find a similar critical strategy productive. This essay will suggest that the development of Jewish feminist theology[1] has been weakened by the Western religious detraditionalization that has been at once its historical context and opportunity. The late or postmodern spiritual "turn to the self," the shift from religious observance as an obligation into a life-style choice, are reflected in liberal feminist affirmations of the individual Jew as an autonomous religious agent, a speaking subject who can only control and define the meanings of a Jewish life for herself by relativizing or disprivileging canonical traditions and focusing on women's experience and texts alone. This focus has been, and remains, necessary, but not to the point where women's religious experience and intellection, as well as the tradition itself, become circumscribed by its ideological confinement to the immediate social context.

Jewish feminism must continue to repudiate and censure Jewish misogyny and discrimination wherever it finds it. Yet radical orthodoxy's posture and aesthetic, its sense of the irreducibility of revelation, may be a timely reminder to Jewish feminists (or at least the religious among them)[2] of the value of what has become, over time, if not dogma, then a body of characteristically Jewish sources, concepts, and motifs with their own mood and temper. For Jewish feminist theology to draw more confidently upon the admittedly androcentric but nonetheless rich theological tradition spanning

---

1. This essay will define Jewish feminist theology inclusively as any Jewish feminist reflection that discourses upon God as the postulate and ground of its values and practices or which interprets experience in the light of Jewish religious narratives and concepts. Such a definition of Jewish feminist theology is not intended to be prescriptive or exhaustive.

2. Not all Jewish feminist thought is religious—Jewishness can be cultural as well as confessional. Likewise, not all Jewish feminists are religious. After experiencing anti-Semitism in the women's movement some Jewish feminists turned to feminist Jewish communities for a more ethnically nuanced identity and support, not to nurture a religious commitment.

the aggadhic (rabbinic, nonlegal) texts of late antiquity to the Jewish theologies of the twentieth century would be neither to deny its patriarchal character nor to reinscribe it. A more thoroughgoing engagement with the whole intra-worldly and extra-worldly range of the tradition could take the Jewish feminist theological repertoire beyond that one motif which (for good relational reasons) most predictably shapes Jewish feminist thinking, namely the covenantal relationship between God and the Jewish people. The covenantal trope and theme is, of course, central to historic and contemporary Judaism and is a fine vehicle for a range of social, political, and sexual perspectives and interests, especially those of the Jewish left. Both the event and notion of covenant denotes the intimacy and reciprocity of the Jewish relationship with God and articulates Jewish fidelities to its natural and supernatural vocation. However, to reduce Judaism to the outworking of a covenant narrows Judaism's imaginal scope and the range of its response to God's self-revelation. God makes a series of different sorts of covenant with Israel in the Bible and the covenantal trope provides but one of the metaphors and schemes for the relation of God and Israel found in the Bible and subsequent Jewish thought, especially that of mysticism, where the covenantal theme is relatively muted.

It may be that the covenantal motif predominates in Jewish feminist religious writing and practice not only because it is inherently relational but also because its consensual dynamic is so amenable to the liberal values of individualism, autonomy, and immanence. I take no issue with covenantal theologies or their immanentist valorization of this world as such. The immanentist tendency to produce theology out of intra-worldly experience and values has shaped Jewish theology since the mid-twentieth-century. Theologians such as Martin Buber, A. J. Heschel, and Eugene Borowitz have offered accessible relational theologies that have made the world a place of welcome both to the human and the divine. Twentieth-century experientialist relational theologies, including those that have characterized Jewish and Christian feminist theology, have been indispensable to much of my own negotiation with the tradition. This essay will not urge the nostalgic rejection of all modern thought and values attributable to some of the more reactionary adherents of radical orthodoxy. Nor will it urge the kind of scripturalism, messianism, and socioreligious insularity characteristic of Jewish ultra-Orthodox groups in Israel and the United States. The problem is rather that Jewish feminist theology's origins in modern egalitarianism and the postmodern pluralization of truth, together with its focus upon the immediacies of women's experience (a deliberate means by which to control the tradition by selecting from it at will and thereby allowing women to operate in a relatively autonomous religious space), has left women religio-intellectually marginalized, and experience of the heteronomous, nonordinary dimension of Jewish revelation has been all but precluded. As Susannah Heschel, herself a Jewish feminist, pointed out nearly twenty years ago, feminists have come to stand in ethical authority over the religious authority of the tradition and its content.[3] Consequently, elements of classical Judaism such as messianic redemption, a final judgment, and resurrection that have been considered rationally or ethically unpalatable and edited out of Jewish thought (if not liturgy) by

---

3. Susannah Heschel, "Current Issues in Jewish Feminist Theology," *Jewish-Christian Relations* 19 (1986): 31.

modern liberal Judaism have, in turn, been further excised by Jewish feminist theology. The eschatological dimension of Jewish thought is, for example, barely referred to at all in Judith Plaskow's 1990 full-length feminist theological text, *Standing Again at Sinai*, even though Jews have been sustained and directed by eschatological hope for most of Judaism's history. (It is surely significant that David Blumenthal's recent theology of the Holocaust is structured around a dialogue not with Jewish feminist theologians but with Christian feminist theologians, suggesting that he considered theodical questions outside the interest or discursive competence of Jewish feminist theology.)[4] Jewish women's religious thought will not attain the status of Torah—broadly conceived as the sum of Israel's body of sacred knowledge—by *alone* insisting on its autonomy, its equality of religious access, its (entirely legitimate) moral quarrel with the gynophobia of tradition, and by the reworking of gender-relevant rituals and stories.

In addition to Jewish feminist scholarship's enquiry into how women's religio-social communities have enabled their spiritual and political self-expression there needs to be an articulation of the transformative immanence of the transcendent that is the *mysterium tremendum* of divine presence, the holy. Yet both Jewish and Christian feminists have been sharply critical of any binary dualisms that produce a hierarchy of values and experience, including such a foundational Jewish theological concept as *kedushah* (holiness). Religious feminism is especially distrustful of the hierarchy of the holy in relation to the profane, claiming that it has sanctioned contempt for the natural, a correlate injustice against women and the God whose image they bear, and an exclusivist religious topography that is spiritually and practically inimical to female social environments. The Jewish concept of holiness is not notably ascetic but distrusts the natural appetites and insists that they are contained within the sanctity of heterosexual marriage and the family home. Qualified to the point of rejection by most Jewish feminists as obsolete, separatist, and gynophobic,[5] it then becomes difficult for feminist discourse to signal the real presence of God in and beyond the assembly of Jewish women and to temper the desacralizing effects of Jewish feminism's alliances with a liberal individualism that prevents the irruption of numinous otherness into history, which has been, from the beginning, the very mission of Israel.

Jewish feminism is found in all but ultra-Orthodox communities (though it is not without influence even in those). As well as Orthodox and Reform Jewish feminism there is also a "postmodern" form of Jewish feminism that has affinities with post-Christian feminist spiritualities.[6] But to varying degrees all types of Jewish feminism have joined the quest of liberal modernity and liberal Jewish feminism and have focused on women's religious liberation, their equality of religious opportunity, and their capacity to reorient the tradition toward the practical needs and conditions of their own lives. Even Orthodox feminist scholars deploy the same historical methods of modern liberal theology. The work of Blu Greenberg and Judith Hauptman, for example, has been to justify women's continuing participation in Jewish life by defending

---

4. David Blumenthal, *Facing the Abusing God: A Theology of Protest* (Louisville: Westminster/John Knox, 1993).

5. See T. Drorah Setel, "Roundtable Discussion: Feminist Reflections on Separation and Unity in Jewish Theology," *Journal of Feminist Studies in Religion* 2 (1986): 113–18.

6. See Melissa Raphael, "Goddess Religion, Postmodern Jewish Feminism, and the Complexity of Alternative Religious Identities," *Nova Religio* 1 (1998): 198–214.

the talmudic rabbis as having been more sensitive to women's needs than other non-Jewish religious authorities of the time. Greenberg, Hauptman, and others develop an essentially modern liberal defense of Judaism, arguing that the discriminatory husk of the tradition can be discarded to reveal its unchanging core: its principles of justice and equality.[7] The two poles (if that is what they are) of modern and postmodern Judaism come together in their rejection of supernatural divine authority, which has, in their view, been at least compromised by the patriarchal nature of Judaism. As a result, Jewish feminist theology is barely or not at all founded in the transcendent obligations to the unheimlich dimension of the holy and the supernatural (rather than merely ethical) vocation of election attending such.

Of course, the more spiritually and politically benign forms of reconstructive postmodernism have rightly disprivileged elite voices and narratives, valorized difference and locality, and affirmed the speaking subjecthood of the silenced Other. Yet I am not alone in opposing postmodernism's dissolution of the categories of shared meaning that are a precondition of the prophetic call to justice and which support a unified and interdependent ecology of Jewishnesses. While difference is properly attended to in so far as Judaism can suffer from a spuriously universalizing, collectivizing notion of Israel that has in practice been exclusively defined by men and marginalizes women, a high ontological theology of the people Israel as collectively representative of God's will and presence in the world could challenge Jewish feminism's postmodern preoccupation with intra-Jewish cultural hybridity and local difference.[8] For without the eschatological accommodation of difference within *klal Yisroel*—the whole people of Israel—that difference will undermine and fragment the historical continuities and solidarities that constitute Jewish women's identity as one half of the Jewish body—the assembly of Israel—before God.

It is hardly surprising that Jewish feminism makes few positive theological claims. Rabbinic Judaism never did consider an explicit theology part of its own project and many in the Orthodox community that endeavor to maintain the spirit and practice of rabbinic Judaism still have reservations about the propriety of Jews doing theology at all ("since its founding, the Hebrew University has barred Jewish 'theology' from its classrooms, lest it offend the custodians of traditional Judaism").[9] Orthodox Judaism prioritizes the clarification and observance of halakah, just as it always has done (even the theosophical schemata of Jewish mysticism did not normally supercede the strict observance of halakah). Liberal theologies are also, if differently, nonconfessional. The best-known and most interesting twentieth-century Jewish theology has a marked

---

7. Heschel, "Current Issues," 27.

8. For example, Esther Schely Newman, *Our Lives Are but Stories: Narratives of Tunisian-Israeli Women* (Detroit: Wayne State University Press, 2002); and Susan Sered, *Women as Ritual Experts: The Religious Lives of Elderly Jewish Women in Jerusalem* (New York: Oxford University Press, 1992). Postmodern Jewish historiography's declaration made over recent years that Jewish history has so many different locations and ethnicities that it does not in any general sense exist is a significant instance of this pluralizing, anti-redemptive stance. See Michael A. Myers, *Judaism within Modernity: Essays on Jewish History and Religion* (Detroit: Wayne State University Press, 2001), 87–88. Compare Yosef Hayim Yerushalmi's unified theological historiography in *Zakhor: Jewish History and Jewish Memory* (Seattle and London: University of Washington Press, 1996).

9. Paul Mendes-Flohr, "Jewish Philosophy and Theology," in *The Oxford Handbook of Jewish Studies* (ed. Martin Goodman; Oxford: Oxford University Press, 2002), 766.

preference for a phenomenological, existential theological epistemology; Reform and Conservative Judaisms remain more or less ethical, practical, and historicist in their still evolving orientation. In their turn, Jewish feminists tend to neglect or dismiss the androcentric tradition as too inhospitable or too negligent of women's experience to be what is ominously termed a "useable" tradition. Jewish feminists have instead concentrated their attentions on the historical Jewish woman as a speaking subject of her own experience, who can from the resources of her own experience and that of her religio-social circle produce alternative models of God and free readings of legendary and biblical texts.[10] All this, as well as postmodern Jewish thought's refusal of normativity, has together rendered Jewish feminist theology—whether as a systematic exposition of faith or more generally as a discourse on the public exteriority of God's relationship with the world—almost an impossibility.

Judith Plaskow's *Standing Again at Sinai*, published in 1990, has become the paradigmatic work of Jewish feminist theology, not least because it is one of the very few works that declares itself to be such. Yet the modern ethical and demythologized stance that shapes Plaskow's work all too often empties the tradition, and with it the category of Jewish womanhood, of numinous otherness by judging all categories, sources, and practice by means of purely ethical criteria of judgment. The chief criterion of these is whether an aspect of tradition does or does not include, serve, and answer the experience of women and the needs of their communities. In *Standing Again at Sinai*, to take one significant instance, Judith Plaskow discounts Michael Wyschogrod's Orthodox theology of Israel as the body in and through which God is present in the world on account of its androcentric emphasis upon the male circumcision that has traditionally marked the body of Israel as holy.[11] It is the narrowness of the modern ethical criteria that, in such instances, is in danger of finally obstructing a re-enchantment of the world as the place of God's indwelling, of occluding the Shekhinah—the female face/presence of God whose presence demands more of Jews than the assertion of their rights to spiritual self-expression (even if it may also confer them).

Jewish feminist theology's Reform terms and assumptions have been established almost single-handedly by Judith Plaskow but have not since been critically interrogated. Jewish feminist theology's historicist, ethicizing Reform legacy has left Jewish feminist theology little discursive room for an intellectual inquiry into the possibility of God's historically and cosmically decisive self-revelation (as distinguishable from that known in and through women's own communities).[12] Rather, the historiographical, hermeneutical, and liturgical energies of Jewish feminist religious studies have been expended in devising the historic grounds and ritual means for sexual equality of religious expression and practice. This body of scholarship has been highly successful in demonstrating how adept women and groups of women are and have been in making Judaism their own through reclaiming traditional practices and festivals such as ritual

---

10. See, for example, Judith Plaskow, "The Coming of Lilith and Eve: Towards a Feminist Theology," in *Womanspirit Rising* (ed. Carol Christ and Judith Plaskow; San Francisco: Harper & Row, 1979), 198–209.

11. Judith Plaskow, *Standing Again at Sinai: Judaism from a Feminist Perspective* (New York: HarperSanFrancisco, 1990), 83–84.

12. My own book *The Female Face of God in Auschwitz: A Jewish Feminist Theology of the Holocaust* (London and New York: Routledge, 2003) attempts to unify cosmic, historic, and domestic revelation. (See especially chap. 6, "The Redemption of God in Auschwitz.")

purification in the mikvah and the celebration of the new moon (Rosh Chodesh). Yet it is questionable whether this socioreligious scholarship has yet succeeded in demonstrating how women's Judaism reveals God's will and presence to Israel as one people within the temporal and post-temporal scheme of Jewish salvation history.

The process of selecting and reclaiming elements of the tradition in accordance with liberationist criteria to produce what is (effectively) a feminist canon and a feminist community is not over and nor should it be. Jewish feminism must continue to repudiate and censure misogynistic texts and traditions and interweave its own female narratives with those of the (masculine) collective. However, the tradition also offers a wholly transcendent sense of the holy that assumes the good but is not reducible to ethical precepts and the interruptive, hierophanic possibilities of a real, personal God.

In 1979 Cynthia Ozick called for the institution of an eleventh commandment for Judaism: "Thou shalt not lessen the humanity of women."[13] Her prophetic rhetoric was a fanfare for the opening of the Jewish feminist project and deployed a classic method of using a Jewish tradition to make another Jewish tradition that is faithful to its own ethical judgment on the world. But Ozick's commandment remains a foundation, not the building itself. Ozick's is a negative commandment that corrects a moral error, a human omission, on God's behalf. Ozick's commandment does not summarize or complete the whole Jewish feminist task. We *also* need a more positive and rigorous feminist engagement with Jewish theology (as distinct from the halakic or biblical studies that are far more commonly undertaken by the feminist academy) that combines justice seeking with a more immediate sense of being addressed by God's self-revelation in history that must accept and then venture beyond Ozick's eleventh commandment.

This essay suggests that Jewish women could usefully attend to radical orthodoxy's refusal of an autonomous secular realm and its renewed confidence in a *sui generis* religious (Christian) voice and teaching that is felt to be its own. However, it must be acknowledged that Jewish theology could not set itself a strictly parallel program to that of radical orthodoxy, since Judaism is a largely non-creedal faith and has different quarrels with modernity than the Church.

First, though, it should be mentioned that Jewish feminism is also differently positioned in relation to Jewish orthodoxy than Christian feminists are to Christian orthodoxy (when the latter is a body of classical texts, not a denomination). The hegemonic masculinity of the Christian theological tradition that has made Christian feminists justifiably suspicious of radical orthodoxy's return to its authority and normativity does not function in the same way in Jewish religious thought. Classical Jewish orthodoxy is certainly androcentric and patriarchal in so far as it "others" and excludes women, but Jewry's precarious positioning within the Christian hegemony means that its theology is not that of the political or cultural masters. Jewish theology is also a theology of the victim: of the marginalized, persecuted, and oppressed; of men who are themselves to a lesser or greater degree socially and culturally excluded from the mainstream, who are feminized both by hostile cultural stereotype and by the marital tropes of their own theology.

If one accepts the patriarchal notion that masculinity is defined by power over the subject other, then it is arguable that until the establishment of the State of Israel in

---

13. Cynthia Ozick, "Notes Toward Finding the Right Question," in *Lilith* 6 (1979): 19–29, reprinted in Susannah Heschel, ed., *On Being a Jewish Feminist: A Reader* (New York: Schocken, 1983), 149.

1948 Jewish men had been emasculated by centuries of persecution in which they showed themselves largely unable to protect their women from humiliation, rape, and murder. Daniel Boyarin's study of Jewish masculinity finds that the postbiblical diasporic exemplar of the ideal male Jew is not an aggressive and domineering figure but a gentle, receptive, and family-oriented figure who is, on that very account, attractive to Jewish women.[14]

Orthodox Jewish theology is not the work of celibates. Judaism has only ever been mildly and occasionally ascetic. Unlike so much of the theology of the classical Christian tradition, Jewish theology has been written by men who were women's husbands. And Jewish masculinity is not traditionally defined economically by a man's being the main bread-winner or by macho physical prowess but by the prestige of his religious scholarship: the pale unworldly scholar was, until the Holocaust, the Ashkenazic religious ideal, not the hunter (identified with Esau) nor even the Israelite man of war. For such and other reasons, modern Judaism, especially in its Zionist forms, found Jewish religious piety to be emasculating. The "feminization" of Jewry is, then, by no means confined to anti-Semitic caricature. Judaism itself casts Israel as God's (sometimes adulterous) wife and the gendered bifurcation of religious emotion in Judaism is further confused by Howard Eilberg-Schwartz's observation that the male Jewish God—especially the anthropomorphic God of ancient Israel—invites men, not women, into a loving, monogamous marital relationship with him. If, in contemporary Judaism, the fatherhood of God is to be taken seriously, Eilberg-Schwartz urges that it should be that of a tender, embracing father whose love for his children affirms rather than derogates female love and which permits intimacy and tenderness in men.[15]

It is for reasons such as these that the historical experience and spirituality of those who have made and sustain Jewish tradition does not stand in a polar relation to that of women. And in its modern form, Jewish theology has been profoundly humane. Its relational turn has been exemplified not only in Buber and Levinas but also in the theology and pacifist stance of Abraham Joshua Heschel (the father of the pioneering feminist scholar Susannah Heschel).[16]

The second reason why radical orthodoxy could not have arisen in Judaism is because, broadly speaking, Judaism is less concerned with orthodoxy than with orthopraxis. Apart from creedal exceptions such as the talmudic text *Sanh.* 10:1, classical Judaism is nondogmatic. There is no essential, normative set of beliefs, as opposed to the practical fulfillment of *mitzvoth* (commandments), that Jews *could* return to as the *fons et origo* of faith. Belief is not so much propositional as attitudinal. *Emunah*—faith—is not the consent or submission of the intellect. This Hebrew term is best translated as trust in God and in the efficacy of Torah to confer blessing. As Arthur Cohen has observed, while it is possible to cull a theology from the aggadic or literary

---

14. Daniel Boyarin, *Unheroic Conduct: The Rise of Heterosexuality and the Invention of the Jewish Man* (Berkeley: University of California Press, 1997).

15. Howard Eilberg-Schwartz, *God's Phallus and Other Problems for Men and Monotheism* (Boston: Beacon, 1994), 5–6, 239–40.

16. Heschel spoke out against the Vietnam War shortly before his death in 1972, refusing to see the Vietnamese communists as anything but his brothers. Heschel reminded American Jewry that Judaism does not absolve anyone from responsibility for her or his own acts and any individual may challenge those in authority who order a Jew to fight.

elements of the classical rabbinic literature (it considers recognizably theological questions such as the nature of God and his providential relation to the world and delineates what it considers to be a proper eschatological hope), the rabbis had little concern for dogmatic consistency or system. Theological enquiry no more than complemented and reinforced exposition of the halakic obligation. The rabbis assumed God's command; they did not apologize for it through rational argument.[17]

It was Moses Maimonides, in the twelfth century, who was the first to set out a fundamental dogmatic theology summarized in the Thirteen Principles that define a Jew and grant him (and presumably her) a place in the world to come.[18] According to Maimonides, even the transgressor who fails to keep all the commandments out of weakness but who understands and adheres to these Thirteen Principles merits a place in the world to come, whereas disbelief, conscious or inadvertent, renders one a heretic. But despite Maimonides' best efforts, Judaism never did become a creedal faith. Jewish philosophers were little interested in either the questions or the imposition of theological orthodoxy and halakhists had little time for purely doctrinal considerations. Although many male Orthodox Jews recited the *Ani Ma'amin* ("I believe")—a short creed based on the article or principle relating to the coming of the Messiah—as they went to their deaths during the Holocaust, very few Jews today, even observant Jews, could recite the Thirteen Principles; they are very far indeed to being the equivalent of, say, the Five Pillars of Islam.

There is, of course, a body of Jewish theology, but until the twentieth century it was all too often apologetic in character. Dogma has been more a historical contingency than a religious necessity. From the medieval era to the early modern period dogmatic systems arose in response to Christian theological polemic against Judaism and attempts to convert the Jews. Not surprisingly, when persecution masqueraded as an intellectual dispute dogmatic theology accrued distasteful associations. Occasionally dogmatic treatises were produced in the course of sectarian quarrels within the Jewish community, but it was not until the rise of Reform Judaism in the late eighteenth century that Judaism adopted a creedal posture. And even then, the concern was largely confined to the period of early "classical" Reform Judaism, when reformers were embroiled in sectarian disputes with Orthodoxy and thinkers such as Moses Mendelssohn and Abraham Geiger were seeking to establish a Jewish civil and religious identity in a period of emancipation that was trading the rights of citizenship for assimilation or the abandonment of cultural and religious difference.

The intra-Judaic struggle to negotiate the relation between ethics and halakah almost overwhelmed modern Jewish religious thought. In the nineteenth century, Reform Jews' Kantian disquiet with what appeared to them to be the archaic, ceremonial, and exclusivist nature of Orthodox Judaism led to an emphasis on the importance

---

17. See further Arthur Cohen, "Theology," in *Contemporary Jewish Religious Thought: Original Essays on Critical Concepts, Movements, and Beliefs* (ed. Arthur A. Cohen and Paul Mendes-Flohr; New York: The Free Press, 1987), 971–72; and Menachem Kellner, "Dogma," in ibid., 141–45.

18. The Thirteen Principles, set out in Maimondes' *Commentary on Helek* (*Sanh.* 10:1), state that God exists, is one, is incorporeal, that he exists prior to the world and is alone a fit object of worship. The principles state further that prophecy occurs, that the prophecy of Moses is superior to that of later prophets, and that the revelation of Torah is from heaven not earth and cannot be altered. The tenth of the principles states that God knows all human acts, that he will reward righteousness and punish the wicked, that the Messiah will come, and that there will be a resurrection of the dead.

of spiritual disposition and motivation rather than on either supernaturalist doctrine or heteronomous law. In an attempt to make Judaism ethically and aesthetically palatable to Western Jews and their Christian neighbors, Judaism was spiritualized and historicized: the critical or scientific study of Judaism (*Wissenschaft des Judentums*) allowed nineteenth-century Jews to explain away reductively such traditional doctrines and practices as belief in a physical resurrection or the cultus of sacrificial worship. The numinous dimension of Judaism was relegated to the primitive period of origins. A thoroughly nineteenth-century ethical evolutionism allowed Jews to adhere only to those aspects of tradition that seemed to them to be morally edifying and in the service of social progress, both within the Jewish community and outside it. It was neither the "iron hand" of halakah (mistranslated by German thinkers such as Buber as law— *Gesetz*) or any transcendental mystery that produced Jewish righteousness, but the uncoerced response of persons to God, liberated by modernity from numinous fear and superstition. The early work of Hermann Cohen was perhaps the most thoroughgoing Kantian rendition of Judaism as a religion of morality par excellence, but it was Emmanuel Levinas who had the greater influence on Jewish religious thought from the second half of the twentieth century onward. Levinas's positioning within the intellectual history of modernity is not always clear, but it is characteristically modern in so far as its ethic is both contemptuous and fearful of the enchanting barbarities of the numinous.[19]

The premodern union of faith and reason that Maimonides and others had sought to establish for Judaism did not, then, survive modernity. Buber's and Rosenzweig's theology—while not strictly denominational—was also informed by Reform Judaism's conviction that Judaism must enable Jews to live well in a modern society. Following Spinoza, Judaism's own modern separation of faith and reason demoted Jewish religious thought from a quest for universal, metaphysical truth to the deployment of central theological motifs such as creation, covenant, and redemption in order to articulate ethical, affective, and existential meaning for the individual Jew.[20]

Jewish feminist thought has not widely questioned the modern. Granted, not all Jewish feminists would style themselves as liberal. Jewish women sympathetic to or participant in the Goddess movement would not do so, nor would the modern Orthodox feminists who wish to adapt Jewish law in women's interests to the degree they consider Torah permits. Nonetheless, self-legislative liberal assumptions about rights and autonomy lie to differing degrees behind all Jewish feminist thought and practice in so far as it is feminist at all. Miriam Peskowitz and Laura Levitt have asked, "Since the majority of work in Jewish feminist studies has been tied either implicitly or explicitly to the Enlightenment's project of emancipation, what are some of the consequences of this strategy? What are some of the alternatives to this way of constructing knowledge?"[21] But there are powerful reasons why Jewish feminists, including its religious thinkers, do not want to surrender the modern advantage. It is, after all, modern Enlightenment thought that has offered all Jews the possibility of civil

19. Emmanuel Levinas, *Difficult Freedom: Essays on Judaism* (ed. Seàn Hand; London: Athlone, 1990), 28–29.

20. See further Paul Mendes-Flohr, "Jewish Philosophy and Theology," 764–65.

21. Miriam Peskowitz and Laura Levitt, eds., "Editors' Introduction," in *Judaism Since Gender* (New York and London: Routledge, 1997) 14.

emancipation and Jewish women an acknowledgment of the irrationality and injustice of premodern gynophobia. There can be little appetite for the premodern when it is in the premodern, "golden" period of classical Judaism that the weight of Jewish authority, that is, rabbinic authority, lies. Furthermore, this is an authority that refuses altogether the terms and much of the content of modern Enlightenment thought. Orthodoxy customarily rejects Jewish feminism because it attributes the movement to the secular humanism of Second Wave feminism, not even giving it credit for being an older product of the Jewish version of Enlightenment: *haskalah*.

Yet Jewish theology would do well to keep modernity at arm's length. As is well known, modernity has both emancipated Jewry and destroyed it. Modernity's rational demystification of the Jew has encouraged Jews themselves in the disenchantment of Judaism. It has conferred rights and made citizens of Jews, but it has also urged, by way of a return on its social investment, the assimilation of Jews to the point of their cultural disappearance. Indeed, loss of faith in God was a casualty of Jewish enlightenment, the Holocaust, and modern technological bureaucracy finally provided the genocidal means to annihilate the European Jewish presence altogether.

In consequence, post-Holocaust theology displays a palpable loss of confidence in its divine object. Having lost faith in the modern promise of society's moral and rational evolution, theologies of the Holocaust most often attribute the catastrophe to God's tendency to hide his face (*hester panim*), not in the biblical manner as a punishment for sin but as an abyssal mystery at the heart of the divine personality. For most post-Holocaust theologians, faith and reason have to be sundered because faith after Auschwitz is not rational.

Whereas the God of classical (rabbinic, premodern) Judaism is more or less consistently the omnipotent God of law and Lord of history, the God of theologians of the Holocaust is all too often a God who is unpredictable, non-omnipotent, and even complicit with evil. While only Richard Rubenstein denied that the Jewish idea of God had survived at all, most other Jewish reflection on the Holocaust (that of Eliezer Berkovits, Martin Buber, David Blumenthal, and Eli Wiesel, among others) presents a remorseful God, in some sense the object of our pity and of our stubborn love, but no guarantor of moral progress. For Irving Greenberg (the husband of pioneering Orthodox feminist Blu Greenberg) the Holocaust has set us free from our obligation to the covenant since God himself fell short of the covenantal promise by averting his eyes from the agony and dereliction of the Holocaust.[22]

Even as I write, on the sixtieth anniversary of the liberation of Auschwitz, Aharon Appelfeld, the Israeli novelist and Holocaust survivor, has declared again that "God did not reveal himself in Auschwitz or in other camps." Betrayed both by God and by liberalism, Jews, he says, did and will henceforth turn to one another, not God, for meaning. Appelfeld tells a story that, from my perspective, sets the historical context and theological agenda for Jewish feminism: he recalls a doctor from an Orthodox background who sailed with him to Israel in 1946. The doctor insisted, "We didn't see God when we expected him, so we have no choice but to do what he was supposed to do: we will protect the weak, we will love, we will comfort. From now on the responsibility is all ours."[23]

---

22. Irving Greenberg, "Voluntary Covenant," in *Contemporary Jewish Religious Responses to the Holocaust* (ed. Steven L. Jacobs; Lanham, Md.: University Press of America, 1993), 92–93.

23. "Always, Darkness Visible," trans. from the Hebrew by Barbara Harshaw, *New York Times*, January 27, 2005.

Jewish feminist theology—if enough of it has been written to merit being termed as a corpus of literature—inherits the post-Holocaust sense of the absence of God from Auschwitz not as his punishment for Jewish sin (as the biblical and rabbinic authors would have had it) but as his moral failure. God's self-revelation in history is neither trusted nor solicited. Consequently, as George Steiner laments, in the post-Holocaust "recession of God," "otherness has withdrawn from the incarnate, leaving only an emptiness which echoes still with the vibrance of departure. . . . Where God's presence is no longer a tenable supposition and where His absence is no longer a felt, indeed overwhelming, weight, certain dimensions of thought and creativity are no longer attainable."[24] Steiner was not speaking of Jewish feminist theology, but his point is painfully relevant. The putative absence of God in and after the Holocaust has made it ever more difficult for Jewish feminism to affirm the witness and judgment of God's presence in the world other than that known indirectly and personally through the human connectivity found in the ordinary social/spiritual communities of women.

It is not only modernity that has undermined Jewish feminist theological confidence in its own voice and purpose.[25] There are other reasons too why Jewish religious thought has made so little impact on Jewish feminism across the denominational spectrum. Not only does the reading, let alone interpretation, of many Jewish sources require technical expertise, Jewish feminist theology is as marginal to Jewish feminism as nonfeminist Jewish theology is to Judaism.[26] Those who would style themselves Jewish feminist theologians could be numbered on one hand, even though women rabbis have a practical or pastoral interest in theology and a substantial number of feminist scholars of the Hebrew Bible assume, even if they do not state, theological positions in their reading of the text.[27] Yet they have little to draw upon.

In an article first published in 1979, Ozick insisted that women's secondary role and status is a historic injury—not a failure of revelation in Torah. It is, she argued, first and foremost a matter for halakic and thereby social reform. Ozick saw no reason to initiate what she felt to be a "pagan" feminization of God. Instead she urged a program of seven points, the first four of which are relevant here:

---

24. George Steiner, *Real Presences* (London: Faber & Faber, 1989), 229.

25. Observe, however, that modernity has indirectly fortified other sectors of Judaism. Orthodoxy has been revived by late modernity's distrust of the modern, something it has urged all along.

26. A significant number of modern Jewish theologians have had an early fascination with Christian theology, Franz Rosenzweig and Eugene Borowitz among them. Buber's thought has been attractive to many Protestants and firmly repudiated by halakically observant Jews. See further Marc A. Krell, *Intersecting Pathways: Modern Jewish Theologians in Conversation with Christianity* (Oxford: Oxford University Press, 2003). Judith Plaskow's and my own interest in Jewish theology developed from an initial academic training in Protestant theology.

27. This theological reticence is not peculiar to Second Wave, post-Holocaust Jewish feminism with its post or late modern decline in confidence in the grand sacral narratives of Western civilization. As Rachel Feldhay Brenner observes in her recent study of Jewish women's writing during the anguished years prior and during the Holocaust, Jewish women intellectuals may have sought consolation and support from God, but it was not that of the Jewish God or the Jewish tradition. Jewish women such as Etty Hillesum and Anne Frank were in fact far more attracted to Christianity perceived as a religion of love and compassion in contrast to the "apparent rigidity and severity of the Jewish Law." Their vision was both humanistic and loosely Christian, emphasizing goodness, kindness, empathy, beauty, inner strength, and self-giving to others (Brenner, *Writing as Resistance: Four Women Confronting the Holocaust: Edith Stein, Simone Weil, Anne Frank, Etty Hillesum* (University Park: Pennsylvania State University Press, 1997), 8, 9, 55, 30, 34–45.

1. The status of women is not "theological." To alter the status of the Jewish woman is not to change one iota of the status of Jewish belief.
2. Therefore the question of the status of Jewish women is "merely" a sociological issue.
3. As a sociological issue, the status of women is the consequence of human decisions amenable to repair by human institutions.
4. In order to satisfy the most traditional members of the community, and also to place the responsibility for injury where it most belongs, the repair must come out of *halakah*, the judicial machinery for change.[28]

In her 1983 response to Ozick, entitled "The Right Question Is Theological,"[29] Judith Plaskow disagreed. Jewish women's status as Other to the male norm is, she claimed, grounded in a masculinist theology of which halakic inequalities are but a symptom. If Jewish women are to have equality of religious opportunity, they would need to begin with a revisioning of the theology that shapes and underpins that law. But, perhaps because both Judaism and Jewish feminism are practiced through and in the practical rather than the theoretical dimension, few seconded Plaskow's point and Jewish feminism remained not so much a form of theological praxis as Christian feminists would understand that term but an essentially social project of establishing religious meaning for women generated in and by the solidarities within their communities.

The dispute between Judith Plaskow and Cynthia Ozick promised much for Jewish feminist theology but delivered relatively little. A year or so after Plaskow had published her response to Ozick, Ellen Umansky published a short article outlining an agenda for Jewish theology, but it was one that foreshadowed more problems than possibilities.[30] Several times in this article Umansky adverts to the "irreconcible" conflict between women's experience and the patriarchal tradition that would at best hamper the development of a Jewish feminist theology. Nor is Umansky convinced that Jewish history is separable from Jewish tradition, leaving Jewish theology without a stable or essential core of revelation.[31] She acknowledges that it is questionable whether the theologian (feminist or otherwise) can claim all personal experience as Jewish, simply because he or she is a Jew; the tradition might impose certain a priori constraints on such. Nonetheless, Umansky leans upon a characteristically Reform equation of revelation with emancipation and rejects Jacob Neusner's view of Jewish theology as that discourse which makes explicit the received, transmitted, and normative statements found within authoritative sources and renewed only in accordance with such norms.

---

28. Ozick, "The Right Question" and Judith Plaskow, "The Right Question Is Theological," in *On Being a Jewish Feminist: A Reader* (ed. Susannah Heschel; New York: Schocken, 1983), 142.

29. Plaskow, "The Right Question Is Theological," 223–33. See also Judith Plaskow, "Jewish Theology in Feminist Perspective," in *Feminist Perspectives on Jewish Studies* (ed. Lynn Davidman and Shelly Tenenbaum; New Haven and London: Yale University Press, 1994), 62–84.

30. Ellen Umansky, "Creating a Jewish Feminist Theology: Possibilities and Problems," first published in 1984 and reprinted in Judith Plaskow and Carol C. Christ, eds., *Weaving the Visions: New Patterns in Feminist Spirituality* (New York: HarperSanFrancisco, 1989), 187–98. See also Alex Wright, "An Approach to Jewish Feminist Theology," in *Women Rabbis Tell Their Stories* (ed. Sybil Sheridan; London: SCM Press, 1994), 152–61.

31. Umansky, "Creating a Jewish Feminist Theology," 187, 189, 193.

Umansky cannot subscribe to a normative theology because its norms have been conceived and written by men. The Jewish feminist theologian must instead formulate what she calls (following Daniel Breslauer) a "responsive" theology. Rather than attempt to construct a normative theology, the feminist theologian should be consciously subjective; she should make no a priori commitment to tradition but listen to her own voice and join with other women in telling stories from their own perspectives and experiences as Jewish women.[32]

Rita Gross's suggestion that Jewish theology could be revitalized by feminists importing Indian Goddess symbols into their feminist conceptions of God has not been acted upon,[33] and very few books have since contributed to the Jewish feminist theological project.[34] It is of course true that most of these foundational articles and texts are precisely foundational and may no longer represent the views of their authors. The problem is that so little has been written to develop and contest these texts toward theology that they remain the constituent corpus of Jewish feminist theology.

Of this corpus, Judith Plaskow's *Standing Again at Sinai* (1990) remains the presiding Jewish feminist theological text and its Reform provenance has not been challenged by the production of theologies from the Orthodox feminist community. As someone who has had a Reform upbringing, Plaskow is, of course, aware that that liberal Judaism has often promised a greater degree of sexual equality than it has always been able or wanted to deliver and that no form of Judaism can supply some form of nonsexist essence of Judaism.[35] She therefore intends her book's vision of Judaism to help "create a Jewish community in which women are present and equal as women" and in which "difference is nurtured and respected."[36]

In this sense, Plaskow had ignored her own argument. Having told the Jewish feminist community that theology must precede sociology, she went on to produce a book that was more an ethically prescriptive sociology of community than a theology (the book is subtitled *Judaism from a Feminist Perspective* and is described by the publishers as a "feminist reevaluation of the role of women in Judaism"). That is, although Plaskow describes the book as a "theology of community," it is in fact a revisioning of community—a rethinking of ideas and experience based on her experience of B'not Esh, the Jewish feminist spirituality collective she helped to establish in the early 1980s, as well as on her participation in the *havurot* (the supportive, informal communities that are centers of alternative thought and practice).[37] No differently than other religious Jewish feminists, Plaskow had continued to justify Judaism to women on ethical, relational grounds, not to explore the intractable questions of what it means to be under judgment, to be subject to God's commandment (perhaps because she did not believe that either was really the case). In the introduction to *Standing Again at Sinai*, Plaskow summarizes Jewish feminism's academic and social achievement in terms of historiography, leadership, literary studies, cultural studies, and sociology—not theology. She

---

32. Ibid., 193–94.
33. Rita Gross, "Steps Toward Feminine Imagery of Deity in Jewish Theology," *Judaism* (1981): 183–93.
34. Rachel Adler, *Engendering Judaism: An Inclusive Theology and Ethics* (Philadelphia: Jewish Publication Society, 1988); Brenner, *Writing as Resistance*.
35. Plaskow, *Standing Again at Sinai*, x, xiii.
36. Ibid., 119.
37. Ibid., vii–ix.

wants to see the transformation of Judaism into a religion that men and women shape together[38] and sees the emphasis on equality of access as an opening move. Yet because her own inspiration and focus is social and practical she is reluctant to move outside its safe, affirmatory space.[39] This is a pity because the Jewish enlightenment had already provided Jews with a reasonable, practical, this-worldly form of religion as a tool of moral and social reform and because Judaism already has a practical theology in halakah's minute attention to the details of everyday life; it does not need another one.

The very organizational framework of Plaskow's book cannot support a theology "proper" (that it requires a special chapter on God is itself an oddity suggesting the subordination of theology to more immediate social concerns). Plaskow sets her chapter on God as the fourth of six chapters: "from the recovery of women's Torah and the reconstruction of Jewish community, we move to the subject of God."[40] Since Judaism gives ontological and theological priority to God without whom no other category (election, law, messiahship, and so forth) makes sense, Plaskow explains the postponement of the theological chapter by saying that her book has no ambition to produce a "reconceptualization of God, nor any account of God's nature that could anchor an understanding of Torah and Israel in some noncircular way." The chapter is "interested instead in exploring and transforming the metaphors for God," about considering Jewish images of God from a feminist perspective in an attempt to "reorient the Jewish conception of deity."[41] This project has been fairly successful, and imaginal and liturgical revisions of "God-She" thrive on the Jewish feminist left. But Jewish feminist theology more or less halted at the place where her book did. Plaskow's now classic study is one upon whose religio-political groundwork Jewish feminism would come to depend. Yet, a decade later, in Danya Ruttenberg's *Yentl's Revenge: The Next Wave of Jewish Feminism*, an edited collection of essays written by the daughters of Second Wave Jewish feminists such as Plaskow, theology shows signs of falling ever further from view.[42] The collection is entertaining, informative, and sometimes moving; it is also refreshingly inclusive of non-Ashkenazic feminist voices, but its discussion of the sexual, political, and cultural identities of the present generation of Jewish feminists is almost devoid of reference to God.

The liberal theme of individual choice (as itself the precondition or substitute for revelation) continues to predominate outside the Jewish feminist literature. Take but one example: American *baalot teshuvah* (secular or Reform Jewish women who have "returned" to Orthodoxy). These women usually return to Judaism because they have experienced a difficult life-changing event or transitional period after which they consciously sought the emotional comfort of order, identity, stability, and community that orthodoxy seems to offer. The secular world had been unable to supply the warmth of a close-knit Jewish family and its respect for the role of wife and mother.[43] What seems

---

38. Ibid., xv–xvi.
39. Plaskow is also handicapped by the range of Jewish feminist religious studies itself, observing that because other women speak more about their lives than about religious issues per se there was "not yet a range of voices" with which she could have a dialogue (ibid., xxi).
40. Ibid., 121.
41. Ibid., 121–23.
42. New York: Seal Press, 2001.
43. Lynn Davidman, *Tradition in a Rootless World: Women Who Turn to Orthodox Judaism* (Berkeley: University of California, 1991), 91, 110; Debra Kaufman, "Women Who Return to Orthodox Judaism: A Feminist Analysis," *Journal of Marriage and the Family* 47 (1985): 547.

significant is that most of these women did not return for reasons of belief. Their choice was just that: a reasoned choice to make Judaism their own. In Lynn Davidman's study, of the non-Hasidic women, half did not believe in God and two-thirds did not consider themselves to have had a religious experience. It was only the Hasidic women (those belonging to pietistic ultra-Orthodox sects) who, by contrast, felt their return to have been to be directed by God.[44]

This more or less universal indifference to the correlation of experience with traditional Jewish teaching is to be found in Jewish feminist studies as well. As an act of political resistance to their status as objects of the law—"silent recipients, outsiders to the process";[45] "absent from the Jewish construction of the universe and God,"[46] contemporary Jewish feminist scholars have instead made Jewish women speaking subjects of their own experience as Jewish women. Study after study has shown how Jewish women have made Judaism their own by its domestication within the home or within the community that comes to be an extended (female) family either by Orthodox ordination or by liberal choice.[47] Other studies have shown how Jewish women balance the demands of Orthodox Judaism with those of their daily lives—not, significantly, by enquiring into the reformulation of belief as such.[48] All of these studies, and others too numerous to mention here, are concerned with the gendering of Jewish practice and with female spiritual intentionality, not with the production of belief in conversation with tradition. This is not the place to assess the intellectual and academic achievements of Jewish women scholars; it needs hardly be said that they are considerable. What needs to be emphasized is the point that Judith Plaskow made over twenty years ago: that, in ignoring the theological and focusing on the phenomenological, Jewish feminism would fail to engage the substantive traditions of belief (whether implicit in the rabbinic literature or, in other texts, theologically and philosophically stated) to which these phenomena indirectly refer. Now, two decades after Plaskow's challenge, the phenomenological, immanentist focus of Jewish feminist scholarship, intensifying that of Jewish modernity in general, has become largely oblivious to that other transcendental trajectory of Judaism and may have left its own feminist theological possibility to wither on the vine.

In this essay it has been necessary to give the diagnosis more space than the prescription. But approaching a conclusion, I want to repeat that this essay has not urged

---

44. Davidman, *Tradition in a Rootless World*, 82–88.

45. Rachel Biale, *Women and Jewish Law: An Exploration of Women's Issues in Halakhic Sources* (New York: Schocken, 1984), 8.

46. Wright, "An Approach to Jewish Feminist Theology," 152.

47. A mere sample of these studies could include Chava Weissler, *Voices of the Matriarchs: Listening to the Prayers of Early Modern Jewish Women* (Boston: Beacon, 1998); Sylvia Rothschild and Sybil Sheridan, eds., *Taking Up the Timbrel: The Challenge of Creating Ritual for Jewish Women Today* (London: SCM Press, 2000); Maurie Sacks, "Computing Community at Purim," *Journal of American Folklore* 102 (1989): 275–79; Rebecca Shulman Herz, "The Transformation of Tallitot: How Jewish Prayer Shawls Have Changed Since Women Began Wearing Them," *Women in Judaism: Contemporary Writings*, online: www.utoronto.ca./wjudaism 10/12/04; Esther M. Broner, *Bringing Home the Light: A Jewish Woman's Handbook of Rituals* (San Francisco: Council Oak Books, 1999); and Tamar El-Or, *Educated and Ignorant: Ultra-Orthodox Women and Their World* (Boulder, Colo., and London: Lynne Reiner Publishers, 1994).

48. See, for example, Orna Blumen, "Criss-Crossing Boundaries: Ultraorthodox Women Go to Work," *Gender, Place, and Culture* 9 (2002): 133–51. The feminist reclamation of traditional practices can be found on websites such as ritualwell.org.

that Judaism cease to be theologically and denominationally plural. Nor does this essay urge that Jewish feminists, among whose number I unequivocally count myself, should now relinquish their feminism. A popular and an academic focus on the diversities and unities of women's experience remains justified and necessary to the production of new Jewish meaning.

However, leaving aside the problem of which Jewish women's experience is selected and articulated as generative of new knowledge and which is not, theologies whose episteme is driven by the community and not by the recognition that God—as God— is not only immanent within that community but also transcendent to it cannot do justice to the tradition. Consistently empirical scholarly enquiry can present a partial, agnostic, horizontal, and even humdrum Judaism that neglects or is not answerable to its exteriority and its more difficult and elusive possibilities of meaning: the missiological question of Israel as supernatural vehicle of revelation and the consequent accommodation of suffering in a soteriological theodicy are but two examples. Questions such as these require waiting upon the kind of irruption of the sublime into the ordinary that was once associated with messianic longing and a sense of being subject to unfulfillable obligations. (Compare, perhaps, Rosenzweig's insistence in *The Star of Redemption* that creation, revelation, and redemption are acts of an excessive, transcendent divine love that abstracts the Jew from the historical world.)

Glancing, indeed, only at twentieth-century Jewish theology, I would want to refer the reader to Michael Wyschogrod, who proposed in his book *The Body of Faith* that God enters the world "through a people whom he chose as his habitation. Thus there came about a visible presence of God in the universe, first in the person of Abraham and later his descendants, as the people of Israel."[49] This account of the body of Israel, like that of Joachim Schoeps, is not the same body as that justly celebrated in so much feminist spirituality; it is an afflicted, hounded body whose affliction is itself a spectacle of revelation. Rosenzweig, also early in the twentieth century, drew upon the convictions of the Jewish philosophers Philo in Roman Alexandria and Yehuda Halevi in tenth-century Spain, who had argued that Jews *had to be* dispersed in order to spread the word of God to the nations. Halevi in particular had portrayed the Jews as each one carrying the seeds of the *amr ilahi* (divine logos) among the nations. Rosenzweig was further indebted to the medieval rabbinic commentator Rashi, who understood the suffering servant of Isaiah 53 to refer to the people Israel, who suffered vicariously for the world. Perhaps para-Christian, this scheme helped Rosenzweig to justify Jewish wandering and its afflictions theologically. Israel is elected to suffer not only for its own sin but for that of the world. God afflicts the body of Israel so that the nations will be healed. The transmissibility of Jewish revelation is dependent on the afflictions that produce Jewish migration.[50]

The implication of Rosezweig's gloss on Halevi and Rashi's missiology is that redemption and diasporic movement are part of the same process. The history of Jewish diaspora, including that endured, managed, and survived by women in their own processes of departure and resettlement, can be read not as a series of disappearances but

---

49. Michael Wyschogrod, *The Body of Faith: Judaism as Corporeal Election* (New York: Seabury, 1983), 36. See also ibid., 57.

50. Franz Rosenzweig, *The Star of Redemption* (trans. W. W. Hallo; Notre Dame, Ind.: Notre Dame Press, 1985), 306–7, 314.

as the purposive dissemination of revelation. The missiology so briefly alluded to here challenges Jewish and Christian feminist theology's insufficiently examined rejection of any redemptive possibility within suffering that has, after all, been a traditional Jewish as well as Christian construal.

Despite his sentimental dismissal of the theological seriousness of the "feminine,"[51] Levinas also prompts the further question of whether Judaism might demand more of us than a celebration of embodiment and the establishment of woman-friendly communities. At his most theologically obnoxious, Levinas denies Jewry any of the consolations of covenantal intimacy or the pleasures of the senses that feminist theology—Jewish or Christian—has sacralized. To take this latter first, Levinas's outburst against visual art, and beautifying sculptural representations of the human body in particular, illustrates my point. While liberal Jews are well disposed to Levinas's congenially ethical theology of the face, they overlook his rejection of art (virtually sacralized by bourgeois moderns as a means by which the individual can announce his or her own perception of the world). Art, for Levinas, is a disengagement and a rendition of life and its discarnate command into the silence of mere spectacle. Art (in general) is the clouding of revelation, "a descent of the night, an invasion of shadow" (tantamount, then, to evil). "To put it in theological terms, which will enable us to delimit however roughly our ideas by contemporary notions: art does not belong to the order of revelation. Nor does it belong to that of creation, which moves in just the opposite direction."[52]

Counterbalancing his own theology of the revelation of the human face, Levinas also pronounces a chilling theology of "the God Who Veils His Face." His is a God who offers "no reprieve, no consolation of presence." There is, he says, to be no expectation of "warm, almost palpable communion with the Divine." On the contrary, it is through the divine word, not the divine presence, that Israel achieves intimacy with its God. The holy is mediated by reason, not by incarnatory presence but in his Torah.[53] God's face is veiled precisely so that he can ask the "superhuman" of "man," that is, to love God in spite of God's turning away.[54] When the Orthodox theologian Michael Wyschogrod dismissed Levinas's account of Judaism as assimilated—worse—"housebroken,"[55] he had in mind Reform Judaism's gratitude to Levinas's central positioning of the ethical. But Levinas's article "Loving the Torah More than God," while objectionable on several counts, signals precisely that haunting, strenuous, elusive strain within Judaism and its afflictions that cannot be domesticated within the warm reciprocities of a covenantal theology. Judaism is not always healing, accessible, and companionable. As Rudolf Otto pointed out at the beginning of the twentieth century, the holy— in which he includes the Jewish *qadosh*—can repel our love as well as attract it; it is terrible as well as lovely.[56] Jewish feminism has done a very great deal to make the holy

---

51. Emmanuel Levinas, "Judaism and the Feminine Element," trans. Edith Wyschogrod, *Judaism* 18 (1969): 30–38.

52. Emmanuel Levinas, "Reality and Its Shadow, in *The Levinas Reader* (ed. Seàn Hand; Oxford and Cambridge, Mass.: Blackwell, 1989), 132.

53. Ibid., 85.

54. Ibid., 86.

55. Wyschogrod, *Body of Faith*, 181.

56. Jewish theology has been both informed by and critical of Rudolf Otto's theological phenomenology of the holy in *The Idea of the Holy: An Inquiry into the Non-rational Factor in the Idea of the Divine and Its Relation to the Rational* (London: Oxford University Press, 1958). Burton M. Leiser's "The Sanctity

community that is Israel attractive to contemporary women. But while Levinas may be right that "on the mean and petty level of day-to-day reality, a human community does not resemble its myth,"[57] Jewish feminism should not demythologize Judaism in deference to its more immediate vision of community.

It is not to be wondered at that Jewish feminism, a child of *haskhalah* (the Jewish Enlightenment), has so often emptied Judaism of its theology, and that even Jewish feminist theology has been so reticent about substantive matters of faith. As we have seen, Jewish feminist theology is, first, a modern response to an Orthodox tradition in which the legal, not the aggadhic, is considered revealed or divinely inspired and which itself encourages legal orthopraxy over creedal orthodoxy. Second, Jewish feminist theology is, by historical chronology, a post-Holocaust theology. This entails that, after Auschwitz, Judaism can no longer be justified either by classical faith in the God of Sinaiatic revelation or by the modern Reform assertion that Judaism underpins the ethical structures of Western civilization. By the end of the twentieth century, Jewish feminist theology could only justify Judaism to other Jewish women on the grounds of its history of prophetic concern for social justice, of its being a source of spiritual and practical connection between the foremothers and the present generation of Jewish women and their daughters, and as a ritual and imaginal focus for women's communal identity—not on the grounds of the truth of its traditional claims. While none of this is to the detriment of Jewish women's immediate experience of Judaism, it has been obstructive to the development of the kind of feminist theology that would refuse to justify belief in God, that would engage and incorporate that nonrational, sui generis element of faith that radical orthodoxy has done so much, in Christian theological circles, to reinstate.

---

of the Profane: A Pharisaic Critique of Rudolf Otto," *Judaism* 20 (1971): 87–92, and Blumenthal's *Facing the Abusing God* are just two examples. As we saw above, Levinas has moral objections to Otto's styling of the numinous, but his own theology is far from devoid of that quality.

57. Levinas, *Difficult Freedom*, 208.

13. Radical Orthodoxy and Feminist Philosophy of Religion

—Beverley Clack

Christian apologetics has taken many varied forms in its attempt to present the Christian message to the wider world. Invariably it has interacted with the major philosophical trends of the day to present the gospel in new and accessible ways.[1] Despite claims that it is not a form of apologetic,[2] the radical orthodoxy movement of the late 1990s has been particularly effective in using the language of radical postmodernist theorists to present a defense of orthodox Christian doctrine.

The use of radical theory to support what is in effect a rather conservative rendition of Christian belief raises significant issues for feminists concerned with developing a feminist philosophy of religion. The work of feminist philosophers of religion has a dual focus: to expose the patriarchal bias of traditional forms of religion, and to advance new ways of approaching religious belief.[3] It is this second concern that forms the basis for this essay, for, far from providing a vision of religion that supports the feminist commitment to liberation, the concern with "orthodoxy" entails that, despite the use of apparently radical theorists, revisionary readings of religion be avoided, with the implication that the status quo can be maintained.

The theorists of radical orthodoxy suggest that the problem for religious belief lies with the central ideas of modernity. They view modernity as posing a rationalist challenge to religion through its commitment to reason and progress. As such, postmodernity presents "a supreme opportunity" for religion.[4] Theorists of radical orthodoxy view the postmodernist rejection of Enlightenment thinking, with its emphasis on the priority of reason, as facilitating a return to the integrated theologies of the premodern period: albeit filtered through the lens of radical "continental" thought. I am not convinced that the only way to secure a religious perspective is to reject the

---

1. See for example Rudolf Bultmann's adaptation of existentialist philosophy in "Jesus and Mythology," in *Kerygma and Myth* (ed. H. W. Barsch; London: SPCK, 1953); and Paul Tillich's application of depth psychology in *The Shaking of the Foundations* (Harmondsworth: Penguin, [1949] 1962).

2. John Milbank, *Theology and Social Theory: Beyond Reason* (Oxford: Blackwell, 1990), 381.

3. For examples of feminist approaches to the philosophy of religion, see P. S. Anderson, *A Feminist Philosophy of Religion* (Oxford: Blackwell, 1998); and Grace Jantzen, *Becoming Divine: Towards a Feminist Philosophy of Religion* (Manchester: Manchester University Press, 1998). For a sense of the diversity of feminist approaches to the philosophy of religion, see P. S. Anderson and B. Clack, eds., *Feminist Philosophy of Religion: Critical Readings* (London: Routledge, 2004).

4. J. Milbank, C. Pickstock, and G. Ward, eds., *Radical Orthodoxy* (London: Routledge, 1999), 1.

Enlightenment and the ideals of modernity. Considering the use of psychoanalytic theory in constructing a meaningful account of religion provides a helpful context for exploring this claim. If Graham Ward uses Jacques Lacan's theories on sexuality for developing his orthodox Christology, I shall suggest that Sigmund Freud's theories of religion provide fertile ground for rethinking the nature of religious belief. Freud is particularly useful for such an enterprise as he stands between modernism and postmodernism: on the one hand he applies a scientific approach to the study of the mind in particular and human life in general; on the other hand his theory of the unconscious challenges the primacy of reason as a way of understanding human life and culture. It is precisely this ambivalence that makes him useful for the development of a feminist philosophy of religion, for he applies critical reason, as well as challenging the view that only reason can make sense of our world. In engaging with Freud, an approach to religion emerges that moves beyond both Christianity and orthodoxy, grounding religion in the habits and peculiarities of the human animal.

Opposing the Modern:
Postmodernity and the Defense of "Orthodox" Religion

It has become something of a commonplace to assert that the values of the Western Enlightenment create a particular set of problems for religious belief. At the heart of the Enlightenment ideal lies the belief that all "men" are rational and autonomous, able to choose their own values and to decide what is correct.[5] Placing the individual center stage in this way causes particular problems for religious traditions. As John Reader puts it, with the Enlightenment came "the triumph of reason over tradition."[6] No longer would the individual bow before any external authority: "the Man of Reason" could make up "his" own mind about all issues, including matters of religion. Coupled with this idealization of the rational individual came the adoption of the scientific worldview with its emphasis on empirical method and verification. In such a context, religious metaphysics and cosmology seemed hackneyed and superstitious. Accepting scientific method led to the rejection of any overarching religious narrative. Religious ways of looking at the world were either outmoded or a matter for private decision making; religious institutions were throwbacks to a "medieval" unenlightened past.

Two rather different approaches to this problem present themselves. One approach is to show that religion can hold its own in the face of critical reasoning. So the philosophy of religion, which emerged as a distinct discipline during the Enlightenment, seeks to show the reasonableness (or otherwise) of religious beliefs. The extent to which it has been successful in defending religious beliefs from the charge of irrationalism is debatable. Emphasizing reason can lead to a rather colorless view of religion that ignores the extent to which ritual is of as much importance as belief.[7]

---

5. Whether "men" included all males and women was a cause for considerable debate. See Immanuel Kant (1763), *Observations on the Beautiful and Sublime*, trans. J. T. Goldthwait (Berkeley: University of California Press, 1960), where women and black men are explicitly excluded from this definition of Enlightenment "man."

6. John Reader, *Beyond All Reason: The Limits of Post-Modern Theology* (Cardiff: Aureus, 1997), 4.

7. Amy Hollywood has powerfully exposed the weaknesses of such an approach. According to Hollywood, religion is not primarily a matter of correct belief but of "body practice." See Hollywood, "Practice, Belief, and Feminist Philosophy of Religion," in Anderson and Clack, *Feminist Philosophy of Religion*, 225–40.

Ignoring the emotive content of religion tends to distort the possibility of a complex understanding of how religiosity relates to the deepest aspects of being human: and these deep (and sometimes disturbing) aspects of our humanity may not conform easily to the dictates of reason.[8]

An alternative approach can be to opt out from any engagement with modernist values whatsoever. Fundamentalist religion pursues this course. An apparently more sophisticated approach is to see postmodernity as providing a way forward for religious belief. Postmodernism, according to Jane Flax, proclaims the death of belief in Man, History, and Metaphysics.[9] The unified, universal figure "Man" has fragmented into different groups and constituencies defined by difference. The downside of such plurality is the lack of meaningful markers for identity. Thus the individual becomes the consumer who defines his- or herself through his or her purchases; who is obsessed by celebrity; who buys designer labels as a way of achieving an identity. Against the backdrop of such triviality, the notion of history as inevitable progress seems ridiculous. But such "self-conscious superficiality"[10] is seen in radical orthodoxy as a means of reasserting the need for some concrete markers that shape self-discovery. Religious tradition becomes the backdrop against which one can shape one's sense of self: and it is this vision of religious orthodoxy that Milbank and his colleagues propose.

Feminist responses to the challenge of postmodernity are varied. Some have responded favorably to the rejection of the rational autonomous self, derived, after all, from the reflections of white privileged males. False universalism, based on the values of one social group, has been exposed and rejected in favor of emphasizing difference. Ellen Armour thus challenges the limitations of "whitefeminist" theology, while Luce Irigaray looks to sexual difference as a way of enabling women to discover a genuine alterity from men. Philosophers of religion such as Grace Jantzen have similarly embraced the critique of "Reason" on the grounds that it has been framed in relation to masculinist ways of thinking (Jantzen 1998).[11]

Other voices resist the idea that Enlightenment values should be given up altogether. Alison Assiter has argued for "a return to 'Enlightenment' values on realism in the theory of meaning, on universalism in feminist theory and on the value of the cognitive domain."[12] While there are things that divide women (race, class, sexual orientation, for example), it is also possible to discern situations when these differences are transcended: "we support one another if one is suffering and we share laughs together."[13] For the liberating power of the feminist project to continue, striving for common ground between women is a necessity. In a similar vein, while accepting criticisms of the Enlightenment, Daphne Hampson has defended its core values as

---

8. See Terrence Tilley (2000), "The Philosophy of Religion and the Concept of Religion: D. Z. Phillips on Religion and Superstition," in *Journal of the American Academy of Religion* 68, no. 2 (2000): 345–56, for a powerful critique of this kind of exclusion.

9. Jane Flax, *Psychology, Feminism, and Postmodernism in the Contemporary West* (Berkeley: University of California Press, 1990): 32–34.

10. Milbank, Pickstock, and Ward, *Radical Orthodoxy*, 1.

11. Ellen Armour, *Deconstruction, Feminist Theology, and the Problem of Difference: Subverting the Race/Gender Divide* (Chicago: University of Chicago Press, 1999); Luce Irigaray, *Sexes and Genealogies* (trans. G. C. Gill; New York: Columbia University Press, 1993); and Jantzen, *Becoming Divine*.

12. Alison Assiter, *Enlightened Women: Modernist Feminism in a Postmodern Age* (London: Routledge, 1996), 7.

13. Ibid., 128.

important for the liberation of women. In particular she reflects on the importance of critiquing tradition: something that should not be underestimated when it comes to considering the ways in which women have been oppressed by habitual views of who they are or should be.[14]

Embracing the postmodern may initially seem to provide a way out of the snares of rationalism for religion: but as Assiter and Hampson suggest, this does not mean that it will necessarily prove helpful for women. Recent feminist work has argued for a renewed connection with, even commitment to, the world's religious traditions.[15] I am not convinced by this imperative to return to tradition for it seems to avoid a critical engagement with the harm that those traditions have historically done to women. Instead, I wish to suggest a different approach. Religion is grounded in human life and culture. It is part of what it means to be a human animal, but this does not mean that it cannot be challenged and criticized. My concern is that movements that reject modernity, including radical orthodoxy, fail to allow for such criticism, and that this has considerable ramifications for women.

The next section of this essay attempts to expose these ramifications by considering the way in which the work of Jacques Lacan is used to develop one such radical orthodox theology. In developing his Christology, Graham Ward, one of the foremost theologians of this movement, uses Lacan's theories on sexuality. In considering his Christology and the ideas that shape it, it is possible to get some sense of why radical orthodoxy is not radical enough when viewed from a feminist perspective. And in part this lack of radicalism arises from the attitude that Lacan takes toward critical reflection. Lacan may have seen himself as the inheritor of Freud's work, but there are considerable differences. If Freud's intention is to uncover the workings of the unconscious with utter clarity, Lacan eschews such an aim in favor of replicating the chaotic, irrational forms of the unconscious.[16] The rejection of reason may suggest the possibility of a highly creative approach to theology, but in practice it enables conservative attitudes both to religion and the position of women to hold sway.[17]

Reworking the Christian God: A Radical (Orthodox) Christology

At the heart of Ward's application of Lacan's theories on sexuality lies the attempt to develop a radical understanding of the body of Christ.[18] This is offered as a response to the feminist criticism of traditional Christologies. Rosemary Radford Ruether, among others, has argued that Christianity is particularly problematic for women, as masculine concepts *and* the male body are divinized in the male body of Christ. Reflecting on the way in which the tradition has used Christ's body to exclude women, both from

---

14. Daphne Hampson, *After Christianity* (2nd ed.; London: SCM Press, 2002), 1–11.

15. S. F. Parson, ed., *Challenging Women's Orthodoxies in the Context of Faith* (Aldershot: Ashgate, 2000).

16. M. Oliner, *Cultivating Freud's Garden in France* (Northvale, N.J.: Jason Aronson, 1988), 7.

17. See, for example, Malcolm Bowie's suggestion that Lacan's comments on women are lacking in depth, for, as he puts it, "scattered sociological observations [are] being passed off as a theory of sexual difference" (Bowie, *Lacan*, 143).

18. See Graham Ward, "The Gendered Body of the Jewish Jesus," in *Religion and Sexuality* (ed. M. Hayes, W. Porter, and D. Tombs; Sheffield: Sheffield Academic Press, 1998); and "Bodies: The Displaced Body of Jesus Christ," in *Radical Orthodoxy* (ed. J. Milbank, C. Pickstock, and G. Ward; London: Routledge, 1999).

positions of leadership and from the development of a specifically Christian anthropology, leads her to ask a crucial question: "Can a male saviour save women?"[19]

Ward's response to such criticisms is to postulate the "subversive" maleness of
Christ's body that calls into question our habitual understanding of what it means to
be embodied. Reflecting on the incarnation leads him to conclude that Christ's body
cannot be read in any simplistic sense as "male": "The XY chromosomal maleness of
Jesus Christ issues from the XX chromosomal femaleness of his mother as miracle, and
so this male body is unlike any male body to date. Its materiality is, from its conception, unstable; though, with the circumcision, its specifically sexed nature is
affirmed."[20] This passage, which attempts to deflect feminist criticisms, requires further
comment. On the one hand, a kind of quasi-scientific reading is given to the (biblical)
events surrounding Christ's birth. Ward seems to take literally the claim that Christ was
"born of a virgin," and this means that his maleness is of a radical kind: without the
male chromosome provided by the father, a male child should not be born. This
means, for Ward, that the preoccupation with Christ's maleness is redundant: Christ is
"unlike" any other male. But this is a somewhat pernicious reading. As Ward has to
admit, Christ's maleness is not *that* odd and is attested to by his body: he is, after all,
capable of being circumcised. This "radical" maleness, it seems, is nothing more than
a convenient metaphor for undercutting feminist criticisms.

Even if we grant that this rereading of the virgin birth is innovative, it ignores the
issue that drives feminist criticisms. The maleness of Christ's body is not a problem *in
and of itself.* What is problematic for feminists is the connection that has been made
between a *male body* and the divine being of God. The debates surrounding the ordination of women bear witness to the continuing power of this connection: because
Christ was male, maleness becomes a prerequisite for the representation of God's representative.[21] Feminists have not created this problem *ex nihilo*: church debates surrounding the leadership of women continue to emphasize the role of Christ's maleness
in determining who may stand as his representative.

To some extent Ward recognizes the complexity of the issue. As he puts it, "the
material orders are inseparable from the symbolic and transcendent orders," a comment that suggests an intimate connection between the realm of the symbolic and
social reality.[22] But having made this connection, he fails to engage with what the history of the church reveals about the way the body of Christ has been read to the detriment of female bodies.[23] Indeed, this failure is evidenced by his attempt to include the
female body within the physical body of Christ. For the medieval church, he argues,
Christ's wounded side was seen as "both lactating breast and a womb from which the
Church is removed."[24] Under this reading, Christ's body incorporates the signs of both
male and female sexual identity. Yet what is ignored is the way in which the "real"

---

19. Rosemary Radford Ruether, *Sexism and God-Talk* (London: SCM Press, 1983), 116.

20. Ward, "Bodies," 164.

21. See Daphne Hampson, *Theology and Feminism* (Oxford: Blackwell, 1990), 50–80, where she considers the way in which Christ's maleness supports the maleness of Christian hierarchies.

22. Ward, "Bodies," 165.

23. See, for example, U. Ranke-Heinemann, *Eunuchs for the Kingdom of Heaven: The Catholic Church
and Sexuality* (Harmondsworth: Penguin, 1990), for discussion of the way in which Christian theology,
read through a masculinist lens, has supported the suppression of women.

24. Ward, "Bodies," 170.

physical markings of Christ's maleness come to be more important than the "symbolic" femaleness of his wounded side.[25]

Reading the body of Christ thus leads Ward to the following conclusion: "God may have a phallus, but he certainly doesn't have a penis."[26] At first reading, this seems a contradictory idea. How can one separate the phallus—the erect, turgid penis—from the penis itself? It is at this point that Ward's debt to Lacan reveals itself. It is through Lacan's theories of sexuality that Ward is able to defend an orthodox commitment to the body of Christ. And this has ramifications for women, as it will leave them, yet again, as rather marginal figures in the development of masculine forms of religiosity.

In order to understand the hazards of employing Lacan's categories for feminist philosophy of religion or indeed theology, it is necessary to explore in detail the Lacanian forms that Ward employs. At the outset, it should be mentioned that Lacan's central concern lies with culture, not with any "determining" biological powers. Thus for some feminists he is simply a cultural critic who exposes the phallocentrism of human culture, while others see him as an enemy to be defeated. At any rate, his interest with the phallus lies not with the biological role of erection but with the cultural power of this image. As such, when he explores the realm of "the Symbolic"—what Malcolm Bowie defines as "a supra-personal structural order"—the phallus becomes the chief signifier for meaning.[27]

In order to understand the role that the phallus plays within human culture, it is important to engage with the key category of the symbolic: "that which makes the Symbolic possible."[28] In Lacan's terms, it is "the Name-of-the-Father" that ensures the development of a human symbolic order. In applying this term, Lacan draws upon the powers that restrict infantile desire by threatening punishment (castration); it is, if you like, the father who comes between the mother and child to stop a too narrow and confining dualism between the pair from developing, thus thrusting the child into the human world of meaning, symbol, and law. In such a context, the phallus becomes "the signifier which holds all signifieds in thrall."[29] At this point, it would seem that the phallus is being distinguished from the penis: to use more traditional language, the phallus operates on a metaphysical rather than a physical level. It represents power, it represents the law to which we are subjects,[30] and it represents that which humanity desires.[31] But the phallus should not be confused with the all too "human" penis. If we consider this dimension of Lacan's thought, some light might be thrown upon Ward's Christology: it is not Christ's penis that identifies him as God. Indeed, God does not have a penis (that which distinguishes the male from the female), but he does have a phallus (in other words, "he" embodies the symbol of power, and is that which humans desire).

25. Feminists will presumably have reservations about reading femaleness purely in terms of a wound, a gash, or a hole. See M. Collins and C. Pierce, "Holes and Slime: Sexism in Sartre's Psychoanalysis," in *Women and Philosophy* (ed. C. C. Gould and M. W. Wartofsky; New York: Pedigree, 1980), 112–27, for a critique of just such a rendition of femaleness as lack.

26. Ward, "The Gendered Body," 173.

27. Malcolm Bowie, *Lacan* (London: Fontana, 1991), 58.

28. Ibid., 108.

29. Ibid., 128.

30. J. Mitchell and J. Rose, eds., *Female Sexuality* (London: Macmillan, 1982), 28.

31. We might at this point think of the way in which the phallus was used as a protective symbol on Greek and Roman amulets. See C. Johns, *Sex or Symbol?: Erotic Images of Greece and Rome* (London: British Museum Press, 1989).

The controlling power of the phallus over human desire should be explored, for it throws further light upon the way in which Ward's Christology is determined by Lacanian categories. It is the phallus, the emblem of power, that human beings want. And this has to be understood differently for men and women. The male, through his body, is capable of "having" the phallus; the female, because she lacks that which has come to be linked with the phallus, the penis, can "be" the phallus (in other words, she can be desired/take the place of the phallus for the male), but she cannot herself possess the phallus. At this point the notion that the phallus can be constructed as a concept distinct from the male body starts to break down. If men and women relate differently to this symbol because of their different bodies, how can we possibly be dealing with a sexually neutral term? Only those with a penis can possess the phallus. And if this is the case for human beings, what are we saying about a God who is described as possessing the phallus? If anything, the route taken by Ward entails an even more male/masculine conceptualization of the divine than that offered within the classical Western tradition: at least for defining figures such as Aquinas, God is understood as incorporeal (without a body),[32] and presumably an incorporeal being can be represented just as well (or badly) by a woman as by a man.

Further analysis of Lacan's work suggests that the notion of a neutral phallus is ultimately impossible to maintain, even within his own theorizing. This impossibility is revealed in his discussion of the relationship between the sexes. "The other," as it has in other Western philosophies,[33] comes to play a key part in Lacan's account of the development of the self. Almost inevitably, it is woman who takes on this role: "The divided subject, haunted by absence and lack, looks to the other not simply to supply his needs but to pay him the compliment of an unconditional yes."[34]

The mother's role in this development is paramount. She constructs "an other" whose first obligation is to be present. Ultimately, the child will lose this all-present other. Then this "pure loss" will become desire. As Lacan puts it, "Desire is neither the appetite for satisfaction, nor the demand for love, but the difference that results from the subtraction of the first from the second, the very phenomenon of their splitting."[35] In such an economy, one begins to see why Ward views Lacan's ideas as helpful when constructing his account of God: God becomes part of the economy of desire. God is the infinitely desirable, in whom we will ultimately find the kind of love demanded by the hungry self.

However, the androcentrism of Lacan's construct of desire should not be underplayed, as it is by Ward. In developing his notion of desire, woman's role looks sadly familiar. In Lacan's universe, women are less subject than men; they are signifiers of desire; they seek the phallus they lack; and so on. Indeed, women's very existence and sexuality are forced into an account of desire and sexuality formed purely by male constructions of what these concepts or realities mean. Consider Lacan's famous reflections upon woman's experience of *jouissance* (or orgasm). Women's sexual experience is defined purely in terms of that which is "not-man's." An unspoken binary comes to

---

32. Thomas Aquinas: "In no sense is God a body," in *Summa Theologica 1a*, 3, article 1, trans. Timothy McDermott (London: Eyre and Spottiswoode, 1964), 21.

33. G. Lloyd, *The Man of Reason* (London: Methuen, 1984).

34. Bowie, *Lacan*, 135.

35. Jacques Lacan, "The Meaning of the Phallus," in *Female Sexuality* (ed. J. Mitchell and J. Rose; London: Macmillan, 1958), 81.

determine his account of human sexuality. Yet his reflections on female *jouissance* begin positively, with a statement that it goes "beyond the phallus": quite a claim for a theorist who argues that the phallus is the prime signifier of the symbolic order.[36] "There is a *jouissance* proper to her, to this 'her' which does not exist and which signifies nothing. There is a *jouissance* proper to her and of which she herself may know nothing, except that she experiences it—that much she does know. She knows it of course when it happens. It does not happen to all of them."[37]

Despite the apparent downplaying of its significance in this passage and in Lacan's economy of desire, it has been argued that he is offering a radical account of female sexuality that undercuts the apparent phallocentrism of his argument. Evidence for such an interpretation comes from his reflections on Bernini's statue of St. Teresa. The clearly sexual nature of her ecstasy forms the basis for the following comment: "Might not this *jouissance* which one experiences and knows nothing of, be that which puts us on the path of ex-istence? And why not interpret one face of the Other, the God face, as supported by feminine *jouissance*?"[38]

Lacan is offering a completely different account of the divine that seems to displace the phallus. There is something mysterious here, something that refutes the clear-cut nature of the role/rule of the phallus. At this point, Lacan seems to be undercutting the phallocentrism of the Western concept of God. He seems to be offering an alternative model for the divine based on the genuine alterity of female sexual experience. How seriously we take this proposal depends upon how we read Lacan. The focus on the phallus could be part of an honest reflection on the nature of Western culture; or it could reflect a patriarchal mindset; or perhaps it reflects both. But his failure to criticize that historical context leaves one uncertain as to what, precisely, one can make of these statements—and particularly the extent to which a feminist can make use of such claims.

I have already drawn attention to Ward's contention that "the material orders are inseparable from the symbolic and transcendent orders."[39] And perhaps this is the problem with defining one's Christology through the ideas of a theorist whom Ward describes as "far more metaphysical" than Freud.[40] The metaphysical cannot help but be bound up with the physical, even if such a distinction is attempted. Consider this example: when reflecting on the way in which the phallus might have become the privileged signifier of human desire, Lacan writes: "One might say that this signifier is chosen as what stands out as most easily seized upon in the realm of sexual copulation, and also as the most symbolic in the literal (typographical) sense of the term, since it is the equivalent in that relation to the (logical) copula. One might say that by virtue of its turgidity, it is the image of the vital flow as it is transmitted in generation."[41]

Despite the claims that he is offering a metaphysic, the account of the phallus/God is located in reflections upon the physical: and not just "any old physical" but the male experience of the body. James Nelson has written compellingly of the way in which

---

36. Jacques Lacan, "God and the *Jouissance* of Woman," in Mitchell and Rose, 145.
37. Ibid.
38. Ibid., 147.
39. Ward, "Bodies," 165.
40. Ibid., 171.
41. Lacan, "Meaning of the Phallus," 82.

male sexual experience is reflected in the emphasis upon lineal, externalized ways of thinking and being.[42] Lacan's words provide a fine example of the kind of thinking that Nelson wishes to challenge. Given this apparent acceptance of masculinist thought forms, it is far from the case that such a viewpoint disrupts accounts of Christ's body in the way that Ward claims.

Considering the theoretical underpinning of Ward's Christology suggests that radical psychoanalytic theory will not necessarily provide feminists with the tools for exposing and challenging patriarchal constructions of religion. Yet this is not to suggest that psychoanalytic theory cannot be applied in a way helpful to feminist aims. Lacan focuses on the language of the unconscious and actively eschews the rational: Freud's position is more ambiguous. Freud can be drawn as both a modernist, seeking a scientific approach to human life and the mind, and as a postmodernist, in that his theory of the unconscious challenges the primacy given to reason and consciousness. In combining aspects of both ways of thinking he provides an approach to religion that disrupts orthodox religious positions *and* provides new directions for understanding the human impulses that lead to religious expression in the first place. It also allows for Freud's own androcentrism to be challenged in a way that moves us beyond the innate conservatism of Lacan's position.

Freud and Feminist Philosophy of Religion: Disrupting Religious Orthodoxy

Having rejected the efficacy of Lacanian theory for shaping a contemporary theology, it may seem perverse to adopt Freud as a conversation partner. If anything, Freud's work seems even more problematic than Lacan's for developing a specifically feminist philosophy of religion. The characterization of Freud as an enemy of feminism is not without grounds. Critical comments concerning feminists abound in his work.[43] More importantly, his theory of sexuality can be seen as unremittingly androcentric. The Oedipal complex deals with the development of *male* sexual identity and seems to be extended to cover female sexuality as an afterthought. But this extension of the theory has implications: while the *fear* of castration determines male sexual and moral development, the female is seen as already castrated. Her sexual and moral development is determined by the extent to which she accepts or rejects this "fact."[44]

If the relationship between Freud and feminism is problematic, Freud's attitude to religion seems similarly unpromising. Freud's characterization of religion as an illusory set of beliefs, grounded in childhood, that should be set aside as we enter maturity, has led philosophers of religion to be rather dismissive of his work.[45] The concept of God as a projection of the father by the frightened child has been categorized as an example of "the genetic fallacy": even if the origins of religion lie in the nursery, it does

---

42. James Nelson, *The Intimate Connection: Male Sexuality, Masculine Spirituality* (Philadelphia: Westminster Press, 1988), 29–46.

43. J. Mitchell, *Psychoanalysis and Feminism* (London: Pelican, 1975), 303.

44. See Sigmund Freud, "Female Sexuality," in *On Sexuality* (Penguin Freud Library 7; Harmondsworth: Penguin, [1931] 1977), 376–83.

45. See Sigmund Freud, "The Future of an Illusion," in *Civilization, Society, and Religion* (Penguin Freud Library 12; Hardmondsworth: Penguin, [1927] 1985).

not follow that God does not exist. Presented in this way, Freud's theories tend to be dismissed as reductive and based upon little real evidence.[46]

Such criticisms have not gone unchallenged. Juliet Mitchell's famous book *Feminism and Psychoanalysis* (1975) offers a systematic defense of Freudian theory in the face of a variety of feminist critiques. Likewise, James DiCenso has rejected the caricature of Freud the arch rationalist, suggesting that "the Other Freud's" ideas on religion are far more complex than mere reductionism.[47]

It is against this background that the use of Freud as a conversation partner begins to make more sense. The complexity of his thought makes him interesting, and nowhere is this more evident than in his ambiguity toward the major tenets of modernism and postmodernism. It is this ambiguity, I shall argue, that allows for both critique and creativity in the study of religion.

Consider, then, the Freud who accepts the modernist attack on religion, and, indeed, extends it. According to Freud, the scientific revolution facilitates the defeat of the superstitious connections that human beings make between their thoughts and the world. It is precisely these connections that support the religious view of the world. A prey to "the elements, which seem to mock all human control," we seek to personalize and "humanise" the forces of nature in order to feel at home in the world.[48] In order to do this, we draw upon our memories of the nursery and the belief we had as children that our father was all-powerful. Thus God is created in the image of an all-powerful human father who is able to protect us. Of course, in Freudian theory the father is not simply protective, and just as during the Oedipal phase of child development the father is viewed with ambivalence, so feelings of guilt and fear come to determine our attitude to the Father-God. The God who has the power to save us is also the God we wish to kill. The God who protects us is also the God who can destroy us/castrate us.

With the advent of science such superstitious views can be eradicated. In this way, religion cannot simply be seen as another (equally valid) way of understanding the world. There are clearly limitations with this view—limitations that shall be addressed in a moment. But what this position does allow for is the *critique* of religious beliefs. So if the virgin birth is considered in the apparently "scientific" way that Ward offers, such a viewpoint can be challenged (and perhaps dismissed) in accordance with scientific principles and empirical evidence. And this critical reflection—precisely the kind that radical orthodoxy seems designed to avoid—is what feminists have been at pains to employ to challenge those religious orthodoxies that have oppressed women in the name of some transcendent "Truth."

Now, we might accept the necessity of criticism in relation to religion but feel that Freud's androcentrism undermines any use to which a feminist might put his theories. It could well be argued that Freud's exclusion of the female from his theory of

---

46. See J. L. Mackie, *The Miracle of Theism* (Oxford: Oxford University Press, 1982), 196; and P. Clarke and P. Byrne, *Religion Defined and Explained* (Basingstoke: Macmillan, 1993), 173–87.

47. See James DiCenso, *The Other Freud: Religion, Culture, and Psychoanalysis* (London: Routledge, 1999). For example, DiCenso argues that Freud's ideas are "quite complex, multileveled and fruitful for ongoing interdisciplinary reflection" (2). At times his comments on religion do suggest a rather limited positivistic and biologistic perspective, but at others Freud's discussion of human beings as "open systems" (ibid.) allows for a more creative understanding of the role that religion plays in human life and culture.

48. Freud, "The Future of an Illusion," 195.

sexuality is even more problematic than the way in which Lacan appropriates the feminine other. After all, it is in Freud's theory that the notion of the female as castrated first presents itself: arguably Lacan is simply building upon Freud's theorizing.

Juliet Mitchell's defense of Freud is particularly helpful at this point. She suggests that Freud's theory of sexuality must be seen against the backdrop of his theory of the unconscious. His theory of sexuality is not *prescriptive* but *descriptive*. He shows us the way in which human self-understanding develops in a particular cultural setting.[49] In this sense, it is not a case of whether we "like" what Freud says about the way in which women in patriarchal society see themselves: it is more a case of analyzing the way in which female identity is shaped in a patriarchal culture. And this does not have simply a social effect: it also shapes the way in which women think about themselves.

In the context of religion, this distinction is significant: not just for defending Freud, but for understanding the nature of traditional religious belief. Rosemary Ruether and Naomi Goldenberg have suggested that patriarchal religion must be read as illustrative of the male attempt to relate to the external world. For Ruether, the question must be asked as to whether religious ritual provides a means by which the male, "marginalized from direct participation in the great mysteries of gestation and birth," attempts to participate imaginatively in the act of creation.[50] Naomi Goldenberg develops such reflections, suggesting that religion arises as "a result of the sustained practise of gender," for men can, in these cultural arenas, "safely pretend to be women, especially in regard to matters of nurture and reproduction."[51] Under these readings, traditional religion is exposed as a peculiarly male way of reflecting upon the external world. This is important, for it suggests that the construction of religion has not been equally dependent upon male and female reflections about the world. In such a context, to argue that the female body can simply be "included" within the transformed body of Christ is to neglect this crucial disparity. Woman has been excluded from the world's religions and her identity shaped in relation to male needs.[52] Exposing the way in which this exclusion has been perpetuated by the central beliefs and rituals of the established world faiths is needed in order that new ways of thinking about religion in the contemporary world can be presented. Freud's commitment to the application of reason means that he is better equipped than Lacan to facilitate a critical discussion of religion that moves beyond the attempt simply to accommodate women within male-determined religious forms.

But Freud's ideas regarding religion are not just useful for criticism. The ideas of "the other Freud" enable a movement beyond simply the critique of traditional forms of religious practice and belief. In particular, his ideas on psychopathology open up other ways of understanding the role that religion plays in the lives of human beings as a whole.

---

49. Mitchell, *Psychoanalysis and Feminism*, xvi.

50. Rosemary Radford Ruether, "Renewal or New Creation?" in *A Reader in Feminist Knowledge* (ed. S. Gunew; London: Routledge, 1991), 238.

51. Naomi Goldenberg, "The Divine Masquerade: A Psychoanalytic Theory about the Play of Gender in Religion," in *Bodies, Lives, Voices: Gender in Theology* (ed. K. O'Grady, A. L. Gilroy, and J. Gray; Sheffield: Sheffield Academic Press, 1998), 193, 199.

52. See, for example, Marina Warner, *Alone of All Her Sex: The Myth and Cult of the Virgin Mary* (London: Picador, 1990), for a detailed analysis of the role that Mary plays in determining the role of women in Christianity.

While advocating the application of reason, Freud also goes some way to destabilizing it as the key category for understanding the nature of human being. Freud suggests that the unconscious is at least as powerful—possibly more powerful—than the conscious world of the rational mind. It is this strand of Freud's thinking that enables a more positive account of the role that religious belief and practice play in human culture. Religion can be seen as one of the peculiarities of "the *sick* animal," "man."[53] Unlike other animals, we are not simply instinctual. In this context, Freud draws our attention to the way in which human beings make connections between disparate things. It is this ability to "only connect" that makes us human.

Grounding religious thought and practice in the human ability to connect entails a return to Freud's criticisms. He argues that at the heart of religious belief lies the idea that we can control our environment through wishes. This mistaken illusion—what Freud calls the "omnipotence of thought"—suggests that by performing certain actions (prayer for example) we are able to control the world about us.

In this sense, religious actions are intimately connected to the practices of magic. But Freud goes further: the actions of the religious are also connected to the "obsessive actions" of neurotics. One of Freud's most famous cases was that of the Rat Man, a young army officer who came to see Freud because he was convinced that his loved ones were in danger. He had been told of a Chinese torture where a pot is filled with rats and tied upside down to the victim's buttocks. In order for the rats to escape they have to gnaw their way through the anus. The Rat Man was convinced that this punishment might befall his loved ones because of his failings as an officer. To avert this danger he followed a set of bizarre, self-imposed "instructions": his "obsessional neuroses." Through analysis, Freud shows that the source of his fears is located in his difficult relationship with his dead father: through revealing their source, he was able to affect a cure.[54]

Now, Freud suggests that religious practices might be seen in the same way: as obsessive actions. Just as the Rat Man sought to resist the power of the father, so the religious seek to stave off the castrating power of the Father-God through enacting certain ritualistic actions: prayer, mass, pilgrimage, and so on. Freud argues that once the childish source of the fears that lead to the construction of religion in the first place has been exposed, religion will no longer be necessary.

Yet running alongside this critical reading of the religious mindset is an approach to religion that could be seen as providing the basis for a more complex engagement where religious practice is grounded in the activities that make us human. In "Obsessive Actions and Religious Practices" (1907), Freud outlines the similarities between religious rituals and the obsessive actions through which the neurotic seeks to render safe his or her frightening world. Neurotic ceremonials "consist in making small adjustments to particular everyday actions, small additions or restrictions or arrangements, which have always to be carried out in the same, or in a methodically varied, manner."[55] These actions might appear meaningless, but for the patient this is far from

53. Friedrich Nietzsche, *The Genealogy of Morals* (New York: Doubleday, [1887] 1956), 257.

54. Sigmund Freud, "Notes upon a Case of Obsessional Neurosis (The 'Rat Man')," in *Case Histories II* (Penguin Freud Library 9; Harmondsworth: Penguin, [1909] 1979), 33–128.

55. Sigmund Freud, "Obsessive Actions and Religious Practices," in *The Origins of Religion* (Penguin Freud Library 13; Harmondsworth: Penguin, [1907] 1985), 32.

the case, for "any deviation from the ceremonial is visited with intolerable anxiety."[56] The ceremonial is "a 'sacred act'"[57] similar to, although not exactly like, a religious ritual, most notably because these actions do not have the public and communal quality of religious practice but are rather forms of "private religion."[58] Freud's work is dedicated to showing how such actions are related to specific repressed events in the patient's life. These actions are thus highly meaningful, providing ways of coping—however inappropriately—with unresolved issues and repressed instincts.

Of course, Freud's intention in exposing the sources of such actions is to break the hold of the obsession: once the origin of the obsessive act is revealed the patient will be able to let go of the action. And the same goes for the illusion that is religion, for religion is "a universal obsessional neurosis."[59] Yet this very description of religion as "a *universal* obsessional neurosis" presumably suggests much about how "normal" humans generally attempt, in much the same way as neurotics, to come to an accommodation with the world that threatens to consume and destroy them. Indeed, Freud's *Psychopathology of Everyday Life* (1901) is committed to showing how we are all to a greater or lesser extent neurotic animals: we are all in some sense mysterious to ourselves, and it is through monitoring slips of the tongue, the things that we lose and forget, that we can come to some sense of who that mysterious person is.[60]

Accepting such a view means that it will be difficult to talk of the human person as in any straightforward way defined by his or her conscious and rational life. Freud seems to struggle with accepting the implications of his own theory on the unconscious, and this is perhaps best seen in his attempt to make a distinction between the superstitious person and the scientific rationalist. This distinction lies in the attitude taken toward chance. For Freud, there are chance events in terms of the things that happen in the external world, but there are no "internal (psychical) accidental events."[61] The superstitious/religious person reverses this position: for this person, there are no accidental events in the external world for all is open to manipulation by the self or, in the case of the religious, by God. Freud sums this difference up in the following way: the superstitious person seeks to "project outwards a motivation which I look for within."[62] But what I find interesting here is that he accepts that there is common ground. Both are attempting to make sense of the world: as Freud puts it, "the compulsion not to let chance count as chance *but to interpret it is common to us both*."[63]

It is this latter point that interests me, for Freud exposes the common ground that lies between the two positions. And reflection on Freud's own behavior underlines precisely those connections. Despite his criticisms, Freud accepts that he is not immune from seeking such connections between his internal and external worlds:

> One morning . . . when I was passing through a room in my dressing-gown with straw slippers on my feet, I yielded to a sudden impulse and hurled one of

---

56. Ibid.
57. Ibid.
58. Ibid., 33.
59. Ibid., 40.
60. Sigmund Freud, *The Psychopathology of Everyday Life* (Penguin Freud Library 5; Harmondsworth: Penguin, [1901] 1991).
61. Ibid., 320.
62. Ibid.
63. Ibid., emphasis mine.

my slippers from my foot at the wall, causing a beautiful little marble Venus to fall down from its bracket. As it broke into pieces, I quoted quite unmoved these lines from Busch: "Oh! The Venus! Lost is she!..." This wild conduct and my calm acceptance of the damage are to be explained in terms of the situation at the time. One of my family was gravely ill, and secretly I had already given up hope of her recovery. That morning I had learned that there had been a great improvement, and I know I had said to myself: "So she is going to live after all!" My attack of destructive fury served therefore to express a feeling of gratitude to fate and allowed me to perform a "sacrificial act"—rather as if I had made a vow to sacrifice something or other as a thank-offering if she recovered her health![64]

Something very powerful is being expressed here: even the most committed rationalist is not able to evade seeking to make an intimate connection between his internal hopes and the external world that surrounds him. In this sense the attempt to divide superstition or religion from other forms of behavior is not particularly helpful. We could consider Freud's action as merely superstitious: the position that Freud encourages us to take by dealing with this story in a light-hearted manner. But we could think about this action rather differently. We could think of it as an action that reveals something of the precarious nature of things, of how we all long for a connection with the world, for a sense that the unfeeling vastness that is the universe might care about us after all; and also how we might attempt to bring about a reconciliation with the powerful forces that threaten to crush us. The religious attempt to connect with the universe is simply one of the ways in which we attempt to do this, and it is by engaging with the different forms that this desire for connection takes—not just with those aspects that are rationally justifiable—that we open up the whole question of what it is to be this strange human animal.

Conclusion: Feminism and Orthodoxy

Radical orthodoxy seeks to maintain the central tenets of Christian theology through applying postmodernist psychoanalytic and literary theory. The application of such ideas sounds innovative, but further analysis suggests that a conservative attitude supports this approach to theology. There is little attempt to deal with the *implications* that belief structures have had for groups excluded from the development of doctrine: and this essay has highlighted the consequences of accepting uncritically religious orthodoxy for the way in which women are portrayed within, and incorporated into, religious traditions.

The ability to critique religious frameworks is fundamental to the feminist analysis of theology and religion. Seeking a return to premodern and pre-Enlightenment ways of thinking significantly undermines the extent to which such a critique can be maintained. Radical orthodoxy proposes that tradition can be accepted—largely wholesale—if it is read through the ideas of postmodernist theorists. In rejecting this approach I have argued that religious beliefs and structures should be challenged. It is important that religious believers and practitioners do not become lazy, believing in

---

64. Ibid., 222–23.

ideas that may be baseless or even unhealthy. It may be difficult to determine the implications and efficacy of belief, but feminists have not shied away from pursuing such
difficult issues. Describing the unconscious or social mores is not enough: there must
also be the possibility of critique. The kind of postmodernist thinking used by the proponents of radical orthodoxy fails to challenge the role that orthodox belief has played
in supporting social injustice. The more ambiguous figure of Freud (as neither modernist nor postmodernist) is helpful for pursuing a feminist philosophy of religion precisely because he does not just describe a state of affairs but offers his own critique.

But more than that, the context against which Freud worked out his theories suggests some parallels with the place that feminist philosophers of religion occupy. In
some autobiographical reflections, Freud comments that from an early age his position
as a Jew and thus as an outsider in nineteenth-century Vienna enabled him to feel
comfortable putting forward unpopular theories.[65] In some ways, the feminist philosopher of religion occupies a similar space: as a woman she stands outside the arena
where religion and theology has, until very recently, been formed. As a philosopher of
religion she need not be bound by commitment to any one religious tradition. And it
is this "outsider" status that provides the best opportunity for developing creative and
challenging approaches to religion. The possibility of critique opens up alternative
ways of seeing the world, and it is through criticism that religion is not overcome but
is shown to be a part of the human world, illuminating, moreover, what it means to be
a human being.

---

65. "At an early age I was made familiar with the fate of being in the Opposition and of being put under
the ban of the 'compact majority.' The foundations were thus laid for a certain degree of independence of
judgment" (Sigmund Freud, "An Autobiographical Study," in *Historical and Expository Works on
Psychoanalysis* [Penguin Freud Library 15; Harmondsworth: Penguin, (1925) 1993], 191).

Contributors

Dr. Marcella Maria Althaus-Reid is an Argentinian theologian, currently a Reader in Theology and Ethics in the School of Divinity, The University of Edinburgh, Scotland. She has written extensively on Liberation Theology and sexuality. Her publications include *Indecent Theology*; *The Queer God*; *From Feminist Theology to Indecent Theology*; and *The Sexual Theologian* (coedited with Lisa Isherwood). She is the associate editor of the journal *Studies in World Christianity* (Edinburgh Press).

Virginia Burrus is Professor of Early Church History at Drew University, where she has taught since 1991. Her teaching and research interests in the field of ancient Christianity include: gender, sexuality, and the body; martyrdom and asceticism; ancient novels and hagiography; constructions of orthodoxy and heresy; histories of theology and historical theologies. She is author, most recently, of *The Sex Lives of Saints: An Erotics of Ancient Hagiography*.

Beverley Clack is Reader in the Philosophy of Religion at Oxford Brookes University, UK. Her publications include *Sex and Death* (2002); *Misogyny in the Western Philosophical Tradition* (1999); and *Feminist Philosophy of Religion: Critical Readings* (2004) co-edited with Pamela Sue Anderson.

Marion Grau, a native of Germany, is Assistant Professor of Theology at the Church Divinity School of the Pacific, a member school of the Graduate Theological Union in Berkeley, where she has taught since 2001. Her essays have appeared in *Strike Terror No More* (2002) and *Postcolonial Theologies: Divinity And Empire* (2004). Her first book, *Of Divine Economy: Refinancing Redemption*, appeared in 2004 with T & T Clark/Continuum.

Mary Grey is an ecofeminist liberation theologian, and professorial research fellow at St. Mary's University College, Strawberry Hill, London (emeritus Professor, University of Wales, Lampeter). Her recent writing includes: *Sacred Longings: Ecofeminist Theology and Globalisation*; *The Unheard Scream: The Struggles of Dalit Women in India*; and *Pursuing the Dream: A Jewish-Christian Conversation* with Rabbi Dan Cohn Sherbok. She and her husband Dr. Nicholas Grey have worked for many years with rural communities in Rajasthan, NW India, through Wells for India, an NGO that creates sustainable water projects.

231

John Hoffmeyer is Associate Professor of Systematic Theology at The Lutheran Theological Seminary at Philadelphia. The author of *The Advent of Freedom: The Presence of the Future in Hegel's Logic*, he is currently writing a book on trinitarian theology and consumer society.

Lisa Isherwood is Senior lecturer in Theology at the College of St. Mark and St. John in Plymouth, England. She is an editor of *An A to Z of Feminist Theology* (1996), *Introducing Body Theology* (1998), *Liberating Christ: Exploring the Christologies of Contemporary Liberation Movements* (1999), *The Good News of the Body: Sexual Theology and Feminism* (2000), and *Introducing Feminist Theology* (2001). She is also an editor of the journal *Feminist Theology*.

Catherine Keller is Professor of Constructive Theology at Drew University, The Theological School and Caspersen Graduate School. Her primary publications include *From a Broken Web: Separation, Sexism and Self*; *Apocalypse Now and Then: A Feminist Guide to the End of the World*; *Face of the Deep: A Theology of Becoming*; and God and Power: Counter-Apocalyptic Journeys.

Melissa Raphael is Professor of Jewish Theology at the University of Gloucestershire, UK. She is the author of a number of books including *The Female Face of God in Auschwitz: A Jewish Feminist Theology of the Holocaust* (2003).

Joerg Rieger is Professor of Systematic Theology at Perkins School of Theology, Southern Methodist University in Dallas, Texas. His books include *God and the Excluded: Visions and Blindspots in Contemporary Theology* and *Remember the Poor: The Challenge to Theology in the Twenty-First Century*. Among his most recent edited volumes are *Opting for the Margins: Postmodernity and Liberation in Christian Theology* and *Methodist and Radical: Rejuvenating a Tradition*. He is currently working on a book on christology and empire.

Mayra Rivera Rivera is currently teaching theology at Drew University. She is author of "Engendering Territory: U.S. Missionaries' Discourse in Puerto Rico (1898–1920)" in *New Horizons in Hispanic/Latino(a) Theology* (2003), and co-editor with Catherine Keller and Michael Nausner of *Post-Colonial Theologies: Divinity and Empire* (2004).

Rosemary Radford Ruether was the Georgia Harkness Professor of Applied Theology at Garrett-Evangelical Theological Seminary (1975–2002) and Carpenter Professor of Feminist Theology at the Graduate Theological Union in Berkeley (2000–2005). She presently teaches feminist theology at the Claremont Graduate University and Claremont School of Theology. She is author or editor of forty books, the most recent being *Integrating Ecofeminism, Globalization and World Religions* (2004) and *Goddesses and the Divine Feminine: A Western Religious History* (2005).

Elina Vuola is research fellow of the Academy of Finland at the Institute of Development Studies at the University of Helsinki, Finland. In 2002–03 she worked as research associate and visiting lecturer at the Women's Studies in Religion Program at the Harvard Divinity School in Cambridge, Massachusetts. She is a regular visiting researcher at the Departamento Ecuménico de Investigaciones in San José, Costa Rica.

Index